ALSO BY KEN GOFFMAN (A.K.A. R. U. SIRIUS)

Mondo 2000: A User's Guide to the New Edge
(with Rudy Rucker and Queen Mu)

Cyberpunk Handbook: The Real Cyberpunk Fakebook
(with St. Jude)

The Revolution®: Quotations from Revolutionary Party Chairman R. U. Sirius

{Counterculture Through the Ages}

VILLARD — Ⓥ — NEW YORK

{Counterculture Through the Ages}

FROM ABRAHAM TO ACID HOUSE

KEN GOFFMAN [A. K. A. R. U. SIRIUS]

AND DAN JOY

FOREWORD BY TIMOTHY LEARY

FROM KEN:

To my fiancée, Eve Berni,
without whom the sun would go out.

To the late Rosemary Woodruff Leary,
who helped make this possible.

To my departed father and very-much-alive mother,
Arnold and Roberta: freethinkers.

To St. Jude, my brilliant, funny writing partner on so many
projects—RIP.

FROM DAN:

To Cate Leggett and Randi Mates, who helped me;
and to Timothy Leary, who showed me.

This book could not have happened if not for the late
Kathy Acker; James Fasci; Douglas Goffman; Harriett Joy;
David Latimer; our wonderfully supportive editor, Bruce Tracy;
and our agent extraordinare, Laurie Fox.

ASSISTANT DEVELOPER:
Leon Fernandez

WRITING ASSISTANCE:
Gracie and Zarkov

Additional thanks to: Lenny Bailes, Ben Ballard, John Perry
Barlow, Claire Burch, the Linda Chester Literary Agency,
Michael Coblentz, Helen Donlon, Benjamin Feen, Steve Follmer,
Norman Girardot, Evan Gourvitz, Peter Hudson, Jason Keehn,
Alison Kennedy, Beth Kennedy, Phil Leggiere, Linda Lowrance,
Sharon Martin, Walter Miles, Jay Schwartz, Dan Sieradski,
Jeremy Tarcher, and Peter Lamborn Wilson.

⊢ FOREWORD

Timothy Leary

Note: This foreword is not a message from beyond the grave, but rather one of Timothy Leary's last pieces of writing, composed when work on the conception of this book first began.

Counterculture blooms wherever and whenever a few members of a society choose lifestyles, artistic expressions, and ways of thinking and being that wholeheartedly embrace the ancient axiom that the only true constant is change itself. The mark of counterculture is not a particular social form or structure, but rather the evanescence of forms and structures, the dazzling rapidity and flexibility with which they appear, mutate, and morph into one another and disappear.

Counterculture is the moving crest of a wave, a zone of uncertainty where culture goes quantum. To borrow the language of Nobel Prize–winning physicist Ilya Prigogine, counterculture is the cultural equivalent of the "third thermodynamic state," the "nonlinear region" where equilibrium and symmetry have given way to a complexity so intense as to appear to the eye as chaos.

Participants in a counterculture thrive in this zone of turbulence. It is their native medium, the only clay malleable enough to be shaped and re-shaped fast enough to keep pace with the flashing of their inner visions.

They are adepts of flux, chaos engineers, migrating in step with the ever-traveling wavefront of maximum change.

In counterculture, social structures are spontaneous and transient. Participants in countercultures are constantly clustering into new molecules, fissioning and regrouping into configurations appropriate to the interests of the moment, like particles jostling in a high-energy accelerator, exchanging dynamic charge. In these configurations they reap the benefits of exchanging ideas and innovations through fast feedback in small groups, affording a synergy that allows their thoughts and visions to grow and mutate almost the instant they are formulated.

Counterculture lacks formal structure and formal leadership. In one sense it is leaderless; in another sense, it is leader-full, all of its participants constantly innovating, pushing into new territory where others may eventually follow.

Counterculture may be found in (sometimes uneasy) alliances with radical, even revolutionary political groups and insurrectionary forces, and the memberships of countercultures and such groups often overlap.

But the focus of counterculture is the power of ideas, images, and artistic expression, not the acquisition of personal and political power. Thus, minority, alternative, and radical political parties are not themselves countercultures. While many countercultural memes have political implications, the seizure and maintenance of political power requires adherence to structures too inflexible to accommodate the innovation and exploration that are basic to the countercultural raison d'être. Organization and institution are anathema to counterculture.

Counterculture—as this book demonstrates—is a perennial phenomenon, probably as old as civilization, and possibly as old as culture itself. In fact, many of the figures who have come to occupy prominent positions in the schoolbooks—from Socrates to Jesus, Galileo, Martin Luther, and Mark Twain—were countercultural in their time.

This book addresses the question "What is counterculture?" and outlines the common themes that weave through countercultures in different times and different places. It also describes the important roles as catalysts of change that countercultures have played in the development of mainstream cultures, showing the ways that culture-at-large emerges from counterculture.

These discussions serve as points of reference in a colorful romp through a crowd of countercultures from Taoism to acid house. I hope that you read and enjoy this book, and that it inspires you to live out the countercultural message of individuality, courage, and creativity with your own personal splendor and glory.

⊦ Contents

⊢ Preface

One beautiful day at the very height of his conquest of the Mediterranean world, Alexander the Great was abroad in the countryside surrounding Athens—which had just surrendered to his forces—surveying the rolling sunlit landscape wrapped around the city that was for him the shining jewel of the vast domain he now controlled.

In the course of this enjoyment, Alexander came upon a man relaxing beside a stream. Basking in the afternoon glow, the man was so absorbed in some kind of bucolic trance that he was clearly indifferent to both the conqueror's presence and the tumult that had freshly engulfed the nearby city. Alexander immediately recognized the man and approached him, saying, "I am Alexander. Is there anything that I may do for you?"

The man lazily opened his eyes, looked up, and replied: "Yes. Get out of my light."

Who was this man, for whom the newly ascended ruler of the known world would interrupt his hour of glory to humbly offer service—only to receive such a casually dismissive response?

The man beside the stream was Diogenes—both a renowned playwright and an utterly impoverished, eccentric Athenian troublemaker with no fixed residence. Diogenes lived out-of-doors, frequenting the streets and public areas of Athens and habitually unsettling its citizens with his sometimes coarse but always brilliantly iconoclastic humor and impish pranks. Famous throughout the Greek world for his aphoristic wisdom and dramaturgic accomplishments, he was also a leading light of the Socratic movement, a Greek counterculture destined to change the face of the Western world forever.

Diogenes' response to Alexander—"Get out of my light"—typifies the attitude of countercultures throughout time to imposed authority: it blocks the light.

The light—the shining forth of unfettered individual expression, the radiant effulgence of human creativity unchained from external agendas and controls. The light—the brilliance released when, individually and especially collectively, human beings freely partake of inner and outer resources to shape their world according to the dictates of the authentic self. And the numinous glow of the world itself in the eyes of those who exercise this kind of freedom.

Had Alexander refused to get out of Diogenes' light, the philosopher-playwright would have been far more likely to pick himself up and move out of the conqueror's shadow than to engage him in fisticuffs. For if Diogenes had responded to the severing of his beloved sunbeam by attempting to vanquish the one who had severed it, the sun—as Diogenes had the wisdom to know—might well have set before the conflict was resolved.

The foremost aim of countercultures is not, therefore, to seize or dismantle the reins of external control or to wage war against those who hold them—although countercultures may passionately participate in such endeavors at times. Rather, countercultures seek primarily to live with as much freedom from constraints on individual creative will as possible, wherever and however it is possible to do so. And when people exercise this kind of freedom with commitment and vigor, they unblock the light so that subsequent generations may bask in its glow.

TRADITION WITHOUT CONVENTION

I deliberately chose to break with traditions in order to be more true to Tradition than current conventions and ideas would permit. The most vital course is usually the rougher one and lies through conventions oftentimes

settled into laws that must be broken, with consequent
liberation of other forces that cannot stand freedom. So
a break of this nature is a thing dangerous, nevertheless
indispensable to society. Society recognizes the danger
and makes the break usually fatal to the man who makes
it. It should not be made without reckoning the danger
and sacrifice, without the ability to stand severe punishment, nor without sincere faith that the end will justify the means, nor do I believe it can be effectively
made without all these.

FRANK LLOYD WRIGHT

Counterculture's lasting impact on history has all too often been dictated
by the adoption of its symbols, artifacts, and practices by mainstream culture in a manner that brutally severs them from their source in living experience. Nevertheless, the historical traces left by countercultures can be
identified by looking at history with an understanding of counterculture's
essence. Reading the cultural record in this way offers an endless source of
inspiration, information, and affirmation, allowing countercultures to derive abundant fuel from earlier historical epochs and figures.

Counterculture is "the cutting edge" by definition, but it is also a kind
of tradition. It is the tradition of breaking with tradition, or crashing
through the conventions of the present to open a window onto that deeper
dimension of human possibility that is the perennial wellspring of the truly
new—and truly great—in human expression and endeavor. As such, counterculture may be a tradition that predates and initiates almost all other
traditions.

THREE CORDS OF CONNECTION

Three distinct strands of connection weave the motley array of countercultures into a continuous tradition: *direct contact, indirect contact,* and *resonance.* The first two are obvious pathways along which ideas, influence,
and inspiration are transmitted from one culture to another, while the
third involves a more subtle and mysterious kind of link between cultures.

DIRECT CONTACT

The most powerful and obvious type of connection between countercultures is direct contact. Here, participants in one counterculture interact
directly with participants in another, opening pathways of communication
that encourage individuality and magnify the countercultural impulse.

Direct contact is prominent in the historical impact of Sufism, the Islamic counterculture that provides the focus for Chapter 6. Through direct
contact with Sufis at the interface of Islamic and Christian cultures in
Western Europe, the troubadours learned the art of testifying to love's primacy in verse and song—a practice that became the hallmark of Christendom's most transcendentally erotic heresy. Influenced by meetings with
Sufi "Illuminates," Friar Roger Bacon subverted the religious authority of
his time by laying the groundwork for the "scientific method." Contact
with Sufi exemplars also inspired St. Francis of Assisi in espousing a radically pacifistic Christianity during that religion's most violent epoch.

Direct contact also comes into play throughout the twentieth century.
Key participants in the European avant-garde movements mingled face-to-
face with American writers in the bookstores, salons, and studios of Paris,
helping to catalyze the Lost Generation literary movement. A few decades
later, many participants in the youth countercultures of the 1960s were
inspired and instructed in person by several of the Lost Generation's "beatnik" literary heirs.

INDIRECT CONTACT

Influence and inspiration are also passed from one counterculture to another through indirect—or mediated—contact. Here, one counterculture
inseminates another across the reaches of time by way of artworks, records,
and legends. In the last one hundred years, as countercultures have prolif-
erated at an unprecedented rate and ease of access to the planetary store-
house of thought and image has evolved to cybernetic levels, this strand of
connection between countercultures has begun to fold back on itself with
dazzling intensity.

While not charged with the vitality and immediacy of direct contact,
mediated contact has been primary in shaping the ideational content of

countercultures. Plato, whose philosophic journey was launched by his involvement with the Socratic counterculture of ancient Greece, left behind a substantial written legacy. Since then, various permutations of Neoplatonic thought have served as a focus for a variety of countercultures, from the Gnosticism of the early Christians to the Transcendentalism of nineteenth-century New England. And in the twentieth century, poet Ezra Pound's writing revived the Sufi-inflected legacy of the troubadours and passed it along to the literary counterculture of the Lost Generation. In all of these examples, an earlier countercultural tradition is revived and a later one shaped and informed through the medium of indirect contact.

RESONANCE

The third connective thread of countercultural continuity is a kind of resonance whose source is a mystery. This is the often compelling similarity of ideas, artistic products, paths of development, and ways of living that occurs between countercultures for which there is no evidence of contact, direct or indirect. The phenomenon of resonance is prominent in congruences between the earliest countercultures discussed at length in these pages, those of the Socratics and the Taoists. Though separated by half the globe's circumference, these philosophic movements appeared at very nearly the same time and were remarkably parallel in their early development.

More than two thousand years later, the life and work of prototypical American counterculturalist Henry David Thoreau resonated strongly with Taoism. As Alan Watts pointed out, Thoreau's particular flavor of anarchism, his pantheism, and his embrace of nature all demonstrated a distinctly Taoist character. Although Thoreau, like other Transcendentalists, immersed himself in Eastern philosophies such as Hinduism and Vedanta, there is no evidence that he studied Taoism. The striking coincidence between Taoism and Thoreau's Transcendentalism can therefore be ascribed only to resonance.

As Thomas Jefferson's writings demonstrate, the revolutionary counterculture of the New World drew significant inspiration and guidance from ways of living and governance practiced by indigenous American peoples. In fact, the Articles of Confederation were structured after a native intertribal agreement. A plethora of the countercultural groups that flourished on the same soil two centuries later during the countercultural explosion of the sixties turned to this same source, loosely modeling tribal living experiments and even modes of dress on Native American custom. It seems unlikely, however, that the widespread enthusiasm among sixties counterculturalists for indigenous American culture somehow took its cues from documents penned by the Founding Fathers. The similarity is once again a matter of resonance.

The key to understanding otherwise mysterious resonances between spatially and temporally disparate countercultures may be the deep, defining values that countercultures share. These values, along with other characteristics that countercultures have in common, are laid forth in Chapter 2.

PREVIEW

Part I of *Counterculture Through the Ages* begins by examining the ancient tales of Prometheus and Abraham. These stories tell us a great deal about the motivations that drive countercultures and the roles they play in culture-at-large. Part I then moves on to identify counterculture's defining elements.

Part II is a chronological account of key countercultures that surfaced from 500 B.C.E. through the early twentieth century, beginning with the movement initiated by Socrates in ancient Greece and concluding with the early-twentieth-century Paris bohemia that produced Cubism, Dadaism, the "Lost Generation," and the one-man alternative language generator named James Joyce (and still other art/cultural trends). Each counterculture discussed in Part II wielded an influence that unrolled across time to achieve tremendous geographic breath.

Part III surveys the thrilling profusion of countercultures that blossomed in the late twentieth century, from the post-Hiroshima stirrings of America's fifties hipsters to the cyberpunks and anti-globalization activists of the 1990s.

SCRATCHING THE SURFACE

As an examination of world countercultures, counterculturalists, and their significance to history, *Counterculture Through the Ages* is necessarily incomplete. Countercultures of some type and magnitude have most likely sprung up in almost every region of the world during almost all epochs of history. Likewise, many isolated individuals with countercultural values and inclinations—in other words, lone counterculturalists—have done important and influential work despite the absence of a supportive countercultural group. It would be nearly impossible to note, within the narrative structure of a single book, every counterculture or counterculturalist that has left a historical trace.

The authors have made many difficult—and, at times, somewhat arbitrary—choices that exclude important countercultural groups and figures. It could easily be argued that many of those left out—from the forest-dwelling sages and early Tantric heretics of ancient India to the towering nineteenth-century American iconoclast Mark Twain—are as important as those that have been included. In a sense, this book can only scratch the surface of its subject without turning into an encyclopedia of brief entries.

A major criterion for including countercultures was their likely familiarity to a broad contemporary readership. The authors assumed that many readers would welcome the truly fresh angle on familiar movements and figures—from Socrates to the beats—provided by the unique framework of world counterculture's progression through time. To the reader disappointed to discover that his or her favorite instance of counterculture is absent from this book, the authors offer their hope that he or she encounters within these pages several rewarding expressions of creativity, courage, and vision closely reflecting the figure or group excluded.

OF LEGACIES AND LIVES

The true poem is not that which the public read. There is always a poem not printed on paper, coincident with the production of this, stereotyped in the poet's life. It is what he has become through his work. Not how the idea is expressed in stone, or on canvas or paper, is the question, but how far it has obtained form and expression in the life of the artist. His true work will not stand in any prince's gallery.

HENRY DAVID THOREAU

Although revolutionary novelty in art, thinking, or spirituality turns out more often than not to have arisen from a countercultural milieu, bold innovation—no matter how contrary to the status quo—does not itself a counterculture make. Authentic counterculture is driven by an impulse even deeper than the desire to innovate or to overturn conventions.

Counterculture cannot be crafted or produced: it must be lived. Where counterculture prizes pushing the boundaries of art, it prizes even more approaching life as an ongoing artistic experiment. Where counterculture values novel thinking, it strives most to express that ideation in the action of the moment. Where counterculture embraces spirit, it does not settle for periodic acknowledgment of divinity through the repetition of some arbitrary gesture, but instead attempts to live each day as a constant, dynamic expression of spirit itself. The artifacts of a particular counterculture are by-products, not end-products, of countercultural living.

For this reason, *Counterculture Through the Ages* emphasizes telling stories as much as analyzing artworks, ideas, and beliefs. Some of the stories included in this book are well documented—Thoreau's experiments in living; the complicated but fertile social interactions of Sylvia Beach, James Joyce, and Ezra Pound; the antics of the Merry Pranksters. Other anecdotes recounted herein are apocryphal in origin—the wry, subversive teaching tales of the Taoist, Zen, and Sufi traditions; the romantic legends left in the troubadours' wake. Both kinds of tale help connect us to the lives that lie beneath the legacies.

It is stories—of those who formed and participated in countercultures; of how such people coexisted, created, risked, dared, sacrificed, succeeded, and failed—that best reveal the living source from which countercultural legacies arise. The trial of Socrates tells us more about the essence of counterculture than Plato's lengthy exfoliations and systematizations of Socratic thought; Timothy Leary's approach to his own death tells us far more than academic manuals on how to use LSD.

The distinction at issue here—the lives of people versus the cultural legacies that their lives produce—highlights the distinction between the formal and informal definitions of the word "culture" itself. Formally, *culture* refers to the beliefs, customs, habits, and mores by which people live, along with the idioms of art and craft that they employ. The word is also used, less formally but perhaps more frequently, to refer to the people themselves, to the individuals, groups, and societies that generate, perpetuate—and sometimes reject—these practices and traditions.

Counterculture Through the Ages encompasses both definitions of culture. While this book tells stories, it also examines modes of custom, systems of belief, and forms of art. But by emphasizing culture's less formal definition, this book seeks to tap the living essence of the cultural episodes it explores.

DAN JOY

6/23/2003

⊢ Dis/Orientation

First of all, thanks to Timothy and Dan for those *too-damned-optimistic* introductions. Like the proverbial fool in many countercultural tales of yore, I have charged headlong into the onrushing chaotic stream of human history armed only with your beautiful visions and maps.

Yes, I set out to knit a lovely symmetrical quilt from the many-colored yarn of these widely varying cultural epochs, hoping finally then to find a shapely finished object whose coherence would be clear to even the meanest intelligence.

But goddamn it, people are funny—and I mean *un*intentionally as well. Oh my maties, the things I found still make me shudder in awe. Great people, smart people, hip people, wildly creative people, flagrantly engaged not only in transformative works but in extravagant folly and contradiction; leaving behind them not just a legacy of spirited runs at authentic countercultural autonomy, but a plethora of unanswered questions. By the god(s), be they dead or alive, they were all human—all too human. And would we have it any other way?

And as for you, dear reader? I can only humbly request that, as you enter this historical narrative, you leave your expectations at the door. You can pick them up unaffected, if you wish, at the end of the trip.

There are many types waiting on line here, and I believe that you will all find many things inside worthy of your interest and attention. But hear me out: as I was writing this over the past two years, I told any number of people the title. As often as not, someone would tell me excitedly about some really obscure, eXXXtreme subculture, usually involving the word "tantric." Among the charms ascribed to these cultures was the fact that they did things like eat brains, or bite the heads off bats and drink their blood. (Insert cheap Ozzy joke here.)

This is not a friggin' freak show, people! While a book about such cultural phenomena does hold a profound fascination for this author (no, I'm not being ironic), this particular work is about cultures whose impact has been more widely distributed. And this point goes also to the style and intent of this book. Sure, I want the hippest of the hipsters—you know, the ones with pictures of Antonin Artaud and Lynette "Squeaky" Fromme on their computer monitors—to find value in this book. But my most treasured hope is that it speaks to ordinary people who have been influenced or impacted by "the counterculture"; that it holds some interest for those who argue *against* counterculture; and finally that it is accessible to the curious, who may not even know what the word represents.

In doing this, I have mostly resisted an urge to engage in the sort of scholarly inquisitions, so popular over the last few decades, that put into doubt our common understandings of certain words that I use frequently in this text, such as individuality and liberty. I don't necessarily reject the value of those discourses, but I've deigned them at least impractical for this disquisition. So if your idea of the Fab Four is Foucault, Deleuze, Derrida, and Lacan, you may find these proceedings a bit jejune.

Okay, now that some of my readers' hipster expectations have been appropriately muted, we can proceed. Welcome to the first-ever history of countercultures.

Dan Joy came up with the idea for this book in 1994 in the course of conversations with Timothy Leary, whose later work in particular provided inspiration for key ideas. Dan developed most of the outline and conceptual foundations for this book and contributed about two chapters as well as other crucial prose passages to the final work. Leon Fernandez provided invaluable input on the outline, selection of countercultures, and basic ideas. I also contributed to the outline and articulation of key concepts, taking over full responsibility for the project in 2001 when it was contracted with the publisher. Gracie and Zarkov contributed a few lines and paragraphs to Chapter 1 and Chapter 8, and Dan rejoined the project for the final round of editorial work. I'm responsible for a large majority of the writing and the specific perspectives expressed therein.

So: when the first-person pronoun "I" is used, it refers to me (R.U. Sirius), and when "we" is used, it refers to Joy and myself. Also, when it comes to gender pronouns like "his" or "her," I like to just mix them up. Sometimes I'll refer to the generic person in the masculine and sometimes in the feminine. Get over it.

KEN GOFFMAN A.K.A. R. U. SIRIUS

6/23/2003

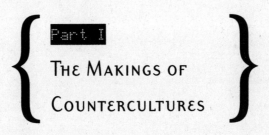

{ Part I

THE MAKINGS OF

COUNTERCULTURES }

CHAPTER ONE

⊢ ABRAHAM AND PROMETHEUS
Mythic Counterculture Rebels

THE MYTHIC COUNTERCULTURES

> A new mythology is possible in the Space Age, where we
> will again have heroes . . . as regards intention towards
> this Planet.
>
> WILLIAM S. BURROUGHS, 1978

> To hell with facts! We need stories!
>
> KEN KESEY, 1987

Myth is as important to counterculturalists as historical fact, and perhaps more poignant. Avant-garde by nature, most countercultures engage
the imaginal and the ideal, as well as the real. In his book *Untimely Meditation: On the Use and Disadvantage of History for Human Life* (1874),
nineteenth-century Promethean philosopher Friedrich Nietzsche even
suggested that we should eschew history in favor of myth. For Nietzsche,
myth created feelings of spiritual community. History deadened such feelings.

With a few exceptions (possibly including our current historical moment), countercultures have been inspired, optimistic, one might say mythical historical episodes. Whenever people courageously and passionately engage in rule-challenging behaviors that attempt to liberate humans from oppressive limitations (or limitations *perceived* as being oppressive), excitement, conflict, and scandal—and therefore engaging stories—are sure to follow. And while modernist and postmodern novelists have shown us that stories can be constructed out of the most ordinary lives—indeed out of banality itself—*myths* emerge from heroism, whether victorious or defeated, whether lived or imagined. Sometimes by design, often by accident, countercultures—even such renunciate, contemplationist countercultures as the Taoists, Zen Buddhists, and Transcendentalists (as we shall later see)—produce legendary heroes who sometimes rise to the level of myth.

In Prometheus and Abraham, we have two of the West's most resonantly countercultural myths. Prometheus is pure story—part of the pantheon of Greek gods—while the narrative of the Tribe of Abraham probably has at least some basis in historical fact.

Although I briefly discuss the possible historic Abraham, I am primarily viewing these apocryphal tales as myths, fulfilling their function as two different rebel archetypes whose styles and trials we still find manifested in countercultures today.

PROMETHEUS: THE HACKER GOD

Prometheus stole fire from the gods on behalf of mankind. That's all some youthful hacker outlaws today need know to inspire them to adapt Prometheus as their icon, and to adapt the Greek deity's name for their online monikers.

The actual Greek myth is a bit more complex. In a reductionist nutshell: Prometheus is a Greek god of Olympus, ruled by Zeus. He initiates animal sacrifices. One day during a sacrifice he sasses Zeus. He cuts up a bull and divides it into two parts: one containing the flesh and intestines wrapped up in the skin; and the other consisting of only bones and fat. Prometheus asks Zeus to choose his share; the rest is to be given to man. Zeus picks the bones and fat, making him bitter against Prometheus and against humankind. Zeus punishes the mortals by withholding from them the gift of fire. Prometheus steals it back. Then Prometheus—who is known to have the gift of foresight—further sasses the great god Zeus by predicting that one of Zeus' children would one day dethrone him, but refusing to say which one. The enraged Zeus punishes Prometheus by binding him in steel chains to a rock in the Caucasus Mountains. There, every day for eternity, an eagle is sent to tear and eat Prometheus' liver. Every night, the god Prometheus' immortal liver renews itself so that he can be tortured again in the next day's light.

This was no mere story to the ancient Greeks. As Carl Kerényi writes in *Prometheus: Archetypal Image of Human Existence,* "This was sacred material. . . . Myth as it exists in its . . . primitive form, is not merely a story but a reality lived." Further, the Greeks did not separate the gods from the humans to the extent that contemporary monotheists separate themselves from their singular deities. As Hesiod wrote, "The gods and mortal men sprang from one source."

Likewise, our understanding of the Prometheus myth springs almost entirely from a single source, the work of the epic storyteller Aeschylus. (Hesiod has had less influence.) While Aeschylus is believed to have written at least four epics about Prometheus, the one that survives intact is *Prometheus Bound. Prometheus Bound* tells the story of Prometheus' great suffering, and his arrogant and insubordinate self-assurance in the face of his tortures, but it does not give us his liberation. That was left to Percy Shelley, who wrote *Prometheus Unbound* in the 1810s.

Our young hacker friends have not deceived themselves in seeing Prometheus' theft of fire from the gods as a metaphor for technology. In Aeschylus' *Prometheus Bound,* Prometheus makes this abundantly clear, saying that he brought humanity architecture—"They knew not how to build brick houses to face the sun, nor work in wood. They lived beneath the earth like swarming ants in sunless caves." And he brought humanity calendars—"They had no certain mark of winter nor of flowery spring nor summer, with its crops, but did all this without intelligence until it was I that showed them—yes, it was I." And he gave them mathematics and writing—"And numbering as well, preeminent of subtle devices, and letter combinations that hold all in memory." And he gave them transportation—"I harnessed to the carriage horses obedient to the rein . . . and carriages that wander on the sea, the ships sail winged, who else but I invented." And most importantly, he gave them medicine—"Greatest was this: when one of mankind was sick, there was no defense for him—neither healing food nor drink nor unguent; for lack of drugs they wasted, until I showed them blendings of mild simples with which they drive away all kinds of sickness."

While Aeschylus' Prometheus is ever the boastful technological and scientific genius, this type was not smiled upon and richly rewarded by the ancient Greeks as it is today. And while Prometheus has been seen as an inspiration to some counterculturalists and artists since the Romantics lionized him in the nineteenth century, for the Greeks this was a cautionary tale. Hubris, or pride, was their greatest sin, and Prometheus was their greatest sinner. As with many followers of Christianity later on, scientific hubris was seen as the overstepping of boundaries that disturbed the divine order. In fact, the Greeks did not fully develop their technical sciences because of their fear of hubris. As R. J. Zwi Werblowski wrote in *Lucifer and Prometheus*, "for Aeschylos . . . Prometheus is in trespass . . . sinner he is, and not merely the hero of a righteous war of liberation against cruel tyrants, as a certain school would have it." But in the following line, Werblowski reveals just cause for rejecting the Greeks' own view of their mythology and adopting the Promethean stance when he writes, "Since Zeus' order is that of a static cosmos, every human aspiration and effort is a revolt."

LOVING PROMETHEUS

The Greeks' greatest sinner started getting some modern love when the Romantics embraced him at the start of the nineteenth century. Percy Shelley's *Prometheus Unbound* got the ball rolling. Shelley completed the missing parts of Aeschylus' tale, liberating the Greek god from his eternal suffering and setting him up as a hero for the post-Enlightenment era. As Theodore Roszak writes, *"Prometheus Unbound* is a song of the heights, a dizzy rhapsody offered to flight and the transcendence of all limits." Indeed, where the Greeks saw hubris, Shelley saw "the highest perfection of moral and intellectual nature, impelled by the purest and the truest motives to the best and noblest ends." If Prometheus is the champion of humankind against the cruel Greek god Zeus, Shelley uses the myth to unite mortals with God, defining man in *Prometheus Unbound* as "one harmonious soul of many a soul, whose nature is its own divine control."

Soon Shelley's friend, the revolutionary rascal Lord Byron, offered his own tribute to the Greek techno-god, offering the lines "Thy Godlike crime was to be kind,/To render with thy precepts less/The Sum of human wretchedness/And strengthen Man with his own mind." Deeper into the nineteenth century, Nietzsche, Keats, and most of all Goethe joined the Promethean ranks. Through the voice of Prometheus, Goethe expresses the Romantics' exhaltation in human experience, their joie de vivre, their lust for life . . . and their revolution against authoritarian gods: "Look down, O Zeus, Upon my world, It *lives*. I have shaped it in my image,/A race like unto me,/to suffer, to weep,/to enjoy and be glad,/and like myself to have no regard of you."

PROMETHEUS AND LUCIFER

Though we are now some four centuries into the Enlightenment, Goethe's use of the Promethean voice to scorn God's authority remains a minority taste. The Promethean view has remained controversial, if not downright unpopular. The archetype that most closely resembles Prometheus in Judeo-Christian mythology is the figure of Lucifer (the angel of light), a.k.a. Satan, and despite the best efforts of Anton LaVey and Marilyn Manson, the Luciferian view is not about to win any elections.

Note the underground, underworld overtones of the Prometheus myth. He suffers his agonies by sunlight. The night heals him. And he is possessed by what Edgar Allan Poe called "the imp of the perverse," the prankster spirit. When he first plays tricks on Zeus, leaving him with the meatless animal gristle, the scene appears without provocation. As Kerényi says, "he is a cheat and a thief. . . . By undertaking to deceive Zeus' mind, Prometheus shows himself to be . . . wanting." He further asserts that Prometheus displays "a certain crookedness of mind, ranging from deceitfulness to inventiveness." Human ambivalence about our own clever aspirations and efforts has created an indelible ideational link between inventiveness and criminality. Nietzsche was moved to embrace the criminality of creativity. In *The Birth of Tragedy* he asserted, "The best and brightest that man can acquire they must obtain by crime." He goes on to quote Shelley's Prometheus in support. As a champion of man, the Greek god might be seen as representing their version of original sin. Kerényi says, "Prometheus shows himself to be man's double, an eternal image of man's basically imperfect form of being."

Werblowski, in his book *Lucifer and Prometheus,* finds correspondences between the Satan of Milton's *Paradise Lost,* the Promethean myth, and the notion of "the cosmogonic jester of primitive peoples." For some cultures, the jester is an acceptable part of the cosmic whole, but in both the Greek pantheon and the Judeo-Christian cosmology he is relegated to the shadows.

For Werblowski, both Prometheus and Milton's Satan appear as rebels against a similar sort of cosmic authority: Prometheus disturbs "the order of Zeus . . . perfect, regulated and static." Milton's Satan, meanwhile, is "a rebel against a rather passive God's immutable decrees, [and he] becomes the symbol of the power-carrier who strains every muscle, nerve and fiber against a supreme and unrelenting, and *ipso facto* cold and hostile fate."

Furthermore, Milton—who despite his rather sympathetic and romantic portrayal of Satan affirmed his Christian faith by also condemning him directly and repeatedly—echoed the Greeks in giving creativity, commerce, and technology to the Prince of Darkness. Werblowski: "the fact that [in *Paradise Lost*] Satan's followers build, dig for gold, make music and philosophize, means that man's total culture is condemned."

Regarding one of Milton's episodes involving warfare between the forces of God and Satan, Werblowski further observes, "The real point of the incident lies in the equation of goodness with nature on the one hand, and of the satanic power-craving and explosive *hubris* of technique and machinery on the other."

And you thought *idle* hands were the Devil's workshop.

THE ANTI-PROMETHEANS VERSUS THE NEW PROMETHEANS

Given the Luciferian echoes of Prometheus, it shouldn't surprise us that conservative theologians abhor the romanticization of this myth. But would you expect enlightened mainstream scholars like Roger Shattuck and counterculturalists like Ted Roszak to also sound the cry of "get thee behind me, Prometheus!"? If a strong anti-Promethean current among sophisticated thinkers surprises you, you must be momentarily forgetting some of those other gifts of scientific discovery and technological invention—the split atom and the hydrogen bomb, global warming, bioweaponry, and corporate technocracy.

Roger Shattuck's *Forbidden Knowledge: From Prometheus to Pornography* presents a 342-page argument, one might even call it a screed, in favor of limiting human knowledge and invention. Shattuck finds some literature answerable for man's hubristic follies, including Shelley's Prometheus, Goethe's Faust, Dante's Ulysses, Byron's Don Juan, Cervantes' Don Quixote, and even the good Christian Milton's glamorized Satan in *Paradise Lost.* Shattuck expresses a longing for a different sort of hero. "Since we seem to be so fascinated by human creatures who aspire to exceed their lot and to attain godhead, how shall we ever reconcile ourselves to a countervailing tradition of heroism in humility and quietism, in finding and in accepting our lot? The line that connects Socrates, Buddha, Jesus, St. Francis, Thoreau, Tolstoy, Gandhi, and Martin Luther King."

As you can see, Shattuck throws up an impressive list of alternative thinkers—one might even call it a list of counterculturalists—in opposition to the Promethean impulse. We can't avoid a startling conclusion: there are anti-Promethean and pro-Promethean countercultures. In fact, the division over the Promethean impulse can be used to characterize the main opposition between the major countercultural tendencies of today.

The anti-Promethean counterculturalists include a whole host of familiar types, including: back-to-the-land hippies, introspective followers of Eastern and Eastern-influenced New Age religions, certain types of feminists, certain types of anarchists, and certain types of environmentalists. We could even make the case that the anti-Promethean countercultures share traits with Abraham's counterculture, discussed later in this chapter. They tend to be anti-urban, primitivistic, tribal, and moralistic. At the extreme of this tendency we find the newly influential (at least within the underground) anti-civilization anarchist theorist John Zerzan, who provides ideological inspiration for Seattle's "black-clad anarchists" who famously rioted at the World Trade Organization conference in their town in 1999, inspiring many imitators around the globe in succeeding years.

A somewhat more moderate representative of the anti-Promethean counterculture is Theodore Roszak, the author whose book *The Making of a Counter Culture* put that word into popular circulation in 1969. Roszak—part of a cabal of countercultural critics of technoculture that also includes Jerry Mander, author of *Four Arguments for the Elimination of Television,* and Neil Postman, author of *Amusing Ourselves to Death*— looks to Mary Shelley's 1804 book, *Frankenstein, or The New Prometheus,* for an unambiguously oppositional take on the Promethean legend.

Ironically, Ms. Shelley was married to Percy Shelley, the man who first portrayed Prometheus as a romantic figure. Mary slyly took her husband's obsession with the glory and power of technology and the Promethean spirit and subverted it. She created the persona of Dr. Frankenstein, a mad scientist whose attempt to engineer new human life (think today of biotech, cloning, artificial life, robotics) backfires, creating a monster that brings death and destruction to Dr. Frankenstein's village, and to the doctor himself. Like Roger Shattuck, Roszak believes that the Greeks were correct in fearing the hubristic pursuit of human knowledge and technological development. But Roszak goes even further, seeing the modern world's obsession with scientific and technological advance as a product of a macho, masculine culture. He contends that "Mary [Shelley] was aware of how easily the line can be crossed between Promethean yearnings and macho posturing." Indeed, Prometheus is a severely masculine God. Sounding not a little like Arnold Schwarzenegger, Aeschylus' Prometheus portrays softness and surrender as womanly characteristics to which he will not succumb, saying, "Deem not that I, to win a smile from Jove,/Will spread a maiden smoothness o'er my soul/And importune the foe whom most I hate/With womanish upliftings of the hand."

While Prometheus' strutting machismo may embarrass some of us today, that's not enough to stop a new culture of wired-up technophiles (women included) from identifying with the Promethean spirit. The New Promethean counterculture is a peculiar conglomeration of: computer hackers and other technological experimenters, upbeat neo-hippie electronic music ravers, digital business mavens, and corporate technocrats who still believe in the power of technology to democratize communications and change the world (while making them extremely rich), political libertarians, and visionary artists using new technology to help us see in different ways. At the extreme of this tendency we find the Extropians, who believe in using technology to give us godlike powers, a notion called transhumanism or posthumanism. Extropians believe that we are on the verge of becoming an immortal, post-biological, spacefaring new species. More popular and diffused are the Promethean countercultural communities that have come together online to steal the fire of music from the gods of the music industry (e.g., Napster and its replacements), and the open source fanatics who believe that all digital code should be shared and used freely. Counterculturalist Robert Anton Wilson spoke for the upcoming wired-up technophile culture back in 1983 when he wrote, "This is not a civilization in collapse but a Prometheus rising!"

Counterculture Is Promethean in Essence

The technological enthusiasts who make up cyberculture, and the political libertarians, are the ones who specifically fly the Promethean flag. But in a broader sense, the Promethean spirit is the essential countercultural spirit, as defined by this book. As explained in the next chapter, we see countercultures as fostering individual freethinking and knowledge, and an aesthetic of constant change. A careful examination of the anti-Promethean countercultures discussed earlier would not only uncover some of these Promethean qualities within them, but would reveal them as Promethean at the core despite their anti-technological bias.

For instance, most of these countercultures show a strongly humanistic character. Prometheus, who deemed humanity worthy of endless gifts and powers as well as a previously unthinkable degree of independence from the gods, is an ancient embodiment of what today has come to be called humanism. And Prometheus' humanism, although to some eyes reckless and libertine, is humanism nonetheless.

But counterculture—including its putatively anti-Promethean forms— is essentially Promethean in an even more important and fundamental way: all countercultures, apparently anti-Promethean or otherwise, are archetypally Promethean in terms of their relationship with authority. This applies to authority in general as well as to the authorities or gods of a specific counterculture's time and place. As Prometheus went against Zeus and the gods of Greece, so today's anti-technological countercultures refuse to blindly worship technology, itself one of the great prevailing gods of our era.

Anti-tech, back-to-the land countercultures often advocate the transfer of agriculture and other fundamentals of survival, like sources of energy and water supply, to the individual domicile or small self-sustaining community. In doing so, they reclaim the capacity for autonomous survival by providing for themselves basic necessities that today are almost universally purchased from a vast agro-industrial establishment. In doing so, they withhold power over individual and community life from that establishment and refuse to feed its authoritarian and economic agendas. Thus, even the low-tech solar power sources and collectivist organic gardens of rural, countercultural, supposedly anti-Promethean alternative communities represent, in their own way, a boldly Promethean gesture.

Finally, as long as the philosophic expansiveness of the Enlightenment project continues to be reduced to a mere obligation to endlessly increase production and consumption without regard for quality of experience or environmental distress, the "anti-technological" counterculture will remain an important countervailing force.

ABRAHAM AND THE FIRST DROPOUTS

> God said to Abraham, go for yourself from your land,
> and from your birthplace, and from your father's house,
> to the land that I will show you.
>
> GENESIS 12:1

> God said to Abraham kill me a son/. . . man, you must be
> putting me on.
>
> BOB DYLAN

While a countercultural rebel iconoclast myth of Abraham comes down to us from the Midrash tales of the second century, Abraham's identity as history's first self-exile, or dropout, is traced all the way back to the Old Testament. In the original Bible, Abraham hears the voice of God and leaves behind his home in Ur in search of spiritual renewal in the land of Canaan. (Later, some Kabbalists interpreted "Canaan" to mean "a place of dynamism, tension, or change.") This simple story has been interpreted by many as the primal exile experience.

Even after leaving Ur for their new home in Canaan, the first Jews maintained their dropout/outsider identity. While generous with the herders living there (at least initially), they separated themselves ideologically. In the Old Testament, Abraham declares, "I dwell among you, but I am an alien." Of course, this sense of intentional otherness echoes down the ages, and remains with us today. Indeed, hipster individuals and communities positively revel in it.

The dropout Abraham was the first Jew. At this essential level, his story has generated a religion of exile and dissent.

While Reform Rabbi Arthur Hertzberg was touring to promote his book *Jews: The Essence and Character of a People,* his overriding message was that Judaism is an "eternal countercultural." In his book, Hertzberg declares, "Abraham, the first Jew, is the archetypal Jewish character. As the leader of a small, dissenting minority living precariously on the margins of society, he defines the enduring role of the Jew as the outsider. The recurring themes of Jewish history—otherness, defiance, fragility, and morality—are present in his life."

Drawing from the Bible, Hertzberg paints a picture that would be familiar to some members of the modern hippie Rainbow Tribe. "God tells Abraham to leave his birthplace to go with his wife Sarah to a distant land. There they dwell in tents like Bedouin. . . . They are strangers among the tribes of idol worshippers." But alien*ness* doesn't necessarily connote alienation. Hertzberg writes, "A man of immense charity, he opens his tent on all four sides. The hungry and miserable can come to him in a straight line, not wasting a step to look for the entrance." Abraham's open-handed generosity and impatience with unnecessary boundaries (tear down the walls!), turnstiles, and formalities are archetypally countercultural. And Abraham goes even further in practicing voluntary communalism. "In the land of Canaan, where water is the most precious of commodities and herders survive only if their flocks can drink, Abraham digs wells and takes the unprecedented step of making them available to everyone."

Rabbi Michael Lerner, a product of the New Left counterculture of the 1960s, views Abraham as the primal revolutionist. In his book *Jewish Renewal,* he asserts, "Almost four thousand years ago, an idol worshipper named Abram revolutionized human history by trusting in a Being he could not see. Together with his wife Sarai, he left civilization behind and became a spiritual pioneer. So began Jewish history."

In her book, *Remember My Soul,* Lori Palatnik asserts that God's command to Abraham in Genesis 12:1 to "go . . . from your birthplace, and from your father's house, to the land that I will show you" demands some interpretation because "at this point in the Torah, Abraham has already left his land and his birthplace." Palatnik believes that God is asking Abraham "to make a journey not just of the body but of the soul. He is asking him to leave the comfort of the assumptions he holds about the meaning of life." She later refers to this process as "leaving the familiar," an apt metaphor for any countercultural process.

The Historical Abraham

With the exception of a shrinking group of religious believers, most historians since 1850 have regarded the story of Abraham as pure myth. Ironically, scientific archaeologists have uncovered increasingly detailed evidence that the Old Testament is, in historian Paul Johnson's terms, a "complex and ambiguous guide to the truth."

The city of Ur was found and excavated by Leonard Woolley in the 1920s, in what is now southern Iraq. Since then, the decipherment of the Sumerian language used on tens of thousands of cuneiform tablets found throughout the region confirms the plausibility of many Genesis stories, including Abraham's. The names Abram (the original spelling of Abraham in the Old Testament), Jacob-el, and Joseph have been found in legal documents from Mesopotamia (between the Tigris and Euphrates rivers in present-day Iraq) and Canaan (modern Israel and Jordan) dating from 2100 to 800 B.C.E. More tellingly, the details of translated marriage and real estate contracts match the sorts of agreements and disputations described in the Old Testament stories.

From the archaeological evidence, it is likely that the historical Abraham dropped out of an advanced Sumerian civilization of the third millennium B.C.E. The economy of Sumer was based on barley and emmer wheat, grown using sophisticated engineered irrigation. Like other Sumerian cities, Ur's farms supported a large population inside fortified walls.

These included professional brewers, bakers, and weavers, as well as artisans in wood, stone, ceramics, metal, and jewelry. Within and between the cities, merchants traveled, trading with the Akkadian cities to the north through the Levant to the even older civilization of Egypt as well as with hill-dwelling barbarians to the east.

The tallest structures were the ziggurats, artificial mountains of mud-brick that supported temples whose priests and scribes organized the annual festivals and controlled the distribution of food. These religious icons towered over the city walls. Warrior-kings ruled over all, protecting the cities from barbarian invasions and waging territorial wars with the other city-states, sometimes becoming overlords of several cities. They were seen as agents of the gods. These rigidly stratified urban theocracies were legalistic, disputatious, hierarchical, and bureaucratic.

The religion was polytheistic—rooted in the myths and cults of each city-state's special gods. Each city had a titular deity. Most inhabitants had a specific role within their divine cult. This included all social classes: farmers bearing grain and fruit; weavers and bakers who provisioned the temples; artisans, scribes, priests, and the royal court. Kings had formal cultic duties, even kings of many city-states, who sometimes installed daughters in high priestly offices with large estates, power, and prestige. Political power was organized around the cult and the court.

There is literary evidence of the existence of a distinct subculture during this time, scattered from Sumer through Mesopotamia to Egypt by way of the Levantine coast. These Habiru (a possible root of the word Hebrew) seem to have been a class of outsiders within Middle Eastern civilization. They were apparently urban gypsies, donkey traders, caravan merchants, government employees, mercenary warriors, and unaffiliated families. Abraham was perhaps a founder of such an alternative "unaffiliated" subculture or counterculture.

LISTENING TO GOD

It is postulated that Abraham rebelled against a polytheistic culture by becoming the first monotheist. Today, of course, many counterculturalists reject monotheism, and some embrace polytheism as an alternative. Clearly, different times and situations provoke wildly dissimilar responses. On the other hand, mere contrariness does not make a counterculture. Wrestling Abraham's presumed history into a countercultural context, we note that he broke away from a culture where all beliefs were dictated by social consensus. In contrast, Abraham's connection to his singular divinity came from listening (literally) to the individual voice in his head, which Abraham interpreted as the voice of God. He courageously ignored his society's ubiquitous consensus reality, and stuck to his individualistic guns. Abraham further proclaimed that access to this direct relationship with the divinity was open to anyone by listening to their own inner voice. Abraham's God was portable rather than fixed, and immediately present rather than distant. The culture of the early Jews was nomadic, tribal, and anti-urban. They were apparently not identified with established political units. Instead, they were mercenaries, troublemakers, slaves, rebels, and stubborn religious visionary fanatics.

The presumptive historical Abraham and his early Jewish tribe manifest some aspects of the counterculture trope: dropping out, or exile from the mainstream society; a direct relationship with the divine without the intercession of icons and idols; and a deeply felt individuality. However, it is impossible to attribute one of the primary characteristics of counterculture—nonauthoritarianism and/or anti-authoritarianism—to the historical Abraham. Abraham's monotheism established a new kind of totalitarianism, a self-declared Patriarchy in which the leader was no longer a divinity himself, but a prophet, a man who could hear the voice of the Divinity. The Jewish cultural identity was established around strict legalistic rules for sex and social behavior, as a portable and permanent way to distinguish themselves from their surrounding cultures.

To find a more purely countercultural Abraham, we return to the realm of myth—the Midrash tales—stories told by rabbis and written down starting in the second century C.E.

THE ICONOCLAST

> If your children ever realize how lame you are, they'll
> slaughter you in your sleep.
>
> FRANK ZAPPA, 1966

The most influential legend surrounding Abraham, taken from Midrash stories written by rabbis in the centuries after the Roman diaspora, sounds like a particularly melodramatic episode from the generational conflicts of the 1960s. It, of course, involves a bratty, self-righteous son who questions his father's tepid sold-out value system and messes with the old man's livelihood. Pops gets so pissed off he turns his son in to the authorities.

Abraham's father, Terah, made a living as a maker of stone icons in polytheistic, idol-worshiping Ur. As a young man, Abraham began doubting the worship of these icons. He started giving his dad a tough time about it. Once, when Dad had left Abe behind to mind the store, Abraham chased away a customer by asking him, " 'How old are you?' 'Fifty years,' was the reply. 'Woe to such a man!' Abraham exclaimed. 'You are fifty years old and would worship a day-old object?' The man became ashamed and left."

One day, while pestering his father about his beliefs, young Abraham asked him "who the God was that had created heaven and earth and the children of men." In response, Terah took him to see twelve great idols and lots of little idols. Terah told Abraham, "Here are they who have made all thou seest on earth, they who have created also me and thee and all men on the earth."

So Abraham went to his mother and asked her to give him some "savory meat" as an offering to his father's gods, to make him "acceptable to them." Abraham took the meat to the icons and saw that "they had no voice, no hearing, no motion, and not one of them stretched forth his hand to eat." Abraham mocked the gods. He made another offering. Then he felt the spirit of God. In the words of the Midrash tale, "he cried out, and said: 'Woe unto my father and his wicked generation, whose hearts are all inclined to vanity, who serve these idols of wood and stone, which cannot eat, nor smell, nor hear, nor speak, which have mouths without speech, eyes without sight, ears without hearing, hands without feeling, and legs without motion!' Abraham then took a hatchet in his hand, and broke all his father's gods, and when he had done breaking them he placed the hatchet in the hand of the biggest god among them all, and he went out."

Even if you're unfamiliar with the story, you can guess the rest. Terah

heard the crashing sounds of sonny boy trashing the family store and ran
to him, shouting, "What is this mischief thou hast done to my gods?"
Abraham replied: "I set savory meat before them, and when I came nigh
unto them, that they might eat, they all stretched out their hands to take
of the meat, before the big one had put forth his hand to eat. This one, enraged against them on account of their behavior, took the hatchet and
broke them all, and, behold, the hatchet is yet in his hands, as thou mayest
see."

In response, Terah proved Abraham's point: "Thou speakest lies unto
me! Is there spirit, soul, or power in these gods to do all thou hast told me?
Are they not wood and stone? and have I not myself made them? It is thou
that didst place the hatchet in the hand of the big god, and thou sayest he
smote them all." And Abraham the bratty countercultural son punctured
his father's argument with his reply: "How, then, canst thou serve these
idols in whom there is no power to do anything? Can these idols in which
thou trustest deliver thee? Can they hear thy prayers when thou callest
upon them?" So Terah busted his son, turning him in to the king for rehab.

While the biblical Abraham displays a modicum of anti-authoritarian
moxie in the Old Testament when he argues with his all-powerful God
about his plans for the destruction of Sodom, it is the mythic Abraham of
the Midrash tales, an iconoclastic generational rebel, who strikes us as
most countercultural.

We all know the history of the 1960s generation gap, but how many of
us who were there remember that feeling, arrogant yet undeniable, that we
young were passionately alive, infused with raw energy and spirit, while
our parents were somewhat deadened? While this observation is outside
the realm of ideational countercultural argument, the ineffable sense of superior vitality as a kind of moral good is frequently shared by the young,
but it both intensifies and spreads to at least some members of all age
groups during periods of countercultural excitement. (Of course, fascist
groups get swept up into this kind of primal, atavistic energy as well, so it
is clearly not an absolute good.)

Michael Lerner implicitly infuses his insights into Abraham and
Terah's ancient generation gap with the spirit of the sixties revolt when he
asserts that "Abraham enters history, aware that something is fundamentally wrong, unwilling to accept idolatry. Abraham can sense . . . some

greater potential than . . . the worship of what is—power, beauty, wealth, etc. In breaking the idols he is symbolically trying to break through to Terah, his father, to say: 'This dead matter that is used to justify an oppressive social order is not real, and you and I don't have to remain stuck in it, do we?' The inability of his father to respond, to see the life energy and reality in his son and to say, 'Yes, son, something else is possible,' means that instead he has to see his son as the problem. For Abraham's father to break through social conventions would require a level of emotional, spiritual, and political aliveness that would be overwhelming and threatening." In emphasizing that this is Abraham, the first Jewish man's entrance into history, Lerner also asserts that the Jewish people are imprinted with a kind of rebellious, justice-seeking spirit.

JEWISH RADICALS

Indeed, Jewish dissent arises throughout history. When Alexander the Great conquered the Near East, the Jews protested. When Greek intellectual culture became the de rigueur trend in Hellenistic Rome, the Jews refused to go along. Their rebellion against Rome unleashed an Imperial backlash that destroyed the Temple and initiated the great diaspora. During the Roman Empire, when Christianity was declared the state religion, the Jews resisted then and through centuries of persecution. Karl Marx, Franz Kafka, and Sigmund Freud, all Jews, raised theoretical and existential hell in the nineteenth and early twentieth centuries.

After the Holocaust of the twentieth century, when William Burroughs, Allen Ginsberg, and Jack Kerouac emerged as the main icons of the beat counterculture, it was the Jewish Ginsberg alone who put himself on the line by agitating for radical social change. (In fact, we might consider Ginsberg the father of the hippie/New Left fusion that gave us the word counterculture. After all, it was Ginsberg's bighearted inclusiveness combined with his characteristically Jewish willingness to insist on actual liberty and justice for all that led the way. Consider the other contenders: Ken Kesey, following his obscurantist tendencies, refused leadership, and Timothy Leary always straddled the line between populism and elitism.)

Jewish comedian Lenny Bruce punctured social and political hypocrisies in the early and mid-1960s with such a rapier wit that he was busted ten times, and hounded by the moral authorities unto death. And those comic absurdist Jewish radicals, Yippies Abbie Hoffman and Jerry Rubin, nagged the hippies—refusing to let them retreat into psychedelic spiritual bliss. Instead, they dragged them off to "levitate the Pentagon," to throw dollar bills onto the floor of the New York Stock Exchange, to battle police in anti-war protest in the streets of Chicago, and to support the campus rebellions and the black militant movement. And finally, the most influential twentieth-century nonconformist Jew, Bob Dylan, has graced us both with his lines of insight and by being possibly the most completely inexplicable person to ever grace the earth.

Rabbi Hertzberg even goes so far as to assert that Jews help spur anti-Semitism by pissing people off with their dissident, questioning intellects. According to Hertzberg, "Jews are critical, subversive." Hertzberg calls on his fellow Jews to honor and continue this very tradition that has placed them in so much danger across history. Within the legends of the Jewish religion, Rabbi Lerner finds opposition to oppression, and the quest for justice: "Judaism's claim that God is the Force that . . . assists us in trans-forming the world . . . [means] we are all required to engage in the strug-gle to change the status quo. Torah's conception of God's kingship tells us . . . that the only real power governing our lives is the Force that makes . . . us leave systems of repression and start over, creating something fundamentally different and new."

Lerner also compares the moral activism implicit in Judaism favorably to contemplationist schools of spiritual cultivation, declaring, "Judaism places transcendence on the human agenda. Human beings need not be stuck in a world of pain and oppression. We can regain contact with a deeper level of being . . . beings who are created in the image of God, who embody an inherent tendency toward goodness and holiness, toward being 'embodied spirituality.' . . . Many other religions had the intuition that something was fundamentally missing from human experience, but then they created 'spiritual experience' by pointing to some higher reality in a . . . spiritual world that was divorced from the world of daily life. Judaism insists this split is *not* an ontological necessity."

Rabbi Lerner lives out his belief in a moral, activist spirituality today by agitating against the militaristic policies of the Israeli government. In this he is joined by Rabbi Hertzberg, and by a substantial minority of Jews in Israel and around the world who can't resist the impulse—bequeathed to them from the Abraham of the Midrash tales—to question authority and stand up against injustice.

COUNTERCULTURE MYTH MIRRORS COUNTERCULTURE HISTORY

This chapter has for the most part dealt with myths as apocryphal tales of larger-than-life heroism. But myth is understood on many levels. At least a brief walk-through of today's predominant approaches to myth is required before the broader implications of counterculture's presence in myth can be assessed.

Contemporary psychologists, anthropologists, and historians—foremost among them twentieth-century psychoanalyst Carl Jung and world-famous mythographer Joseph Campbell—assign enormous importance to myth. Many scholars view myths as keys to the soul of humanity, as symbolic doorways into our individual and collective deeper nature.

World mythology features certain mythic archetypes that are universal to nearly all human cultures. The countercultural Trickster, for instance, has been blowing the minds of human beings with his quicksilver elusiveness in frequent appearances around the globe since before the dawn of history. Campbell and his legions of followers take such presences in world mythology as indications of basic human qualities that transcend cultural and temporal barriers. In the hands of Jung, Campbell, and others, myth becomes a kind of racial pre- or extra-historical memory, not so much of *what has happened* as of *what we are*.

This viewpoint reads myths as narrative encodings of humanity's most basic beliefs, drives, aspirations, yearnings, and fears. More simply, myths are the stories we tell ourselves about ourselves, about our fundamental nature and the things that are important to us.

This chapter has located symbols of counterculture in the mythic foundations of the two great historical streams from which modern Western civilization has emerged: the Classical and the Judeo-Christian traditions. Here, the roles of Prometheus and Abraham are hardly peripheral, walk-on parts. Instead, they are central to their respective mythologies. If myth, as so widely held today, tells us about the psychic makeup of humanity, then the towering mythic presences of Abraham and Prometheus, along with the prominence of the Trickster and other countercultural figures in world myth at large, point to the countercultural impulse as an integral element of human nature. Counterculture, myth tells us, is very important indeed.

Some scholars see myth as relevant to virtually every aspect of human existence. Joseph Campbell has famously said: "The latest incarnation of Oedipus, the continued romance of Beauty and the Beast, stands this afternoon on the corner of 42nd Street and Fifth Avenue, waiting for the traffic light to change." Campbell is telling us: as in myth, so in human life.

And as in myth, so in human history. The stories of Prometheus and Abraham mirror the historical reality of counterculture in telling ways. In the myth of Prometheus, the countercultural figure is viewed—at least in the ancient accounts—as an overwhelmingly evil influence on humankind. In the story of Abraham, the countercultural figure's role is profoundly positive; he is the source of a vast legacy embraced as a foundation for living by an entire people. This disparity reflects the oppositional feelings, the fierce enmity and sacrificial loyalty, that historical countercultures evoke in the times and places in which they arise.

More importantly, the tales of Prometheus and Abraham are about beginnings, origins, and sources. Abraham appears as the literal and spiritual progenitor of the great tribe whose story provides the focus for one of world's most important documents. Prometheus, with his spirit of rebellion, innovation, and revolutionary humanism, is cast as the bringer of everything from writing and mathematics to transport and medicine (before all of which, as quoted earlier, human beings "lived beneath the earth . . . in sunless caves"). It is no great stretch to read the Prometheus tale as suggesting that the innovations now associated with the Neolithic Era, and then civilization itself, arose from the countercultural impulse.

The role and prominence of counterculture in the mythic dimension explored by this chapter are mirrored in the historical ground mapped by the rest of this book. The chapters that follow show counterculture as a crucial source of change at the very center stage of history.

OTHER COUNTERCULTURAL MYTHS

Before we step away from pure mythology and into the world of actual historic countercultures, we should mention some other mythological figures who strike us as countercultural. We think of Eve, the first woman, who took a bite of that forbidden Schedule One fruit of all knowledge, setting off the first drug bust. And we think of that other naughty chick Pandora, who casually opened her box one day, setting loose the evils of the world. (Notice how these mythologies like to blame the women!) We think of Jim Morrison's favorite, Dionysius, the oversexed imbiber of wine and hallucinogens who got torn apart by wild groupies. We think of the Sorceress Circe with her magic potions. We think of Goethe's immortality-seeking bad boy Faust. We think of Robin Hood and his merry band of Weathermen. We think of Alfred E. Neuman . . .

CHAPTER TWO

⊦ A DIFFERENT TYPE OF HUMAN EXCELLENCE

Defining Counterculture

> There is a different type of human excellence . . . a conception of humanity as having its nature bestowed on it for other purposes than merely to be abnegated. . . .
>
> It is not by wearing down into uniformity all that is individual in themselves, but by cultivating it and calling it forth . . . that human beings become a noble and beautiful object of contemplation . . . and whatever crushes individuality is despotism, by whatever name it may be called and whether it professes to be enforcing the will of God or the injunctions of men.
>
> JOHN STUART MILL, "OF INDIVIDUALITY"

From one perspective, counterculture appears to be a challenge to the very notion of history. To rebels against tradition, explorers lighting out for new conceptual territories, and (in some cases) advocates of the Eternal Now, history may seem, at best, quaint, and, at worst, the enemy. At the very least, the Western concept of history as a narrative progression primarily defined by big-name leaders, varying social structures writ large, and the changing boundaries among warring nation-states seems almost explicitly designed to bind us to a mainstream vision of humanity's (very limited) potential. In this context, the historical record conspires to convince us that the dominance of noncountercultural behaviors, like conformism and authoritarianism, defines humanity. We are sometimes tempted to say that those who *remember* history are, in fact, the ones condemned to repeat it.

But as Western culture, and particularly its younger generations, speed toward increasingly ahistoric times, the picture doesn't look pretty. For one thing, short historical memories decontextualize volatile situations in the contemporary world, producing negative results. So we might, for instance, respond to the rage of the colonized (or formerly colonized) with uncomprehending irritation, as if their lack of passivity is a shortcoming in character, an inexplicable rudeness that sometimes reaches the level of violence. Or we (in the U.S.) may simply accept the common wisdom that our nation-state is "the land of the free," without really understanding the rights guaranteed in our Constitution and Bill of Rights and the ways in which they have been both expanded and diminished.

At the level of counterculture, we may find lots of young people influenced by hippie hedonism, but with no real awareness of that movement's deeper philosophic tenets. Even more dangerous, they may consume that movement's sacramental plants and chemicals without adequate practical information about safety, or how to harmoniously integrate their experiences into their daily lives.

This rush toward ahistoricity even deprives some of today's countercultural youth movements of some depth and humanity. Throughout the 1990s, Generation X/technoculture embraced a cult of the new. *Wired* magazine, sounding exactly like Chairman Mao during his brutal sixties Cultural Revolution in China, celebrated rapid technological change as a "typhoon" wiping away all remnants of the past. This rejection of all things past reached its apotheosis in that glorious outburst of countercultural exuberance known as the rave movement. By the mid-1990s, the most devastating putdown in this culture's arsenal was the phrase "That's so five minutes ago."

By ignoring history, even recent history, "cult of the new" counterculturalists deprive themselves of splendid things—like the mind-expanding wonders of the music of John Cage and Iannis Xenakis, or the intensely countercultural statements made by the Rolling Stones' *Beggars Banquet* or the Sex Pistols' *Never Mind the Bollocks Here's the Sex Pistols,* or even Tricky's astounding *Pre-Millennium Tension,* which is now like *sooo* five years ago. Of course, each generation likes to feel that it's invented its own rebel culture, and as this book will illustrate, they're mostly correct. The essential countercultural spirit perpetually reinvents itself in unpredictable ways, outrageous styles, and novel forms. Nevertheless, many twenty-first-century youth counterculturalists could benefit from learning the history of their late-twentieth-century antecedents, and we could all benefit from learning about countercultural movements from the depths of time.

WHAT IS HIP?

> I walk forty-seven miles of barbed wire/Use a cobra snake for a necktie
>
> BO DIDDLEY

Very few people have an exact, handy definition for what counterculture is, but they're pretty certain that they know it when they see it. In fact, when Theodore Roszak popularized the term in his 1969 book, *The Making of a Counter Culture,* we could *literally* see who the people were that fit into his conception. Any male with long hair and possibly a beard, wearing raggedy-assed patched jeans, a bandanna, and maybe a tie-dyed T-shirt was almost certainly a counterculturalist. Any woman with even longer hair, wearing the same thing as the guy, or alternatively a peasant dress, was also probably a counterculturalist . . . in other words, almost everyone in college at that time. These people represented a synthesis of the hippie movement—dedicated to mind-expanding drug experimentation and going with the flow, and the New Left/peace movement—dedicated to challenging authority, ending imperialism and war, and an ill-defined communalism.

From Roszak's perspective, theirs was a revolt against an alienating, mechanized, overly materialistic civilization in favor of a more natural, intuitive, harmonious, and generous way of life. But to others, like Tim Leary and (to a lesser extent) the Yippies and the Diggers, they were pre-capitulating a world in which technology liberated us from human scarcity and alienating labor, granting us a life of spontaneous, playful self-exploration and, indeed, self-indulgence. Whatever vision (and there were thousands of others) of the baby boomers' counterculture we subscribe to, we can be sure of one thing: Newt Gingrich believes it ruined America.

Of course, cultural characteristics that are first perceived as challenging, novel, and even revolutionary may eventually strike us as stale—a caricature. Today, a long-haired guy is just as likely to be a reactionary redneck, and the hippie countercultural zeitgeist has been supplanted by a broader, more eclectic alternative culture composed of counterculturally inflected subcultures. Punks, avant-garde artists, the hip-hop underground, anti-globalization activists and Black Bloc anarchists, *Wired*-reading technoculturalists and hackers, club culture trendoids, conscious rappers, educated psychedelicists, Burning Man, modern primitives with steel implants and piercings dangling from every organ, denizens of the sexual underground, pagans, postmodern academics, funkateers, New Agers, riot grrls, slackers, ravers, natty dreadsters, Zen Buddhists, Gnostics, lonely iconoclasts, Deadheads, poetry slammers, goths, tree huggers, libertines and libertarians—all are sometimes defined (and self-defined) as countercultural.

As if this laundry list of "weirdos" isn't enough to contend with, some traditionalist groups—fundamentalist Christian and orthodox Jewish groups—have started to refer to themselves as countercultures. *Webster's New World Dictionary* defines counterculture as "a culture with a lifestyle that is opposed to the prevailing culture," so it's not surprising that groups who are deeply opposed to pluralism, abortion, rationalism, sexual freedom, science, materialistic self-indulgence, free speech, and many other aspects of our culture that are more or less mainstream, would see themselves as countercultural. By this definition, even Islamic jihadists who live in Western lands constitute a counterculture.

"COUNTERCULTURE" IS UP FOR GRABS

While a few similarities can be found between some countercultural elements and these fundamentalist groups, we reject the definition of counterculture as simply any lifestyle that differs from the prevailing culture. Clearly, the definition of counterculture is up for grabs, but we contend that, whatever their differences, there was a singular mutual intention motivating nearly all who defined themselves in countercultural terms up until the last few years. They were all anti-authoritarian or nonauthoritarian. Our defining vision asserts that the essence of counterculture as a perennial historical phenomenon is characterized by the affirmation of the individual's power to create his own life rather than accepting the dictates of surrounding social authorities and conventions, be they mainstream or subcultural. We further assert that freedom of communication is an essential characteristic of counterculture, since affirmative contact holds the key to liberating each individual's creative power. (Throughout the rest of this book, we will be making declarative statements about the nature of counterculture. We acknowledge that these observations are rooted in our own point of view, and other views are possible. However, qualifying all of our statements with that awareness would become tiresome to both the readers and the writers.)

Cultural phenomena are extremely multiplex entities. This fact presents enormous challenges to any effort to define and make generalizations about cultural movements. These difficulties are described by Roszak in the Preface to *The Making of a Counter Culture*:

> I have colleagues in the academy who have come within an ace of convincing me that no such things as "the Romantic Movement" or "the Renaissance" ever existed—not if one gets down to scrutinizing the microscopic phenomena of history. At that level, one tends only to see many different people doing many different things and thinking many different thoughts. . . . It would surely be convenient if these perversely ectoplasmic Zeitgeists were card-carrying movements, with a headquarters, an executive board, and a file of official manifestoes. But of course they aren't. One is therefore forced to take hold of them with a certain trepidation, allowing expectations to slip through the sieve of one's generalizations in great numbers, but hoping always that more that is solid and valuable remains behind than filters away.

The problems Roszak bemoans multiply themselves as we attempt to define not just a single cultural episode, but instead a whole category of historical cultural occurrences.

A cursory glance at the table of contents for this book could easily give rise to confusion regarding the vast range of social phenomena we've defined as countercultural. The countercultures we've chosen are extremely diverse and disparate—for example, it's hard to see an immediate relationship between the Age of Reason, the Sufis, and the Surrealists. Some movements are remembered as primarily spiritual, while others are known for their artistic, political, and philosophical contributions. Some contradict others in certain aspects. The Socratics introduced deductive reasoning while the Dadaists exploded it. The seventeenth-century libertines mocked spirituality while the Sufis pursued it in a sometimes libertine manner.

This sometimes contradictory diversity might lead some readers to conclude that we basically rounded up all the cultural and political movements we found cool or interesting, and called it a history of counterculture. Not true. Counterculture movements, no matter how different they seem from one another, arise from variable combinations of the same principles and values.

COUNTERCULTURE'S DEFINING PRINCIPLES

Humans are multifaceted, perversely unsituatable beings, and countercultural types tend to be among the most difficult to pin down. Nevertheless, there are certain root principles, or meta-values, that distinguish countercultures from mainstream society, as well as from subcultures, religious and ethnic minorities, and noncountercultural dissident groups. The primary characteristics of counterculture are threefold:

- Countercultures assign primacy to individuality at the expense of social conventions and governmental constraints.
- Countercultures challenge authoritarianism in both obvious and subtle forms.
- Countercultures embrace individual and social change.

Individuality is central to counterculture. In some sense, we could have easily called this a history of freethinkers and free thought. Assigning primacy to individuality entails the cultivation, encouragement, and defense of individual self-expression, not only in terms of "freedom of speech" but in regard to belief, personal appearance, sexuality, and all other aspects of living. The countercultural spirit denies only those expressions of individuality that clearly oppress others.

Our vision of counterculture centered on individuality is admittedly fraught with dangers. Many dissidents and counterculturalists have come to associate the word individualism with greed, selfishness, a lack of compassion, and the existential loneliness that comes from rejecting (or being rejected by) community. Countercultural individuality does not embrace mere self-centeredness. Countercultural individuality is deep individuality, shared. It includes people and cultures that follow the Socratic admonition to "know thyself." This distinction brings to mind an interview I (Ken) once read in an underground newspaper with avant-garde filmmaker Kenneth Anger. Commenting on Aleister Crowley's famous phrase "Do what thou wilt shall be the whole of the law," Anger said (I'm paraphrasing) that this doesn't mean you should just do whatever the hell you want. The purpose of the magickal exploration is to find your "true will" through deep, disciplined self-exploration. The seeker must first find out what her will *is,* before doing it.

Despite these qualifiers, our interpretation of counterculture undeniably reads a bit (small l) libertarian. We are not going to discuss here whether the right to infinitely accumulate personal property and wealth is a necessary guarantor of individual liberty or, in fact, inimical to it. But we will assert that just as we reject mere selfishness, we also exclude mere communalism from our definition. Cultures that prevent or discourage individuals from fully exploring and expressing their authentic being—whether through direct coercion or populist peer pressure—can't be considered countercultural. Participation in most quintessential countercultures therefore rarely requires that the individuals do, say, think, or believe anything precisely. All that is demanded is a commitment to the process of stripping away the bondage of both externally enforced and internally inculcated authority so that authentic individuality can blossom.

—

Another primary characteristic of countercultures—one that flows directly from their individualism—is that they challenge authoritarianism in both its obvious and its subtle forms. Some countercultures might challenge the overt control of individuals by state or religious powers. But all challenge the more subtle authoritarianism exerted by rigid belief systems, widely accepted conventions, inflexible aesthetic paradigms, and both spoken and unspoken taboos.

The broad compass of authoritarian phenomena that countercultures challenge is suggested by the continuum of New World countercultural movements beginning with the American democratic uprising and proceeding through New England Transcendentalism to the Lost Generation literary experiment. The first of these episodes threw off the authority of the British Empire over its colonies. The Transcendentalists liberated individual spirituality from the authority of organized religion. And the romantics of the Lost Generation challenged the tyranny of syntax over thought, overturning literary conventions in search of a natural language of the mind.

Counterculture's anti-authoritarian humanism is sometimes asserted through outright rebellion and revolution. But unlike most revolutionists, the revolutionary counterculturalist doesn't seek to establish an alternative authoritarian regime in place of the old, but rather to move toward ever-increasing freedom and democratic empowerment for the greatest number of people.

Some counterculturalist groups and individuals are self-identified as anarchists. Today, anarchy is generally associated with violent, chaotic situations, periods when—in the absence of authority—people engage in destructive, "lawless" activities that make it difficult, or impossible, for most folks to obtain necessities for living. When we say, for instance, "Iraq is in a state of anarchy," we know that this is not a good thing. The common belief is that an anarchist is a person who advocates "no government." This is generally true, but the phrase "no governor" is more exact, since there may be agreed-upon rules (preferably by consensus) and ways of enforcing those rules when absolutely necessary.

Anarchists believe that people can best live and organize their lives without hierarchy or coercion. There are dozens of different theories about how this ideal should be realized and what form it should take. Anarchism epitomizes nonauthoritarian political philosophy. The question that remains is whether it is practicable, particularly among large populations. Many anti-authoritarians believe that idealistic attempts to practice pure anarchy on a large scale would prove disastrous and only lead to a mass demand for renewed, strong, authoritarian governance. Most would try to severely limit hierarchy and coercion through vastly expanded democratic and civil libertarian means.

Another primary characteristic of all countercultural episodes is an enthusiasm for personal and social change. This embrace may be formulated quite abstractly, as in Taoist philosopher Lao-tzu's insight that change is the only constant, or the ancient Greek Heraclitus' similar proclamation that "everything changes; nothing remains." In Taoist counterculture, this wisdom was associated with an anarchistic but ultimately passive politics. Other counterculturalists have opted to embody the principle of change in concrete, large-scale social action.

On the individual level, counterculturalists demonstrate changeability: a fluid, chameleon-like process of perpetual transformation in personal identity, interests, and pursuits. Counterculturalists passionately perform what Nietzsche called "transvaluation"—a philosophy and a way of life that involve continual experimentation with changing value systems, perceptions, and beliefs as an end in itself.

Here, activist countercultures like sixties radicalism and passive countercultures like Taoism find some common ground. Just as many well-known sixties counterculturalists progressed through an astonishing series of permutations in style, aesthetics, politics, and philosophy over a few short years, the most celebrated exemplars of Taoism and Zen have traditionally been inscrutable to others because of their unpredictable and contradictory behavior from moment to moment, day to day, and year to year.

The countercultural embrace of constant change is sometimes confused with trendiness or the acceptance of *any* change. Particularly today, whatever activity is au courant in media and youthful culture (which extends almost into old age) may be described as "hip"—joining the Marines, racing cars in the streets, engaging in intimacy contests on national TV, or following around the rock band Phish. At the risk of being obvious, some changes, like a change from democracy to dictatorship, or from a libertine to a martial culture, are clearly not countercultural in nature.

Naturally, all primary countercultural principles are expressed within parameters that are shaped by the historical moment. Specific historical countercultures represent the underlying directives of counterculture through aspiration and direction, but the animation of these principles in the world is limited by human imperfection. Indeed, the very human contradictions and imperfections found within these historic episodes provide this narrative with opportunities for irreverent criticism, hopefully giving it more of an authentic countercultural character than a mere exercise in cheerleading—or a dry recitation of facts—would have provided.

NEARLY UNIVERSAL FEATURES OF COUNTERCULTURE

Other characteristics manifested by most of the countercultures in this book arise from the fundamental defining principles we just covered. These nearly universal features of counterculture are:

▌ Breakthroughs and radical innovations in art, science, spirituality, philosophy, and living.
▌ Diversity.
▌ Authentic, open communication and profound interpersonal contact. Also, generosity and the democratic sharing of tools.
▌ Persecution by mainstream culture of contemporaneous subcultures.
▌ Exile or dropping out.

Countercultures are transgressive, avant-garde movements. The countercultural embrace of change and experimentation inevitably results in pushing beyond accepted views and aesthetics. The most outstanding examples of countercultural discovery and invention resulting from this impulse—taken together—form one of the major narrative lines in this book. We are looking at boundary transgressions that change history.

The innovations might be political, spiritual, philosophical, artistic, or indeed difficult to pigeonhole. Examples extend from the formation of the Socratic method at the foundations of Western thought to the aesthetic accomplishments arising from Sufism (the verse of Rumi, for instance—currently the world's best-selling poet), and to the democratic ideals that receive universal lip service across the planet today.

If a seeming counterculture looks like a conformist monoculture, it is probably either a genuine counterculture struggling with mass popularization, or a subculture. Countercultures display an exceptional diversity. In contrast, subcultures are usually defined by a kind of alternative or minority conformism.

On the other hand, any gathering into a self-defined cultural group is going to be motivated by *some* commonality, even if it's a gathering of people who—like Groucho Marx—wouldn't want to join any group that would have them as a member. Also, particularly during adolescence and early adulthood, there tends to be a groping after identity. Genuine nonconformists may still feel some need to flaunt the styles and badges of some flavor of contemporary alternativeness. At the other extreme, some counterculturalists are clearly identifiable by their absolute refusal to acknowledge that they're countercultural at all. Why would they choose to so fit in? They are *such* counterculturalists! Anyway, the distinction between subculture and counterculture can be subtle and subject to debate.

Open communication—the free exchange of art and thought between like minds—is often an important element in spawning countercultural communities. Intellectual communication is key to the formation of countercultures. When one counterculturalist dares to divulge his or her heretical notions to a sympathetic ear, a link is created that might become the first in a chain of countercultural community.

The value that counterculturalists place on interpersonal communication is reflected in Sufi Caliph Ali Ben Ali's declaration "A subtle conversation—Ah! That is the true Garden of Eden!" And Ralph Waldo

Emerson said he'd walk a hundred miles through a snowstorm for one good conversation.

Intimate emotional communication—the practice of profound soul baring—is as important as intellectual communication in most of these communities. Recall how the tender courage to bare one's deepest secrets was at the core of the beat movement, and not just in the public, published confessionals of Ginsberg, Kerouac, Diane di Prima, and others. Before their works received wide circulation, the beats spent hundreds of nights talking intimately with each other until dawn.

The beat movement, of course, did emerge from its private hipster intimacy and into the glaring media spotlight. Most countercultural eruptions were, indeed, propelled by the creative use of whatever media or public fora were available. Socrates acquired his students by holding forth in the public gymnasia and markets of Athens. The troubadours spread a new concept of love throughout Europe by traveling and singing songs. There would have been no American Revolution without unflagging pamphleteering. Picasso bent the world's visual perception forever through the medium of the canvas. And the 1960s might have been a firecracker instead of a fusion bomb if not for the sublime sonic subversion etched into the grooves of mass-marketed vinyl records.

Most counterculturalists believe in unqualified liberty to communicate the contents of their minds and imaginations. It's not surprising, then, that countercultures are usually subjected to some level of persecution. When a counterculture is born, a society finds foreigners in its midst. Breaking taboos, violating norms, challenging sacrosanct ideas: the anti-authoritarian spirit inherent in counterculture potentially threatens any established order. Suppression frequently follows.

Types of persecution range from official campaigns of mass obliteration by state authorities to social ostracism and the rejection of the countercultural individual by his peers and family. The degree to which a given counterculture was or is persecuted depends significantly on the extent to which that movement engages in open social activism, and how widely it broadcasts its messages.

When persecution fails to stamp out an active counterculture, the dominant culture tends to assimilate it, subtly weakening, distorting, or sometimes inverting its memes, robbing them of their subversive power.

Establishment forces integrate countercultural phraseology into their own propaganda, while economic powers reduce countercultural art and aesthetics to a mass-marketed commodity. Theodore Roszak writes in *The Making of a Counter Culture,* "it is the cultural experimentation of the young that often runs the worst risks of commercial verminization—and so of having the force of its dissent dissipated." New Left philosopher Herbert Marcuse called this process co-optation.

On the other hand, even the most commercialized aspects of the countercultural meme were profoundly subversive to the totalitarian Stalinist states that fell at the end of the 1980s. And even in the relatively open corporate democracies, co-optation may yet backfire. Has the commercialization of anti-authoritarian irreverence through music, comedy, children's animation, and so many other media given bad attitude to an even more widespread and tougher counterculture among many of today's young, as manifested by Gen X skepticism, open source culture, raving, and the anti-globalization movement? And can the countercultural spirit survive war fever in a nation under attack by an invisible enemy? These questions remain unanswered.

Dropping out is one frequent countercultural response to these difficulties. Even when not forced into exile, countercultures often seek greater freedom to explore and live according to their values by separating themselves from the mainstream. This secession can involve geographic isolation, or it can occur by more subtle methods.

Like the American Transcendentalists before them, many members of the sixties youth counterculture took the geographic route by establishing experimental communes in remote rural areas. The American writers and artists of the Lost Generation chose complete exile, expatriating to the more sophisticated territories of Paris and other European locales.

Other counterculturalists dropped out of the mainstream while continuing to live in its midst. The beats separated themselves from America's hyper-conformist fifties society through distinctive dialect, unusual modes of dress, and a refusal to participate in the corporate rat race even at the cost of poverty. (Some may sneer that the major beat figures eventually became financially comfortable as the result of their writings and lectures. However, Allen Ginsberg was the only one who was ever in any danger of having a genuinely high freelance income, and he gave most of his money away.) But most beats remained in the cities instead of heading for the hills. Similarly, punk squats, urban "hippie" communes, and illegal warehouse takeovers by ravers have carved out "temporary autonomous zones"— places and moments of self-selected liberty from the rule of law—in the heart of mainstream power.

Generosity is another important and nearly universal feature of counterculture. Abraham opened up his tents to feed the poor. The Zen bodhisattva lives a life of service, without succumbing to the self-righteousness of the charitable. Gertrude Stein and Ezra Pound generated support for boundary-defying artists in early-twentieth-century Paris. Countercultures tend to value humanity over property, and many love nothing as much as giving stuff away for free. Other countercultures express their generosity through the Promethean impulse to democratically share technological innovation and discovery, ideas, visions, and artwork. The famous hacker slogan "Information wants to be free" is very much a core countercultural concept.

THE PERSONALITIES OF COUNTERCULTURISTS

You see this one-eyed midget shouting the word "Now."

BOB DYLAN

Counterculturalists tend to be jokers, bohemians, and libertines. These qualities subvert serious analyses, but we shouldn't diminish the importance of these stylistic undercurrents. The antic behaviors and easy sensuality found in countercultures across time are, in some ways, the special ingredients that make many countercultures attractive.

Pranksters, cosmic jesters, yarn-spinning riddlers, and defiant mockers of all that's pompous populate many of our stories. Countercultural playfulness represents the nonauthoritarian refusal to take oneself, any ideology, or any code of righteousness too seriously.

Among the Socratics, we recall the philosophically pointed pranks that Diogenes played on Plato's Academy. Humor was an instrument for transmitting profound wisdom in the teaching tales of Taoism, Sufism, and Zen. The stories from all these traditions similarly rely on existential, mind-twisting punch lines to alter the listener's perceptions.

Turning the Boston Harbor into a giant cup of tea to mock British rule was both an act of radical civil disobedience and wry irony on the part of eighteenth-century American revolutionary counterculturalists. In the 1960s, humor was at the heart of the radical activism of Abbie Hoffman's Yippies. The Yippies drove the authorities nuts, attempting to "levitate the Pentagon," bringing a pig into the streets of Chicago as their 1968 presidential candidate, throwing dollar bills from the top floor of the New York Stock Exchange, and performing other political acts of absurdity too numerous to list. Ken Kesey's band of Merry Pranksters took many young Americans into a raucous and sublimely silly LSD wonderland. And in the late 1960s, the world's most popular performers, the Beatles, released scads of impish songs riddled with psychedelic in-jokes and double entendres. Today, playful ravers dress like children attending a birthday party in some science-fictive future, wearing flashing lights, iridescent accessories, and sucking on the glow-in-the-dark pacifiers strung around their necks.

Persecution failed to suppress the sixties counterculturalists' irreverent fun. The defendants in the Chicago Seven trial turned the proceedings into an outrageous comedy play—even as their freedom was on the line. Timothy Leary, repeatedly taken into custody by the authorities, always flashed a wild grin for the media cameras. The famous picture of a protester placing a flower in the barrel of a soldier's rifle stands as an archetypal lighthearted response to grim authority.

For some otherwise jaded postmodern citizens—who have long since digested absolute freedom of expression, and the death of both ideology and (the conventional monotheistic) God—it is only the hedonism of some of our counterculturists that still disturbs. Honesty compels us to admit that libertine lifestyles tend to produce ambiguous results. Nineteenth-century philosopher Søren Kierkegaard engaged in a disquisition that tried to show that a pleasure-oriented lifestyle is unsustainable. The great boho decadent Oscar Wilde expressed his own ambiguities in his classic *The Picture of Dorian Gray.* Throughout the latter half of the twentieth century, conservatives have whined—and not without cause—about some of the more sordid results of mass bohemianism.

Countercultural liberties can open pathways to well-being that aren't recognized by mainstream culture—but can also result in a reckless disregard for self and others. The freedom to self-cultivate in new ways and the freedom to self-destruct through socially unacceptable channels were both evident in sixties Haight-Ashbury. While throngs of Haightsters were taking up yoga, vegetarianism, and the careful, thoughtful use of mind-manifesting plants and chemicals for self-discovery—all practices the American mainstream had barely even heard of—equal numbers were falling prey to heroin, methamphetamine, and sexually transmitted diseases—issues equally foreign to middle-class culture. The liberty to explore alternative ways of living manifested in a complex blend of opposing tendencies. Some junkies became yogis; some yogis became junkies; and others sat piously in the lotus posture injecting speedballs into their veins. Even some who practiced newfound methods for self-discovery and well-being did so in a destructive manner. Vegetarians starved themselves of protein. Meditators and acidheads let themselves be brainwashed into corrupt or psychotic cults. Spiritual seekers embraced various permutations of the new mysticism so self-righteously that they became rigid, oppressive "White Light Nazis."

Whether following libertine countercultural impulses—in comparison to more self-disciplined paths—is desirable is ultimately a personal, existential question. Should intensity of experience be privileged over health and longevity? Jack Kerouac famously wrote, "the only people for me are the mad ones, the ones who are mad to live, mad to talk, mad to be saved, desirous of everything at the same time, the ones who never yawn or say a commonplace thing, but burn, burn, burn." Can the road of excess truly lead to the palace of wisdom or—as in the case of Jerry Garcia and other psychedelic veterans who ultimately pitched their tents in the land of Oblivia—vice versa?

COUNTERCULTURE AND DRUGS IN PERSPECTIVE

Drug use, of course, is the great bugaboo, the contentious issue that lurks in any discussion of contemporary counterculture. What surprises here, perhaps, is the extent to which drug use is *not* central to this exploration (at least not until we get into the twentieth century). Still, mind-affecting plants and chemicals do pop up across countercultural history, so it is necessary to give a perspective on how they fit into the countercultural picture.

In counterculture since the beats, so-called hard drugs—stimulants and narcotics like speed, heroin, and cocaine—have occasionally fostered fruitful creative frenzy (some beat poetry) or provided a context for narratives of hilarious morbidity and artful gloom (William Burroughs). These drugs have been used with enjoyment and apparent impunity by some. But because of the syndromes of dissolution so often connected with their long-term use, such substances have generally undermined the project of embodying the countercultural impulse in effective action and sustainable modes of living. Counterculture by definition strives toward freedom, while drug addiction is a kind of slavery. In this sense, addictive drug use can ultimately be assessed as anathema to counterculture despite its widespread presence in recent countercultural episodes.

There is a vast history regarding the use of psychedelic (mindmanifesting) plants like psilocybin, peyote, and marijuana to obtain spiritual and religious visions and shamanic healing powers, allowing individuals and groups access to the numinous realm without the intercession of any religious authority. This history is widely disregarded within the mainstream culture, but readers can learn all they need to know simply by reading Huston Smith's *Cleansing the Doors of Perception: The Religious Significance of Entheogenic Plants and Chemicals.*

More to the point of this particular narrative, altered states of consciousness can sometimes help people conceive alternative truths or open them up to multiple perspectives. In *High Frontiers* magazine, Bruce Eisner and Peter Stafford described the use of various mind-altering drugs as being "like changing the perceptual filters on your camera to give you a variety of pictures of reality." Psychedelics like LSD, mescaline, and later MDMA (or Ecstasy), while certainly presenting some hazards, have fueled the countercultural drive by illuminating utopian visions, inspiring artistic departures, and exposing consensus reality as a buffoon emperor with clay feet and minimal clothing. Even the dark side of the psychedelic experience has made its contribution, infusing the desire for radical change with electric urgency by rendering the horrors of modern life in the vivid, pulsing close-up images of a trip focused on harsh negative realities.

Within these contexts, the use of certain plants and drugs, particularly but not necessarily the psychedelics, is presumed to be understood as an indicator of a particularly unrestrained example of counterculturalness. At the same time, let's stipulate that this is not always the case for all individuals and cultures, historically or currently. Even the relatively drug-saturated counterculturals of recent decades have given place to counterculturalists who had nothing to do with drugs. For example, adherents of the France-centered Situationist movement—a pivotal influence on much of the sixties youth counterculture—pointedly eschewed drugs. Similarly, the influential early-eighties "straight edge" element of hard-core punk rock provided a powerful anti-drug voice, although its members usually evinced an appropriately countercultural tolerance toward drug users themselves.

At its best—again mostly, but not exclusively, with the psychedelics—counterculture drug exploration goes beyond the usual chemical quest for recreation, relief, or oblivion. Instead, it becomes a manifestation of counterculture's great perennial embrace of new ideas, technologies, experiences, and modes of being. It is from this context that works like Aldous Huxley's *The Doors of Perception,* Daniel Pinchbeck's *Breaking Open the Head,* and the classic Beatles song "Tomorrow Never Knows" have arisen, evincing the same quality of greatness that so often appears when the countercultural impulse is followed with passion and courage.

Is Counterculture Counter Anymore?

Western and global culture today is a confusion of values. But who can deny that—within the chaotic complexity of this New World Disorder—ever more individuals have increased individual freedom to nonconform to conventions and to communicate their own eccentric ideas? Before the popularization of the Internet and the easy availability of other types of communications technology, most Western civilians didn't have convenient means for expressing themselves, or for distributing the results. Today, while free speech and thought, questioning authority, constant change, sexual liberty, and most other aspects of counterculturalness are not quite majority tastes, these liberties *are* permitted and available to a tremendous number of global citizens, if not the majority. Perhaps counterculture is no longer counter.

On the other hand, we continue to experience backlashes against liberty. Cultural conservatives are particularly up in arms about the progress counterculture has made in softening popular attachments to rigid, absolutist belief structures. The conservatives feel this "moral relativism" is responsible for an ethical vacuum. They assert that people in a mass society need precise dictates and codes to live by—preferably decreed by religious authority and enforced by the fear of a judgmental, punishing God. They see the lack of a highly defined, inflexible social ideology as responsible for social anomie and decadence, drug abuse, sexual abuse, gangstaism, and the general rudeness extant in Western culture today. They blame the 1960s. While we could list a number of other factors that are equally to blame for these troubling and troubled behaviors that concern everyone who wants to live in peace and prosperity, not just culture conservatives, we won't deny that liberty plays a role in all this "chaos."

Despite the apparent embrace of the Enlightenment doctrine of individual liberty in the eighteenth century, most people since have lived in societies and communities that imposed fairly well-defined social conventions and offered them productive lifelong roles. As the conventions, roles, communities, and families that have sustained stable conformist identities crumble under the strain of whirlwind technological development, global cultural interpenetration, and individual liberty, many—maybe even most—postmodern citizens find themselves thrown for a loss. The Taoist idea of flowing with constant change, the scientific method of experimentally seeking knowledge rather than arriving at certainty, the Surrealist's gift for turning chaos into art and "meaningless meaning"—these ways of seeing and being in the world are not yet understood by most people living in the (relatively) free lands. And even when they're understood intellectually, it's not easy to truly live free.

The true countercultural path is a difficult one. It's doubtful whether a majority will be happy living without some sort of externally dictated belief system anytime soon. Freedom from certitude and rigid behavioral codes will undoubtedly continue to provoke confusion, angst, and destructive behavior in many. And at a mass level, in post-9/11 America, the whole project of spreading, and expanding, the boundaries of nonconformism and autonomy has been vastly complexified. Perhaps the best that counterculture can hope for is to persevere, although another view sees opportunities for radical shifts within the turbulence. In either case, surf's up!

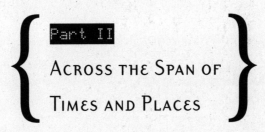

Part II

ACROSS THE SPAN OF

TIMES AND PLACES

CHAPTER THREE

⊢ POLITICALLY INCORRECT
Socrates and the Socratic
Counterculture

I did not care for the things that most people care about—making money, having a comfortable home, high military or civilian rank, and all the other activities, political appointments, secret societies, party organizations, which go on in our city.

SOCRATES, VIA PLATO

Socrates held that the aim of human life is to search for the truth to the nature of things as they are, not as they are interpreted by the conventional mind. . . . Like the Pied Piper, Socrates was a juvenilization agent, accused by conservative minds of the dangerous game of discomfiting all authority before a circle of impressionable youths and subtracting from the state the stability of tradition . . . his unsettling effect on the young and his persistent criticism were intolerable to any establishment.

TIMOTHY LEARY

> Who was Socrates, anyhow? A very argumentative Greek
> who had a nagging wife and was finally compelled to
> commit suicide because he was a nuisance!... Evidently
> Socrates had called something into being long ago
> which was very explosive. Intellectual dynamite! A moral
> bomb!
>
> WINSTON CHURCHILL

In 369 B.C.E., the Western world's first democracy in Athens, Greece, executed a seventy-year-old man for the crime of philosophy. The actual charges were: "Socrates is guilty of refusing to recognize the gods recognized by the State and introducing other, new divinities. He is also guilty of corrupting youth." In point of fact, the charges were brought at least partly in vengeance over a political conflict that Socrates played no direct role in.

On the day he was to die by drinking poison hemlock, young admirers gathered around him, just as they had for forty years, to speak of life and its deepest and truest meanings. While some of his followers wept, Socrates maintained the same playful spirit of reflective inquiry in the face of death that had seen him through his life. The wise old man led his young followers through a dialectical discussion about justice, death, and the afterlife and told them that he was looking forward to going to a place "where they don't murder people for asking questions." This was the end of the life of Socrates the Greek, the man who brought independent critical thinking into Western culture, casting a long shadow that is still vital today. The brave, Christ-like serenity he displayed in his final moments is as important to the Socratic legend as his ideals, exemplifying the authenticity that he preached.

At least that's one way of looking at it. The Socratic counterculture is not an easy one for children of democracy to endorse. Issues around class and elitism raised by the Socrates story will lead this exploration necessarily into a perhaps discomfiting examination of the inherent conflict between exuberant, "self-centered" (i.e., focused within the individual) nonconformism and "the common people."

A Bunch of Greek Guys Sitting Around Talking

Socrates was an odd duck, a town character, a famous eccentric, admired by a few but a figure of fun to the masses. Incapable of ordinary social pretense, he was often seen in public sitting or standing perfectly still for hours, tranced out on his own thoughts. When not so self-entranced, he spent all his time walking around Athens barefoot, eagerly seeking out conversation. He owned only one coat that he wore continually, and frequently was in need of a bath. Comedic plays (Athens' most popular entertainment medium) frequently ridiculed his compact, homely, rugged features and his peculiar ways.

Since he chose not to write down his ideas and experiences, what we know about Socrates comes from words, voluminous but sometimes contradictory, passed down by several of his followers, most prominently Plato and Xenophon. "Socrates is a very difficult subject for historians," wrote Bertrand Russell. "There are many men concerning whom it is certain that very little is known, and other men concerning whom it is very certain a great deal is known. But in the case of Socrates, the uncertainty is as to whether we know very little or a great deal."

We do know that he was born to relatively humble origins in Athens, Greece, 469 B.C.E. His father is believed to have been a stonecutter. His upbringing would have been middle class—he was neither part of the aristocracy nor one of the poor majority. He inherited a modest home from his father, which would offer him all the comfort and security he seemed to require. After a stint as a soldier in the Peloponnesian War—where he was noted for his physical prowess and disciplined ability to ignore the extreme discomforts that raised the complaints of the other soldiers—he may have made a brief attempt to take up his father's craft. But Socrates swiftly abandoned any thoughts of a career. For most of his life, he chose to live as a penniless (albeit not homeless) itinerant street philosopher. He spent his days in the agorae and gymnasia talking to anyone and everyone, and frequently spent his evenings as the guest of aristocratic friends, talking and drinking.

Athens of the fifth century B.C.E. was a city awash in the glory of the Periclean Age. Freshly liberated from challenges to independent development by the decisive defeat of invading Persian and Carthaginian armies, the Greeks had adopted a remarkable new system—democracy. Male citizens of all classes were given not only a vote but a direct participation in policy-making that is unmatched in the Western democracies today. Citizens could generally speak freely (although, as we shall see later, a formal concept of individual civil liberties had not yet been developed). Athenian culture exercised its freedom to reach new heights in art, architecture, and scholarship.

On a gloomier note, Athens was warlike and imperialistic, ruthlessly colonizing other Greek city-states, and in perpetual conflict with the equally powerful Sparta for domination over the rest of the Greek world. Defeated enemies were kept as slaves. Nobody in this great democracy ever questioned the institution of slavery, not even Socrates.

While their Spartan enemies epitomized a renunciate culture in which the enjoyment of fleshly pleasures and material well-being was verboten, Athens was culturally liberal, if not libertine. A lively free market (pottery, fish, crafts) attracted visitors from all nearby ports. Many Athenians participated in nightly feasts. Wine flowed at public (gymnasia) and private (symposia) parties. Aside from the enjoyment of food and wine, these feasts revolved around public conversation and debate—but would also feature music, dancing girls, and comedy. Male citizens, whether married or not, were considered entitled to a full sexual smorgasbord, including unmarried women, prostitutes, and—most prominently—their fellow males. Male beauty was prized, particularly within the aristocracy.

Women, on the other hand, did not receive such liberal treatment. They were excluded from the public realm and not allowed to be educated. Around the age of fourteen, an Athenian girl would be married, by arrangement, to a man approximately twice her age. Women stayed indoors, cooked, and spun clothes. Socrates alone opined that women were equal, and should be treated as such, although there is no evidence that he kicked up a big fuss about it.

Despite democracy, male Athenian aristocrats lived in a different world from the average citizen. Within the wealthy culture, homosexuality was particularly endemic, usually coupling older men and adolescent boys. And their symposia, or drinking parties, were private, invitational affairs. Since exclusivity of any sort was something of an offense within the hyper-democratic city-state, majority Athenians imagined the aristocrats' symposia as decadent scenes of drunkenness, sexual exploits, and political treachery against democracy. These visions, while exaggerated, were not entirely incorrect.

The Greek aristocrats associated the beautiful with the good. Well-born bisexual pretty boys, strutting their stuff in the gymnasia and on horseback, were granted a sort of moral superiority to the average. These young aristocratic men were expected to compete with one another in exhibiting arete (excellence). Excellence was proved by bravery in battle, high performance in sporting events, and generosity in public service. The aristocracy pursued excellence largely to affirm their superiority over the common folk.

Into this world of "the beautiful people" wandered the homely itinerant philosopher Socrates. Perhaps he was attracted by the easy abundance of food and drink (although he preached and practiced moderation). He was definitely attracted to the notion of pursuing excellence. He would take the idea in his own direction, applying it to the life of the mind. And undoubtedly, all those pretty boys played a role in drawing him into the aristocratic milieu.

While his core group contained a few itinerant seekers like himself, Socrates' following—the Socratic counterculture—would develop primarily among these children of the aristocracy. This earned him not only mockery and contempt from the masses, but also some suspicion among parents and others within the elite. Clearly, like so many counterculturalists across history, the good-natured thinker named Socrates was destined to wind up on the shit list of all political and economic factions.

THE SOCRATIC PHILOSOPHY: THINK FOR YOURSELF AND QUESTION EVERYTHING

The unexamined life is not worth living.

SOCRATES, VIA PLATO

Socrates was, first and foremost, a critic. He questioned everything and everyone and never received a single answer that satisfied him. He didn't exclude himself from this total rejection of what passed for human knowledge. Having been declared the wisest man alive by the Oracle of Delphi, he maintained that he had received the honor only because he was wise enough to know that he didn't know anything. Although he was developing a philosophy, one that evolved a dialectical process for seeking the truth and the pursuit of self-knowledge, Socrates asserted no *doctrine*.

In the twentieth century, the Marxist revolutionary Vladimir Lenin (who presumed himself to know just about everything) said that the way to get people to understand was to "explain, explain, and then explain again." Socrates, whose goal was to lead people toward self-understanding by exposing the fallacies of what they presumed to know, might have said "question, question, and then question again." This was what came to be known as the Socratic method at its most raw, as practiced by the man himself—relentlessly inquiring, and ridiculing each answer within the context of yet another question.

Plato scholar Walter J. Black describes the Socratic method:

> Start with a simple question suggested by something someone else has said. Ask him innocently to explain what he thinks is the meaning of some familiar word, the name of something immaterial but regarded commonly as important—friendship, courage, justice, truth. Show him by more probing questions how stupid his conventional definition is and kindle his interest to try for something better, something that will pierce down to the very heart of the problem of human values. Even if he reaches no positive conclusion, both he and the listening circle will have realized for a moment, at least, how foolishly they have taken for granted habits, opinions, and attitudes that were prejudiced, harmful, and false, and how thrilling and inspiring may be the hunt for truth and honesty.

In the Athenian democracy, citizens were free to have opinions, but the value of that liberty was limited because nobody yet knew how to really think for himself. Until Socrates, and another contemporary philosophic school, the Sophists, nobody had ever asserted that the received assumptions about the nature of things that had been handed down from generation to generation were inadequate or open to debate. As Aristotle, a second-generation student of Socrates (he was a student of Socrates' follower Plato), would claim, "There are two things which may justly be credited to Socrates, inductive reasoning and general definition."

In other words, Socrates taught the Greeks how to think, and how to think about thinking. Abstract values that had received labels like truth, justice, love, goodness, and beauty could no longer simply be asserted. What did you *mean* by truth, etc.? And the point had to be proved. As George Santayana would later assert, "Socrates rescued logic and ethics forever from authority."

But while he doubted—and even ridiculed—all existing knowledge, Socrates did believe—like Fox Mulder—that the truth is out there . . . somewhere. He was not an absolute philosophic relativist. That role was fulfilled by the Sophists, another group of wandering teachers who made their home in Athens. The Sophists denied that there was any ultimate unchangeable truth, any absolute right and wrong. They saw truth, justice, and all other values as consensual-social—temporary agreements without any ultimate referent or source of legitimacy. Indeed, the Sophists were, in many ways, the West's first "postmodernists." However, the Sophists were not inclined toward obscure academic theorizing or exposing prejudices toward alien cultures. Athens was a litigious, highly politicized society. Ordinary citizens could bring one another to court, and all participated in public political debates and decision-making processes. So Sophist teachers applied their belief in the elasticity of basic concepts pragmatically. They were paid by their young students to teach them the art of persuasion.

Socrates found the Sophist approach ignoble and shallow. Rather than questioning values in the pursuit of something better, some sort of intellectual excellence, Socrates saw that the Sophists were merely advocating and practicing opportunism in the absence of any ultimate values. Since there was no truth, the clever Sophist could use rhetoric and seductive-sounding logic to get his own way, to win an argument, with no regard to truth.

So while he shared with the Sophists the obsession with challenging and, indeed, demolishing received wisdom, for Socrates the process of winnowing away falsehoods was part of a deep intellectual search for knowledge, rather than something to be used for personal advantage. In a passage from Plato, Socrates explained why his notion that the truth is ultimately knowable served mankind better than the Sophists' claim that it is not: "We shall be better, braver, and less helpless if we think that we ought to inquire than we should have been if we indulged in the idle fancy that there was no knowing and no use trying to know."

It is difficult for us today to understand how radical Socrates' message was. In a very real sense, Socrates was the first individual. Up until the Socratics, the collective culture of the city-state, whether autocratic or democratic, was the locus of thought and identity. You were who your tribe was, even if you were the leader. The individual functioned as an indistinct molecule in the singular entity that made up a particular community, programmed by the habits, rituals, beliefs, and assigned roles of that culture. Socrates was the first to suggest that an individual could "know thyself," that there was potentially something unique within every human being. In the words of nineteenth-century Austrian philosopher Frank Brentano, "He tore the individual out of his historical context."

So—by thinking about how to think—Socrates didn't only give birth to the Aristotelian logic that would become the dominant mode for philosophical inquiry at least up until the twentieth century (and which, in turn, would produce the eternally practicable scientific method). Socrates gave us the discrete human psyche, in essence inventing psychology and human potential. We owe the entire notion of introspection, as it's understood in the West, to Socrates.

And we could go even further. Since mainstream psychology has developed into methods for helping individuals to conform and adapt to the social customs and agreements of the time—or just plain making it through the daily stress of the ever-accelerating weirdness—Socrates can be seen as the godfather of alternative psychology. He was the first Western rascal to use shock tactics to deprogram individuals away from the beliefs and habits of their culture, a project now associated with the likes of Georges Gurdjieff, Aleister Crowley, R. D. Laing, William S. Burroughs, and Genesis P-Orridge. Possession of your own independent psyche remains controversial, and sometimes punishable, to this very day.

COUNTERCULTURAL ELITIST

It is within the realm of political philosophy that the Socratic story darkens and becomes complicated. It's clear that Socrates was basically apolitical. Repeatedly, his various students report that he rejected participation in politics in favor of "the perfection of the soul." In Plato's *Apology*—the Platonic discourse generally believed by most scholars and historians to have been closest to Socrates' word—the character Socrates says, "Perhaps it may seem strange that I go about and interfere in other people's affairs to give advice in private, but do not venture to come before your assembly and advise the state." As the great American leftist journalist I. F. Stone pointed out in his book *The Trial of Socrates,* his use of the phrase "*your* assembly" is telling. The assembly belonged to all the people of Athens, but Socrates held himself apart from the politicized mass.

He was essentially a political dropout who criticized all systems. But like most natural dissidents and gadflies, he would have directed his harshest opprobrium toward his own society, which happened to be a participatory democracy. So the Socratic politic emerges—both from the literature and as the result of a series of incidents that took place during his lifetime—as blatantly anti-democratic.

Any discussion of the Socratic political problem has to, first of all, contend with the distinctions between Socrates and his star student, Plato, a task that is technically impossible. Socrates, as we've already noted, didn't write anything down. After Socrates' death in 399 B.C.E., Plato began his long career as a philosopher. And he wrote *everything* down. He wrote voluminously. While he was inspired by Socrates, it is common knowledge that he also developed his own ideas. After all, Plato was the initiator and leading professor in the world's first public academy, so his evolution was observed. Indeed, differences between Plato and Socrates were commented on by no less a figure than Aristotle, who, as a student in Plato's institute, had some inside knowledge.

But Plato used Socrates as his mouthpiece in *all* his works, making no distinction between his ideas and those attributed to his lead character, "Socrates." Scholars have conjectured as to where the dividing line between Socrates and Plato may lie. It is all guesswork, but it seems that we could draw some likely conclusions by presuming a tremendous difference in temperament between the two men.

Socrates was an extreme eccentric, a dropout. He could not bear to participate in any sort of official function, and rejected all notions of material success. He refused all payment for his teachings. His was a life of perpetual spontaneity. He wandered and talked. He considered all ideas aloud. He was a provocateur, joking, teasing, and intentionally outraging listeners. Nothing was beyond his consideration, yet nothing was found to be true.

Plato, by contrast, was dashing, socially adept, and rather conformist—a well-bred child of the aristocracy. He possessed the bureaucratic skills necessary to open and run the world's first academy. He lectured in an institutionalized formal setting, taking money for his wisdom. And he froze his thoughts onto the static format of print.

There's probably a reason why Socrates didn't write it all down. He himself said that he didn't know anything. Socrates was all about process. Each discussion he engaged in was an experiment, and the discourse might range in any direction over any terrain in its attempt to arrive at truth. And even as recorded in the writing of the earnest Plato, the playfulness of Socrates comes through. He tried ideas out, toyed with them. Yet, by the time Plato writes *The Republic*, his character "Socrates" has become a highly proscriptive philosopher full of rules, laws, and explicit recommendations for organizing the good society; in fact, laying out a rather fascistic path to utopia in detail.

We can safely assume that this is the work of Plato. As William K. C. Guthrie points out in *Socrates*, "His [Socrates'] mission was not to impart any body of positive doctrine, but to bring home to men their intellectual need, and then invite them to join him in the search for truth." But that doesn't let Socrates completely off the hook. Clearly, the man who chose to throw in his lot with the aristocratic youths of Athens expressed some degree of contempt for democracy, and along with that a prejudice in favor of some sort of ruling elite. The part of Socrates that we should probably accept on face value from Plato is that he believed in a meritocracy, rulership by "those who know" how to rule. This would be in keeping with the Athenian aristocratic ideal of excellence that Socrates had adopted and applied to the cultivation of the mind.

What we have here is your basic "theory of the leisure class" situation. It was inevitable that the philosopher of deep contemplation would wind up teaching the children of the aristocracy in Athens, Greece, in the fifth century B.C.E. Only the aristocracy had time for the luxury of pursuing self-knowledge and improvement. For this very reason, bohemias, countercultures, and subcultures throughout history have tended to be the province of the economically privileged (although, as we shall see throughout this book, some stout and dedicated working-class heroes have had their historic countercultural movements too). One of the reasons the counterculture of the 1960s became so powerful and massive was the presence of a healthy economy and a decent social welfare system that allowed middle-class children and even some poor people the luxury of "searching for themselves."

Even so, elitism of one sort or another is an undeniable and basic element of counterculture. Any honest, freethinking nonconformist must admit to some degree of contempt for the average, and must experience periods of alienation from the political judgments of the democratic masses. Indeed, the very name counterculture implies a thrust in opposition to the presumed popular culture of the people. And anytime someone stands up and says, "I think all your commonly accepted and treasured beliefs are bunk and I might have a better approach," she is scorning the common folk to some degree.

Imagine yourself in the society that Socrates was facing. There's no concept of individual civil liberties or civil rights. There's a vague set of laws, but essentially the only law is whatever the majority decides on that particular day. Taxes are sometimes imposed upon specific individuals for personal reasons. And if the majority wants to vote that nose rings are ugly and therefore no one should wear one, you could be arrested for that offense. Or even if they don't vote to ban nose rings, anybody can take anybody else to court and press charges, any charges. It's up to a jury of five hundred to decide—by majority rule—not only your guilt or innocence, but whether wearing nose rings is, in fact, criminal or not, and worthy of the death penalty or a punch in that nose. Everything is perpetually up for grabs by a majority vote. The personal is indeed political in fifth-century B.C.E. Athens, and now you can discover just how intrusive that concept is!

Athens also was possessed by an unhappy pathology that has manifested in many hyper-egalitarian cultures ranging from the French Revolution, to Mao's China, to the German Green Party in the 1970s. The people were hostile toward anybody standing out, achieving too much, being too charismatic, doing anything so well that it made the ordinary folks feel inferior. And jealous revenge was easy to exact within the Athenian court system. The aristocrat's cult of excellence, in fact, was partly an understandable rebellion against this popular suppression of any extraordinariness.

Although most of his criticisms maintained a humorous tone, Socrates must have grown bitter, over time, with the tyranny of the majority. But it seems unlikely that this good-natured philosopher, in his pursuit of authentic goodness, was out to oppress the masses. Socrates was simply trying to liberate the evolution of thought itself from the grip of mass ignorance and reaction. As Bertrand Russell pointed out, "It should be observed that the view which substitutes consensus of opinion for an objective standard has certain consequences that few would accept. What are we to say of scientific innovators like Galileo?" It is, most likely, this objective standard that Socrates was striving to bring into the political realm when he argued for government by expertise. It was a bit of a domain error on his part, but one committed in self-defense against the overextension of democracy into areas best left to individuals. Remember, nobody had yet suggested a system wherein majoritarian rule could be balanced against individual rights. The notion that an advocate of democracy could have said, as did Thomas Jefferson, "He who governs best governs least," would have been utterly alien to the Athenians. Only authoritarian alternatives were on the political menu. And so we confront the fact that Socrates, while trying to remain above the fray, implicitly sided with the aristocratic elitists against democracy. As we shall see later, these leanings came to a sorry end.

Here, through Socrates' dilemma, we confront one of the major contradictions inherent in counterculture within democracy. Nonconformist freethinkers are outsiders, alien by nature. It's worth repeating: the very assumption that an individual, or small group, can criticize and propose alternatives to mass politics and culture *is* elitist. Countercultures *do* hold themselves apart. At the same time, as countercultures have evolved, most have advocated a kind of egalitarianism. They tend to believe that wealth should be shared, if not equally, at least generously, and that all people should be treated as fully human, regardless of class, race, gender, nationality, etc. Resultantly, we have witnessed many countercultural self-professed advocates for "the people." And we have also observed that many of these nonconformists are despised by the very people they see themselves as witnessing for. In some ways, this contradiction reached its apotheosis during the New Left counterculture of the late 1960s/early 1970s. While the New Leftists were chanting "Power to the people," polls showed that the people approved of beating the hell out of them (Chicago Democratic convention 1968) and even shooting them dead (Kent State, Black Panther Party).

Historical moments like the New Left "revolution" to the contrary, these contradictions have generally been less severe during the contemporary post-Enlightenment era, with the advent of civil liberties, the spread of literacy and education, and the evolution of technology. (These observations get a bit wavy and wonky particularly in the post-9/11 era. Many of us are nervously watching the evolution of "the new normal" for its impact on civil liberties.) Indeed, many contemporary counterculturalists resolve this contradiction—at least to their own satisfaction—by advocating equality almost entirely in terms of access to ideas and tools, and even by developing tools that democratize that access. The computer and the Internet have emerged as a sort-of salve. On the one hand, countercultural elitists can claim even greater independence from the mass culture by ignoring mainstream media—establishing their own mediated autonomous zones. And on the other hand, they can offer regular folks the opportunity to do the same (or the opposite if they prefer) by making these tools cheap and easy to use. Still, tensions and contradictions remain between the individualistic nonconformist nature and the democratizing spirit of counterculture. Particularly those counterculturalists who identify with leftist egalitarian democratic views have to contend with both the animosity they feel toward mass culture and the animosity that mass culture feels toward them.

SMARTYRDOM

Meanwhile, back in Athens, Socrates' scathing critique of mass culture came to a bad end, both for the city and for himself. Various students of

Socrates, and hangers-on amidst the Socratic counterculture, grew into nasty adults. Some brought shame upon themselves. Others brought murder and tyranny to their city-state. Between them, they brought the aging philosopher down with them.

Alcibiades was the first product of the Socratic counterculture to fall from grace. As a young aristocrat, Alcibiades was the prettiest boy in all of Athens. He was also witty, an excellent sportsman, and possessed of the sort of arrogance and extravagance that is so often the privilege of beauty and talent combined with youth and wealth. Irreverent from the get-go, Alcibiades was that rare Socratic follower who could trade barbs with the master himself, and Socrates loved him for it. In Plato's *Dialogues,* Alcibiades appears as quite possibly Socrates' favorite young follower.

As an adult, Alcibiades became one of Athens' military leaders, but this didn't change his self-indulgent ways. He possessed a colossal sexual appetite and was an immoderate drinker. He was also a show-off, a drama queen, with a rock-star-like propensity for minor acts of rebellious antisocial behavior. So despite his generally excellent record of service to Athenian society, he accumulated enemies, particularly among the dour egalitarians.

He finally found himself in serious hot water just as he was about to depart Athens as one of the commanders in a military expedition against Sicily. He was accused of vandalizing a sacred statue of Hermes. Some demos (pro-egalitarians) believed that rebel aristocrats had formed a "Socratized" secret society dedicated to such activities, and historians still argue about whether the charges against him were true. In any case, he was convicted in absentia while leading Athenian troops into battle. Rather than returning home to face punishment, he took up exile with Athens' mortal enemy, Sparta, further sullying not only his own reputation but that of his old teacher, Socrates. Although he would return to Athens, even reclaiming positions within its military leadership for a while, the rest of Alcibiades' career was marked by occasional exiles, and marred by his peculiar and counterintuitive advocacy of Sparta's highly disciplined and severely authoritarian culture.

Alcibiades' checkered career went a long way toward gaining Socrates a reputation for corrupting youths with philosophic heresies that led to dangerous antisocial behavior. But it was the actions of the Thirty Tyrants that cemented his bad rap. In 404 B.C.E., after nearly two centuries as one of the two successful civilizations in Greece, Athens was finally defeated in war by the other one—Sparta. Upon defeat, Athenian aristocrats, in collaboration with the Spartan victors, dissolved the democratic state and established their own oligarchy. The anti-democratic coup was led by Critias and Charmides, both either former followers or hangers-on amidst the Socratic circle—depending on whom you read. They were also both close relatives of Plato, then a young member of the Socratic circle.

This group came to be known as the Thirty Tyrants. They established a reign of terror that, while denying democratic rights to the many, was focused primarily on their fellow aristocratic property owners. Corrupt to the core, Critias and company used false charges and judicial death sentence decrees to kill and rob many of the other wealthy citizens of Athens.

Socrates, of course, remained true to his nature. He criticized the new bosses just like the old bosses. In fact, one of the tactics the Thirty used to confiscate property was forcing or intimidating citizens to act as their police. The citizens would be sent to the homes of propertied aristocrats to accuse them, and arrest them for crimes. The death penalty would be imposed, and the ruling oligarchs would seize the aristocrat's wealth. One day, the Thirty called upon Socrates to join with a group of four other citizens to do their heinous bidding for them. While the others followed orders, Socrates simply walked away. Gandhi would later call this an inspiring act of nonviolent resistance.

The only reason Socrates was not put to death by his former students was that they were soon thereafter overthrown. The tyranny had lasted only one year. Democracy was reestablished. Socrates didn't miss a beat, criticizing and ridiculing the new government as he had all previous. Meanwhile, in establishing the peace, the new democracy had agreed to a general amnesty for the oligarchs—those who had terrorized Athens could not be tried for their political crimes. However, in litigious democratic Athens, citizens soon found other excuses to bring some of their former oppressors, and those who associated with them, to trial. Among the criminal tyrants, the name of Socrates kept cropping up. As youths, many of the offenders had fallen under the Socratic spell. Despite his having been a lonely resister to the tyranny when called upon to act as one of its thugs, Socrates was eventually held to blame for his wayward students. As noted at the beginning of this chapter, he was put on trial for corrupting youth and for heresy. But mainly, he was tried and convicted because of the terrible actions of his former followers and friends.

However wrongheaded some of his political theories may have been, few have ever questioned Socrates' integrity. While he firmly believed that the important truths were within, and that politics was to be avoided whenever possible, Socrates had almost gotten himself into political hot water with the democracy earlier in his life by remaining true to his principles. Forced into the Athenian equivalent of jury duty, he did something virtually unheard of. He stood alone, in opposition to 499 other voters, voting not to convict an old war hero who, in the frenzy of a necessary retreat during a battle, left behind dead and wounded soldiers, a violation of the Athenian code of honor in warfare.

The trial of Socrates for heresy and the corruption of youth took place in a public forum before an enormous audience of followers and critics. Indeed, however scandalized the Athenian masses might have been by Socrates, they loved to listen to the man. His statement at the trial, as reported by Plato in *The Apology* (believed to be the closest Plato ever came to remaining strictly true to Socrates' own words), remains an inspiration for those who would defy authority by remaining true to their deep self, regardless of the risk. *The Apology* only occasionally lapses into the sort of shrill self-righteousness one would expect from one about to be martyred for his beliefs. Remaining true to his inner voice, much of Socrates' self-defense is playful. He continues asking his damned questions. At times, he is almost like a bullfighter, teasing the enraged public with his impudent contempt for public figures, statesmen, and any "who consider themselves wise, but are not." Despite his brazen attitude, Socrates was convicted by only a 56 percent majority vote of the jurors. Socrates was then given the opportunity to suggest an alternative to the death penalty, and it is generally believed that the democratic authorities hoped he would suggest exile, which would have been accepted. They did not want to go down in history as the executioners of the great philosopher. But Socrates stubbornly argued that he should actually be *rewarded* for playing the "gadfly," and proposed—as a compromise—that he pay only a small fine. This last bit of insolence proved more than the jury could tolerate. Even more jurors voted for the death penalty than had voted to convict him in the first place.

Many scholars and historians surmise that Socrates rejected exile in favor of the death penalty to prove his virtue, which had been called into question by the behavior of some of his intellectual progeny. And his bravery and dignity while waiting to die accomplished precisely that on a historic level. As his young followers visited him daily inside the prison walls, he continued his question-filled discourse. With death approaching, discussion frequently turned to questions of god and the afterlife. Typically, Socrates entertained these questions good-naturedly, not by asserting any sort of certainty but by calmly listing the likely possibilities and then declaring that none of them would leave him any worse off than he was alive. He died as he had lived, encouraging his followers to know themselves and to fearlessly seek truths.

SOCRATIC COUNTERCULTURES THROUGH THE AGES

It could be argued that while Socrates, as a world-historic philosopher, was a raging success, the Socratic counterculture itself was a disaster. But surely most of the youths within the Socratic circle quietly used the valuable Socratic lessons in self-examination to lead more thoughtful and fulfilling lives, without becoming arrogant murderous tyrants. And beyond that, Socrates' words and deeds have echoed down through history, inspiring freethinkers and brilliant spirits like Coleridge, Byron, Shelley, Popper, Emerson, Whitman, Rabelais, and Voltaire. Indeed, to this day, whenever we find pesky, politically incorrect individualists irritating all factions by thinking for themselves and questioning everything, we witness a still-lively Socratic counterculture.

CHAPTER FOUR

⊢ LEAP INTO THE BOUNDLESS
Taoism

Happiness is lighter than a feather, but no one knows how to carry it.

"CHUANG-TZU"

The central theme of the Chuang Tzu may be summed up in a single word: freedom.

BURTON WATSON

"Go with the flow." The popular sixties aphorism was a gift from Taoism, the Chinese philosophy of gentle and graceful spontaneity. Its ur-texts having first appeared approximately five hundred years before the birth of Christ, Taoism remains to this day one of history's most exquisite and advanced expressions of what Timothy Leary called "chaotics"—the practice of embracing and skillfully surfing the waves of change. True practitioners of the Tao (which simply means "the way") recognize the impossibility of concretizing its wisdom as dogma. Dogma dams the flow. Even language itself fixates the mind and interrupts the flowing Tao. The primary Taoist philosopher "Lao-tzu" (in fact, probably a combination of many Chinese sages) said, "The tao that can be spoken is not the true tao." Nevertheless, we use language to place Taoism within a history of cultures practicing freedom of thought and perception, nonauthoritarian behavior, and constant change.

While most of the countercultures in this book were historical epochs, cultural movements that can be located within certain periods of time, Taoist history is as diffuse as its philosophy. Its beginnings are difficult to pinpoint, and it is still debated whether the main written texts, *Tao teh Ching* by "Lao-tzu" and the stories of "Chuang-tzu," were actually created by singular individuals or were passed down by various sages and simply assigned to a name. Taoist history is shrouded in mystery; not surprising for a philosophy that shuns public attention. Yet Taoist influence permeates Chinese history and thought, and seeped into Western discourse, particularly during the twentieth century. Oddly, although the details of Taoism's evolution are mysterious, Taoist spirituality is not transcendental or particularly abstract. In fact, it rejects any notion of a great transcendent or metaphysical beyond, and is firmly rooted in the art of living in the body.

With its consistent denial of the ordinary boundaries of language, logic, and morality on thought in favor of raw, undifferentiating, and unfettered experience, Taoism is perhaps the most psychedelic of our pre-1960s countercultures. Readers who have journeyed to the antipodes of consciousness, who have felt every belief—every sense of self and the world—dissolve, only to find themselves still very much embodied, alive, and in fact refreshed and liberated by the experience, will be particularly receptive to the Tao.

THE PHILOSOPHICAL TAOISM OF "LAO TZU" AND "CHUANG TZU"

> When they lose their sense of awe,
> people turn to religion.
> When they no longer trust themselves,
> they begin to depend upon authority.
>
> "LAO-TZU," *Tao teh Ching*

So many countercultural tropes are loosed in the *Tao teh Ching* and the *Chuang-tzu* that one is tempted to assign one of the many translations of these two books to his readers and be done with it. "Lao-tzu's" every word challenges conventional strivings for success and control, and dares us to relax and harmonize with the flow of nature and events. That great English authority on irreverence, Oscar Wilde, called "Lao-tzu's" *Tao teh Ching* "the most caustic criticism of modern life I have met."

Almost equal in influence, the collected stories of "Chuang-tzu" are humorous, puckish teaching tales that, as we shall see in later chapters, bear a resemblance to Zen koans and the Sufi tales of Nasruddin. They are frequently described as a work of "anarchistic individualism"; Chinese scholar Wu Zhuangzi was moved to call them "a satirical stab in the back of our convention and common sense." One would have to wait for the libertine movement in seventeenth-century France before this sort of extreme statement was legitimately provoked in the West.

In Chapter 2, we asserted that a primary value in countercultures is that they assign primacy to individuality at the expense of social conventions and governmental constraints. J. J. Clarke, author of *The Tao of the West,* finds in Taoism "a valuing and cultivation of the personal life above service to the state." Taoist individualism, however, differs from Western individualism, with its attachment to the sturdy ego and the romantic self. Kristofer Schipper, the dean of Western Taoist scholars, and possibly the first one who actually apprenticed in a Taoist religious school in China, asserts, "Too often men define their personalities by their tastes. They are wont to say 'I don't like this and I like that,' so as to set themselves apart and to try to maintain a semblance of individuality. But this way of choosing, of cutting up existence into pieces, and using one's body in the search for some hypothetical satisfaction is fatal." And yet Schipper also maintains that "the *Tao teh Ching* . . . considers the human being in his role as sovereign." There is no contradiction. Despite recommending that we rid ourselves of (what Taoists see as) an illusory sense of a well-contained selfhood, Taoism pronounces humanity free of the dictates of a ruling god that dispenses morality (frequently as enforced by the state) and encourages gently spontaneous human eccentricity.

Not surprisingly, Taoism is sometimes looked upon by many conventional Chinese as an embarrassment. In 1961, Chinese historian C. K.

Yang described it as a "humiliation . . . its activities have not benefited the nation at all [but] have repeatedly misled the people by their pagan magic." Westerner Athanasius Kirchner, writing in 1667, described Taoism as "full of abominable falsehoods [practicing] repulsive rituals." A more sympathetic Chinese commentator complained that it is "the least understood and most commonly ignored and maligned, of all the major religions of the world." Nevertheless, the Taoists have been treated mostly as a kind of welcomed random element by Chinese traditionalists across history.

IGNORE AUTHORITY

> When rich speculators prosper
> While farmers lose their land;
> When government officials spend money
> On weapons instead of cures;
> When the upper class is extravagant and irresponsible
> While the poor have nowhere to turn—
> All is robbery and chaos.
> It is not in keeping with the Tao.
>
> "LAO-TZU," *Tao teh Ching*

The above "Lao-tzu" quote would fit comfortably in a contemporary radical left manifesto. But don't start waving the red and black flags around the Taoist altar quite yet. The Taoist relationship to political and social authority is complex and ambiguous.

Taoists' nonauthoritarianism is largely conceptual in nature. It originates from their view of the universe. Rather than worshiping a creator, Taoists view the universe as emerging out of chaos, and they worship only the ever-changing life process. Contrasting this view with that of the Western monotheisms, the great countercultural orientalist Alan Watts said, "Tao cannot be understood as . . . ruler, monarch, commander, architect, and maker of the universe. The image of the military and political overlord, or of a creator external to nature, has no place in the tao." Similarly, Joseph Needham compared the Taoist vision favorably to the Christian God, whom he termed "a ruthless Caesar."

Across Chinese history, Taoism has had a varied relationship with authority; sometimes complementing and cooperating with it, sometimes resisting it, frequently ignoring it. Despite the fact that much of the *Chuang-tzu* was, in the words of Edouard Chavannes, "a condemnation of the intelligence, filial piety, and loyalism that are the essential principles of Confucius's teachings" (Confucianism was the powerful, dominant, conservative philosophy of China), "Chuang-tzu" seems to advocate conformity and going along: "the sage will keep to customs . . . even though men's preferences appear ridiculous to him." There is, in fact, a delightful aspect of getting away with it in the Taoist stance. Taoists offer a mirthful and ruthless critique of convention and power, yet follow the "path of least resistance," which most frequently means not resisting at all. As Stephen Mitchell—an American whose translation of *Tao teh Ching,* although controversial among Taoist scholars, was a number-one-selling book in the mid-1980s—says, "The master simply responds to circumstances in the appropriate way. If the President or the Pope or a border guard has a question, he will be glad to answer it. Otherwise, he minds his business and leaves it to the tao." Modern revolutionists will also find little affinity for "Chuang-tzu's" embrace of the class system; "ruler and subject, superior and inferior, hand and foot, external and internal, conform to a natural principle of Heaven. . . . Let the servants simply accept their own lot . . . without dissatisfaction."

Still, as with so many aspects of Taoist philosophy and history, for every example there is a counterexample. (In fact, please assume that almost everything I say about Taoism has been contradicted or modified by some scholar or another somewhere within the literature.) And so, the Taoist philosophy has been used occasionally in the service of insurgency against grim authority and pitiless class oppression.

Besides their participation in the occasional revolt, Taoists' cultivation of nonconformist eccentricity sometimes produced smaller, personal revolutions. Indeed, despite the path of least resistance, Taoism tended to produce individuals who were thorns in the side of the powerful. One example: during the Chou Dynasty (1122–256 B.C.E.), a pair of Taoist brothers became heroes among the local masses through their passive resistance. When they learned that the founder of the new Chou Dynasty had launched an unwarranted military campaign, they refused to eat the produce of the kingdom, subsisting instead on "a blameless diet of doe's milk and ferns." To take their minds off their hunger, they sang a little protest song: "Climb that west slope/Pinch those ferns/Trading evil for evil/Don't they know is wrong?" Eventually they starved to death, but the populace honored them more in death than the ruler they protested against, who died soon thereafter.

Occasional exceptions aside, Taoists were more likely to be advisors to the ruling courts than revolutionary activists. Indeed, much of the *Tao teh Ching* is formulated as advice to those who govern, although the advice is to govern as little as possible: "Let go the fixed plans and concepts, and the world will govern itself. . . . The more prohibitions you have, the less virtuous people will be. The more weapons you have, the less secure people will be. The more subsidies you have, the less self-reliant people will be. Therefore the Master says: I let go of the law, and people become honest." And: "The Master understands that the universe is forever out of control, and that trying to dominate events goes against the current of the tao." For centuries most Chinese rulers maintained a contingent of Taoist advisors in their courts, both in recognition of their sagacity and to provide a minority counterpoint to the stodgy Confucian majority whose advice usually prevailed. The often inebriated antics of the Taoist advisory faction fulfilled a role in many ways akin to that of the court jesters of medieval Europe, who spoke with a forthrightness that would have endangered them but for the impunity their buffoonery afforded.

The Taoist relationship with the ultra-conformist philosophy of Confucianism, which generally ruled the empire, ebbed and flowed much like the Tao itself. More often than not, there was cooperation, collaboration, and even a kind of merging between the two opposing tendencies. Even Chu Hsi, leader of a rather hard-line Neo-Confucian orthodoxy in the twelfth century, wrote commentaries on the sacred books of Taoism. The *I Ching* is the most familiar product of the interplay between these two philosophies. Here, the idea of letting the Tao "speak" through its ordering of "randomly" cast yarrow stalks or pennies reflects both the magical and philosophical Taoist streams, while the values of conduct expressed in the textual passages that accompany the hexagrams are often Confucian in character.

This reflects the Chinese concept of Yin/Yang, the union of comple-

mentary opposites, a philosophy quite distinct from the West, where opposing philosophies are expected to "duke it out" to see which one is right.
(Of course, Hegel's dialectic suggested that opposing forces, struggle as
they might, usually wind up in synthesis, but there's no evidence that the
rock-solid German philosopher knew of the Tao.) Schipper noted that a
peculiar dynamic between Confucianism and Taoism came into play after
Confucianism was established as the official state ideology (in 140 B.C.E.):
"On the one hand, there was the state and its administration, the official
country, claiming the 'Confucian' tradition. . . . On the other was the real
country, local structures being expressed in regional and unofficial forms
of religion." In other words, aside from frequently being advisors to the
ruling elite, Taoists were able to have relative autonomy over certain locales
across Chinese history.

BEYOND FREETHINKING

Earlier, we asserted that this book might as easily have been called "a history of freethinkers." It's roughly true, although with Taoism, "thinking" is
kind of beside the point. The mental liberty asserted by the Taoists is so
extreme that they could be seen as the perfect target for that popular as-
persion "Your mind is so open, your brains are gonna fall out."

Leaving aside their mutual anti-authoritarianism, the Taoist conception of mental liberty is almost the diametrical opposite of Promethean
countercultures like the Enlightenment, with their emphasis on rational
freethinking and scientific method. In fact, Taoism in many ways predicts
post-Enlightenment Western countercultures that revolted against rationalism and the limits of language, such as the Surrealists and the members
of the Lost Generation. As "Chuang-tzu" put it: "The fish trap exists because of the fish; once you've gotten the fish, you can forget the trap. . . .
Words exist because of meaning; once you've gotten the meaning, you
can forget the words." In typically playful fashion, "Chuang-tzu" adds,
"Where can I find a man who has forgotten words that I might have a
word with him?" For "Chuang-tzu" scholar A. C. Graham, Taoist philosophy represents the "liberation of experience from thought and language"
and "loosens the grip of categories made habitual by naming [and] frees
the current of thought." Despite their differences, many Enlightenment

thinkers were romantically attracted to Taoism, as one element of the philosophic and religious pluralism they perceived in Chinese history. (The fact that Chinese rulers supported the arts and sometimes heeded the advice of visionary sages undoubtedly also had a fundamental appeal to men who were sometimes able to influence their own "enlightened despots.")

By the late twentieth century, the Taoists' subversion of language and rational narrative discourse was taken up by some in the academic post-modernist deconstructionist movement. J. J. Clarke perceives an almost textbook definition of the postmodern aesthetic in his reading of "Chuang-tzu," writing, "There is a form of epistemological pluralism, the belief that there are many possible perspectives on the world, that there is no rational means of discriminating between these perspectives, and hence that there is no way of identifying the one correct way of conceptualizing reality. Human conventions are historically contingent in a radical sense. . . . What is common to Taoism and postmodernism . . . is that they are both concerned, not with establishing a new and more legitimate way of conceptualizing the world, but rather with subverting the very possibility of doing so."

As with the mix-and-match aesthetics of today's postmodernists, Taoists practiced a broad eclecticism, drawing into Taoism elements from Chinese shamanistic and magical traditions, as well as sampling bits of its Confucian opposite. Later, Buddhism was added to the mix. In the words of Clarke, "Taoism reveals a strong syncretistic tendency to draw inspiration from a seemingly incompatible variety of sources. . . . [Taoists practice] sheer promiscuity . . . which embraces not only a variety of religious and philosophical teachings but also draws on the methods of dietetics, medicine, gymnastics, breathing exercises and meditation techniques."

Among postmodernists, the lack of objective certainty is sometimes experienced as a vertiginous terror of falling into a fearsome void, what Richard Bernstein referred to as "the Cartesian anxiety." But for the Taoists, it represented a liberation—the annihilation of the conceptual mind was viewed as a way to allow the natural mind to roam free.

Psychedelic postmodernists are more likely to be able to groove with the Tao than the academics. When Burton Watson, who translated the *Chuang-tzu,* wrote that it was "one of the fiercest and most dazzling assaults ever made not only upon man's conventional system of values, but upon his conventional concepts of time, space, reality, and causation as well," we enter the hallucinatory terrain that psychedelic philosopher Terence McKenna called "boundary dissolution." "Chuang-tzu" explicitly stated, "The Way has never known boundaries . . . forget the years; forget distractions. Leap into the boundless and make it your home!" He also captures the feeling—familiar to people on the drug path—of becoming a clear channel by exorcising the reason and ego-bound self through extreme and even assaultive methods, writing, "I smash up my limbs and body, drive out perception and intellect, cast off form, do away with understanding, and make myself identical with the Great Thoroughfare." Kristofer Schipper says, "He [the Taoist sage] *survives* [emphasis his] the breakdown of values." And Ziggy Stardust sang, "I busted up my brains for the world."

ÉPATER LE BOURGEOIS

There are aspects of Taoist nonconformism that remind us of some of the more severe anti-bourgeois sentiments expressed by twentieth-century radical left-wing intellectuals like Jean Genet, who glorified criminality as the only honorable refuge from hypocrisy. Watson writes, "In order to pry men loose from their conventional concepts of goodness and beauty, 'Chuang-tzu' deliberately glorifies everything that to ordinary eyes appears sordid, base, or bizarre—ex-criminals who have suffered mutilating punishments, men who are horribly ugly or deformed, creatures of grotesque shape and size." "Chuang-tzu" himself wrote, "Who can convince me . . . that benevolence and righteousness are not in fact the loop and lock of these fetters and manacles." Robert Anton Wilson put it this way: "Convictions cause convicts."

"Lao-tzu" put the Taoist rejection of morality in a more positive light, writing, "Throw away holiness and wisdom, and people will be a hundred times happier. Throw away morality and justice and people will do the right thing. Throw away industry and profit, and there won't be any thieves." This anti-moralism isn't merely another attempt by Taoist sages to blow our conceptual minds. There is also a kind of spiritual democratization at work here. The Taoist vision of divinity is funky, earthy, and available to the lowest of the low. "Chuang-tzu" wrote, "This thing called The Way—where does it exist? . . . It is in the piss and shit."

Giving Peace a Chance

In no way should we take the Taoist assault on ordinary morals as excusing coercive, violent behavior. The Taoists, like so many countercultural social critics across history, were merely exposing the hypocrisies of the "good and decent" high-society folk. "Chuang-tzu's" comment that "He who steals a belt buckle pays with his life; he who steals a state gets to be a feudal lord" reminds us of nothing so much as Woody Guthrie's famous lines, "Some will rob you with a six-gun/And some with a fountain pen."

In fact, Taoism embraces a unique form of relative pacifism (you wouldn't expect them to be absolutist about *anything,* would you?). The *Tao teh Ching* says, "Weapons are the tools of violence; all decent men detest them. . . . Peace is his highest value." But Taoists don't codify their rejection of violence. Violence is to be avoided simply because it interferes with the art of living well. In Clarke's words, "Taoists . . . attempt to formulate a means of dealing with conflict in the least destructive of ways and rely on the refinement of defensive techniques which minimize the use of force." Today, with many cultural conservatives asserting that the only way to minimize destructive, violent, antisocial behaviors is by convincing the rabble to return to the strict moral codes of the established authoritarian monotheisms, the pragmatic Taoist approach—seeking peace simply because it is the best way to live—strikes us as a happier and more realizable alternative.

The Tao is all about ease in living, taking the path of least resistance. Strife, conflict, and warfare simply don't fit the profile. The flexibility of Taoist "ethics" is well expressed by this marvelous *Chuang-tzu* tale, justifying a king who—in keeping to the path of least resistance—uses a white lie to avoid a hassle:

> King Wen was seeing the sights at Tsang when he spied
> an old man fishing. Yet his fishing wasn't really fishing.
> He didn't fish as though he were fishing for anything,
> but as though it were his constant occupation to fish.

King Wen wanted to summon him and hand over the government to him, but he was afraid that the high officials and his uncles and brothers would be uneasy. He thought perhaps he had better forget the matter and let it rest, and yet he couldn't bear to deprive the hundred clans of such a Heaven-sent opportunity. At dawn the next day he therefore reported to his ministers, saying, "Last night I dreamed I saw a fine man, dark-complexioned and bearded, mounted on a dappled horse that had red hoofs on one side. He commanded me, saying, 'Hand over your rule to the old man of Tsang—then perhaps the ills of the people may be cured!'"

The ministers, awestruck, said, "It was the king, your late father!"

"Then perhaps we should divine to see what ought to be done," said King Wen.

"It is the command of your late father!" said the ministers. "Your Majesty must have no second thoughts. What need is there for divination?"

In the end, therefore, the king had the old man of Tsang escorted to the capital and handed over the government to him.

At the end of three years, King Wen made an inspection tour of the state. He found that the local officials had smashed their gate bars and disbanded their cliques, that the heads of government bureaus achieved no special distinction, and that persons entering the four borders from other states no longer ventured to bring their own measuring cups and bushels with them. The local officials had smashed their gate bars and disbanded their cliques because they had learned to identify with their superiors. The heads of government bureaus achieved no special distinction because they looked on all tasks as being of equal distinction. Persons entering the four borders from other states no longer ventured to bring their own measuring cups and bushels with them because the feudal lords had ceased to distrust the local measures.

King Wen thereupon concluded that he had found a great Teacher and, facing north as a sign of respect, he asked, "Could these methods of government be extended to the whole world?"

But the old man of Tsang looked bland and gave no answer, evasively mumbling some excuse; and when orders went out the next morning to make the attempt, the old man ran away . . . and was never heard from again.

Yen Yuian questioned Confucius [note: "Chuang-tzu" inserted real historical figures into his teaching tales] about this story, saying: "King Wen didn't amount to very much after all, did he! And why did he resort to that business about the dream?"

"Quiet!" said Confucius. "No more talk from you! King Wen was perfection itself—how can there be any room for carping and criticism! The dream—that was just a way of getting out of a moment's difficulty."

Indeed, the whole macho attitude of the perfectly righteous and steadfast warrior has no place in the Taoist tradition. Taoism is one of the few philosophies in recorded history that privileges what are generally labeled feminine qualities. "Lao-tzu" asserts, "Nothing in the world is as soft and yielding as water. Yet for dissolving the hard and inflexible, nothing can surpass it. The soft overcomes the hard; the gentle overcomes the rigid."

According to Schipper, this sort of "feminism" was reflected in actual Taoist culture. He asserts, "The movement of the Heavenly Master was organized on the basis of absolute equality between men and women who shared . . . leadership. Instructed to keep to the feminine, religious leaders from the Heavenly Master school instructed male followers to never stare, carry arms, hunt, or urinate while standing up." (All this, in the land of foot-binding! Among the non-Taoist Chinese, women through much of history were reduced to the status of virtual slavery.)

Far from developing a violently nihilistic culture in the absence of rigid belief structures and disciplined obedience to rules, Taoists avoided conflict, cultivating qualities such as softness, stillness, and yielding. Indeed, in Taoism, the macho martial assumptions of mainstream "heroism" are utterly upended, turned upside down.

WE DON'T NEED NO EDUCATION

Some aspects of Taoism's conceptual radicalism drift a bit outside the pale even for some beyond-freethinkers (such as your humble author). For instance, Taoists express a sort of hostility toward most accepted notions of education. "Chaung-tzu" praised the days before people were led astray by knowledge, writing, "They stayed at home without knowing how to do the least thing, they strolled around without knowledge where they were going. They stuffed themselves with food, slapped each other on the back, and lived free and easy. They had no talent for anything else." And "Lao-tzu" rejected scientific and technological progress, as most of us understand it, when he wrote that content people "enjoy the labor of their hands and don't waste time inventing labor-saving machines." In *Lao Tzu and Taoism*, Max Kaltenmark observes, "The Taoists condemn mere learning as dangerous, for it is a source of dissipation." And Watson observes that parts of the *Chuang-tzu* "attack all man's inventions, all human civilization and culture with a shrill, almost pathological fury."

However, Schipper argues that the Taoist advocacy of what some might call a kind of ignorance is "nothing more than a healthy mistrust of all established ideas and prejudices, a way of introducing a strong relativity into all that men pretend to know something about." And "Lao-tzu" actually showed an appreciation for science when he wrote, "A good scientist has freed himself of concepts and keeps his mind open to what is." In fact, as naturalists, Taoists were often the scientists of China. Theirs was a different conception of science, based not on the exploration of the underlying laws of phenomena, but on the observation of the behavior of animals, plants, the elements, and the heavens. Watts observes that "what is important is to understand the winds, the tides, the currents, the seasons, and the principles of growth and decay. . . . The Taoist attitude is not opposed to technology per se. . . . The point is that technology is destructive only in the hands of people who do not realize that they are one and the same process as the universe." Joseph Needham, in fact, was a great defender of the notion that the Taoists were the first scientists.

Still, Taoist philosophy seems fundamentally uninterested in the free and open sharing of information. This doesn't come from an authoritarian desire to disempower people, but out of a belief that pure knowledge is impossible to language and most approximate knowledge is a useless distraction. As Clarke writes, "The fundamental goal of Taoism, namely self-transformation, is completely different from that of the quest for objective knowledge."

THE TAO FLOWS THROUGH HISTORY

As asserted earlier, the history of Taoism is diffuse and difficult to pin down. As Clarke says, "What we are engaged in is not the interpretation of a single cultural entity, or the reading of a single set of texts, but rather with an intertextual sequence of readings, a mosaic of citations, interpretations, translations and reconstructions which can be traced back over more than two millennia of cultural and intellectual history." The way Taoism ebbs and flows (that Taoist quality!) in and out of Confucianism and Chinese Buddhism adds to the complexity.

Hundreds, perhaps thousands, of distinct Taoist cultures have come and gone over the millennia. Sinologist Holmes Welch was moved to complain about the promiscuous variability in Taoist history, pointing out that—over time—the term embraced "the science of alchemy; maritime expeditions in the Isles of the Blest; an indigenous Chinese form of yoga; a cult of wine and poetry; collective sexual orgies; church armies defending a theocratic state; revolutionary secret societies."

It is not my intention here to nail down Taoist history. Still, a necessarily fragmentary overview serves to get us into a few nitty-gritty episodes in Taoist counterculture.

While it was preceded and influenced by shamanism, the expressions that would become Taoism are generally seen as emerging during the fifth century B.C.E. in China, around the same time that Confucius formed the Wisdom School that was destined to dominate China's culture and philosophy until Mao. It was, in fact, a renaissance period in Chinese culture that witnessed an abundance of philosophical schools including the Legal-ists, the Sophists, and the stoic, militaristic Mo Ti school. Confucianism and Taoism were the only ones to survive, although—in typically Chinese fashion—both philosophical movements absorbed aspects of these other schools as their own. The *Tao teh Ching* is generally believed to have been passed down by various sages, and completed about 400 B.C.E., while the *Chuang-tzu* is generally believed to be written sometime about 300 B.C.E. Little is known about early "Taoism," although it might be envisioned as more a school of philosophy than a religion. (The distinction would likely have been meaningless to the Chinese participants of the time.)

A school called Neo-Taoism seems to have emerged during the first century B.C.E., with the spread of Buddhism from India. Neo-Taoism is believed to have been a syncretic mix of Taoism, Buddhism, and Confu-cianism. Some of its adherents believed that Buddha and "Lao-tzu" were the same person. By this point, Confucius was well established in Chinese culture as the one great sage. In *A History of Chinese Philosophy, Volume II*, Fung Yu-lan notes that many Neo-Taoists viewed Confucius as the ruler, and "Lao-tzu" and "Chuang-tzu" as his counselors.

Although there were probably a few previous organized cults, religious Taoism seems to have emerged into the historical record during the "Pe-riod of Disunity" (221–589 C.E.). According to University of Georgia pro-fessor Russell Kirkland, this "Celestial Masters Tradition" was "systematic and hierarchical down to the laity. . . . The Celestial Masters school re-garded itself as an orthodoxy, opposing other religions." Like Christians, church members sought salvation from illness and inherited sins through confession and good works, and they believed in a coming apocalypse dur-ing which only the elect would be saved.

This orthodoxy was relieved by a sort-of "reform" Taoist church under the leadership of Ling-pao in the late fourth century C.E. Deeply influ-enced by Buddhism, this was the beginning of what's come to be known as "Organized Taoism." In the words of Professor Kirkland, "Taoism became an ecumenical, non-sectarian tradition, in which any text or group de-voted to higher spiritual goals found a place. During this period, Taoism generally maintained close ties to the government and the cultural elite. This 'New Taoism' was oriented towards spiritual cultivation through meditation and 'inner alchemy.' " The Taoist monasteries that exist in China today are, more or less, survivors of this tradition.

THAT OLD-TIME RELIGION

One of our assertions is that liberating countercultures tend to get reined in over time. The majoritarian impulse to create dominator mythologies and rigid authoritarian structures reasserts itself, even around the most boundary-defying notions. Certainly there were enormous differences between the straightforward, lucid ideas expressed in the *Tao teh Ching* and what Edouard Chavannes called the "hodgepodge of coarse-grained superstitions" of the religious Taoists.

This Taoist religious text, filled with busy visions of a sort of powerfully deistic "Lao-tzu," provides an example of how far they had wandered from the simple clarity of their original text: "Lao-tzu transformed his body. His left eye became the sun; his right eye, the moon; his head became Mount K'un-lun; his beard, the planets and constellations; his bones, dragons; his flesh, four-footed creatures; his intestines, snakes; his stomach, the sea; his fingers, the Five Peaks; his hair, trees and grass; his heart, the Flowery Dais; as to his two kidneys, they were united and became one, the Real and True Father and Mother." This is not to say that there isn't something delightful and poetic about these visions. But whereas *Tao teh Ching* tends to snap you to attention, an hour spent with these texts puts one's head into a fog bank.

Religious Taoism brought deistic mythologies and ritualism into the Taoist mix, seemingly ignoring "Lao-tzu's" warning that "ritual is the husk of true faith." But despite these contradictions, it would be a mistake to presume that Taoism ever took to the authoritarian extremes of the Western monotheisms. Clarke writes, "There were indeed many Taoist religious sects which emerged and flourished in the period following the foundation of the Celestial Masters sect which bear obvious analogies with Christian sectarianism, but these Taoism movements constituted a loose collectivity which lacked any tendency towards *strong* [emphasis mine] doctrinal coherence or institutional hierarchy."

Taoist scholar Norman Girardot asserts that after Taoism became institutionalized into a religion, it still maintained its playful antic qualities "to some degree . . . there was always an individualistic dimension to being Taoist. Moreover, one didn't really belong to some sort of Taoist Church. Rather you were part of a local community where Taoist ritual was a part of the ongoing life of the community."

Fortunately, the distinctions between the liberating philosophies of "Lao-tzu" and "Chuang-tzu" and the formal religious Taoism are nowhere near as drastic as, for instance, the distinction between the progressive humanism of the historical Jesus Christ and the Spanish Inquisition. In fact, the Taoist anarchist impulse survived its many transitions.

TAOIST ANARCHISM

Hakim Bey, whose *The Temporary Autonomous Zone* manifesto became a defining text of 1990s countercultural anarchism, has asserted that "The earliest definitions of anarchy are found in the *Chuang-tzu* and other taoist texts." Schipper observes that the "management of the common property—buildings, land, furnishings and revenue—was strictly egalitarian. . . . The society was made up of countless communities, all linked together by a very dense network of alliances. This network of religious and liturgical organizations, whose economic and cultural importance was paramount, maintained itself almost entirely outside the control of the state." Indeed, the organizational forms of many Taoist religious enclaves sound like the decentralized, networked society of a contemporary anarchist's wet dream (and they did it without the Internet). The temple identities centered around celebratory festivals involving "reading, chess, charity, pilgrimages, writing, medical research, kite flying." Similarly, many twentieth-century anarchist individuals and groups, ranging from Georges Bataille to the Yippies, have proposed anarchist utopias centered around community festivities.

Taoist libertarian policy was first institutionalized by the emperor Han Kao-tzu, founder of the Han Dynasty in 206 B.C.E. Han proclaimed that "hereafter only three simple laws shall prevail: namely, that manslaughter shall be punished by death, and that assault and theft shall be punished according to the facts of each case." As some readers will know, a pure form of libertarianism today advocates this very notion—although its adherents express it in terms of there being just two laws: one against violence and one against theft/fraud. (Believe it or not, I first read this idea advocated by Andy Warhol and Truman Capote in a co-authored guest editorial in *High Times* magazine in the late 1970s.)

According to Chinese historian Lin Yu-lan, in 201 B.C.E., "a General Ts'ao . . . was made governor of the populous and economically advanced state of Ch'i on the eastern coast. He selected an old philosopher . . . follower of 'Lao Tzu' . . . to be his chief advisor. . . . [The advisor] told the Governor that the best way to govern his great state compromising seventy cities was to do nothing and give the people a rest. The Governor religiously carried out his advice throughout his nine years of governorship. The people became prosperous, and his administration was rated the best in the empire."

In 179 B.C.E., the emperor Wen Ti and his Taoist empress Tou ascended the throne. Their liberal regime abolished collective family responsibility for crime, torture as punishment, and taxes on interstate commerce. They radically reduced land taxes and tried as best they could to avoid warfare on the borders of the empire. Empress Tou persuaded her whole court to read "Lao-tzu."

The first actual recorded Taoist-led insurrection was the Yellow Turban rebellion, which started in 182 C.E. The revolt had a wide appeal among all classes and was suppressed only after spreading through many provinces in China. Not only did it severely weaken the Han Dynasty, it succeeded in establishing a number of autonomous, self-governing, quasi-anarchistic communities. A state based explicitly on libertarian Taoist ideals was briefly established within China by the Taoist Celestial Masters movement during this period. According to Isabel Robinet, "Within the wider political context of China it proved to be unsustainable, but it merited imperial interest and patronage."

During the fifth century, a utopian school of Taoism inspired rebellions aimed at establishing the reign of the "Way of Great Peace," a dream of a return to a society free from oppressive state interference and economic exploitation. A series of fourteenth-century peasant revolts were linked to the Taoist-inspired Buddhist Sect of the White Lotus.

These Taoist revolts were the exception rather than the rule. As we've already asserted, the Taoists generally advocated accommodation. And when they did lead an insurrection, it was usually aimed only at changing the behavior of an oppressive empire, not at overthrowing the regime and replacing it with a "Taoist system." Clarke suggests that the Taoists were not really political anarchists, in the Western sense of the word. "The ideal society for Western anarchists is one in which the role of government is reduced to a minimum or abolished altogether, whereas a Taoist is concerned more with removing supposedly artificial hindrances to the spontaneous and natural working of the state than with abolishing it completely." Indeed, my reading of "Lao-tzu" suggests that Taoism might prefer an *extremely* benevolent and nonauthoritarian—yet all-powerful—matriarch to the tedious and nerve-shattering processes of egalitarian, participatory, democratic decision-making. Still, anarchist and libertarian ideas and impulses are obviously contained within the Taoist philosophy, and current and future anarchists will certainly make use of those ideas.

THE BOHO DANCE

Dedicated to the life of ease and the art of living, the Taoist lifestyle, in many cases, was not so different from the various bohemian art and countercultural communities we are familiar with in the West.

One of the earliest examples has a particularly modern ring to it. Sometime about 100 B.C.E., the Neo-Taoists developed an intellectual trend that was called "Pure Talk." It was popular among dispossessed and out-of-office intelligentsia; its most widely known exponents were known as the Seven Sages of the Bamboo Grove. Reminiscent of the Socratics, these nonconformists sponsored informal and convivial, wine-fueled, outdoor discussions about spiritual and literary topics. The participants in this culture were, according to Clarke, "intentionally eccentric and antiestablishment."

In some ways, Pure Talk, and Neo-Taoism as a whole, preached a kind of desperate Taoism that is strikingly similar to twentieth-century Existentialism and nihilism. Sounding a bit Beckettian, Neo-Taoist philosopher Lieh-tzu wrote, "Natural changes and human activities are equally mechanistic in their operation, and there is no such thing as divine or human freedom, divine or human purpose. . . . Helpless infancy and doddering old age take up about half of this [our] time. The time that is obliterated while asleep during the night, and that which is wasted while awake during the day, again amounts to another half of the rest. And yet again, grief and fear fill up about another half. Thus, then, there is only a space of some ten-odd years which one really gets (for his own enjoyment), and even then there is not one hour which is not linked to anxiety" (and these poor bastards didn't even have Prozac).

Some Taoists' solution to this existential misery was "abandonment," which really pretty much meant unrestrained hedonistic indulgence. Contextualized by his pessimistic view of the human situation, Lieh-tzu advocated pleasures that are immediate and easily gratified—primarily bodily pleasures. But all is not necessarily lost. In a nice twist, Lieh-tzu tried to show how selfish hedonism could improve the world. As interpreted by the historian Lin, Lieh-tzu believed that "once it is assumed that everybody in the world seeks only his own immediate pleasure, this automatically eliminates the struggle for power and self-profit among men, since such power and profit can only be gained as the result of troublesome preparation and laborious effort." This "playboy" philosophy of licentious self-indulgence as a path to peace and ease of living will surely remind readers of various currents in twentieth-century hedonism.

One passage from Chinese historian Liu Hsün captures the state of liberty of Pure Talk devotees in particularly colorful terms: "Juan Chi used to indulge himself in wine and wild abandonment. He would uncover his head, let loose his hair, take off his outer clothes, and lie sprawled on the ground. Later on the youth of the nobility . . . were all followers of his example. They said this was the way to attain the origin of the great Tao. Therefore they would get rid of their caps, pull off their clothes, and exhibit shameful behavior, as if they were birds and beasts. Doing this to an extreme degree was called 'understanding'; doing it to a lesser degree was called 'comprehension.' "

As the twelfth-century patriarch of the Taoist Total Perfection movement Wang Ch'ung-yang put it, "Everyone should first learn to loosen up and to abandon oneself." The Tao, indeed, rocks.

SEX AND DRUGS

Taoism, in its embrace of all that is natural, is a sex-positive spiritual path. However, with the exception of those certain periods of orgiastic "abandonment," most Taoists have not approached sexuality with the sort of wantonness that contemporary sexual liberationists do. In Taoism, sexual intercourse reflects the harmony of heaven and earth. Therefore, in the words of Schipper, "The exalted status and even sacredness accorded sexuality meant that it was not practiced with the kind of personal freedom we have come to value in the modern world." On the other hand, Clarke describes "sexual practices . . . incorporated into public rituals . . . liturgies turned into sexual orgies . . . condemned by the Confucians." On the whole, it seems that the Taoists took a balanced approach toward sex, finding it, in Schipper's words, "beautiful, good for the health, and right," but practicing more extreme forms of sexual libertinism only at rare historic intervals.

Which brings us, naturally, to drugs. As implicitly psychedelic as the boundary-smashing vision of the Taoists is, there is evidence of only rare involvement in mind-altering drugs. According to Bill Porter, author of *Road to Heaven: Encounters with Chinese Hermits,* "The only female member of a mythical Taoist group that, during the thirteenth century, came to be known as the Eight Immortals, was sometimes depicted holding a magic [*Amanita muscaria*] mushroom." Hakim Bey reports that the only certifiable personification of cannabis as a deity in any religion is Ma Ku, "Miss Hemp," from the Mao Shan school of Taoism. According to Bey, their style of meditation involved inhaling hemp incense and aimlessly wandering "in a world of imagination that was shared by all initiates and codified in elaborate fantasy, geographies of mountains, grottoes, undersea cities, distant island utopias, the hollow earth, the cloud palaces of the sky, and outer space."

BURNOUTS AND DROPOUTS

While the Tao has a relatively exalted place among some Chinese historians, and a kind of mysterious, upbeat New Age gloss now in the West, some aspects of the Taoist mind-set actually seem strikingly similar to the state sixties veterans refer to as "hippie burnout" or "acid casualty." As someone who, more or less, abandoned all ambition during my early twenties, and spent a few afternoons unable to speak, pouring sand from one hand into another (sometimes without any plant or chemical assistance), tales of (in the words of Michel Strickman) "Taoist fools and blockheads" carry a peculiar resonance. Lieh-tzu expressed it this way: "Internal and External were blended into Unity. After that, there was no distinction between eye and ear, ear and nose, nose and mouth: all were the same. My mind was frozen, my body in dissolution, my flesh and bones all melted together. I was wholly unconscious of what my body was resting on, or what was under my feet. I was borne this way and that on the wind, like dry chaff or leaves falling from a tree. In fact, I knew not whether the wind was riding on me or I on the wind." To the Western mind, this reads like a description of a total psychological breakdown. For Lieh-tzu, it described an exalted state.

Indeed, when one abandons one's instinct for status and allows all thought and categorization to dissolve, one is sometimes left simply staring at the proverbial blade of grass, looking to all the world like a useless idiot. In fact, perhaps even *being* a useless idiot. Within a Western culture that's paranoid about beggars, bums, welfare recipients, drifters, and losers, this is simply not to be tolerated. Within other cultures, including the culture that prevailed in China for thousands of years, allowances are made for the holy fools. Somehow, despite the fact that they lacked central heating, electric door openers, designer jeans, computers, and transgenic salmon, the Chinese did not live in fear that their world would fall apart if a few among them were not the least bit industrious.

Taoism prized uselessness. The dropout, fool, hermit, joker is—in some ways—the supreme Taoist. "Chuang-tzu" wrote,

> [Chuang-tzu] was traveling over a mountain when he saw a huge tree with splendid foliage. Some woodsmen who were there seemed to disdain it. He asked them why. "It's no good for anything," came the reply.
>
> Thereupon "Chuang-tzu" said: "This tree, because its wood is good for nothing, will die a natural death."

In another passage that will appeal to contemporary slackers almost as much as it does to unrepentant draft dodgers of yore, he spoke of the virtues of being a hunchback, pointing out that healthy upright humans are conscripted as soldiers or made to work on Maggie's Farm as servants. Instead, like the twentieth-century anti-work-ethic anarchists, the Situationists, Lieh-tzu advocated "going rambling without a destination." And "Lao-tzu" wrote, "Other people are bright; I alone am dark. Other people are sharp; I alone am dull. Other people have a purpose; I alone don't know. I drift like a wave on the ocean, I blow as aimless as the wind." Watts' description of the honored Taoist fool is perhaps the most extreme: "The fool . . . sits by the side of the road talking nonsense. The fool is like a Mongoloid child who is not interested in survival, and who will take a plate of food and run his finger around in it, make a wonderful slosh with the stew, and then watch it drip from the tip of his finger."

The typical Westerner will object, asserting that if everyone is allowed to play around like a gibbering child, who will do the hard work of survival? Even beat icon Jack Kerouac objected to the oncoming psychedelic hippie dropout culture by asking, "Who will lick the stamps?" But Taoists don't worry because . . . *Taoists don't worry.* (HA!) Most people, following the course of their nature, will be industrious enough. They will farm, they will nurture children, they will build shelters, chop wood, and carry water. Taoist communities have survived and thrived. Some do more. Some do less. A few do nothing. Taoists don't indulge in invidious comparisons and jealousy. They don't care for the stress.

Hermits are the honored dropouts of Taoism. The first known Taoist hermitage started in the third century C.E. According to Porter, "Some retired to achieve their ideals, some bowed out to maintain their principles, some chose quiet to still their passions, some chose escape to preserve their lives, some to shame others into changing their ways, some to cleanse themselves." Many viewed their hermitage as a renunciation of greed and believed they could change society by changing themselves first.

As with contemporary countercultures, most dropouts came from the privileged classes. Porter lists those who took to hermitage as "aristocrats tired of court life, would-be officials unable to pass the exams, scholars unwilling to compromise their principles, exhausted bureaucrats, exiled ministers, men one step ahead of the executioner." But unlike today, China's

LEAP INTO THE BOUNDLESS {85}

dropouts were perceived as great benefactors. Their pursuit of the pure Tao—and the more eccentric and reclusive the better—was seen as a good influence.

PRANKSTERS AND JESTERS

There is little in the West that compares with the space the Chinese made for Taoist dropouts and fools. The quietist monastic traditions of our leading religions perhaps bear some resemblance, but they're too somber, lacking in the playful sense of outrage that was the Taoists' metier. Closer to the mark are the Western traditions of the clown and the jester. While in China, the Tao might be permitted to hide away; in the West, its spontaneous wandering spirit might be found among show folk, or sideshow folk. Here, the free spirit must contribute at least something to "the economy," even if it's just our amusement.

Taoism itself is full of the trickster spirit. Lin Yu-lan speaks of "a certain roguish nonchalance, a confounded and devastating skepticism . . . [and] impish humor." In fact, Clarke was moved to ask: "Is Taoism, with its deconstructive humor and irreverent skepticism, anything more than a glorious hoax, the product perhaps not so much of philosophical ironists as of philosophical pranksters?"

The answer is blowing in the wind that the Taoist sage is riding on.

CHAPTER FIVE

⊢ THE HAND THAT STOPPED THE MIND

The Zen Counterculture

Once we have realized the comedy of our situation we
are already on our way to Zen.

CONRAD HYERS,
THE LAUGHING BUDDHA: ZEN AND THE COMIC SPIRIT

One day, sometime around 500 B.C.E., more than one thousand
disciples of Siddhārtha Gautama (the Buddha) gathered at the Mount of
the Holy Vulture to hear their enlightened master deliver one of his famous lectures. But on that day, the enlightened one simply stood up before his audience and held up a flower. One member of the audience—a
monk named Kashyapa—smiled. He "got it." Conrad Hyers writes of
Kashyapa's smile, "It is the glad reception of that moment of insight which
has taken the whole world by surprise, a moment of seeing with the freshness and immediacy of the little child, full of amazement and wonder—a
'holy yea' which is capable of transforming even specks of dust into stars
and frogs into Buddhas." Kashyapa's spontaneous transcendence of the
symbolic/verbal in favor of a direct acknowledgment of the divine perfection of nature is said to be the inspiration for Zen Buddhism.

NOTHING IS SACRED

Birthed in neighboring India, Buddhism slowly slipped into China over the long centuries following Gautama's life. For centuries, the relatively few Chinese practitioners apparently accepted the conventions that had been established by various Buddhist schools in India, where Gautama's simple message of inner peace through the transcendence of the desiring, suffering ego had become freighted down with a multitude of rituals and deities. But sometime in the sixth century C.E., the Chinese developed an authentically indigenous Chinese Buddhism called Zen. In fact, the birth of Zen (initially called Ch'an) has been described by D. T. Suzuki—the Japanese Zen monk largely responsible for the West's twentieth-century quantum leap in awareness of the spiritual practice—as a Chinese "revolution" against Indian Buddhism.

Legend has it that a traveling monk named Bodhidharma brought Zen from India to China in 520. Zen iconography renders Bodhidharma as a wild vagabond carrying his rucksack over his shoulder. Alan Watts describes him as "a fierce-looking fellow with a bushy beard and wide-open, penetrating eyes—in which, however, there is just the hint of a twinkle."

While some believe Bodhidharma is a myth, invented to link Zen directly to the land of Gautama, it hardly matters. The Bodhidharma story embodies the playful, countercultural nature of Zen. In one Bodhidharma tale, the Chinese emperor Wu bragged to Bodhidharma about the many ways he had promoted Buddhism under his rule. The emperor, of course, was fishing for a generous, expert assessment of his good *karma,* this concept of cumulative spiritual brownie points being central to the kind of Buddhism that Wu was familiar with.

The emperor asked the monk, "What spiritual merit has my sponsorship of Buddhism gained for me?" Bodhidharma answered, "No merit whatever!" Shaken, the emperor asked, "Then what is the first principle of the sacred doctrine?" Bodhidharma replied, "It is empty. Nothing is sacred." The emperor demanded, "Then who are you to stand before us?" Bodhidharma answered, "I don't know"—an apparent flippancy expressing the Zen view that the belief in an ego-bound "self" is absurd.

The Bodhidharma description of the Way became the classic definition of Zen: "Outside teaching; apart from tradition./Not founded on words and letters./Pointing directly to the human mind./Seeing into one's nature and attaining Buddhahood."

In the two centuries following Bodhidharma's appearance, Chinese Zen exploded into a vast populist movement. The most recognizable character from this era is Hotei, "the laughing Buddha." The familiar images of a smiling, joyous, potbellied Buddha—his arms raised skyward in ecstasy—are not, as widely believed, portraits of Gautama. They depict Hotei.

The legend of Hotei is supposedly based on the life of Keish, an itinerant Zen monk. Keish set out to demonstrate that Buddhist awakening gives rise to playful, humorous spontaneity, not rigid, dour-faced monasticism. In his book, *Crazy Wisdom,* Wes Nisker credits Keish with showing "You can have great realizations of suffering and emptiness and yet emerge a . . . joyous fat man who drinks a little wine now and then and would rather play hide and seek with children all day than chant sutras with a bunch of old monks in a stifling hot temple."

Uninterested in any formal recognition of his enlightenment, Keish refused the Zen "master" appellation and chose to remain outside the confines of Zen monastic life. "Instead," Conrad Hyers, author of *The Laughing Buddha,* writes, "[he] walked the streets with his sack over his shoulder, giving gifts to children." Hotei, the laughing archetype that posterity has fashioned from the life of Keish, incarnates the inexhaustible, cheerful generosity of awakened, spontaneous "Buddha Nature."

Then there were the Laurel and Hardy of Zen, "Cold Mountain" and "Pick Up." Zen tales portray these two as always singing, joking, and poking fun at the more self-serious monks. Iconography portrays them wild-eyed, leaning on brooms and laughing uproariously. This Zen laughter is entirely subversive. Hyers: "[Zen] laughter leads toward the debunking of pride and the deflating of ego. It mocks grasping and clinging, and cools desire. . . . It turns hierarchies upside down as a prelude to collapsing them. . . . The whole intellectual and valuation structure of the discriminating mind is challenged, with a result that is enlightening and liberating."

Besides deflating the cultured ego, Chinese Zen laughter also mocked the class prejudices that had infused Indian Buddhism. The Indians had defined six kinds of laughter, ranging from the classy, a faint, barely perceptible smile; to the déclassé, what Hyers calls "boisterous . . . raucous guffawing, convulsions, knee-slapping and hysterics." Naturally, the Zennists indulged in the latter.

Despite his constant buffoonery, Cold Mountain was widely known for his deep insights and the profound poetry he composed under his real name—Han Shan (Han Shan means "cold mountain"). His high reputation resulted in an unexpected visit from a renowned Zen priest. But Cold Mountain was so repulsed by the notion of associating with formal authorities that, when the priest appeared, he fled to the remote highlands. He spent the remainder of his life there, writing poetry on rocks and wood.

In one of his poems, Cold Mountain describes the bliss that his drop-out status afforded him: freely drifting, "I prowl the woods and streams./ And linger watching things themselves./Men don't get this far into the mountains,/White clouds gather and billow,/Thin grass does for a mattress,/ The blue sky makes a good quilt./Happy with a stone underhead,/Let heaven and earth go about their changes."

While we see Zen as a counterculture within the broader culture of Buddhism, the Chinese were simply reifying the original spirit of primal Buddhism. Gautama himself was a counterculturalist within the context of the Hindu orthodoxy. He was a Hindu sadhu (wandering renunciate beggar), whose transformative visionary experience occurred soon after he had violated the extreme asceticism of his sect of forest yogis by eating sweets. Sitting under a tree, Gautama had slipped into a natural "altered state." He saw and understood the endless suffering and striving of humanity, yet this state of consciousness allowed him to feel peaceful, nonattached compassion toward this collective misery, as well as toward his own personal difficulties. He abandoned Hinduism's complex systems and mythologies in favor of teaching others how to directly experience this new way of seeing and being in the world.

The Chinese Zennists took a Buddhism that had grown fabulously baroque in India and brought it back to its experiential baseline by reenvisioning it through a Taoist lens. The parallels are clear. As A. C. Graham said (in the previous chapter), "Taoist philosophy represents the liberation of experience from thought and language." Given the notorious syncretic tendencies of the Chinese, it is not particularly odd that India's Buddhism was shaken out of its ideology-laden slumber and brought back to its primal roots under the influence of the Taoist sages.

In *An Outline of History*, H. G. Wells is both opinionated and eloquent regarding the absence of belief in primal Buddhism. "There was to be no clinging to tawdry superstitions," he tells us. "It was primarily a religion of conduct, not a religion of observances and sacrifices. It had no temples . . . it had no sacred order of priests. Nor had it any theology. It neither asserted nor denied the reality of the innumerable and often grotesque gods who were worshipped in India at that time. It passed them by."

With a respect for experimental truth that in some ways prefigured the scientific method, Gautama ignored cosmologies or theologies, instead teaching the results of his lifelong examination of human suffering and its causes. This examination culminated with the Eightfold Path, a set of principles for living that promised release from suffering. Liberation was not reserved for some indeterminate future or for an afterlife, nor was it dependent on the duration and quality of one's adherence to certain behaviors or doctrines. This salvation was available in the present—through, as Wells puts it, "the merger of the narrow globe of individual experience in a wider being."

While, at its point of origin, Buddhism was hardly even a religion, as we usually understand it, it rapidly became one. Wells writes, "From the very first this new teaching was misconceived . . . a vast accumulation of vulgar marvels . . . presently sprang up around the memory of Gautama." Gautama's followers wasted no time enshrouding his simple, direct teaching within a densely populated tapestry of gods, demigods, demons, institutions, hierarchies, rituals, beliefs, and occult mysteries that reflected the Hindu religious culture Gautama had tried to deconstruct.

Although he had rejected that Hindu concept, his followers even declared that Gautama was the reincarnation of the Buddha, a great being who periodically returned to earth to reveal divine wisdom to mankind. History, of course, now remembers Gautama as "the Buddha."

REPRESSED ZEN

In 845, under Emperor Wu-tsung, the rapid popularization of Zen was challenged by an intense, widespread persecution. Zen temples were burned down, their treasures seized.

Fortunately, at least for the fate of Zen, Wu-tsung died young from the ingestion of a poisonous herb. His spiritual loyalties lay in a conventionalized occultist school of Taoism, and the self-poisoning was the result of his search for an alchemical elixir of immortality.

Zen survived this emperor's attempt to obliterate it, entering a second period of growth and prosperity. But damage was done. Partly as a defensive reaction to Wu-tsung's persecution, the character of Zen in China changed. It became cautious, tame, and formal. Much of its countercultural flavor was sacrificed to what some Zen scholars call the "clerical faction."

This formalization of the Zen monastic teaching tradition was also an almost inevitable result of popularization. Alan Watts describes this transformation in a manner broadly illustrative of the processes by which countercultures go "mainstream":

> . . . the fortunes of the [Zen] school so prospered and its numbers so increased that the preservation of its spirit became a very serious problem.
>
> Popularity almost invariably leads to a deterioration of quality, and as Zen became less of an informal spiritual movement and more of a settled institution . . . [it] became necessary to "standardize" its methods and to find means for the masters to handle students in large numbers. There were also the special problems which arise for monastic communities when their membership increases, their traditions harden, and their novices tend more and more to be mere boys without natural vocation, sent for training by their pious families. The effect of this last factor on the development of institutional Zen can hardly be underestimated. For the Zen community became less of an association of mature men with spiritual interests, and more of an ecclesiastical boarding school for adolescent boys.

As Zen became heavily structured, it came to resemble other forms of Buddhism, and religions per se, more closely. Eventually, Chinese Zen simply disappeared, dissolving into Chinese Buddhism in general. To the best of our knowledge, there are no distinctly Zen schools in China today (although some Buddhist schools incorporate Zen thinking and practice).

TURNING JAPANESE

As is so frequently the case, the Zen countercultural strain didn't die, it migrated. Tao-flavored Buddhism reemerged in Japan in the twelfth and thirteenth centuries.

On its arrival in Japan, Zen almost immediately bifurcated. A monk named Essai guided an establishment Zen, with monasteries sponsored by the Japanese emperor. But Zen master Dogen refused offers of similar sponsorship, upholding radical Zen's tradition of maintaining distance from both secular and spiritual authorities.

Japanese Zen is populated by a host of colorfully countercultural figures who expressed Zen awareness in unique, eccentric, individual styles. One was the fifteenth-century Zen teacher Ikkyu Sojun, who called himself "Crazy Cloud." John Stevens describes him in *Zen Masters:* "Radical Ikkyu . . . was unconventional, uncompromising, and combative. He relentlessly attacked sham and hypocrisy, concealing nothing himself, even his sex life, which makes him unique among stony-faced Zen priests, who usually mask their emotions so well."

Ikkyu did his best to subvert the formalities that had, by then, crept into Japanese Zen. For instance, Zen schools had started handing out diplomas to represent the attainment of enlightenment. Ikkyu loudly denounced this practice, refusing the *inka* presented to him by his own teacher and offering no form of certification to his own students. In the spirit of true Zen, Suzuki comments, "Copying is slavery. The letter must never be followed."

Then there was Bankei, a seventeenth-century populist Zen country preacher. He was known for his straightforward, unpretentious, often coarse articulation of Zen precepts; his sermons attracted great crowds from the lower classes, but students of social rank avoided him. The rough-hewn wise man's powerful but unmannered presence frightened away members of the upper class and others who valued conventional nicety. "He spoke to large audiences of farmers and country folk," Watts tells us, "but no one 'important' seems to have dared follow him."

As has been already implied, Zen was—by its very nature—something of a spiritual class revolution against Indian Buddhism. Zen stripped away the images of ethereal, unapproachable, bejeweled demigods that had infested the Indian iconography. In its place, it gave us what Hyers calls "the celebration of the ordinary." The new icons were poor humble monks. And the Zen saying "Before enlightenment, chop wood and carry water. After enlightenment, chop wood and carry water" tells us that this was a path for common working folk.

The poet Ryokan was another Zen master who kept company exclusively with common folk. A gentle wanderer with a reputation for spiritual mastery, he refused high positions in the hierarchies of Zen schools and temples. Instead, the childlike, self-effacing Ryokan labeled himself "The Great Fool," and shunned the company of monks and priests. His penchant for drinking sake with villagers and farmers, his special delight in playing with children, and his generous manner—he could always be counted on to recite his poetry upon request—make Ryokan something of a Japanese counterpart to Keish.

Ryokan's love for nature and animals has also earned him comparisons to St. Francis. He worshiped nature as it was, without romantic illusions. In one poem, he compared the lice on his chest to insects in the grass. And nature was all Ryokan needed to dispel his grief when he was robbed: "Left behind by the thief—/The moon/In the window."

Zen took hold in Japan, becoming an integral aspect of Japanese culture, and so it remains today. Alan Watts writes that in Japan, Zen "has entered into almost every aspect of the people's life—their architecture, poetry, painting, gardening, their athletics, crafts, and trades; it has penetrated the everyday language and thought of the most ordinary folk." (One, of course, wonders then about the Japanese penchant for conformity. I will leave this ambiguity hanging . . . Zen-like.)

NOTHING REALLY IS SACRED

> What is the first principle of the sacred doctrine? Vast
> emptiness and nothing sacred in it.
>
> FROM THE LEGEND OF BODHIDHARMA

Zen philosophy centers on the notion of emptiness, making it even more difficult to discuss than Taoism. While the Taoists viewed the world as emerging out of meaningless chaos, they emphasized life's processes. Zen reverses emphasis, focusing on the ontological void Zennists see as the existential bottom line. In essence, Zen believes that only after one empties oneself out, becoming utterly detached from significance, can one experience life's flow from an enlightened perspective. Zen rejects metaphysics and theism—belief systems that construct meaning out of the manipulation of symbols. In the words of R. H. Blythe, author of *Zen in English Literature and the Oriental Classics,* "Zen is the unsymbolization of the world and all things in it." And it's not just symbols and beliefs that get the axe. As Suzuki put it, "the whole structure of personality is overturned." Zennists have described enlightenment as being like "the bottom of a tub falling out."

Like Gautama's original Buddhism, Zen attempts to evoke (or indeed *pro*voke) a liberated mind state. While not necessarily free from the experience of pain, this consciousness isn't in bondage to it. And in accordance with the countercultural principle of open, democratic access, Zen declares this awareness available to all human beings at all times. But Zen awareness can't be actively sought. In fact, it can't be generated by any form of activity. It is simply possible, to be entered spontaneously—when the activities of the ordinary rational mind are abandoned. Suzuki explained the anti-authoritarian nature of the Zen concept of spontaneous satori: "When the doctrine of enlightenment . . . is to be grasped immediately without any conceptual medium, the sole authority in his [the Zen practitioner's] spiritual life will have to be found within himself; traditionalism or institutionalism will naturally lose all its binding force."

Whether sixth-century Chinese, twelfth-century Japanese, or contemporary Westerners, humans lose themselves in the exigencies of civic life and personal survival. We become so immersed in worry and need, thought and symbol, that we confuse the identities we carry into our social interactions with our essence. These identities bind us to the past. Our desires bind us to the future. On rare occasions, the mental activity generated by these issues may cease, and we awaken to our extraordinary presence in the moment. This experience is but a hint of satori, and Zen invites us to experience this state as a way of being in the world. The world tries to convince us that this is impractical, but as Zen master Hui-neng pointed out, "so long as our minds remain unattached to any particular thought, it is capable of thinking all thoughts suitable to all situations."

BEING THERE

We've already noted that Zen awareness can't be sought after—striving can't achieve satori. But Zen doesn't leave us stranded in confusion, hoping that a lightning bolt of spontaneous enlightenment will suddenly strike. Zen has developed practices and techniques for achieving that which cannot be achieved through practices and techniques. (If you can't handle blatantly absurd contradictions, there's a chapter about the European Age of Reason coming up soon!)

There are two primary Zen practices. Zazen, the prolonged, silent sitting meditation that has become the central Zen activity, increases the likelihood that the practitioner will take notice of moments when her consciousness spontaneously becomes centered in the present. Practicing zazen gives us time to notice *now*.

The second technique involves forcibly interrupting mental activity so that the present is experienced. Zen masters and adherents who use this technique are like spiritual Surrealist pranksters, dedicating their lives to shocking students and seekers out of their mental habits. A primary tool of this methodology is the koan—jokes without clear punch lines, riddles without obvious answers—that short-circuit ordinary thought processes and trick rational minds into giving up. The famous example is "What is the sound of one hand clapping?" Equally striking is Zen master Hui-chung's declaration: "When you have a staff, I will give you one; when you have none, I will take it away from you."

And then there are the Zen parables and teaching tales—stories without obvious meaning, generally consisting of brief snippets of interaction between a master and a student. These stories shatter rational complacency with sudden, unexpected explosions of absurdity, paradox, and sometimes violence. One such tale is retold by Alan Watts: "Master Shih-kung asked the disciple if he could take hold of empty space. The disciple made a grasping movement in the air with this hand but Shih-kung exclaimed, 'you got nothing!' The disciple then asked, 'What, then, is your way?' Whereupon Shih-kung took hold of the disciple's nose, gave it a sharp twist and called out, 'That is the way to take hold of empty space!' "

In many Zen narratives, the student's satori is achieved only after he rebels against his teacher's authority. For instance, when one master asserted that all speech somehow relates to ultimate truth, his monk inquired, "Then may I call you a donkey?" Playful disrespect appears frequently in the discourses of radical Zen. Leave your self-importance at the door along with your shoes.

Another Zen mind-stopping method that will intrigue lawyers but horrify contemporary social workers involves waking up seekers to the current moment by delivering sharp blows to the head, usually with a hard wooden stick. This practice is characteristic of Rinzai, the "hard school" of Zen. While it is well known that Zen teachers would smite their students in this manner, it is less known that students would also hit each other, and sometimes even hit their master! (Rinzai monasteries sound like veritable "Fight Clubs"!) In this Zen practice, the hand that holds the stick quite literally becomes the hand that stops the mind.

Some Zen masters have also been known to use uproarious, loud shouting and, in the words of Nisker, "belly laughs and blasphemy" to interrupt cognition. Not surprisingly, these behaviors were seen as bizarre, threatening, and uncouth by conventional Chinese society.

Zen Versus Authority

> There has probably never been a religious movement
> more sweepingly iconoclastic than Zen.
>
> CONRAD HYERS

Its radical techniques have made Zen a countercultural threat to established orders. Jung observed, "If Buddhism were a 'Church' in our sense of the word, the Zen movement would certainly have been an intolerable burden to her." But the more radical strains of Zen threaten even *Zen's* established order. Radical Zennists dismiss all conventional and spiritual authority. Its practitioners even reject the power of the "Patriarchs," a lineage of masters acknowledged within Zen tradition as leaders of the entire Zen movement for their respective generations. And—as expressed by the famous Zen aphorism "If you meet the Buddha on the road, kill him"—radical Zen even rejects the authority of the Buddha himself. Zen master Feng once announced, "The Buddha is a bull-headed jail-keeper, and the Patriarchs are horse-faced old maids!" And in response to the question

"What is the Buddha?" Zen master Ummon is alleged to have answered, "A dried dung-stick!" This, of course, echoes the earlier Taoist "Chuang-tzu" quote "This thing called The Way—where does it exist? . . . It is in the piss and shit." Both Zen and Taoism aim to upset spiritual elitism—the assumption that the Way, or Buddha Nature, is available only to the good and the beautiful.

In *The Laughing Buddha: Zen and the Comic Spirit*, Conrad Hyers retells the following story from the annals of Zen: "Yun-men once related the legend to his monks, according to which the Buddha at his birth pointed toward heaven with one hand and the earth with the other, and taking seven steps forward looked toward the four quarters of the earth, exclaiming, 'Above and beneath heaven, I alone am the honored one.' Yun-men then declared, 'If I had seen him at the time, I would have cut him down with my staff, and given his flesh to dogs to eat, so that peace could prevail over all the world.' "

Alan Watts, discussing monasteries that practice radical Zen, writes: "The student . . . is free to challenge the master, and one can imagine that in the days when Zen training was less formal the members of Zen communities must have had enormous fun laying traps for each other. To some extent this type of relationship still exists. . . . The late Kozuki Roshi was entertaining two American monks at tea when he casually asked, 'And what do you gentlemen know about Zen?' One of the monks flung his closed fan straight at the master's face. All in the same instant the master inclined his head slightly to one side, the fan shot straight through the paper *shoji* behind him, and he burst into a ripple of laughter."

Many of Zen's most widely celebrated figures remained true to its countercultural essence, refusing the formal titles, certifications of enlightenment, and high positions within priestly hierarchies offered them by the Zen schools and establishments of their day.

Zen Beats a Westward Path

Happy. Just in my swim shorts, barefooted, wild-haired,
in the red fire dark, singing, swigging wine, spitting,
jumping, running—that's the way to live. All alone and
free in the soft sands of the beach by the sigh of the sea

out there, with the Ma-Wink fallopian virgin warm stars
reflecting on the outer channel fluid belly waters.

JACK KEROUAC, *THE DHARMA BUMS*

Zen came into contemporary Western civilization when Suzuki published
an English-language version of *Essays in Zen Buddhism*. Suzuki subse-
quently traveled frequently to America and Europe to speak about Zen.
He was a walking advertisement for enlightenment. Even more than his
learned discourse, Western intellectuals and spiritual seekers were awed by
his presence—his serene demeanor, quiet dignity, and wit. Zen's popularity in the West has grown so rapidly since the appearance of *Essays in
Zen Buddhism* that some have predicted that its publication—along with
Suzuki's later activities—will be seen by future generations as comparable
to Bodhidharma's epic (if mythical) journey into China.

As the result of Suzuki's efforts, Zen became a major force in the beat
and sixties countercultures. Jack Kerouac, the first beat writer to excite
public interest (and opprobrium), was particularly enamored with Zen.
His popular novel *The Dharma Bums* articulated this love. Indeed, Zen
was embraced to a greater or lesser degree by many major beat figures, including Neal Cassady and poets Allen Ginsberg and Gary Snyder.

One can easily imagine how excited these dropouts from conservative,
capitalistic fifties America must have been with the words of Suzuki: "The
desire to possess is considered by Buddhism to be one of the worst passions
with which mortals are apt to be obsessed. What, in fact, causes so much
misery in the world is the universal impulse of acquisition . . . as wealth is
coveted, the rich and poor are always crossing swords in bitter enmity.
International wars rage, social unrest ever increases, unless this impulse to
get and to hold is completely uprooted. Cannot society be reorganized
upon an entirely different basis . . . ? . . . The Zen ideal of putting a monk's
belongings into a tiny box is his mute protest . . . against the present order
of society."

Nobody turned sixties youth counterculture on to Zen more than Alan
Watts. A former Episcopalian minister, Watts emigrated from his native
England to California and became the West's most popular exponent of
Eastern philosophies. And, like millions of much younger people in the
1960s, Watts experimented extensively with psychedelic drugs and plants.

In *The Joyous Cosmology*, he documented his LSD journeys, linking them to various forms of Eastern mysticism. Naturally, this book captured the attention of the emerging, acid-saturated sixties counterculture, turning Watts into a popular freelance spiritual leader. Watts, in turn, directed the hippies' attention toward Zen.

Zen's influence in the West continues to grow today. Before the latter half of the twentieth century, the New World and the European continent had no Zen schools, temples, and monasteries of their own. Now there are hundreds, if not thousands, of such establishments. And, as in Japan, Zen practices have escaped the monastery. Tens of thousands of active U.S. citizens, for instance, practice Zen techniques while otherwise going about the busy life of an average contemporary person.

Scholar of comparative religion Huston Smith has eloquently identified the source of Zen's appeal to the Western world:

> We understand the specific attraction of [Zen] when we realize the extent to which the contemporary West is animated by "prophetic faith," the sense of the holiness of the *ought*, the pull of the way things could be and should be but as yet are not. Such faith has obvious virtues, but unless it is balanced by a companion sense of the holiness of the *is*, it becomes top-heavy. If one's eyes are always on tomorrows, todays slip by unperceived. To a West which in its concern to refashion heaven and earth is in danger of letting the presentness of life—the only life we really have—slip through its fingers, Zen comes as a reminder that if we do not learn to perceive the mystery of our *present* life, our *present* hour, we shall not perceive the worth of *any* life, of *any* hour.

CHAPTER SIX

⊢ LOVE AND EVOLUTION

The Occult Counterculture of the Sufis

Come, let's scatter roses and pour wine in the glass;/
We'll shatter heaven's roof and lay a new foundation./
If sorrow raises armies to shed the blood of lovers,/I'll
join with the wine bearer so we can overthrow them./
With a sweet string at hand, play a sweet song, my
friend, So we can clap and sing a song, and lose our
heads in dancing.

HAFIZ

If a bush can say, "I am Truth," so can a man.

SUFI SAYING

Of all countercultures, perhaps Sufism is the one that most
closely resembles a quantum event. Sufism is nearly impossible to define
and even harder to locate, seeming at once everywhere and nowhere. Its
exact origins are lost within a cloud of probabilities. We know of its presence largely through its interpenetration with other cultures, the distinc-

tive quality of the signatures it leaves in the properties and patterns of the cultures it collides with.

Even the origin of the word Sufi is ambiguous. Early Sufis wore humble wool clothes, and most say Sufi is simply the Arabic word for wool. But others claim it comes from the Persian word for pure.

According to Richard Smoley and Jay Kinney's *Hidden Wisdom,* "The first historical traces of sufism as a mystical path appeared within two centuries of the founding of Islam in the seventh century A.D. . . . It is said that the Prophet Muhammad instructed his son-in-law, Hazrati Ali, in the techniques and inner truth of his mysticism. Ali in turn instructed other Muslims before he was killed in one of the power struggles that overtook Islam in the decades after the Prophet's death. Today, nearly every Sufi order traces . . . back to Ali."

A slightly different historical narrative locates Sufi origins among an entire circle of friends who regularly sat with Muhammad during his final years. This communion was said to have been cultivated by the Prophet to seed within the hearts of his associates an organic, vital awareness that would continue to unfold and be transmitted to others after his death as his dynamic spiritual legacy. Yet another alternate history from within Sufism traces it all the way back to the building of the Temple of Solomon (an event also mythologized as the birth of Freemasonry). This historical account casts Muhammad as an initiate, rather than the initiator, of Sufism and claims Jesus himself as a Sufi dervish.

In the seventh century, Muslim mystics, in the words of Smoley and Kinney, "attracted followers on the strength of their personal saintliness. These illumined beings taught their students the techniques they had employed to become 'friends of God,' and those who attained spiritual realization in turn taught others." In the eighth century, these casual associations evolved into formal communities called Sufiyay. By the late thirteenth century, Sufi orders became a force to contend with in the Arab world and India.

Conventional religious history characterizes Sufism as a sect of Islam, and the original mystics were almost certainly Muslims. However, many Sufis refuse this sectarian limitation, acknowledging the divine genesis of all religions and rejecting claims of superiority or exclusivity on the part of any. A number of Sufi masters have worked within Jewish or Christian tradition.

Indeed, Sufism views itself as going to the very root of all religions. Sufi master Hazrat Inayat Khan wrote, "There is one religion and there are many covers. Each of these covers has a name: Christianity, Buddhism, Judaism, Islam, etc. and when you take off these covers, you find that there is one religion, and it is that religion which is the religion of Sufi." According to Khan, Sufis claimed Jesus as one of their own, a "Master of the Way." The *Jewish Encyclopaedia* tells us that the Kabala is also rooted in the Sufi practices.

Of course, as with all quantum events, for every express opinion there are those who rise up with a different view. Contemporary Islamic scholar Othman Ali argues that "Orientalist stereotypes of legalistic, unbending and militant literalists and eclectic, compassionate, peaceful Sufis distort. . . . Sufis could and did belong to literalist schools of law; some led jihad movements and many advocated implementing the Shari'ah [Islamic law] as vigorously as any literalist."

The features that enshroud Sufism within this mist of quantum uncertainty also illustrate its radically countercultural nature. However many versions arise across history, Sufism started out—informal and unauthorized—on the fringes of the Muslim religion. It was—and remains—grounded in experience. Thus, its interpretation remains mutable.

GOD IS LOVE

> Islam admits no original sin, only forgetfulness of the Real.
>
> PETER LAMBORN WILSON,
> *SCANDAL: ESSAYS IN ISLAMIC HERESY*

> Love/ripped open the curtain/of puritanism/and revealed my desire/for paradise—/My bathtub fell off/the roof!
>
> SALMAN SAVAJI, IN HIS CLASSIC FOURTEENTH-CENTURY
> PERSIAN SUFI POEM "THE DRUNKEN UNIVERSE"

Unlike Taoism and Zen Buddhism, which might comfortably be defined as philosophies, or even methods, Sufism—with few exceptions—defines itself as a religion. Sufis are involved with God (singular). Indeed, Sufis are amorous toward God and all his creation.

Sufism is a religion of passion, a religion of the heart. Whereas the Buddhist seeks the "cessation of desire," Sufis lose the self through the intensity of their desire for union with God and, frequently, with the beloved representative of God's beauty—the human subject of the practitioner's ardor. You might say that the Sufi burns the candle of his heart on both ends, ultimately burning out his ego, allowing for fusion with the One. The great Sufi poet Ibn al-'Arabi, in his "The Young Woman at the Ka'ba," describes the intensity of his passion: "Amazing! How could it be that the one pierced through the heart by love has any remainder of self left to be bewildered? Love's character is to be all-consuming. It numbs the senses, drives away the intellect, astonishes thoughts. . . . Where is bewilderment and who is left to be bewildered?"

In his introduction to Arabi's book of poems *Stations of Desire,* Michael Sells puts it this way:

> When the mystic lover is thinned away and broken down, when he can no longer hold on to his self or his thoughts, when he is emptied of his own words and arguments, the beloved reveals herself.
> . . . this is the moment of love-madness. For the Sufis in general and Ibn al-'Arabi in particular, love-madness is analogous to the mystical bewilderment that occurs as the normal boundaries of identity, reason, and will are melted. The self of the lover passes away. In this "annihilation" he becomes one with the divine beloved.

The thirteenth-century Sufi Rumi expressed the vigilance of the passionate seeker when he wrote: "If love slips out of your hand/Don't fall into Despair. Keep searching. Fight to find it/Until you reach Him, see Him, Don't sleep, don't eat, don't relax." This fragment works as easily as a straightforward romantic poem as a love poem for God. And in fact, Sufic devotion is intended to work in both ways. In some of Arabi's work, he creates a sort of dialectic, or argument, around the question of whether the beloved is the present human form or God. Arabi seems to spin the reader around, dervish-style, until all is a blur and we can no longer worry the distinction. The human beloved and God are one and the same . . . or the human beloved is a sign of God, depending on the interpretation.

There is frequently—although not always—an erotic component to Sufic love. Both Rumi's and Arabi's poetics are saturated with sexual imagery. Arabi wrote, "When a man loves a woman, he seeks union with her, that is to say the most complete union possible in love, and there is . . . no union greater than that between the sexes," and Rumi illustrates the sensibility more vividly: "laughing crazily,/moaning in the spreading union of lover and beloved/This is the true religion. All others/are thrown-away bandages beside it."

Today's Islamic fundamentalists are paradigmatic of anti-sexual hysteria—their panic particularly aimed at feminine desire. But Peter Lamborn Wilson, American counterculturalist and Sufi scholar, claims: "The model of Islam was never chastity. The prophet spoke of 'pleasures which are seemly in the eyes of God,' by which he meant polygamy and concubinage. . . . Sex is a mode of worship or contemplation. You make love because God is love."

Sufic love—sometimes polygamous and sometimes monogamous—shouldn't be confused with pure erotomania. Sufis espouse *all* the attributes commonly associated with love. Wilson: "Love is important . . . for nearly all sufis, who accept that God's qualities of love and generosity outweigh his qualities of justice and fear . . . sufism offers a general mystical interpretation of the psychological experience of love . . . between husband and wife, master and disciple, or lover and beloved."

While Sufic eroticism never, in Wilson's words, "led to a sex cult," there have been episodes of what he has waggishly labeled "Sacred Pedophilia." (It needs to be noted that Wilson's provocative use of this word can't be understood in the same way that it is used today, to describe a pathological sexual obsession and/or criminal exploitation of the young. It should also be noted that this practice was marginal within historic Sufism.) A practice called *nazar ill'al-murd,* or "contemplation of the unbearded," involved male initiates meditating on attractive young boys—

some of them barely on the verge of puberty—as a sign of God's beauty. Also called "The Witness Game," it was not quite as scandalous within early Islam as it would be to most Westerners today. Ahmad Ghazali, a major Sufi figure from Persia in the twelfth century, was an early supporter of "the game." Wilson describes a Sufi portrait in which Ghazali is portrayed "seated in his cell-retreat, staring at a young boy, with a single rose on the floor between them."

Ibn Taymiyya, a fourteenth-century arch-conservative enemy of Sufism, charged that kissing and embracing were also a part of these ceremonies, and Wilson allows that, "when overcome by ecstasy during the sama ('spiritual concert'), [some] were inclined to rend the shirts of the unbearded and dance with them breast to breast."

Given the peculiar sexual climate current in the United States—combining hysteria about adolescent sexuality with ubiquitous commercial public titillation around same—it is perhaps worth noting that this is pretty mild stuff. It seems likely that most of the God/love-intoxicated mystics separated their appreciation of prepubescent beauty from any lustful compulsions for sexual penetration, although according to Wilson, "One sufi, accused by the arch-puritan Taymiyya of sexual immorality, replied, 'And so what if I did?'"

Clearly we are on an emotionally (and legally) tender terrain within a contemporary context, but at that time, according to Wilson, "The ultimate problem for the Islamic moralists . . . was not pederasty or pedophilia *per se* . . . The real danger in 'sacred pedophilia' was the claim that human beings can realize themselves in love more perfectly than in religious practices." The Sufis were accused of the heresy of Incarnationism. While conservative theologians claimed that God could be seen only after death, the Sufis professed to witness God with their eyes; in the words of one shocked conservative, "while gazing at a comely slave boy."

For Sufis, this eroticism isn't about self-gratification. (Well, at least not consciously.) After all, the idea is to lose the self, the ego, in one's passion for God. Like the Buddhists and Hindus, Sufis are among the "grateful dead." They seek liberation from the self while incarnate. Rumi wrote, "Die now, die now, in this Love die; when you have died in this Love, you will all receive new life." And Wilson echoes him, writing, "The seeker must renounce his own self. . . . He must travel from things to

Nothing, from existence to non-existence. How does one get lost on purpose?"

The Sufis take a romantic approach toward losing themselves in God. Like the Buddhists, most Sufis renounce material desire and easy pleasure. But rather than trying to center their minds on the void, Sufis' enlightenment is aesthetic as well as ascetic. They "dig" God everywhere, as manifested in the physical world. To the extent that they are averse to materialism and mere pleasure seeking, it is only because these attributes interfere with their complete devotion to the God that made the existing world manifest. The phrase "complete devotion" is key. The Sufis are fervent lovers of God. Like the pining romantic, they are finally disinterested in lesser pursuits.

The Sufi cosmogony is too complex to do justice to in one chapter dedicated to its countercultural aspects. But I will make a brief attempt. In a complicated trick of the tail, the Sufic God inheres in a mysterious metaphysical place that humans can barely fathom, and can begin to approach only through lifelong study and devotion. At the same time, Sufism also maintains that "all is one," that is, everything existing is a manifestation of God. Incarnate things are viewed as similar to God, while at the same time God is "incomparable" to incarnate things. In other words, the physical world is not God *per se*, but God's semiotics/hermeneutics. Henry Bayman, a Western writer who trained with Sufi masters in Central Anatolia, writes, "In Islamic and Sufic thought, the world of meaning completes the world of matter, precisely because it supplies the meaning that is missing from the material world."

HIGH ISLAM

A pound of roast meat, a few loaves of bread/A jug of wine, at least one willing boy,/A pipe of hashish. Now the picnic's spread/My garden beggars paradise's joy.

ABU NUWAS, SEVENTH/EIGHTH CENTURY,
TRANSLATION BY HAKIM BEY

Close the shop of argument and mystery. Open the teahouse of experience.

IDRIES SHAH

Sufis seek intoxication. In other words, they formulate the experience of losing oneself in love and God in terms of getting high. While most Sufis aim for a natural buzz, a minority of Sufic circles across history literally get intoxicated with wine, hashish, marijuana, or even coffee as part of their spiritual practice.

The Shari'ah, the central document of Islamic law, condemns intoxication of any sort. However, many Sufic circles simply don't follow the Shari'ah. A few don't self-define as Muslims. In any case, most "lawless Sufis" believe that once you attain a certain level of illumination, there are no rules. Al-Iraqi, a much respected Sufi master and poet from the thirteenth century, wrote: "We've moved our bedrolls from the mosque to the tavern of ruin/we've scribbled over pages of asceticism and erased all miracles of piety./Now we sit in the ranks of lovers in the Magi's lane/And drink a cup from the hands of the dissolute haunters of the tavern./If the heart should tweak the ear of respectability now, why not?/For we've raised the flag of our fortune to high heavens./We've passed beyond all self-denial, all mystical stations."

A primary historical order that embraced hashish as part of their process, the Qalanadars, seem(ed) like hard-core hippies. According to Islamic historian Dr. Carl W. Ernst, starting in the late thirteenth century, "Wandering groups of ascetics wearing animal skins . . . shaving all body hair, and generally acting in an outrageous fashion, began to be seen all over the Middle East and South Asia. . . . They were careless about . . . Islamic ritual . . . frequently went naked . . . and were renown for . . . use of hallucinogens and intoxicants. . . . Known as Qalandars, they . . . were viewed as . . . dangerous by political authorities [and] . . . were associated with peasant uprisings, particularly in Anatolia."

Wilson, an unabashed wine and THC enthusiast, came across any number of quasi-secret wine-imbibing and hashish-smoking Sufi orders in the Islamic world during his travels there in the 1970s. He portrays a gathering of Qalandars in a cemetery with "the right sort of people . . . intoxicated fakirs and transvestite dancers—it was more a public festival than a private gathering. . . .

"The affair was devoted to ecstatic dancing of a more or less impromptu nature. . . . Miniaturists loved to show wild dervishes whirling round and round, the long sleeves of their robes flying out like wings. The

aim of the music is to impel the user towards a spiritual experience." Sufi
ecstatic dancers, of course, came to be known as whirling dervishes in the
West, due to the circular and (sometimes) spinning movements that some
use(d) as part of their ritual. Although most sects were pacifistic, early
Western colonialists were so shocked by the ecstatic dancing they halluci-
nated that the dervishes were dangerously insane and "bloodthirsty."

In 1973, Peter Lamborn Wilson witnessed what he called an "impressive" THC-suffused ceremony at a Sufi shrine in Lahore, Pakistan, in
honor of Madho Lal Husayn. Wilson: "A great deal of bhang [a marijuana-
based drink] was consumed in a very brotherly—if somewhat insane—
ambiance. Qawwali music was played and transvestite whirling dervishes
performed."

For Wilson, Husayn

> seemed to exemplify the Qalander spirit . . . wild
> dervish, intoxicated and erotic.
> . . . a pious and ascetic sufi who used to spend every
> night immersed to his waist in the river, reading the
> Koran. One night however he suddenly laughed and
> hurled the Book into the water, where it sank beneath
> the waves.
> He shaved his beard and took to wearing bright
> ruby-red robes, wandering around Lahore spouting po-
> etry and nonsense. One day he saw a beautiful young
> Brahmin boy named Madho and fell in love with him . . .
> [and] became his spiritual master and lover.

The Qalandariya continue as a Sufi order in Pakistan. Wilson: "All over
Afghanistan and Pakistan the most popular prayer before lighting a pipe of
charas [hashish] or taking a cup of bhang is, 'Ya! Lal Shabaz Qalandar!' "

The Turkish poet Fuzuli, who wrote the famous Sufic treatise *Layla
and Majnun* (yes, Virginia, Eric Clapton had this Sufi story in mind when
he titled his big pop hit with Derek and the Dominos), said that wine was
only "an eager disciple setting the world afire, but hashish is the sufi master himself."

According to Idries Shah, twenty-first-century America's favorite drug—

coffee—was discovered by Abu-el Hasan Shadhilli, a dervish sheikh. Some Sufis used it ceremonially to increase their awareness.

Is it not interesting that a common theme within most of the counter-cultural spiritual practices we discuss involves practitioners experiencing ecstasy—people feeling really good, high, and happy—while at the same time, these same people have renounced material greed, and the ego gratification of social success and fame? Perhaps there's a message in there for us.

WAKING THE SLEEPWALKER WITHIN

Once upon a time Kidr, the Teacher of Moses, called upon mankind with a warning. At a certain date, he said, all the water in the world which had not been specially hoarded, would disappear. It would then be renewed, with different water, which would drive men mad.

Only one man listened to the meaning of this advice. He collected water and went to a secure place where he stored it, and waited for the water to change its character.

On the appointed date the streams stopped running, the wells went dry, and the man who had listened, seeing this happening, went to his retreat and drank his preserved water.

When he saw, from his security, the waterfalls again beginning to flow, this man descended among the other sons of men. He found that they were thinking and talking in an entirely different way from before, yet they had no memory of what had happened, nor of having been warned. When he tried to talk to them, he realized that they thought that he was mad, and they showed hostility or compassion, not understanding.

At first, he drank none of the new water, but went back to his concealment, to draw on his supplies, every day. Finally, however, he took the decision to drink the new water because he could not bear the loneliness of

living, behaving and thinking in a different way from
everyone else. He drank the new water, and became like
the rest. He forgot all about his own store of special
water, and his fellows began to look upon him as a madman who had miraculously been restored to sanity.

IDRIES SHAH, *TALES OF THE DERVISHES*

I must discover, at all costs, some manner or means for
destroying in people the predilection for suggestibility
which causes them to fall under the influence of mass
hypnosis.

G. I. GURDJIEFF, AT THE START OF THE TWENTIETH CENTURY

Many contemporary counterculturalists—and psychologists who trend
toward the "human potential" camp of that vocation—are obsessed with
the idea that people need to be deprogrammed or debrainwashed from the
inherited percepts of their culture, as well as from the lazy habits of mind
that naturally accrue to anyone's psyche during the process of living and
using language. A particularly hard-core dilatation of this notion posits
that we are all sleepwalking through life, and desperate measures are required to wake us up. James Joyce, William Butler Yeats, G. I. Gurdjieff,
Aleister Crowley, and Timothy Leary are among the twentieth-century
thinkers who employed the "sleepwalker" trope. Gurdjieff and Crowley
were infected with the idea through their study of Sufism (and Leary
through his study of Gurdjieff in the mid-1960s). As Shah writes, "Sufism
sees ordinary consciousness as unconsciousness. All our waking days we are
literally asleep. The project of Sufism is to wake us up and to keep us awake
to 'the Real.' "

Overcoming brainwashing and remaining "awake"—not falling back
into lazy conditioned responses—seems to require something of a tough-
love approach. Shah writes, "Sufism doesn't trade in airy-fairyness, mutual
admiration, or lukewarm generalities, when the bite disappears . . . so does
the Sufi element . . . the Sufi teacher cannot supply his disciple with only
a small quantity of Sufism."

According to one of Gurdjieff's famous students, J. G. Bennett, the
Khwajagan school of Sufism that influenced his teacher emphasized "con-

stant vigilance, and . . . struggle with one's own weaknesses. They also used methods of awakening involving shocks and surprises." One technique Gurdjieff employed in his wisdom schools was to frequently ring a loud bell. Students going about their daily business had to freeze where they were and bring their presumably wandering minds back into the present. Crowley, ever the drama queen, would sometimes cut himself during meditations when he noticed his mind meandering off into old familiar patterns. In one poem, Rumi recommends a different kind of cutting—old familial ties: "The mother and father are your attachment/to beliefs and bloodties/and desires and comforting habits./Don't listen to them!/They seem to protect,/but they imprison./They are your worst enemies."

Sufic vigilance frequently requires the neglect of ordinary social vigilance, the diligence called for in the workaday (or war-a-day) world. Shah: "The Sufi is asleep to 'things of the day'—the familiar struggle for existence which the ordinary man finds all-important—and vigilant while others are asleep. In other words, he keeps awake the spiritual attention dormant in others."

OF MASTERS AND AUTHORITY

God does not need our worship, we do.

HENRY BAYMAN

Sufism, at its essence, opposes authoritarianism. Most Sufis don't formally recognize degrees of spiritual achievement with the assignation of titles, status, or positions of relative responsibility or privilege; they don't acknowledge any absolute spiritual authority in human form, or empower any persons as ultimate arbiters of spiritual matters in human affairs. While affirming that divine inspiration has guided the lives of the prophets of all great religions, Sufism also affirms that any and all human beings can be divinely inspired. This leveling leaves egalitarian brotherhood—according to Sufism, the very fountain of spiritual life—as the root principle of genuine Sufi community and social expression.

Still, in exploring Sufism as a nonauthoritarian path, one can't avoid one seeming contradiction: the requirement that the individual Sufi initiate surrender himself absolutely to the instructions of a teacher or master.

As we have seen, the Sufi initiate requires constant surprise to remain awake. A prepackaged program of meditations, procedures, and/or exercises isn't going to suffice. Even more than Zen or Taoist enlightenment, Sufi illumination depends upon a relationship with a living master. (As with nearly everything in this book, there are exceptions to the rule. In *Sacred Drift*, Wilson discusses a Sufi way that is without gurus.) It is perhaps a peculiar conundrum for a nondoctrinaire religion. But then it is precisely the absence of doctrine and rote rituals that leaves the Sufic hopeful no other way in. The true Sufi master works intuitively with each initiate, teasing his psyche out of its slumber—putting him through practices and processes specifically designed to decondition that individual.

Shah wrote, "People . . . attempt to enroll themselves in mysticism on their own terms. . . . The [Sufi] disciple . . . can make no conditions. . . . In the development of the human mind, there is a constant change and limit to the usefulness of any particular technique. This characteristic of Sufi practice is ignored in a repetitious system." Shah goes on to quote a Sufi initiate who seems to have been successfully deconditioned: "My teacher liberated me from the captivity in which . . . I thought I was free, when in fact I was actually revolving within a pattern."

Westerners who have witnessed several generations of spiritual and psychological mindfuckers—the gurus and the Werner Erhard types who proved to be in it for money and power—are understandably cautious about surrendering to a "master." Indeed, given human tendencies, one can only assume that, across history and to this day, some con artists have passed themselves off as Sufi masters (and some great Sufi adepts with Trickster tendencies have passed themselves off as con artists). The initiate must rely on her own intelligence and intuition in choosing a teacher, or leave the Sufi process alone. And, unlike Islamic fundamentalism, no one that we know of has ever attempted to coerce people into practicing Sufism (it wouldn't work) or killed "infidels" for not participating.

Historically, Sufis insisted that some enlightened individuals could interpret the Qur'an, while fundamentalists insisted that their "authoritative" view was not an interpretation at all, but the *essence of the book itself*. However, the authoritarian interpretation of the Muslim religion may not be rooted in the Qu'ran at all. According to Ernst, "the Arabic term Islam [meaning surrender] . . . was of . . . minor importance in classical theologies based on the Qur'an; and denotes the minimal external forms of compliance with religious duty. . . . The key term of religious identity is not Islam but imam, or faith. . . . Faith is . . . mentioned hundreds of times [in the Qur'an]. Islam is mentioned only eight times."

In fact, Ernst avers that the emphasis on Islam was a gift from European Orientalists and was used to define Muslim culture as backward in comparison to the post-Enlightenment West. Ernst adds that, in light of the horrors of its present dominant form, many who (quietly) embrace Sufism within the Islamic world today refuse to believe that their loving poetic practice ever had anything to do with the Muslim religion.

The sacred status assigned to the individual will in Sufism is also reflected in the practice of Sufi medicine. Here, the demand for cure, as well as the diagnosis and prescription, must originate with the patient, leaving the physician in the role of advisor and facilitator.

Despite their obvious differences, Sufis and conservative Muslims lived in relative mutual tolerance through most of the religion's history. Serious trouble came in the person of a fundamentalist Muslim scholar by the name of Muhammad ibn Abd al-Wahhab in the late seventeenth/early eighteenth century. Wahhabism is at the heart of the most virulently authoritarian fundamentalist Islamic movements today. Islamic suppression of Sufism reached a contemporary historical peak during the Ayatollah Khomeini's rule over Iran after the 1978 revolution.

The conflict continues today. In a lecture on Islamic extremism before the U.S. State Department in 1999, Shaykh Muhammad Hisham Kabbani remarked that the Wahhabists are "completely against Sufism because they think that you can go directly to God without the intercession of any saint."

HIDDEN IN PLAIN VIEW

The occult (literally "hidden") character of Sufism seems to diverge from a significant secondary countercultural characteristic (as we've defined them). Sufism does not advocate the open sharing of information, per se. There is, within the Sufi belief system, a meritocratic hierarchy in which information is presumably doled out to initiates based on how prepared they are to receive it. But there is very little commentary on this in the literature. It does not seem to be an important point of emphasis. In point of fact, since the religion includes more than its share of writers and poets, Sufis probably share all their secrets to excess. The occult dimension appears mostly due to the inability of anyone outside the experience to *understand* what is being revealed. In other words, the unilluminated can't receive certain types of information not so much due to suppression as to their own incapacity.

Consider again Henry Bayman's words, quoted earlier in this chapter: "In Islamic and Sufic thought, the world of meaning completes the world of matter, precisely because it supplies the meaning that is missing from the material world." This concept of creation as God's manifest signification gives an occult spin to Sufi cosmogony. For Sufis, illumination requires not just liberation from ego, but study and effort in uncovering God's message. Mathematical, numerological, cosmological, linguistic, alchemical, and scientific investigation, both "sacred" and practical, proceed naturally from this challenge.

THE MORE THINGS CHANGE . . .

Personal evolution—the primary countercultural characteristic of constant change—plays a significant role in the Sufi order. But Sufi evolution operates in an unusual way. On the one hand, Shah distinguishes the Sufi from the anti-dynamism of conventional Buddhism or Hinduism, and states that "The sufi . . . is *going somewhere,* not being kept at . . . some sort of norm." And he enlarges this point beyond the personal to include social evolution: "Sufis believe that . . . humanity is evolving to a certain destiny. We are all taking part in that evolution. Organs come into being as the result of the need for specific organs. The human being's organism is producing new organs in response to such a need." Indeed, this and other extraordinary pre-Darwinian Sufic anticipations of evolutionary theory caused Shah to assert that "the earliest known theory of . . . evolution is of Sufi origin."

On the other hand, Shah declares, "Psychology learns as it goes along. Sufism already knows." Presumably, God knows, and humans evolve toward God. Or perhaps the truth embraces raw contradiction—the truth is enigmatic. Let's leave it at that.

SUFI AT PLAY

Given the no-nonsense character of Sufi deconditioning practices, we might conclude that this is a dry and humorless (if occasionally stoned) religious philosophy. But this is not the case. In fact, besides Rumi, the most popular public manifestation of Sufic thought is the tales of Nasruddin, humorous teaching tales based on a wandering itinerant mulla. The Nasruddin tales are similar to Zen koans and the Taoist stories of "Chuang-tzu." However, rather than playing the inscrutably wise master, Nasruddin plays the fool, mimicking rote behavior. The famous example has Nasruddin searching for his keys in one spot, despite the fact that he had dropped them elsewhere, because a light is shining in the place where he is conducting his futile search. We laugh, but we are also being subtly shown how we stay (physically, psychologically, and/or spiritually) where it is convenient and pointlessly attempt to resolve problems that can be overcome only by moving on.

Nasruddin was an exemplar of the Sufi prankster spirit. Echoing our earlier descriptions of radical Zen masters, Ernst writes that "Mulla [Nasruddin] stepped upon the fool's path to wisdom and survival. In the face of the vicissitudes of his time, he maintained a serene, ironic smile and adopted a protean approach to life. . . . He traveled about regularly. With a keen mind, a sharp wit . . . he also had the unabashed naïveté of a child."

THE SUFIC INFECTION

Sufi influence on Western culture runs deep, but is difficult to trace with any precision. Most historians see Sufism as traveling up from Arab Morocco to Spain. Annemarie Schimmel, author of *Mystical Dimensions of Islam*, says that the late-thirteenth-century Catalonian scholar Ramon Lull was the first European to show Sufi influence. A few centuries later, Schimmel writes, the chancellor of Louis IX transmitted the legend of Rabia al-Adawiyya, a woman Sufi saint from the eighth century, to Europe.

The historical diffusion of Sufism is manifold and impressive. The *Tale of the Thousand and One Nights,* the story of William Tell, and much of Cervantes' *Don Quixote* show Sufic influence. In about 1000, the Sufis produced the first encyclopedia to appear in the Western world. Had it not been for the documentation and preservation of the Kabbala that formed part of this work, the nineteenth-century democratization and renaissance of Judaism through the advent of Hasidism, to which Kabbalism is central, might never have occurred. In the next chapter, we show the influence Sufism is believed to have had on the troubadours, and therefore on Western music, poetry, and romance.

British consul, explorer, and prototypical ethnographer Sir Richard Burton noted that Sufism was "the Eastern parent of Freemasonry." In fact, a close examination of Sufism's influence reveals a multifaceted role in grand-parenting Western democratic thought. (Wilson suggests that it was technically probably a related, more radical Muslim heresy that influenced these apostate Europeans—an Ismaeli sect descended from the hashish guerrilla potentate Hassan I Sabbah, much mythologized by William S. Burroughs. The Ismaelis are close cousins of the Sufis who—from time to time—hide their even more subversive philosophy under Sufi cover.) Burton, himself a Sufi initiate, integrated the Sufic transcendence of religious and ethnic myopias into his nineteenth-century studies of indigenous cultures. This established a naturalistic—although not uncritical—counterpoint to the ethnocentric paradigms being developed by many of his contemporaries in anthropological study.

Sufism's emphasis on individual experience as a means of arriving at truth played a direct role in originating the empirical method at the basis of modern science. Friar Roger Bacon, who laid out the foundations of the scientific method in the thirteenth century, credited certain Eastern "Illuminates" in his famous Oxford lectures. These cryptic references have been claimed as allusions to a Sufi brotherhood also revered by St. Francis of Assisi—another key portal for the influx of Sufic ideas into the West. (Both Bacon and St. Francis belonged to the same order of monks—one that was clearly subject to some form of Sufi schooling for at least a few generations.)

WHAT GOES AROUND COMES AROUND

For better or worse, the U.S.-supported (one might indeed say imposed) Afghan government apparently thought a little counterculture influence would be tonic for the people in the aftermath of the ultra-puritanical Taliban regime. An article in the April 24, 2002, edition of the *Financial Times* titled "Afghans Offered Sensual Antidote to the Taliban" stated,

> Afghanistan's interim government is trying to break the moral and intellectual hold of the Taliban on Afghan society by promoting the poetry of 13th-century poet Jalal al-Din Rumi, who advocated use of narcotics and wine, sensual love and whirling as an antidote to religious intolerance. Afghanistan was long a center of Sufism.
>
> Staging a two-day conference on Rumi financed by UNESCO, the Ministry of Information would like to bring about a resurgence of Sufi heterodoxy: in short, the construction of a post-Muslim social and cultural order. Chairman Hamid Karzai opened the conference noting that Rumi's Sufism "will rehabilitate the self and [post-Taliban] society as a whole." Rumi was even renamed Jalal al-Din al-Balkhi for his origin in Balkh of Afghanistan. The conference included traditional Turkish [Mevlevi] Whirling Dervishes.
>
> As Rumi observed in one poem: "I am neither a Muslim nor a Hindu./I am not Christian, Zoroastrian, not a Jew,/I am neither East nor West/. . . I am of the divine whole.' In another poem Rumi observes: 'When we become wine in attribute,/wine will be abolished!/When we become totally hashish,/hashish will be overthrown!"

U.S. Attorney General John Ashcroft (from the George W. Bush administration) did not attend.

CHAPTER SEVEN

REMAKING LOVE

The Troubadours and the
Heretic Spirit of Provence

> For the first time people wrote about love: courtly love,
> fine love, adulterous love, love of the troubadours, and
> they went a long way into things. The troubadours for
> example were people who wrote about "tremendous,"
> "inaccessible" love and respect for the lady. For the first
> time the lady is elevated to the level of the man and this
> is the most important thing in the culture and is per-
> haps the symbolic thing about the cultural efferves-
> cence of the twelfth and thirteenth centuries.
>
> GERARD ZUCCHERO, *ROSAMUNDA*

The troubadours were poet-songwriters who crisscrossed southern France, Mediterranean Spain, and northern Italy from 1100 to 1300,
performing compositions devoted to the Feminine Spirit and its fleshly in-
carnations. Centered in the Provence region that later became part of
France, the troubadours were sponsored by lords and ladies, traveled with
them, and entertained in their courts. The word troubadour itself is rooted

in Arabic, translating roughly as "inventor of songs," and carrying conno-
tations of creativity, discovery, and originality. The historical record numbers the troubadours at about four hundred individuals who lived during
the two-century span known as the High Middle Ages.

The troubadours expressed their worship of womankind by writing
songs directed at a chosen living female—specifically, a noblewoman who
was already betrothed. The wonderment with which the troubadour regarded the woman who inspired his song is exemplified in this verse by Arnaut Daniel, considered by many to have been the movement's premier
poet, in praise of his young beloved:

> I am blind to others, and their retort
> I hear not. In her alone, I see, I move,
> Wonder. . . . And jest not. And the words dilate
> Not truth; but mouth speaks not the heart outright:
> I could not walk roads, flats, dales, hills, by chance,
> To find charm's sum within one single frame
> As God hath set in her t'assay and test it.
>
> And I have passed in many a goodly court
> To find in hers more charm than rumor thereof. . . .
> In solely hers. Measure and sense to mate,
> Youth and beauty learned in all delight,
> Gentrice did nurse her up, and so advance
> Her fair beyond all reach of evil name,
> To clear her worth, no shadow hath oppresst it.

The troubadour love of woman rose to the level of religious devotion.
As French scholar Louis Gillet puts it, "While addressing an audience of
women, [the troubadours] had invented the cult of women. . . . Woman
became a religion." Inspired by this spiritual devotion, their songs were so
fresh, so innovative, so unprecedented, that the ears of Europe were soon
seduced.

LAUGHTER AND DEVOTION

The troubadour movement's earnest devotion to all things female did not render them humorless. To the contrary, they were wags. One chronicler describes the frivolity of Guilhem IX, believed to be the first troubadour: "He took nothing seriously, he turned everything into a joke and made his listeners laugh uncontrollably."

The troubadour movement evinced a most important countercultural quality, the ability to laugh at itself. Arnaut Daniel satirized the counterculture that gave him his fame. Since the troubadour's way of life was based on devotion and service to the lady of his affections, it was customary that he always do this lady's bidding, no matter what that might entail. In one of his poems, Arnaut makes humor out of the dilemmas of this practice.

In Arnaut's tale, one Lady Edna demands that her troubadour suitor participate in a sexual act he finds distasteful—so distasteful, in fact, that he refuses her. His refusal, as a complete violation of the troubadour code of love, tosses the entire troubadour culture into heated controversy. In Arnaut's story, the troubadours divide into two camps: one defending the refusal, the other attacking it. The ensuing debate is summarized in five randy verses exploring the merit (or lack of it) associated with the sexual act in question, whose precise nature can be deduced from the puns Arnaut makes about the suitor's place of origin, "Cornil"—a near homonym of "corn-hole," a colloquial term for anal sex.

TAKING LIBERTIES

The frank eroticism and boldly adulterous sentiments of troubadour song were utterly revolutionary for their time and place. Consider, for instance, the following lines composed by Cercamon in the twelfth century, rendered as prose in the Middle English of the same period by Robert Briffault: "Send God the saviour I may hoste there as my gentle lady wones; and may she lap me in her fold, and yield the thing she hath fore gaged; apert let her forth uncoyed, eft shot the bolt, and ill betide her jealous dolt."

During roughly the same period, Guilhem IX was more direct, declaring: "I shall tell you about the cunt, what its nature is. . . . Although any other thing decreases if someone else steals from it, the cunt increases."

The complete disruption of contemporary convention and morality represented by such blatant eroticism is just one demonstration of the troubadour movement's distinctly countercultural character. The troubadours also granted themselves an unusual freedom of speech and self-expression in matters of politics, religion, and even the business of the noble courts they entertained.

The troubadours were tolerated—and often, it seems, actually encouraged in taking these liberties—by the princesses and princes who sponsored them. A new, counterculturally inclined nobility had arisen in Provence who admired the troubadours' courageous art and worldly eloquence.

The troubadours used their freedom of expression to challenge the character of mainstream culture. In his classic, lyrically written 1945 study *The Troubadours,* Robert Briffault describes their wide-ranging, quintessentially countercultural critique: "[The troubadour] hits with scourge all forms of egoism, deceit, and insincerity, whether in women, or in great lords or commoners, and his revolt imparts to this archaic poet a modern flavor." Briffault's characterization brings to mind Socratic iconoclasm, the "Howl" of the beats against the injustice and hypocrisy of their times, and the antisocial provocations of the punk movement.

Like counterculturalists of other periods, many troubadours were essentially itinerants. Troubadour performers traveled widely, welcomed and supported by cities, towns, and noble courts throughout their land by virtue of their charm and the powerful appeal of their bold new music.

And as in many countercultures, the troubadours' embrace of liberty sometimes led to what many would consider "irresponsibility" and libertine excess. The following description of Arnaut Daniel, written by one of his contemporaries in the troubadour movement, portrays a familiar kind of countercultural dissipation: "Arnaut the scholar who is ruined by dice and Backgammon, and goes about like a penitent, poor in clothes and money." The troubadour who penned these words might have been writing about beat icon Neal Cassady or uncounted other well-known countercultural figures.

COURTLY COUNTERCULTURE

The troubadours were supported by elements of the Spanish nobility that also formed alliances with heretical groups and sometimes openly scorned the Church. Additionally, highborn women had assumed powerful positions within the noble hierarchies. Feudal inheritance laws in Provence, the home of the troubadour movement—especially in Aquitaine, the part of Provence that was the movement's precise point of origin—were far more liberal to women than in other regions. In these areas, women were not merely allowed to steward property during periods when a ruling male was unavailable, they were permitted to inherit, own, and run properties themselves. Some historians have credited this happy legal deviation to a cumulative series of "mistakes" that became established as precedents over time, while others credit a general open-mindedness that took hold during that time.

With a severe loss of male lives resulting from the Crusades, the potential for women to take power under the laws of these regions reached fruition. Countercultural tendencies among the nobility were stimulated by an influx of fresh perspectives from a new breed of empowered noblewomen, who provided crucial support for the troubadours' art by vigorously cultivating its presence in their courts.

These new, very bold, and sometimes very young princesses of feminine power wrapped troubadour song around themselves like a symbolic shroud, signifying their stature and affirming their worthiness for leadership. The troubadour's elevation and veneration of woman served as a propagandistic balm that soothed and subtly indoctrinated the more conservative elements of society. Troubadour song, manner, and style charmed, distracted, and entranced—softening conservative fears of this transformation.

THE MAGIC OF PROVENCE

Provence of the High Middle Ages was the product of a dazzlingly multifaceted, culturally dynamic, and historically pivotal Islamic-Christian interface. The Moors, the branch of the Islamic "empire" that held sway over much of Spain during this epoch, were characterized by a profound appreciation and cultivation of the arts and all forms of scholarship, as well as a refined devotion to the art of living. Also, among the Moors, women were accorded an unusually high status for the time in artistic, political, and intellectual arenas.

Meanwhile, feudalism and knighthood were evolving and spreading throughout Christian Europe. With women rising to levels of economic and political power unprecedented in Christendom, the status of noblewomen in Provence and other regions soon came to mirror and even exceed the stature of their sisters among the Moors.

Foremost among Christendom's newly empowered women was Eleanor of Aquitaine, who became queen of France and later queen of England. Eleanor's courts were significant sponsors of the troubadour movement and its art.

Extraordinarily similar in temperament, Christian Europe and Moorish Islam commingled and cross-fertilized harmoniously along the borders between Provence and Moorish Spain. As Briffault puts it: "Nothing of . . . fanaticism existed in the course of the three centuries during which the two peoples, Christian and Muslim, lived side by side. The question of religion did not enter into the policy of the Spanish rulers; they made no claim to be defenders of the faith. . . . Even after the Christian kingdoms had begun to expand, the Christian kings were nowise concerned to expel the Moors from the peninsula."

Influenced by close interaction with the tolerant, artistically and spiritually refined Moorish wing of the Islamic empire, Christian Provence became a haven of heresy. Alfonso the Battler overthrew the local Catholic archbishop and severed relations between the Spanish branch of the Church and "Mother Rome." The Cathars and the Knights Templar, heretical groups whose presence spread from the Holy Land to Germany, received sanctuary and support in Provence, cultivating allies and sponsors among the same freethinking nobles who supported the irreverent, subversive troubadour movement. And the troubadours were exposed to Moorish poetic and musical influences, passing them along to Western Europe. In doing so, the troubadours opened a conduit of cultural insemination that would play several formative roles in the rapid developments taking place in European Christendom.

TRUE LOVE

At a time when pairing and marriage had long been dictated by economic and political-familial agendas, the troubadours injected—or at least reinjected—the notion of romantic love into Western culture. This kind of love had been neglected in the West since the Greco-Roman mythos—characterized by passionate, stormy romances between its goddesses and gods—was replaced by Christendom's romantically arid theology.

In fact, when the troubadours first appeared, around the opening of the twelfth century, the idea that coupling could arise from choices of the heart—as opposed to material necessity or the forces of social convention—was profoundly novel and deeply opposed to centuries of prevailing tradition.

However, as the troubadours gained popularity, they changed the culture. The concept of romantic love rose like a blazing sun over the Western world, assuming its current position as the primary driving force behind courtship and union—the underlying rhythm propelling the entire dance that blossoms as intimate partnership. Thanks to the troubadours, Western partnerships today are not arranged and imposed by societal interests, but out of love (at least ideally) between two people who *choose* each other.

Today, of course, some counterculturalists see romantic love, limited to two individuals, as bourgeois and reactionary, or at least emptied of meaning by an avalanche of banality and over-commercialization. But in the context of that time, the troubadours' reinvention, or remaking, of love for the entire Western world was, as Gillet wrote, "an immensely far-reaching revolution. Those archaic poets, whom no one now reads . . . wrote their works for a posterity of centuries and carved deep in our souls the fundamental feature of our civilization. . . . They brought about a change so unprecedented that its effects have been incalculable. It was a genuine act of moral creation, the most original in the Middle Ages, a kind of love entirely detached from all idea of generation and the reproduction of species."

SUFI ROOTS

Accurate characterization of the troubadour movement is complicated by a confusing—albeit richly ambiguous—historical record, laden with legend, hyperbole, and apocrypha. In fact, scholars documenting this group through the seven centuries since its disappearance have divided into opposing camps over fundamental issues regarding the nature of the troubadours and the agendas and influences that drove their art.

One division involves the origin of troubadour verse and song. Traditionally, historians presumed that it sprang from nowhere—the troubadours simply invented it from whole cloth. Historian Frances Gies notes that troubadour poetry has often been compared to "a flower that seems suddenly to appear without root or stalk."

This view clearly reflects a severe Western bias. One need look no further than the Moorish presence in Provence for the roots of the troubadour idiom. The troubadours used Moorish musical instruments(!), including the rebec, an ancestor of the violin.

In *The Troubadours,* Robert Briffault offers a lengthy and convincing argument for the Moorish origins of troubadour art. His detailed examination takes a particularly close look at song structure, line structure, and meter, demonstrating how the troubadours' work replicates distinctively Moorish idioms.

Sufi presence in the culture of Moorish Spain was strong, and Briffault specifically cites Sufi forms of devotional verse and song as roots of troubadour art. In *The Sufis,* Idries Shah—the twentieth century's preeminent exponent and historian of radical Sufism—focuses on linguistic and semantic correspondences between the Sufi and troubadour idioms, tracing the Provençal words, syllables, and phrases repeatedly used in troubadour songs to Arabic roots and underlying Sufic meanings. Historian Robert Graves has endorsed Shah's work in this area. The works of Briffault, Shah, and Graves have shown—almost indisputably—that troubadour art was seeded by mystic Sufism's devotional expressions.

While troubadour and Sufi songs were closely connected in form, they differed in content. Still, both idioms were devotional in nature: while the Sufis sang praise to the Divine Being of esoteric Islam, the troubadours sang praise to their living female muses.

Street musicians provide the final link in the chain between the Sufi counterculture of Islam and the troubadour counterculture of Christendom. The first generation of troubadours picked up their idiom from the streets of Provence. Here, wandering lower-class musicians—today they might be called "buskers"—had begun singing their own versions of Moorish and Sufi songs in their native Provençal tongue.

Christendom's scholarly elite sneered at this street idiom, finding it base, vulgar, and unworthy of notice. But the young nobles of Provence found it entrancing. They dismissed the opinions of the scholarly elite, shedding their noble pretensions to learn the new art from the itinerant songsters of the street. These young nobles refined and promoted the form until, within a few generations, it became the favored court musical entertainment for a broad segment of regional noble Christendom.

Sex, God, or Both?

The women toward whom the troubadours directed their love poems were invariably married—usually to a powerful noble lord. Some troubadours even wrote rather explicit accounts of their affairs with these women.

The adulterous sentiments professed in troubadour verse—along with the frank eroticism of the movement's poetry in general—are at the center of another major scholarly division. There are two completely opposite views regarding how literally we are to understand troubadour erotic imagery.

Some scholars, with attitudes ranging from moral condemnation to active adulation, take quite literally the troubadours' expressed desire for—and occasional accounts of their sexual liaisons with—the wedded highborn women of their time. The troubadours have thus been called a "cult of adultery."

Traditionally, however, most scholars have insisted on a strictly metaphoric interpretation of the erotic content of troubadour verse, promoting a perspective reminiscent of many Judeo-Christian interpretations of the vividly sexual imagery contained in the biblical Song of Solomon. These scholars hold that the troubadours were mystic celibates whose erotic images were metaphors for the purely spiritual intercourse that can occur between a deeply religious man's soul and the deity he surrenders it to.

This chaste spiritual approach to the troubadours' sexual poetry is consistent with the influence of devotional Sufi songs on the movement's work and with the overlap between the troubadours and the Cathar heretics of the same period. The Cathars embraced a form of Gnosticism that held a deeply dualistic conception of the relationship between spirit and matter. They shunned the flesh and its desires as part of the material realm, which they viewed as a corrupt, degraded, and distorted reflection of the pure and perfect realm of spirit.

Nevertheless, this view of the troubadours as chaste practitioners of a purely metaphoric erotic poetry is difficult to support. Troubadour poetry demonstrates detailed knowledge of both the bodily mechanics and psychological dynamics of human sexual relations. And while the troubadour's desire for his lady was often voiced in transcendently spiritual tones, it was also sometimes expressed in coarse and vulgar terms that hardly suggest a purely chaste erotic mysticism.

Lastly, we have the (hopefully apocryphal) tale of the demise, at the close of the twelfth century, of a troubadour named Guilhem de Cabestanh. Guilhem, we are told, met his end when the jealous husband of the object of his love songs killed him—and gave Guilhem's heart to his wife, intending that she make a meal of the departed troubadour's vital organ. True or not, this tale of adulterousness avenged is not the sort that we would expect to find surrounding the life (or death) of a chaste and pure composer of devotional mystic poetry.

In fact, historical documentation clearly suggests that the exclusively metaphoric interpretation of troubadour eroticism first appeared *after* the troubadour movement itself had dissipated. As Briffault states, prior to "the annihilation . . . of the society which brought about the development of [troubadour] literature . . . there is nothing to be found in the poetry of the troubadours that suggests a platonic idealization of passion."

The influence of the Catholic Church in this ex post facto sanitization of the troubadour legacy can't be underestimated. After the troubadour movement per se had come to a close, the Church was still faced with a tremendous challenge: the troubadours' artistic legacy—completely at odds with the sexual mores that the Church was trying to enforce—remained enormously popular.

The interests of the Church were well served by a school of Italian scribes who took on the troubadour compositional tradition after the movement itself had died away. They were orthodox Catholics—in Briffault's words, "conforming exponents of ecclesiastical taste." This group promoted the chaste, Catholicized interpretation of troubadour erotic imagery.

This distortion of the troubadour heritage typifies the way the cultural mainstream copes with a countercultural eruption so powerful that its impact can't simply be erased—and therefore has to be integrated in a fashion that still protects the establishment's interests. The establishment propagates a dishonest, conservative interpretation of a countercultural legacy and, through its dominance, turns it into the reigning "truth."

Our arguments against a strictly metaphoric approach to troubadour erotica are not intended to advocate a purely literal interpretation. A spiritual dimension clearly suffuses much of the troubadours' sexual imagery. As K. H. Maahs describes the devotion of one German *minnesinger* to his lady: "His love is shot through with strands of visionary experience and almost religious fervor."

Rather than interpreting the troubadours' erotic poetry as exclusively literal or exclusively metaphoric, we propose a synthesis. Perhaps many— or even most—troubadours were *both* Cathar or Sufi-influenced mystics *and* daring sexual adventurers. Maybe the troubadours were a mystic-carnal hybrid species, intrepid explorers of the heights and depths of human sexual experience who—like the Tantrists of India or those initiated by the "sacred prostitutes" of the ancient Mystery Cults—found a gateway to spiritual ecstasy in sexual union with a woman whom they approached as an incarnation of the Divine Feminine.

Any erotic verse to flow from the pens of such mystic sexualists would—like most worthwhile poetry—enfold multiple levels of meaning, opening itself to simultaneously literal and metaphoric readings. It therefore seems likely that *both* raw carnal lust *and* transcendent Cathar-Gnostic communion with God suffuse the body of troubadour erotica, to differing degrees depending on the work at hand.

TROUBATRIXES

The troubadours are generally documented as if their movement was composed entirely of men. But there were significant female contributors to the troubadour idiom. They were known as troubatrixes. In fact, prior to their work, women poets were unheard of. Not surprisingly, all but one of the nine known troubatrixes lived in Aquitaine—the region where the blossoming of High Middle Ages feminine power reached its pinnacle.

The work of the troubatrixes is just as bold, frank, and adulterous as their male counterparts'. For example, have a look at the following lines composed by the Countess of Dia in the twelfth century, containing what historian Gilda Lerner calls "unusually frank expressions of the sexual power game": "Handsome friend, charming and kind,/when shall I have you in my power?/ If only I could lie beside you for an hour/and embrace you lovingly/know this, that I'd give almost anything/to have you in my husband's place,/but only under the condition/that you swear to do my bidding."

It's unfortunate, though predictable, that male transcribers of the troubatrixes' work frequently claimed credit for it themselves. Thus, the verses of the troubatrixes have often been credited to male troubadours presumed to be writing in a female voice.

To Sir with Love: Troubadours and Knights

The troubadour movement's close relationship with the contemporaneously evolving knightly class has tremendous historical significance. Many troubadours were knights, and many knights were troubadours. In addition to the more popular love ballads, the troubadours wrote and sang accounts of battle and war that celebrated knighthood and soldierly courage.

As Frances Gies tells us, "The most important influence of the twelfth century on the knightly class lay in . . . the outpouring of chivalric literature, above all that of troubadour poetry." Under troubadour influence, the knightly class developed their influential ethic of "chivalry" toward women, also known as the etiquette of knightly or "courtly" love. This highly structured set of behaviors—whose present-day remnants include the custom of men opening doors for women—cast the knight into the role of servant, protector, and (if need be) rescuer of the female.

The chivalric ethic adopted by the knights represented a formalization and codification of the more individualized, more fluid, and spontaneously organic style of romance practiced by the troubadours. In other words, the ethic of courtly love was a co-option or "mainstreaming" of the troubadours' countercultural romantic and sexual ways.

As opposed to the uncontrolled, unpredictable, and often adulterous erotic escapades of troubadour counterculture, the chivalric code was acceptable to mainstream Christendom. Indeed, the reformulation of troubadour romantic style into the institution of chivalry was created, and imposed on the rising knightly class, by the Catholic Church.

This maneuver allowed the Catholic establishment to at least partially defuse the threat presented by the increasingly popular troubadour erotic ethic. By perpetrating a sleight-of-hand through which the troubadour "cult of adultery" reappeared as the knightly "cult of the dame," the Church provided a relatively tame, acceptable substitute focus.

The second reason that the Church created knightly chivalry from the raw materials of the troubadour counterculture had to do with the nature of early knighthood itself. Like the troubadour approach to romance and sexuality, knighthood somehow had to be tamed to suit the aims of the Church.

The practice of knighthood had emerged during the ninth and tenth centuries as a form of mercenary employment pursued by materially ambitious members of the peasant underclass. Only later did knights rise into their long-term position as the lowest—although highly honored—rung of feudal nobility. The first knights were generally willful, independent, uncontrollable, armed (and often violent) ruffians. Volatile in disposition, they were certainly not "chivalrous" in the least. Their antics, adventures, and internecine disputes frequently disrupted the civic peace of their communities. As far as the Church was concerned, the early knights represented a threat to Catholic codes of behavior as well as to Church property in the towns where knights dwelled or came to fight.

Frances Gies vividly summarizes the crisis that arose: "the real-life knight of tenth century . . . [was] ignorant and unlettered, rough in speech and manners; he earned his living largely by violence, uncontrolled by a public justice that had virtually disappeared. Civil disputes and criminal cases alike had ceased to be adjudicated by the enfeebled royal power and instead were settled by the sword. The unarmed segment of the population, the Church and the peasants, were victims or bystanders. . . . The prevailing anarchy stimulated remedial action. This came from the Church."

In a masterly ploy designed to tame the threat represented by the rising class of professional knights—and to harness its coarse but considerable energies in service of the Catholic-controlled feudal establishment—the Church moved to embrace (and thereby civilize and control) the knightly class. The Church converted the image of knighthood from that of peasant mercenary to courageous and courtly servant of nobility by sponsoring those who wanted to be knights, putting them through Church-designed training, and instituting the initiation ritual wherein aspirants were "dubbed" into knighthood and assigned the title "Sir."

The Church trained knights in a code of chivalry they created by transmogrifying the troubadour ethic of romance for its own purposes. Knights who might otherwise have been inspired by the troubadour model to undertake adulterous romantic adventures—executed with the brute force of the armed peasant as opposed to the refined lyric prowess of the troubadour—were indoctrinated by the Church into believing that they had been trained as exemplars of the best the troubadour had to offer.

Knighthood became genuinely refined through churchly influence and further elevated by absorption into the echelons of nobility. As this process took place, the troubadour movement and the knightly class came to intermingle and overlap.

Today—as reflected in movies, novels, and other media—we remember and celebrate the conservative ethic of chivalry much more frequently than we recall chivalry's origin in the bold but exquisite eroticism of the troubadours. In this sense, the troubadour counterculture achieves its most visible historical impact through mainstream revisions of its legacy—instead of through the continued cultivation of that counterculture's original essence by subsequent generations.

A Chain of Heresies

No counterculturally oriented look at the High Middle Ages would be complete without some acknowledgment of the important precedents for Freemasonry that were set during this period. Although the first Masonic lodges were not officially established until 1717, Freemasonry was modeled to a significant degree after the Cathar and especially the Knights Templar groups. In fact, the eradication of the Templars by the Catholic Church probably played an important role in the decision by the founders of Freemasonry to protect their organization by operating as a "secret society."

Like the troubadours, the Cathar and Knights Templar movements were heavily inflected by the esoteric Sufism they were exposed to through their contact with Islamic culture. These groups provided stepping-stones for the distinct Sufic imprint on Freemasonry. The connection between Sufism and Freemasonry is visible to anyone familiar with the basic tenets of both movements, and has been pointed out by historian Robert Graves, Sufi exponent Idries Shah, and ethnographer Sir Richard Burton—who was both a Freemason and Sufi initiate.

While certainly heretical, the Knights Templar, the Cathars, and the later Freemasons were too formal in structure to qualify as true counter-cultures. But eighteenth-century Freemasonry played an important role in the countercultural democratic uprisings covered in the next chapter of this book, "Cultural and Political Revolution." Due to the chain of connection running from Sufism through the Cathars and Templars to Freemasonry and democratic idealism, today's concept of democracy still echoes with the egalitarian embrace of humanity that was expounded and practiced by the Sufis.

NOBODY EXPECTS THE SPANISH INQUISITION

By the end of the twelfth century, the specter of persecution by the Catholic establishment loomed large for the troubadour movement. The Church, in fact, had launched an organized campaign against all manner of heresy. This Spanish Inquisition was largely a punitive response to the cauldron of heresy that Provence had become.

The Catholic Church declared open war on the Knights Templar in response to the threat presented by the formidable combination of wealth, independence from external authority, and military prowess that the Templars had achieved. The Church was also incensed by the alliances and holdings that the Templars had acquired in the Islamic east, where the group had been charged by the Catholic establishment with maintaining safety for Christian pilgrims along the routes opened up by the First Crusade.

At the same time, the Church went after the Cathars for their dangerously attractive heretic rekindling of Gnostic Christianity. Troubadour songs had become a part of Cathar worship. The visibility of the connection between the Cathars and the troubadours certainly did not bode well for the troubadours.

Religious authorities began declaring that poetry itself was a sin. The Church forced knights to take an oath that they would never compose verses again. The threat that the new Catholic militarism represented to the troubadours is reflected in the actions of Guilhem de Montanhagol, who might be described as the Benedict Arnold of the troubadour movement. A leading troubadour himself, Montanhagol, who had composed a tirade against Catholic monks, fled Provence and took refuge in Moorish Spain when the Inquisition began.

But after a time he returned to Provence and attempted to mollify the Catholic authorities by claiming that the troubadour movement had originated in a chaste and pure vision of love. While the movement may have become corrupted, Montanhagol insisted it could be reformed—with his help—and realigned with its original values. In the verse composed by Montanhagol during this period we find the first use of the word chastity in troubadour poetry.

Sordello and others who initiated the Italian school that promoted the puritanical interpretation of troubadour poetry were, in fact, disciples and friends of Montanhagol. Briffault refers to the sanitized version of the troubadours' concept of love as "Montanhagol's pious fraud." Thus the Catholicized distortion of the troubadour legacy began.

It seems clear that the troubadours were a major underlying target of the Catholic campaigns against the Cathars and the Templars. But as a loose-knit, unorganized, and nonhierarchical group, the troubadours didn't provide a focus for direct attack.

However, to dismantle the Templars and Cathars, the Church took aim at their established sponsors and allies among the nobility—frequently the same royals who provided the cultural venue for the troubadour movement. The Church charged large numbers of nobles with various crimes and heresies, seized their properties, and imprisoned and sometimes executed them. This strategy succeeded in eradicating the troubadour threat as well. The utter collapse of its well-heeled sponsoring subculture precipitated the troubadour movement's rapid disappearance.

"In France," Briffault laments, "troubadour poetry was not merely allowed to fall into oblivion; it was willfully put aside and buried in complete neglect." But, as he affirms, "Before sinking into the abyss of oblivion, the art of the troubadours had laid its imprint on all lyrical literatures of Europe."

THE TROUBADOUR REVIVAL

> [Troubadour] poetry's historical importance . . . is perhaps greater than that of any other single agency that has been influential upon the course of development of our literatures.
>
> ROBERT BRIFFAULT, *THE TROUBADOURS*

Aside from all other aspects of their movement's influence, the troubadours' compositional legacy alone forever changed the face of poetry and song in the Western world. Over two centuries, they practiced, advanced, and refined a style of verse and song that became foundational to many subsequent developments in Western literature and folk and popular music. The troubadour idiom is, for instance, the origin of the love ballad in all its myriad forms.

By the time the troubadours themselves passed, their idiom had already been picked up and was being developed by the *minnesingers* of Germany and the *trouveres* of northern France. The folk music of the British Isles was revolutionized by troubadour forms and sensibilities, which had been transported from Provence by Eleanor of Aquitaine—the great royal champion of troubadour culture—when she arrived in England to serve as its queen. Through these and other pathways, the troubadour influence spread, working its way into the underlying matrix of Western music and poetry.

After the original troubadours disappeared, Italy became a crucial nexus for the preservation and extension of their art form. As Briffault explains, "Italy was the heir of the troubadour heritage, and became, as it were, the executrix of that legacy." For example, the indebtedness of Dante's work to troubadour poetry is immense. Of Arnaut Daniel, Dante said, "In the poetry of love . . . [he] surpasses them all." Generations of poets and writers were, in turn, influenced by Dante's corpus.

The troubadour movement has provided a key archetype for a broad range of twentieth-century countercultures and counterculturalists. Vachel Lindsay, the influential American visionary poet-artist who wandered the country "penniless and afoot" to spread his prophecy of an imminent countercultural revolution, called himself a "troubadour" and used the troubadour as the central image in describing his mission. And Ezra Pound—often enshrined as the greatest English-language poet of the twentieth century—wrote volumes analyzing and paying tribute to the troubadour poetic legacy.

As provocative road-bound songsters, the troubadours provided a model for the countercultural folk uprising of the American 1960s. Traveling sixties folksingers frequently invoked the troubadour identity, and the journalists who documented the movement echoed their claim. Bob Dylan and Donovan, among others, were labeled troubadours. A popular folk club in Los Angeles was named the Troubadour, and a briefly successful American band of the period actually called itself the Troubadours.

As the 1960s progressed, Dylan, Donovan, the Byrds, Jefferson Airplane, and many troubadour-styled folk musicians created a bolder, harder-edged musical backdrop to propel their increasingly complex poetic assaults on rigidity and convention. Electrified and psychedelicized, these folk-to-rock innovators combined with British pop stars and blues-influenced musicians to create the technologically driven soundtrack for a broad, nearly global countercultural explosion. This revolution in sound may be as historically important as the original troubadour movement, since it birthed a rock idiom now heard every day all over the world.

And in many rock compositions, the discerning ear can still detect echoes of the troubadour songs of medieval Provence. Among the virtually endless examples that could be cited is the mid-sixties Rolling Stones hit "Lady Jane": "Your servant am I and will humbly remain. . . . / I pledge myself to Lady Jane."

These lyrics exemplify the troubadour's complete surrender to the woman of his heart's desire. Sentiments of this kind were absent from Western poetry and song prior to the troubadour era.

What is perhaps most remarkable about the depth and breadth of the original troubadours' impact on history is the size of the movement itself. It consisted of only about four hundred individuals distributed across two centuries in a relatively small geographic area. Like the few score original

Socratics, the slightly more than a dozen initiators of Christianity, the perhaps one hundred participants in the Lost Generation, and other countercultures covered in this book, the troubadours were actually a very small group. Here is proof that a handful of individuals can in fact change the course of history—especially if they are energized by the bold self-expression, willingness to innovate, and the freedom from social convention that characterize counterculture.

CHAPTER EIGHT

⊦ CULTURAL AND POLITICAL REVOLUTION

The Enlightenment of the Seventeenth and Eighteenth Centuries

[Leibniz] wrote that original sin necessarily was a part of the best of worlds . . . What!? To be chased out of a place of delights, where we would have lived forever if we hadn't eaten an apple! What!? To produce in misery miserable children, who will suffer everything, who will make others suffer everything! What!? To undergo all illnesses, feel all sorrows, die in pain, and for refreshment to be burned in the eternity for centuries! Is this really the best of available lots?

VOLTAIRE, *THE PHILOSOPHICAL DICTIONARY*, 1765

We have it in our power to begin the world over again.

THOMAS PAINE, *COMMON SENSE*, 1776

The European Enlightenment/Age of Reason of the seventeenth and eighteenth centuries is perhaps the most important and influential counterculture presented in this book, and the one whose status as a counterculture will be most contested. It institutionalized many of the values we have already discussed, but did so unevenly, indeed exclusively for white males (and often only for certain *privileged* white males), an opportunistic blindness that still repercusses today. It also institutionalized rationalism, attempting—despite all the natural resistances of cussed, uncooperative human beings—to place deductive logic in the ultimate seat of *authority.* And perhaps most importantly, its very formalization of the linguistic and legalistic construct "liberty" was formulated as a social contract that—in concert with the technological developments of its time—slowly but surely roped everybody into society, from which there was increasingly no escape. The unknown, hidden spaces outside of history and Western civilization were slowly incorporated into this dubious and very poorly realized "contract"-based system that—while declaring and indeed sometimes diligently attempting to established a "consent of the governed"— coerced people from birth to participate by their very presence within its territory. The French philosopher Michel Foucault showed how, within this social contract, "an implicit system of obligation was established: he [those outside the elite; the indigent poor] had the right to be fed, but he must accept the physical and moral constraint of confinement." Liberty and justice *for all* sometimes required mass incarceration, as we witness today in the United States.

Still, as deep as this objection (which is in some ways a nutshell description of the contemporary academic left's view) may run, it presumes the wide existence of something better, more autarkic or more intrinsically cooperative, before, or outside of, the Age of Reason's grasp. While it is virtually impossible for us to measure the qualities of life and freedom experienced by those utterly outside the territories (Europe and America) where the Age of Enlightenment took place, we do know about the world in which it took place. And it is in contrast with—and in the context of that world—*our* historical world that this counterculture represents an explosion of novelty, individual autonomy, and anti-authoritarian revolution that has not yet been *successfully* surpassed.

THE SOCIAL CONTRACT

Imagine living in a place where daily life and its institutions are organized around the idea that there is one true faith that provides all the answers;

that all authority and tradition are a direct result of God's plan; that prayer and ringing church bells are the only way to ward off plague and famine. Imagine a world where almost all intellectual discussion and publication concerns matters of religious doctrine; where hierarchy, inequality, suffering, and everyone's place is preordained by God and cannot be questioned or changed. Imagine living in a world where almost all political power is concentrated in a very small number of hereditary aristocrats who have been chosen by God to wield power as they see fit in this world. This power is especially to be used to enforce religious conformity even to the point of coordinated massacres of other religious sects. Imagine living in a world where, in some regions, religious warfare kills off nearly 50 percent of the population, and expressing an opinion on the nature of the Trinity might get you burned at the stake.

Welcome to continental Europe on the eve of the Enlightenment.

Now imagine that, in the course of about one hundred years, things changed. Now there was an increasingly popular acceptance of the idea that the universe runs according to readily understood laws that do not require the intervention of God; that the application of reason through science could improve the life of every individual in this world; and that every man should have identical legal and political rights. And perhaps the most shocking change of all, the ruling authorities allowed thinkers a great deal of freedom to discuss and spread these subversive notions.

NEW PHILOSOPHY OF THE LATE SEVENTEENTH CENTURY

The Age of Reason really began in earnest during the second half of the seventeenth century. From about 1650, various proponents of a new philosophy espoused a worldview that supplanted the absolute hegemony of religious faith and the Bible with reason, skeptical inquiry, and scientific method. Among these, Descartes was the first to systematically propose that reason could understand the physical world, including humans, and explicitly theorized a mathematical physics as a way of understanding nature. John Locke regularized the idea of civil government based on the consent and contract of the governed instead of hereditary divine right. The direct descendants are of his thinking are the Declaration of Independence and all civil constitutions based on individual sovereignty. And Benedict Spinoza proposed a basis for ethics and morality that had no use or place for God. John Amos Comenius advocated liberal educational ideas like abandoning rote discipline and instead playfully engaging students' interests and imaginations. Isaac Newton showed that the motion of all material objects, from water waves, to apples, to the moon and planets, always obeyed a few very simple rules. After that, the universe did not need angels to keep it going, it needed only Newton's law (as Alexander Pope, the English poet, put Newton's contribution to banishing superstition from the worldview: "God said, Let Newton be! and all was light").

Finally, there was no more important figure in this seventeenth-century emergence than Francis Bacon. While Bacon made no scientific discoveries or technical advancements, he invented the philosophy of modern science and technology that completely reversed the medieval beliefs that God, angels, and Satan continually intervene in the world. According to the medievalist conception, there was no point in studying the world for patterns, since all causality comes from these supernatural beings. There is therefore *no* way to manipulate this world to decrease human suffering or increase happiness. Happiness was available only by getting in accordance with God's plan: suffering, dying, and going to heaven. God's plan is revealed only through ecclesiastical authority.

Bacon argued that nature, though complex, was consistent, therefore studying nature through the technique of experimental method was the only path to true knowledge. He believed that through a coordinated and free exchange of the results of these scientific studies, communities of scientists—using inductive logic—would make steady and true progress toward increasingly accurate knowledge. Finally and most importantly, he believed that this knowledge could be used for the practical benefit of humanity, ameliorating suffering and increasing well-being. This assertion is the core of the Enlightenment heresy: that the here-and-now can be improved—we need not wait for heaven.

Commenting on what Bacon had to say to his time, historian Jacques Barzun reveals essential countercultural qualities: "Authority is worthless. The notion that something is true because a wise man said it is a bad principle." And, "The free exchange of ideas and results corrects errors and speeds up discovery."

CULTURAL AND POLITICAL REVOLUTION {141}

This incipient age of freethinking individualism had been gathering steam for centuries. As early as the fourteenth century, Francesco Petrarch had declared, "Everyone should write in his own style." Early in the sixteenth century, Martin Luther chipped away at absolute, centralized religious authority by declaring that every Christian has equal access to God. Also in the sixteenth century, the Spaniard Juan Luis Vives anticipated Baconian science by encouraging his contemporaries to be more aggressive and confident in presenting observations regarding the laws of nature, liberating them from the worship of antiquity. In the words of Barzun, "He disputed the philosopher's cliché of the time that said present generations were 'dwarfs standing on the shoulders of giants.' "

In the second half of the seventeenth century, freethinking began to spread beyond the few remembered by history. Many now-forgotten radical intellectuals began the attack on revealed religion; denying miracles, the Devil, and the need for God's continuing intervention in the world. For most, this was not necessarily an atheistic philosophic divergence. Newton, for instance, believed that the planets were hurled from the hand of God at creation, but that God did not need to intervene any further in his celestial "clockwork."

This vision, called deism, became the favored religious bias of the Enlightenment era. It was, on the whole, a rather vague cosmogony (think today of the Unitarians). It seems that deism was a hedge against saying what they were not quite ready to say.

No . . . *not* that God is dead or nonexistent, but that knowing the nature of all things; the meaning of life; what God is—is a *science project*. On its face, this can sound terribly cold and banal. But in fact, this exercising of the experimental human mind has given birth to elegant, beatific mathematics and physics that sometimes even claim to prove the immanence of a divinely guided symmetry or even divine chaos at work in our universe.

From the attack on religion and church authority, targets expanded to include politics. Philosophers started questioning traditional hierarchy and advocating that the interests of the individual should be primary. Some radical Spinozaists went so far as to question the whole structure of traditional and divinely supported morality and behavior. To the horror of the elites, by 1700 the most radical philosophers seemed to be pushing for a world where the pursuit of individual happiness in this life was displacing the command to please God.

In many ways, it was the Englishman John Locke who initiated the political change. In *Two Treatises of Civil Government* and other tracts, he described man as having the right to believe, say, and do what he pleases within certain reasonable limits of civil society. Locke was not an advocate of democracy or a civil libertarian per se; his liberties and democratic powers were still to be confined to an elite of "notables." But his ideas were a giant step along the path.

Perhaps more importantly, in his *Essay Concerning Human Understanding*, Locke presented arguments that would liberate humanity from the tyranny of its belief in such absolute inborn limitations as original sin. In *The Culture of Power and the Power of Culture*, T. C. W. Blanning wrote that Locke presented us with the idea that "Children currently picked up their habits and prejudices from their elders, so the human race was caught in a vicious circle of brutality, ignorance, superstition, vice, and misery. It could be broken . . . if an educator intervened to open a window to alternative experience."

This fertile late-seventeenth-century discourse was still limited to the intellectual elite. Discussions were conducted primarily in dense philosophical Latin texts, privately circulated manuscripts, and debates at the various learned academies. But while the number of participants was few, the impact on the highly centralized intelligentsia was overwhelming. By the end of the seventeenth century, the spread of the freethinking Enlightenment to broader segments of society was probably inevitable.

The Church hierarchy attempted to eradicate the heresy, but the proponents of the new philosophy and science outmaneuvered them. For one thing, thinkers like Locke and Newton explicitly stressed that their views, no matter how radical they seemed to conservative churchmen, were compatible with a Christianity freed from superstition. In general, the profusion of original thinking must have had a corrosive effect on the unity of those opposed to the new philosophers, since Christian sects fought and argued over which parts of the new philosophy were, in fact, compatible with their beliefs.

Many, perhaps most, of the late-seventeenth-century freethinkers (and indeed those of the eighteenth-century Enlightenment) emphasized their oppositional position toward the totalizing religious philosophies of the past even over the production of novel ideas. Locke wrote that it was "ambition enough to be employed as an underlaborer in clearing the ground a little, and removing some of the rubbish that lies in the way of knowledge." But as Enlightenment historian Peter Gay, in his introduction to his biography of Voltaire, commented, "The philosophes have often been accused of being 'merely negative' . . . but in fact the energy that animated them was a drive for knowledge and control, a restless Faustian dissatisfaction with appearance. Their favorite instrument was analysis, their essential atmosphere, freedom; their goal, reality. The most popular metaphors were not merely metaphors of battle but metaphors of penetration: they spoke of the light that pierces the corner of darkness, the blows that level barriers of censorship, the fresh wind that lifts the veil of religious authority, the surgical knife that cuts away the accumulation of tradition . . . the eye that sees through the mask of political mystery-mongers."

The Festive Court of King Louis XIV

> While the poor people sleepin' all the stars come out at
> night.
>
> DONALD FAGEN AND WALTER BECKER, STEELY DAN

The cultural revolution that blossomed in the eighteenth century was also ironically fostered by the interests and cultural perversity of an absolutist monarch from the seventeenth. France's King Louis XIV, possessed of a massive and energetic egoism, birthed a lively court scene, complete with tightly constructed and highly ritualized nightly ceremonial feasts and celebrations that gave many artists a forum for presentation and provided them with a generous livelihood. Frederick the Great, an eighteenth-century Prussian "enlightened despot" who was himself a culture vulture of the highest order, would speak fondly of King Louis' court, saying, "Greedy for every kind of glory, he wanted to make his nation as supreme in matters of taste and literature as it was already in power, conquest, politics and commerce." (Among the artists sponsored by Louis XIV was the playwright Molière, whose work survives and still interests us today.)

Louis' court scene was an antecedent for the bohemian nightlife trope and seems like something Elton John might have dreamed up during the 1970s. Blanning writes:

> The first great set-piece [at Versailles was] evocatively named 'Pleasures of the Enchanted Isle.' . . . At the all night celebrations held in 1668 . . . all the senses of the 600 guests were titillated—by a banquet, a ball, a comedy (Molière's *George Dandin*) and a fireworks display. . . . Music was omnipresent . . . all taking place in a park transformed into fairyland by illuminated transparencies. . . . This move to nocturnal festivities also served to distance the leisured world of the court from the round of mundane toil. . . . The courtiers were going home to sleep as lesser mortals were leaving home to work. For the ordinary royal subject, there was a strict division between festive days and working days, between festive spaces and working spaces, but in the world of the court, every space is a festive space and every time is a festive time. Court life was totally festive.

Amidst the debauchery, something substantial was happening. Creative artists were becoming an important element in the pride of kingdom. Louis' influence in this regard would infect the kingdoms of Prussia and Russia in the next century, and by that time, the artists would explicitly have become vectors of the Enlightenment contagion.

Early whisperings of the political revolutions against religious absolutism and monarchy that would prevail toward the end of the eighteenth century had preceded Louis XIV's reign. In 1598 in France, King Henry issued the Edict of Nantes, declaring that the government should not prescribe religious belief and conduct. The edict was not completely followed. (In 1685 the edict was revoked, and resulting persecutions caused the mass emigration of Huguenots, so that entire cities and regions were ruined and depopulated.) Nevertheless, it shows that notions related to the separation of church and state were already gaining currency. In England in 1688, a rebellion led by the landed gentry and supported by the (at that time small in numbers) middle class placed constitutionally significant legal and practical limitations on the monarchy of William of Orange. Called the Glorious Revolution, the uprising took primary governmental authority away from the monarchy and put it into the hands of the propertied and commercial classes. At least as historically significant, the Glorious Revolution showed that monarchy, generally believed ordained by God, was actually vulnerable to insurrection.

Revolting Writers

More extreme countercultural currents could also be found during the seventeenth century. A circle of French poets who came to be known as the libertines anticipated certain nihilistic currents in contemporary culture. As Louis Gottschalk wrote in *The Foundations of the Modern World, 1300–1775,* "They were free-thinking, unconventional, even atheistic writers, of whom one of the most prominent was Theophile de Viau. They rejected, along with traditional religion, much of the faith in man, his morality, and secular authority, thus appearing to the devout in . . . France . . . to be a conspiracy against God, man, and government. . . . [Later] new writers came to be charged with it [being libertines], Cyrano de Bergerac among them—composers of light verse, risqué or even obscene poems, irreligious burlesques, and broad satires."

Cultural Revolution in the Eighteenth Century

By the turn of the eighteenth century, the hundred years of intermittent religious warfare, the scientific revolution, and the intellectual ferment of the accompanying new philosophy had caused a crisis of belief among the elites. The courtiers, officials, scholars, clergy, and other privileged types could no longer believe unconditionally in the traditional worldview. There was no consensus on how to come to terms with the new philosophy. The Western worldview had been shattered and the elites were unsure what would take its place.

Into this epistemological chaos stepped hundreds of rebellious thinkers, artists, and ultimately political activists ready to consolidate, popularize, and expand on the work that had begun with the likes of Locke, Descartes, Spinoza, and others.

One great act of consolidation and popularization was the 1751 publication of Denis Diderot's *Encyclopédie*. Diderot was a notorious critic of conventional morality and religion who was briefly imprisoned for his outrages (freedom of speech was an ambiguous terrain in France throughout the century). Besides offering a fair measure of post-Lockean antiauthoritarian polemic, the *Encyclopédie* attempted to organize all knowledge and make it accessible to common readers. In the process, Diderot revealed an abundance of information that had been the exclusive province of various specialists and guilds. Diderot's *Encyclopédie* was the signature opening act in the long process of democratizing information that has continued to be a major theme, and source of conflict, right into this so-called communications era. For his efforts, he was hounded by French censors.

In the 1720s, Jonathan Swift raised the stakes in the philosophic conflict between old power and new philosophy when he wrote "A Modest Proposal," a vicious satire of the cruelty and pomposity of the privileged that suggested quite pragmatically that the many starving children of Ireland could make themselves useful as food. The bitterness and utter irreverence expressed by Swift's writing, and soon thereafter by Voltaire, marked an important escalation in the rebellion against authoritarian elites. Unlike the seventeenth-century freethinkers, many of the new century's radicals didn't just question authority. They were inclined to give it the finger.

Another major figure of the Enlightenment, Jean-Jacques Rousseau, was a contemporary and sometimes friend of other Enlightenment figures. But Rousseau forged his own path, and in the process created a distinct philosophic line of thought that has generated its own legacy, one associated largely with what we now call the political left. In common with other Enlightenment figures, Rousseau threw brickbats against religious dogma and advocated free speech and discourse. But Rousseau focused his passions on economic inequities and the plight of the poor. And while the idea that science could light the darkness of the human condition was central to most Enlightenment opinion, Rousseau, in his 1750 essay, "Discourse on the Arts and Sciences," questioned the new tenets. In fact, Rousseau was in some ways the father of a very contemporary critique that views science and technology as invasive tools that replace the old tyranny with a new and more insidious one. He believed that science and pure reason had the effect of alienating people from themselves and each other and concerned himself with finding the "natural" way to live. Rousseau also diverged from the central Enlightenment tenet that enlightened self-interest and private property helped to guarantee liberty and advance the public good. In his essay *The Social Contract*, Rousseau advocated less freedom to pursue self-interest and greater collective responsibility.

Some other important eighteenth-century figures included Paul Holbach, a German by descent but a French citizen, who shocked European society with his widely distributed advocacy of atheism; the Prussian/German Johann Wolfgang von Goethe, who romanticized Prometheus' revolt against a despotic God and created the daemonic fictional seeker of immortality called Faust; and philosopher Immanuel Kant, who summed up the zeitgeist in the first paragraph of his essay "What Is Enlightenment?": "Enlightenment is mankind's exit from its self-incurred immaturity. Think Courageously! Have the courage to use your own understanding! Is the motto of enlightenment." But no figure is more representative of the eighteenth-century zeitgeist than the "Apostle of Doubt," Voltaire.

THE BRAZENLY DISDAINFUL BUT WELL-DRESSED M. VOLTAIRE

> The marvelous part of this infernal enterprise is that every murderer's chief has his flags blessed, and solemnly invokes the Lord before he goes out to exterminate his neighbors. . . . Moral philosophers, burn all your books. As long as thousands of our brothers are honestly butchered at the caprice of some men, the part of mankind consecrated to heroism will be the most horrible thing in all nature.
>
> VOLTAIRE, *PHILOSOPHICAL DICTIONARY*, "WAR"

Voltaire, born François-Marie Arouet, was not a particularly original philosopher. But he gathered together the rebellious thoughts and attitudes of his times and expressed them through his writing with such a pungent wit that he is celebrated as *the* representative of eighteenth-century cultural insubordination. He has been called "the philosopher-punk of the Age of Reason." Indeed, his name is still emblematic of philosophical bad attitude for all the ages.

As a young man, Voltaire quit law school, where he had developed what would be a lifelong contempt for pomposity and hypocrisy, and took to hanging out in the salons of a notorious society lady named Ninon de l'Enclos. Through her, Voltaire found himself moving amidst a leisured social circle wherein trading nasty witticisms was the main hobby. Discovering himself to be better at this than all others, Voltaire quickly focused his derogative skills on assaulting the sacred cows of his time—particularly religion—through literary satire. In 1717, at the age of twenty-three, accused of authoring some satirical poems mocking the recently deceased King Louis XVI, he was tossed in the Bastille for over a year.

From that point on, Voltaire's life would be one of very occasional, brief imprisonments and frequent exile, the result not only of his insolent pen but of his unwillingness to employ diplomacy in personal and philosophical conflicts with his (off-and-on) friends and contemporaries. Those years not spent in France were spent in England, the part of Prussia that is now Germany, and Switzerland. Besides having writerly skills, Voltaire was such a sharp business investor and speculator that he made himself very wealthy. Unlike most of the other philosophes, and despite his somewhat nomadic existence, he was able to live comfortably wherever he was, holding court as a sort of philosopher-king. Gay paints this picture of Voltaire in semiexile: "In the 1750's he . . . settled in Ferney . . . on French soil near the Genevan border . . . [with] its stream of distinguished visitors and its unceasing flow of correspondence. It became a kind of literary government in exile. Where Voltaire was, there was Paris."

In a sense, Voltaire's character marks the first emergence in this book of an amusing countercultural archetype. For all his completely sincere radicalism, Voltaire was also a man who consciously cultivated his bad-boy image with the establishment. Biographer A. J. Ayer, in his book *Voltaire*, refers to his "addiction to mischief." Dressing all his life in the dandyish style of his youth, he was a man who thoroughly enjoyed public (and female) attention. As an author and playwright, he followed his "press clippings" closely and reacted emotionally to criticism. In other words, he was, in every way, a contemporary commercial rebel artiste.

As a playwright, Voltaire catered to the overly formal tastes of the salon and aristocratic set. History has judged his plays to be fussy and rather mediocre. He had but two great literary achievements. First, there was the novel *Candide,* in which Voltaire explored his main themes: in a nutshell, optimism is foolish and philosophical speculation is useless; and everywhere the individual suffers pointlessly due to political and religious oppression. But, through practical effort, groups of individuals can become happy. And then there was his collection of short essays, *Philosophical Dictionary,* in which Voltaire organized his irreverent commentaries on a series of topics in alphabetical order.

While it was obvious to everyone that the *Philosophical Dictionary* was a product of Voltaire's inimitable impertinent stylings, Voltaire denied being the author . . . while publicly delighting in its success. Partly this was because French censorship, however unpredictably utilized, could sometimes escalate into imprisonment of the author. But mostly, it was just another example of Voltaire brazenly toying with his public. Indeed, when the initial book run was released in Paris in 1734, it was burned as subversive.

Voltaire's main target was the absurdities of religion, particularly the Christian and Jewish traditions (although Islam received a few jabs of the doubter's pen as well). And his method of attack was to hoist any belief system on its own petard. Peter Gay wrote, "His performances were dominated by a single pervasive technique: irony. In a world of censorship, of ecclesiastics hunting heretics, and of influential readers to be appeased, irony was an agent of twofold liberation; it freed the writer to speak the truth and it freed the reader to see it."

Note the sardonic tone as Voltaire retells the tale of Abraham in a way that exposes its irrationality: "He brought his wife Sarah along . . . she was extremely young and almost a child compared to him, for she was only sixty-five. Since she was very beautiful, he resolved to turn her beauty to account. 'Say that you are my sister so that it may go well with me because of you.' Rather he should have said, 'Claim to be my daughter.' The king fell in love with Sarah and gave the alleged brother 'many sheep, oxen, servants, and maids': which proves that Egypt was then a very powerful and highly civilized and consequently very ancient kingdom, and that brothers who came and offered their sisters to the kings . . . were rewarded munificently."

With a few words of sarcasm, Voltaire could skewer any religious source: "Saint Thomas . . . says that . . . there are three vegetative souls, namely, the nutritive, the augmentative, the generative; that the memory of spiritual things is spiritual and the memory of corporeal things is corporeal, that the rational soul is a form 'immaterial as to operations and material as to being.' Saint Thomas wrote two thousand pages as forceful and clear as this, besides, he is the angel of the schoolmen."

As anti-religious as Voltaire's pen was (Gay called his essay "The Sermon" a "declaration of war against Christianity"), he was not an atheist. Gay again: "He was in favor of toleration and simple, reasonable beliefs . . . he opposed fanaticism, persecution, and superstition. . . . Voltaire attacked the idea of a cruel god." In *Philosophical Dictionary*, Voltaire himself wrote, "Fanaticism is surely a thousand times more disastrous [than atheism], for atheism inspires no sanguinary passion, as fanaticism does; atheism does not inhibit crimes, but fanaticism sees that they are committed." Like so many during this epoch, Voltaire was a deist.

While he was the consummate eighteenth-century cultural revolutionary, Voltaire died before the political revolutions in the English colonies of America and in France, and he showed no inclination toward democracy. In fact, Voltaire was a great supporter of benevolent absolute monarchy. It's not surprising. He was, on occasion, offered asylum, feted, and supported by the eighteenth century's greatest "enlightened despot," Prussia's King Frederick, with whom he had a complex, sometimes feuding friendship. Russia's Catherine the Great was also a fan and correspondent.

DESPOTS MAKE THE (CULTURAL) REVOLUTION

It is one of the peculiar ironies of the Enlightenment that many of its ideas were propagated by absolute monarchies, a system that Enlightenment doctrines would ultimately consign to history's proverbial dustbin. Prussia's King Frederick was the personification of enlightened despotism. A respectable intellectual in his own right, Frederick read tirelessly and wrote essays on aesthetics (including passionately negative critiques regarding the quality of his Prussian/Germanic writers, whom he accused of excessive pedantry and pomposity, favoring the frisky irreverence of the Frenchman Voltaire).

Upon taking the throne, Frederick issued an edict that "All religions must be tolerated and the sole concern of officials is to ensure that one denomination does not interfere with another, for here everyone can seek salvation in the manner that seems best to him." Frederick preached religious tolerance to such an extent that—at a time when Turks and Prussians had some degree of mutual hostility—he declaimed, "If the Turks . . . came and wanted to populate this country, then we would build mosques and temples for them."

Historians paint Prussia in the eighteenth century as something of a golden age of free worship and free thought, a society—reminiscent of Socrates' Greece—in which the exploration of philosophy was the primary concern. However, Frederick's reign should not be viewed through rose-tinted glasses. Like that of King Louis XIV of France, whom he so admired, Frederick's cultured regime also pursued vicious wars of conquest against foreign enemies. And any right that could be granted, like freedom of the press (1740), could just as easily be revoked (1743). A despot, after all, was still a despot.

Still, a fecund cultural revolution was taking place, and Immanuel Kant and C. P. E. Bach were among the important figures who thrived under Frederick's patronage. (Other great artists like Haydn, Goethe, and Mozart also flourished during the regime, although their relationships with the king were chilly.)

Meanwhile, Russia's Catherine the Great also spread the Enlightenment meme by publishing its works. Diderot was given sanctuary in her court, and Rousseau and Voltaire were both beneficiaries of her enthusiasm.

In conformity with ideas we've expressed in earlier chapters, readers may expect us to conclude that Frederick and Catherine, each in their way, were trying to co-opt the dangerously liberal ideals of the Enlightenment, but the historical evidence is that they were actual genuine enthusiasts for these ideas. I will not conjecture as to whether they were aware of their Gorbachev-like role in dismantling monarchy as a viable institution.

SEEDS OF THE NEXT COUNTERCULTURAL REVOLT

Twenty-first-century countercultural writer Erik Davis wrote in a 2003 issue of *Bookforum* magazine, "The West left the universe in the dust when it followed Descartes down his disenchanted road of mechanistic rationality. . . . Up to that point, Europe had maintained an uneasy if productive dialectic between materialism and mysticism . . . *episteme* and *gnosis*." It is easy for us to forget how revolutionary reason and irreligiousness were during the sixteenth and seventeenth centuries. In the light of previous centuries of various religious absolutisms, complete with a frequent and stultifying taboo against using logic to examine reality and solve problems, mere common sense was a liberating blast, bringing clarity and social change. Still, even then, the seeds of later countercultural rebellions against the limits of rationality were already evident.

Rousseau and Goethe, for instance, both saw limits to reason and sought a unity of mind and heart. The Marquis de Sade, meanwhile, expanded on the outrages of the seventeenth-century libertines. Sade's writing would attempt to challenge the very foundations of the civilized personality. His vile and pornographic attacks on authority advocated total liberty over moral restraint. His was a particular response to being born to the elite in a brutal and extremely hierarchical culture, and he reacted by making its brutality explicit in both his personal behavior and his writing. In contrast to Enlightenment philosophes, Sade used reason against itself; he reveled in carnal violence and perversity, but often acted out his tastes in peculiarly structured episodes. In the words of the online site Art and Culture Network,

> de Sade's irony challenges the very distinction between reason and perversion, between the upright bourgeois citizen and the perverted criminal. In *120 Days of Sodom*, de Sade's subject is a rigidly stratified group of people who've fled from the social world to a remote castle. Everyday life is structured with meticulous and unwavering precision, with this subtle twist: these quotidian customs are completely perverse. The inhabitants of the castle are bent upon living out their devotion to

vice to the fullest, but they do so inside a fastidious order that is maintained despite the unrelenting debauchery. Rather than reject order and reason in his valuation of the criminal instincts, de Sade opted for a parodic synthesis: an affirmation of the powers of both reason and vulgar passion capable of constructing the appropriately perverted soul.

Sade himself wrote, "All universal moral principles are idle fantasies," and described himself as "irascible, extreme in everything, with a dissolute imagination the like of which has never been seen, atheistic to the point of fanaticism." While Sade obviously was too lacking in idealism to be anything but an ambiguous bystander and occasional fringe participant in the political revolutions of his time, he has proved to be a world-historic mythic counterculture unto himself. Sade's sex revolt should probably be contextualized. Most of the enlightened revolutionists of the eighteenth century, for instance, still renounced masturbation.

The ideas of Rousseau and Goethe would seep into the Romantic movement of the early nineteenth century, and beyond that into Transcendentalism and the psychedelic movement, and Sade's perverse mutations of rationalism would affect the Surrealist and punk cultures.

THE POLITICAL REVOLUTIONS OF AMERICA AND FRANCE

> We hold these truths to be self-evident, that all men are created equal, that they are endowed by their Creator with certain unalienable Rights, that among these are Life, Liberty and the pursuit of Happiness.
>
> THOMAS JEFFERSON, DECLARATION OF INDEPENDENCE

> A filthy little atheist.
>
> PRESIDENT THEODORE ROOSEVELT ABOUT THOMAS PAINE

The first great revolution against monarchy to apply Enlightenment principles took place not in Europe but in the American colonies. The colonies were inhabited by former Europeans who were very much a product of that continent's long history of godly monarchy, with all its pomp, circumstance, and the kind of reflexive respect for antiquity still evident in Great Britain today. But time, distance, and the wide-open spaces of the American continent had given the colonists an independence of psyche and spirit that allowed them to apply Europe's newest export—Enlightenment beliefs—more effectively than the originators.

The settling of America began with a group of exiles who were, in many ways, the diametrical opposite of countercultural. The Puritans had turned their backs on European decadence and come to the New World to live according to strict authoritarian religious principles. (In *From Dawn to Decadence,* Barzun goes to some lengths to show that the Puritans were not quite as tight-assed as folk history imagines them. Still, they were very much pointing away from any freethinking—or freewheelin'—tendencies.) But when the Puritans' legacy of hard work and independent self-reliance synergized with the classical liberal ideals coming from Europe, something explosive occurred. It was a new kind of classical liberalism, less abstract and effete, guided by rough-hewn colonists accustomed to dealing with comparatively primitive conditions. This characteristic, this rugged individual stoicism, proved to be just the ticket for making libertarian ideas work in the late eighteenth century.

The American Revolution, like the rest of the country's history, is rich with irony and contradiction. On the one hand, its liberating ideology really began to spread when the Cato Letters, published anonymously in *The London Journal* from 1720 to 1723, became a monster hit in the colonies. The Cato Letters criticized England's Glorious Revolution for failing to live up to its promise, advocated absolute free thought and speech, and criticized pretentiousness in an accessible style that appealed to the colonists. On the other hand, the revolt against England was actually *pro*-expansionist, gaining momentum when King George III signed the Proclamation of 1763, prohibiting any English settlement west of the Appalachian Mountains. The purpose of the proclamation was to prevent the colonists from conquering any more Native American lands.

For all the contradictions, the countercultural character of the American Revolution really comes from the freethinkers like Jefferson, Franklin, and Paine who made it happen. The makers of the Revolution were renaissance men who—besides being thinkers—were savvy businessmen, scientific dabblers, and members of their colonial assemblies. Most were deists (though the Puritan influence lingered in the form of a strong work ethic), and many were high livers, known for their fondness of wine, woman, and song. (None, however, *were* women.)

The well-born Thomas Jefferson, author of the Declaration of Independence, who would become the third president, was undoubtedly the most eloquent and philosophically sophisticated leader of the Revolution. But plainspoken middle-class Thomas Paine strikes us as the more approachable representative. The rest of the Founding Fathers focused on the elites. Paine was unique in focusing on common working people. Paine's idealism and archetypally American optimism provided the enthusiasm needed to make a freethinkers' revolution. (Voltaire had written, "It is extremely rare to find reason joined with enthusiasm." In other words, it's crazy to get fanatical about a political position opposing fanaticism, but sometimes, in the course of events, it becomes necessary.)

Paine was an author of clarion calls, particularly *Common Sense*. This small-book-length essay was published in January 1776, just a half year before independence was declared. It sold half a million copies, an absolutely enormous number for that time (the total population was only 2.5 million). Virtually every literate person in the colonies read *Common Sense,* including the British loyalists, who howled like stuck pigs for Paine's head. General George Washington committed himself to the cause after reading it. The Revolution truly might not have happened without it.

It takes a certain passionate cast of mind to pen clarion calls. As Sidney Hook wrote, "He was the great phrasemaker of his age." Consider this passage from *Common Sense:* "O ye that love mankind! Ye that dare oppose, not only the tyranny, but the tyrant, stand forth. Every spot of the old world is overrun with oppression. Freedom hath been hunted round the globe. Asia, and Africa, have long expelled her—Europe regards her like a stranger, and England hath given her warning to depart. O! receive the fugitive, and prepare in time an asylum for mankind." A close parsing of this hyperventilating rhetoric raises minor quibbles. For instance, for freedom to be hunted and expelled, it has to exist in the first place. But who would change a word of it?

Paine is recalled for his enormous faith in the essential goodness of mankind. This legacy was reified, as we shall see, during the Transcenden-talist/abolitionist movements, and during the early phases of the hippie and New Left countercultures of the 1960s. Paine's idealism shouldn't be mistaken for naïveté or gullibility. For instance, he wrote, "This is suppos-ing the present race of kings in the world to have had an honourable ori-gin; whereas it is more than probable, that could we take off the dark covering of antiquities, and trace them to their first rise, that we should find the first of them nothing better than the principal ruffian of some restless gang." This critique—finding thuggery and gangsterism at the root of state political power—remains a sophisticated countercultural view to this day.

Another irony of American history is that many of our Founding Fa-thers were "blasphemers." In other words, they said things about God and religion that would get them run out of Washington on a rail in the twenty-first century. Jefferson wrote that the Book of Revelation was "merely the ravings of a maniac, no more worthy nor capable of explana-tion than the incoherence of our own nightly dreams." And James Madi-son wrote,

> During almost fifteen centuries has the legal establish-ment of Christianity been on trial. What have been its fruits? More or less in all places, pride and indolence in the Clergy, ignorance and servility in the laity; in both, superstition, bigotry and persecution.
>
> What influence, in fact, have ecclesiastical estab-lishments had on society? In some instances they have been seen to erect a spiritual tyranny on the ruins of the civil authority; on many instances they have been seen upholding the thrones of political tyranny; in no instance have they been the guardians of the liberties of the people. Rulers who wish to subvert the public liberty may have found an established clergy convenient auxil-iaries. A just government, instituted to secure and per-petuate it, needs them not.

Spread the word!

America's revolution fulfilled the Glorious Revolution's promise of the separation of church and state. Over the years, the quality of the nation's adherence to this principle (like many others) has had its ups and downs. Indeed, we should currently keep a wary eye on the situation.

CLASS CONFLICT: THE OTHER HISTORY OF THE UNITED STATES

As we've already observed, while the Enlightenment raised the banner of equal and democratic rights, it still excluded the majority from them. The American Revolution did little to change that. The democratic governing rights afforded in the Constitution were the exclusive province of property-owning white men. Poor people, Native Americans, women, and obviously the African slaves who made up approximately 25 percent of the population were excluded. On the other hand, the Bill of Rights was intended to apply to a broader segment of the population, essentially excluding only slaves and Native Americans (who were considered foreign nationals) from its civil libertarian protections. (Technically, until the Civil War, the states—which had a high degree of independence—could ignore the Bill of Rights, and its application varied wildly.)

According to Howard Zinn, the influential alternative leftist historian who has written books like *A People's History of the United States,* which tells America's history from the view of the oppressed and dispossessed, America's revolutionaries were coping with serious insurrectionary violence from below, at the same time that they were building their revolution.

> Starting with Bacon's Rebellion in Virginia, by 1760, there had been eighteen uprisings aimed at overthrowing colonial governments. There had also been six black rebellions, from South Carolina to New York, and forty riots of various origins.
>
> Mechanics were demanding political democracy in the colonial cities: open meetings of representative assemblies, public galleries in the legislative halls, and the publishing of roll-call votes, so that constituents

> could check on representatives. They wanted open-air
> meetings where the population could participate in
> making policy, more equitable taxes, price controls, and
> the election of mechanics and other ordinary people to
> government posts.

After the Revolution, the common workers and farmers took the Declaration seriously and immediately started pressuring the oligopoly for inclusion. Riots and armed rebellions (including the Whiskey Rebellion) by the lower classes were a part of the nation's early political landscape. Few among America's elite of revolutionary activists supported the lower-class rebellions, but Thomas Paine was frequently among them. Among other reforms, Paine proposed dropping the Constitution's property requirements for working people's inclusion and opposed a tax structure that was unfair to common laborers.

Despite the enormity of the New World revolutionaries' blind spots, they were the effective freethinkers of their time, moving individual liberty, the free exchange of ideas, and the spirit of social transformation radically forward. The ideas of the Founding Fathers would be used by those who sought and received inclusion within its principles: first the nonpropertied males, then the abolitionists, woman's suffrage, unionists, and civil rights activists all adopted the ideals of the American Revolution to gain greater participation in this system.

FRANCE LOSES ITS HEAD OVER THE ENLIGHTENMENT

The birthplace of Diderot, Rousseau, Voltaire, and so many other lights of the Age of Reason was the next nation to experience a political revolution in the name of liberty at the close of the eighteenth century. In fact, the French Revolution was a series of revolutions.

General dissatisfaction with the French monarchy had been growing amongst all factions of the populace since the death of Louis XIV in 1715. Louis' successors—Louis XV and Louis XVI—were not particularly competent managers of the affairs of state at home, and they also suffered humiliating defeats in wars with England and Prussia. Combined with lavish spending on their courts, these international adventures brought France to bankruptcy.

Noble families were still smarting from the usurpation of their political powers by absolute monarchy in the middle of the previous century. Meanwhile, ordinary working people groaned under the feudal economic privileges and powers still held by the nobility, who were largely exempt from taxes and military services, and controlled the trade guilds and a great portion of the country's wealth.

The first phase of France's political revolution began in May of 1789 when a group of nobles convinced the king that the only way out of the political doldrums was to convene the Estates-General, the parliamentary assembly that had been empowered to represent the interests of the three French estates: church nobles, hereditary nobles, and the bourgeoisie, before it was eliminated by the imposition of the absolutist monarchy. During the following month, the bourgeois estate secretly convened and took the Tennis Court Oath to form a constitutional government. (The meeting had taken place on a tennis court. Could there be a more appropriate site to launch a bourgeois revolution? The Golf Course Insurrection perhaps?)

On July 14, 1789, the rabble got into the spirit of things when they famously stormed and destroyed the Bastille, an act still celebrated today with drunken abandon by Frenchmen and miscellaneous revolt groupies everywhere. While the storming of the Bastille remains a potent symbol of insurrection against the aristocracy, the practical purpose of the action was that the gunpowder used by the king's (mostly German mercenary) militia was stored there. Immediately after the storming of the Bastille, the Paris Commune was constituted, establishing Paris as territory liberated from the monarchy's rule. (This Paris Commune should not be confused with the legendary Paris Commune of the late nineteenth century, whose overall boho ambience and attempt to live according to anarcho-communist theory has inspired romantic tributes from twentieth-century Situationists and other far-left dreamers and radicals.)

In August 1789, the National Assembly wrote the Declaration of the Rights of Man, a document influenced by the U.S. Constitution and Bill of Rights that declared freedom of speech, freedom of the press, religious liberty, and protection against unlawful imprisonment. In fact, the original draft was composed with the help of Jefferson (the American ambassador to France at the time). However, in the hands of the factionalized assembly, it lost much of its definition, becoming a rather fuzzy moralistic statement about the common good and universal rights. Distinct from the American Revolution's documents, the Declaration also announced the intention to abolish the class system. (Not in the Marxist sense. The idea was merely that everybody would have equal rights to participate in the state, and to achieve and acquire regardless of their parentage.)

Olympia de Gorges answered the French Declaration of the Rights of Man with a Declaration of Women's Rights. According to Barzun, "She proposed for marriage a single form of contract with reciprocal rights, recourse to the law in cases of seduction and paternity, and . . . participation in government. More radical was Theroigne de Mericourt. Her organization, called Amazons, participated in protests with a single breast bared." This powerful image is frequently repeated in paintings and drawings referring to the French Revolution. Mericourt was a leader in the march to Versailles to protest bread shortages that brought the king back to Paris, where the Revolution could keep an eye on him.

In 1791, a faction of the National Assembly, a coalition of the bourgeoisie called the Girondins, established a constitutional monarchy, sharing power uneasily with the king, but the attempt to compromise with monarchy was doomed to failure. Historians differ as to whether it was the nobles or the king who didn't want to compromise, but in either case, the commoners were getting restless and demanding an end to the monarchy.

Eventually, the mob revolution became irresistible. The Girondins were removed from power by the Jacobins, a cabal with (pre-Marx) communist leanings who were deeply influenced by Rousseau, led by Jean-Paul Marat and a dyspeptic, self-righteous judge named Robespierre. Part of the Jacobins' attraction was that they promised to end the chaos and restore order to France. Highly organized and popular among the artillerymen (members of the "armed forces") and with the denizens of the Paris Commune, they were indeed well positioned to bring about order. All they had to do was give the people what they wanted.

And what they wanted was blood. In the Reign of Terror, thousands of aristocrats and other political enemies of the regime were sent to the guillotine. Now, instead of rationalism being suppressed by religious authority, religion was suppressed and "the Goddess of reason" was enthroned in Notre Dame.

The time of the Terror was both a season of horrific madness and an extraordinary attempt to accelerate toward a set of utopian goals that included complete equality and what might be idealistically viewed as participatory democracy at the level of the street (although it looked more like mob rule). Robespierre declared, "The French people seem to have outdistanced the rest of the human race by 2,000 years; one is tempted to regard it as a different species," and Enlightenment figures abroad—ranging from Thomas Jefferson to Goethe—enthused over the French Revolution almost until the bitter end.

Within two years, the Jacobin rulers had turned on each other and, one by one, their heads also rolled into the basket. Their failure led, a few years later, to the reign of a new kind of despot, the emperor Napoleon. And while most associate the name Napoleon with short dudes who want to rule the world, he maintained and extended (and sometimes retracted, at his whim) many of the features of the Enlightenment revolution while pursuing his international conquests.

In reductive terms, the French Revolution was proto-communist and the American Revolution was proto-libertarian. The American Revolution was birthed out of a peculiar mix of Enlightenment idealism about the rights of every individual and a seemingly contradictory set of elitist and oligopolistic beliefs held by most of the Founding Fathers. The French revolutionaries were influenced by the same ideas about individual rights, but—in the long run—were more focused on the needs and wants of the dispossessed as an enraged *group,* and in their attack on elitism and oligopoly, individual rights wound up being savaged.

The French Revolution collapsed where the American Revolution succeeded. Readers are certainly welcome to find an absolute historic syllogism here, but we'll give that a pass. History is long and unfinished, and the countercultural view—at least when it comes to politics—should be omni-skeptical and perpetually dissatisfied. Still, the issues raised by these divergent, ultimately oppositional, political currents that emerged from Enlightenment thought recall observations made about the Socratic counterculture in Chapter 3. Counterculture's essential characteristic, deep radical individualism, has complicated and ambivalent relationships with both populism and elitism that may never be resolved. Clearly, the counter-cultural value of nonauthoritarianism is very difficult to institutionalize politically in large societies. Both the elites and the mobs must be watched closely. Liberty requires vigilance.

THE FIRST MEDIA REVOLUTION

Media, as we know it, first emerged at the beginning of the eighteenth century. Papers, journals, broadsheets, all became widely available in the newly created public space of the coffeehouse. By the middle of the century, publishing had almost completely abandoned the previously pro forma use of Latin, instead employing the popular vernacular. And it wasn't just text that was being popularized. Media was transforming the public sphere. Blanning observed, "Cultural media . . . now became accessible to the public—reading societies, lecture halls, theatres, museums and concerts. What these various spaces had in common was the sovereignty of rational argument . . . outranking claims of status or wealth."

The popular market for art and literature liberated writers and artists from the need for court patronage. No longer having to please their sponsors, they could experiment, and speak out as brashly as they wished. Of course, the exigencies of the market created new pressures to please the public that we're all familiar with today, but on the whole, the transition led to a great flowering of creative forms and dissident visions.

Amsterdam's capitalist publishers didn't care about the radicalness of your ideas as long as the printing bill was paid. And the ancien régime of the eighteenth century had become a very inefficient and sporadic oppressor. Book smugglers and publishers played cat-and-mouse games with the authorities. The authorities themselves were deeply conflicted, oftentimes giving prior warning of their raids. All of the radical early Enlightenment thought that had been safely encrypted in the mostly unfamiliar Latin was now the subject of "popular" debate. A *Lady's Guide to Newtonian Physics* was a hot topic in the fashionable salons as early as the 1730s.

The spread of radical ideas was no accident. During the course of the eighteenth century, individuals dedicated themselves to spreading the Enlightenment cause. Self-conscious and increasingly organized sets of individuals, often centered around Masonic lodges (the secret society of the

Freemasons), agitated for radical change. Many Enlightenment figures were Freemasons, including Wolfgang Mozart, George Washington, Benjamin Franklin, Isaac Newton, Voltaire, Diderot, and Frederick the Great, and it's known that nearly 150 lodges existed throughout the Americas at mid-century. Historians disagree on the importance of the secret society. For some, who would likely point out that these values were being expressed quite openly and boldly by Masons and others alike during this time, Freemasonry is a mere historical sideshow. For others, inclined to see history in conspiratorial terms, the age of Enlightenment itself—and the cultural and political revolutions it fostered—was a Freemasonic "operation." In reality, it was inevitable that thinkers and talented writers and artists who were passionate about the new spirit of liberty would "conspire" to spread the word. The fact that Masonic lodges, complete with occultish rituals, became one of the centers for propagandizing activities has intrigued weirdos and spooked religious fundamentalists ever since.

Technological and media revolution characterized the eighteenth century. As always, it was a double-edged sword. Blanning: "Just as the public sphere was socially heterogeneous, so was it politically multi-directional. It was not an agenda but a space in which all kinds of opinions could be expressed, including those which were supportive of the status quo." Additionally, the same technologies that spread the liberating power of the media and commerce were already starting to show a negative side. As uber-technophobe Jeremy Rifkin has correctly asserted, pre-industrial laborers paid little attention to time, and took frequent holidays, but the market culture lashed most citizens to the clock. The Germans began conceiving of education primarily as a means of instilling obedience, and for the most part the world followed suit. Gloomy industrialism, with its "dark satanic mills," loomed on the horizon. A factory conformist culture of mass production would inspire new countercultural rebellions.

Blanning argues that "the cultural emancipation of the masses has been a dismal failure. Mass culture has become manipulated culture; its recipients have been degraded as passive consumers. The culture industry is just a prop of the status quo." This is certainly a popular contemporary countercultural view, although a consideration of any number of pop cultural phenomena, such as the popularity of the neo-Situationist film *Fight Club* among young adults, and the wickedly satiric hit television show *The*

Simpsons, combined with the still-lively culture of dissident activism, argues for a slightly more nuanced analysis.

Many of the factions of the modern world—leftism, centrism, libertarianism, neo-primitivism, scientism, hedonism, romanticism, and materialism—were present in the Enlightenment. Freethinking produced thought and (surprise!) much of it was contradictory. Like countercultures discussed earlier in this book, the Enlightenment expanded the boundaries for personal behavior, freedom of association, free thought, open communication . . . pretty much all the primary and secondary countercultural characteristics discussed in the second chapter of this book coalesce within its ideals.

And yet, Reason (the heart has its own) has left many feeling bereft. The shadow side of the Enlightenment's political legacy—racism, colonialism, economic inequities, environmental devastation—remains unresolved. Biological and nuclear holocausts haunt our dreams, radical religionists pursue theocracy (some violently) with increasing vigor, and "the Enlightenment" is armed to the teeth. And so, it is now trendy among postmodern intellectuals to look upon the Enlightenment as the deficient product of dead white males, while some spiritual New Agers and environmentalists also dismiss Western culture in its entirety as a wrong turn. Good for them! All opinions and points of view are tolerated, even welcomed. And if we were to try to shut them up, their response would be the same as ours:

I KNOW MY RIGHTS!

CHAPTER NINE

⊢ TO EACH HIS OWN GOD

The American Transcendentalists

There are always two parties, the party of the Past and the party of the Future: the Establishment and the Movement. At times the resistance is reanimated, the schism runs under the world and appears in Literature, Philosophy, Church, State and social custom.

RALPH WALDO EMERSON

A common and natural result of an undue respect for law is, that you may see a file of soldiers, colonel, captain, corporal, privates, powder-monkeys, and all, marching in admirable order over hill and dale to the wars, against their wills, ay, against their common sense and consciences.... They have no doubt that it is a damnable business in which they are concerned; they are all peaceably inclined. Now, what are they? Men at all? or small movable forts ... at the service of some unscrupulous man in power? Visit the Navy-Yard, and behold a marine, such a man as an American government can make ... a mere shadow and reminiscence of humanity....

> The mass of men serve the state thus, not as men,
> mainly, but as machines.
>
> HENRY DAVID THOREAU

> The great gifts are not got by analysis. Everything good
> is on the highway.
>
> RALPH WALDO EMERSON

By the 1830s, the American Revolution, based on the principles of the eighteenth-century Enlightenment, was well secured. Democracy and basic political liberty muddled along, albeit imperfectly achieved and riddled with contradictions that we are still trying to sort out today. The Enlightenment's assault on religious dogma was less successful. The great mass of men and women were no more engaged in independent thought about the cosmogonic origins of the universe and their place in it than they were in the sixteenth century. Most—particularly in America, land born of the Puritans' pilgrimage—entrusted their relationship with the presumed divine creator to the church they inherited by birth, and accepted—at least superficially—its still quite rigid codes of conduct and ritual.

Despite a veneer of the religiosity and piety that had characterized the early American settlers, God was in reality no longer at the center of American life. The pursuit of money, possessions, and status were manifestly the real values of the time. Meanwhile the Unitarians, a mostly New England–based religion rooted in an austere Calvinism, had taken some baby steps toward relaxing that religious philosophy's strict codes, although by today's standards they were still quite orthodox. (Absolute adherence to certain traditional rituals remained compulsory and Jesus Christ was still the only Savior, demanding obedience and formal respect.)

A small crack in the coherence between the Christian cosmology and that of some Unitarians first revealed itself in the person of William Ellery Channing in an 1819 sermon. The Unitarian minister knocked God off his heavenly throne, preaching, in the words of Perry Miller, the existence of "an indwelling God and the significance of intuitive thought . . . the unity of the world and God, and the immanence of God in the world." Although the Transcendentalist moniker would not be affixed to this notion (and a whole host of others) for another seventeen years, this was in essence the beginning of the movement. Retrospectively, Channing would comment, "Transcendentalism, as viewed by its disciples, was a pilgrimage from the idolatrous world of creeds and rituals to the temple of the Living God in the soul. It was a putting to silence of tradition and formulas, that the Sacred Oracle might be heard through intuitions of the single-eyed and pure-hearted. Amidst materialists, zealots, and skeptics, the Transcendentalist believed in perpetual inspiration, the miraculous power of will, and a birthright to universal good. He sought to hold communion face to face with the unnamable Spirit of his spirit, and gave himself up to the embrace of nature's perfect joy."

A few Unitarians were impressed by Channing's breakaway ideas, including a very bright if somewhat timid young sprout named Ralph Waldo Emerson, who became a minister in the mid-1820s. By the middle of the next decade, a few who were so influenced started gathering together, mostly at Emerson's home, for free-flowing discussions about philosophy and spirituality.

This group of Unitarians, soon joined by other intellectual seekers, was also greatly influenced by German Romanticism. Inspired by Immanuel Kant's *A Critique of Pure Reason* in 1781, the Romantics had formed a countercurrent to John Locke's empirical rationalism, which dominated the Enlightenment. As Paula Blanchard, author of *Margaret Fuller: From Transcendentalism to Revolution,* explains it, Kant "shook up the prevailing rationalists by claiming that consciousness . . . cannot be explained by science or theology . . . it simply exists. Kant called the mysterious . . . power of the mind 'transcendental knowledge' because it transcends all rational attempts to analyze it."

Early in the nineteenth century, German Romantics, particularly Goethe, privileged intuition and the "logic of the heart"—as expressed through poetry and other arts—over the cold calculations of reason. To Goethe, the natural world was divine, infused with wonder, and man should feel exalted by his presence as an active participant.

While Channing's cosmological meditations initiated this convergence of nascent freethinking spiritualists, it was Emerson who energized the group with the publication of his monograph *Nature* in 1836. In this tome, Emerson beautifully expressed the group's Kantian belief in a divinity that couldn't be apprehended by the logical examination of the material world yet was immanent in nature. And he married these spiritual insights to a critique of the greed, small-minded hypocrisy, and prevalent unconsciousness of the society that surrounded them.

It was the oppositional elements of *Nature* that galvanized the group, making explicit their alienation from the majority and their concurrent sense of uniqueness. Of course, the neighbors started to gossip about these strange men and, by now, women, who could not help but occasionally start spouting their "un-Christian" maverick philosophies in the shops and public spaces of New England, and who gathered together conspiratorially at the house of the dissident (by now former) Unitarian minister, Emerson. The neighbors christened them "The Transcendentalist Club."

Like "beatniks" and "hippies," the group had been labeled by outsiders whose only intention was to have a spot of fun at their expense. Still, give the neighbors some credit for having the sophistication to apply a worthy name. The gang did not object and soon adopted the moniker. Transcendentalism would become an influential and much debated philosophy for the mid-nineteenth century, adding its own distinct flavor to what would evolve into a period of radical unrest in America that culminated in the Civil War.

COME TOGETHER: THE FRIENDS

> Friendship, like the immortality of the soul, is too good to be believed.
>
> RALPH WALDO EMERSON

> Emerson had a habit of discovering promising young men.
>
> RALPH RUSK, *THE LIFE OF RALPH WALDO EMERSON*

However much they may have looked like a conspiracy of freaks to some of Emerson's neighbors in Concord, Massachusetts, in the mid-1830s, the Transcendentalists were really just a small circle of friends, growing larger. But because they valued friendship so deeply, and because they felt compelled to live out their values, the Transcendentalists would soon evolve into a recognizable counterculture, even in the 1960s sense, complete with underground periodicals and communes.

At the beginning, A. Bronson Alcott, a gentle, dreamy spiritualist, was the group's central figure, a role later taken over by Emerson. Around the time of the advent of the Transcendentalist Club, he had gotten into controversy with the publication of his *Conversations on the Gospels*. His sins included calling Christ by his first name, and what Paula Blanchard called "several mild hints . . . that babies were born by women and not found under cabbage leaves." The Unitarians were outraged, as was a reviewer for a Presbyterian newspaper who, according to Blanchard, "declared *Conversations* the most obscene and indecent book yet published in America and suggested that Alcott be prosecuted for blasphemy."

Margaret Fuller, a homely woman whose intellect and personal power dazzled nearly everybody she met, entered the Transcendental circle soon after meeting Emerson in the summer of 1836. Fuller was, in many ways, Emerson's opposite. While he was fundamentally withdrawn, she was what we would today call a natural networker. Even with people who were reticent, she would persist in breaking down boundaries and developing intimate friendships. Blanchard: "Socially she broadened his [Emerson] experience, bringing to Concord a choice succession of those friends whom [it was said] she wore like 'a necklace of diamonds around her neck.' " Fuller rapidly became a central figure in the club's conversations, taking on the Socratic role of asking provocative questions and leading discussions. By 1840, recognizing that some women who were unaccustomed to expressing their views in public were intimidated in the presence of so many learned men, she started a separate series of conversations for women. The women idolized her, some going so far as to express a romantic longing . . . "if only she were a man." Fuller was a one-woman Transcendentalist recruitment drive, bringing lots of promising young people of both genders around, many of whom became an important part of this circle of friends.

And then there was the Transcendentalists' greatest writer, Henry David Thoreau. Thoreau was a blunt and impetuous young man; the intensity of his alienation from society made the other Transcendentalists look like Boy Scouts. And while his participation in the community was somewhat limited by his reclusiveness, Thoreau has emerged in history as

Emerson's equal as a leading light of the Transcendentalist movement, thanks to the power of his pen.

The great American writer Nathaniel Hawthorne was an odd presence in Transcendentalist circles. Although he did not subscribe to their philosophy in the least, he was completely accepted as a part of the community. He even helped to form the Brook Farm commune, where he lived for several years, not out of idealism but out of need (he was perpetually broke), and out of an appreciation for good company. And while he grudgingly admired Emerson as "a great original thinker," Hawthorne was basically a stoic who could sometimes excoriate the Transcendentalist followers. In one essay, he wrote that his "poor country village [was] infested with . . . a variety of queer, strangely dressed, oddly behaved mortals, most of whom took upon themselves to be important agents of the world's destiny, yet were simply bores."

Like the beats in the 1950s, the Transcendentalists placed tremendous import on friendship and were inclined to share each other's deepest thoughts and hopes. Emerson, Thoreau, Fuller, and Alcott, for instance, shared their intimate private journals. And Transcendentalist gatherings weren't merely intellectual colloquies. They quickly took on a celebratory aspect, helped along by Emerson's wife, Lidian. Blanchard: "These were . . . among the first Americans to be liberated from the belief that anything pleasant must be sinful. Lidian Emerson [was] a bountiful hostess . . . when her guests gathered for the midday at the September meal they found the table loaded down with beef, boiled muttons with caper sauce, ham, tongue, corn, beans, tomatoes, macaroni, cucumbers, lettuce, applesauce, puddings, custards, fruits and nuts." An independent thinker in her own right, Lidian Emerson held beliefs that fell somewhere between the Transcendentalists' liberality and more traditional Christian views, but she enjoyed being a part of this budding community.

By the end of the 1830s, the small circle of New England–based friends had become a crowd and its influence had spread further, mostly due to the popularity of Emerson's books and lecture appearances in the wider world. As with any aggregation of nonconformists, they started to attract some dodgy characters and genuine lunatics. Ellery Channing (nephew of William Ellery Channing), for instance, was a second-rate poet who took Emerson's and Thoreau's ideas to an extreme. He refused to deal with work or money, but unlike Thoreau, he didn't have the discipline and survival skills to be self-reliant outside the system. Much to Margaret Fuller's displeasure, he married her sister. In a striking display of tolerance, Emerson and (grudgingly) Fuller helped the couple along through life. And then there was Jones Very, a talented visionary poet who one day decided that he was the second coming of Christ. Emerson was his great defender. At one point, Emerson wrote of a gathering, "Very charmed us all by telling us that he hates us all." In reality, his delusions of grandeur and insistence on receiving special attention irritated many in the Transcendentalist community. Even Emerson, while entertaining the validity of Very's claim, refused his occasional demand to be treated as the reborn Messiah.

Today, Very would probably be labeled a schizophrenic and his delusional genius would be flattened by psychiatric drugs in hope of making him fit for society. A more complicated relationship exists between abnormal mind states and counterculture. What a dreary world it would be if all eccentricities were suppressed. And when society's norm is understood to be pathological, the issue of sanity is up for grabs. Indeed, some of Very's visions were decidedly prescient: "In the physical world we are driving to annihilation of space and time." On the other hand, severely disturbed people tend to engage in coercive behaviors (a decidedly noncountercultural trait) and frequently bring trouble to countercultural movements.

COME TOGETHER: THE IDENTITY

It's no small irony that a man as naturally aloof as Emerson became a sort of den mother to a community of dreamers and lunatics, but it is true. He, and his equally brave and generous wife, Lidian, maintained something of an open house across the Transcendentalist era, and Emerson used his considerable influence to get his fellows heard and published (a very similar role was played more comfortably by the gregarious Allen Ginsberg in the 1950s and beyond). Just as interesting was the way that Emerson—despite his strongly individualistic suspicion of group identity and collective thinking—embraced the opportunity to speak for this movement. While he refused the public's desire that he speak directly about Transcendentalism at every lecture, he did speak to his peers' identity on occasion. In

1842, he finally bit off the whole tamale, delivering a lecture titled "The Transcendentalist," where he lovingly described his compatriots:

> ... they shun general society; they incline to shut them-
> selves in their chamber in the house, to live in the country
> rather than in the town, and to find their tasks and amuse-
> ments in solitude. Society, to be sure, does not like this
> very well; it saith, Whoso goes to walk alone, accuses the
> whole world; he declares all to be unfit to be his compan-
> ions; it is very uncivil, nay, insulting; Society will retali-
> ate ... [but] these persons are not by nature melancholy,
> sour, and unsocial—they are not stockish or brute,—but
> joyous, susceptible, affectionate; they have more than
> others a great wish to be loved. Like the young Mozart,
> they are rather ready to cry ten times a day, "but are you
> sure you love me?" They wish a just and even fellowship,
> or none. They cannot gossip with you, and they do not
> wish ... to gratify any mere curiosity which you may en-
> tertain. Like Fairies, they do not wish to be spoken of.

In the same lecture, Emerson also indicated that the Transcendentalists were not merely a collection of sensitive types but quite possibly a movement for social transformation: "In liberated moments, we know that a new picture of life . . . is already possible; the elements already exist in many minds around you, of a doctrine of life which shall transcend any written record we have."

Ralph Rusk, in his biography *The Life of Ralph Waldo Emerson*, eloquently explored the genesis of the Transcendentalist identity, writing,

> If the Symposium was an amorphous club with no dues
> to collect and no regular members, the persons taking
> part in its discussions were nevertheless easily identi-
> fied and their intellectual orientation gradually came to
> be understood. The [early] Transcendentalists appeared
> to be mostly extremely liberal Unitarian ministers who

were quite as much interested in literature, philosophy or even social reform as in the church. Many . . . were seekers after new truths and were impatient of restraint by any creed. . . . Though they wouldn't let God be human, they tended to make man divine; and their incipient divine man had it as one of his duties to get his own most important revelations without depending on a middleman between himself and God. They had the fervor and conscience of the seventeenth-century Puritan. . . . Their intellectual horizons were broadened by the rationalism of the eighteenth century and by the new theories of the natural scientists. They felt the liberalizing pull of political democracy and the expansiveness of the Romantic movement in literature. But they also drew much from the potent essences of various idealisms, mysticisms, pantheisms, and Platonisms. . . . They had the conviction that the world was their province, and they foraged through it for spiritual and mental food. They were not, however, in so much danger of overindulgence as one might have supposed. Even if Transcendentalism sometimes seemed to be the saturnalia of faith, the members of the Transcendental club were, after all, mostly intellectuals who exercised a good deal of judgment and self-restraint.

As is frequently the case with avant-gardists, the high-spirited Transcendentalists weren't averse to declaiming their own specialness. Emerson saw himself and his friends as a "natural aristocracy," and declared that "the persons who constitute the natural aristocracy are not found in the actual aristocracy, or, only on its edge; as the chemical energy of the spectrum is found to be greatest just outside the spectrum. . . . I have seen an individual, whose manners, though wholly within the conventions of elegant society . . . were original and commanding . . . one who . . . carried the holiday in his eye, who exhilarated the fancy by flinging wide the doors of new modes of existence . . . with happy, spirited bearing, good-natured and free as Robin Hood; yet with the port of an emperor, —if need be, calm, serious, and fit to stand the gaze of millions."

If the Transcendentalists were bent on transforming American society, conventional logic would decree that one of their shared traits was not conducive to this lofty ambition. The group was in revolt against the Protestant work ethic. In fact, they sometimes advocated outright laziness. The Transcendentalists didn't like the way industrial capitalism had imposed its tyranny of the time clock. Additionally, by the mid-1800s the transformation of the societal ethos that is more or less completed today was just beginning. "Make money" was becoming the absolute reigning command program of American society. All other considerations, however well spoken of, were, in reality, moving to the periphery. The Transcendentalists believed that constant busyness (business) shriveled the soul and closed the mind. Time was best spent in contemplation, reading, appreciating nature, and sharing intimate thoughts with other human beings. As Ralph Gabriel wrote in his 1940 essay "Emerson and Thoreau," "To spend a weekday alone or with a friend, as both Emerson and Thoreau frequently did, loitering about Walden Pond without even the excuse of hunting or fishing, was little short of a sin." In this regard, Thoreau was the slacker king right from the start. As a Harvard graduate, he was chosen for the honor of speaking at his graduate commencement. Thoreau took the opportunity to suggest that the biblical command should be reversed, and we should work one day a week and rest six!

As an adult, Thoreau liberated himself from the workaday world. According to Carl Bode, editor of a collection of Thoreau's works, he set out to "reduce his wants and live a simple life." In *Walden,* Thoreau wrote, "I am convinced, both by faith and experience, that to maintain oneself on this earth is not a hardship but a pastime, if we live simply and wisely. . . . It is not necessary that a man should earn his living by the sweat of his brow, unless he sweats more easily than I do." He also described his plain diet as "rye and Indian meal without yeast, potatoes, rice, a very little salt pork, molasses, and salt; and my drink, water." But he did confess to rare occasional visits to restaurants in town.

The desire to get out from underneath the drudgery associated with Western civilization is an ongoing theme in counterculture, but thinkers diverge radically about how to get there. Anti-Prometheans would like to see us return to an earlier, less hurried mode of existence. Some, in fact, would lead us back to the hunter-gatherer era, while others would like to somehow combine that lifestyle's charms with ubiquitous computer communications technology, an aesthetic that is one among several definitions of "modern primitivism." Promethean opponents of the work ethic, on the other hand, want to speed the production of technologies that theoretically would do the drudge work for us (but which under our current social system only seem to accelerate competition, forcing us to be on the job 24/7). These contrasting approaches were already visible in the mid-nineteenth century. One inventor, J. A. Etzler, declared, "I promise to show the means of creating a paradise within ten years, where everything desirable for human life may be had for every man in superabundance, without labor and without pay." He was taken to task by the anti-Promethean Thoreau. Gabriel comments, "For Thoreau machines were gadgets which made life so complicated that they made living difficult; they were burdens which men carried on their backs. They blighted alike the lives of the children who tended them in factories and of the entrepreneurs who had them built. Thoreau never compromised with the machine; he never ceased to despise—and pity—those men whose days were filled with business and whose goal was wealth."

COME TOGETHER: THE MOVEMENT

> It was a time when the air was full of reform. . . . Madmen , madwomen, men with beards, Dunkers, Muggletonians, Come-outers, Groaners, Agrarians, Seventh-Day Baptists, Quakers, Abolitionists, Calvinists, Unitarians and Philosophers, —all came successively to the top, and seized their moment, if not their hour, wherein to chide, or pray, or preach, or protest.
>
> RALPH WALDO EMERSON

> We had a great deal of company, —curious tourists from abroad, artistic people, and socialists.
>
> ARTHUR SUMNER,
> REMINISCING ABOUT THE BROOK FARM COMMUNE

In 1840, the Transcendentalists became a true social movement with the publication of their own journal, *The Dial*. Margaret Fuller was pressed into service as the editor. In her opening statement, she wrote that the journal should be "A perfectly free organ . . . for the expression of individual thought and character. There are no party measures to be curried, no particular standard to be set up." This medium for a movement without ideology went on to publish signature works by all the leading Transcendentalists, as well as the words of hangers-on like Hawthorne and even a few liberal politicians. Emerson wrote of how it captivated "all the bright boys and girls in New England, quite ignorant of each other, [who] take the world as so . . . the boys that . . . do not wish to go into trade, the girls that . . . do not like morning calls and evening parties. They are all religious, but hate the churches; they reject all the ways of living of other men." Other Transcendentalist journals, with titles like *The Western Messenger, Harbinger, Aesthetic Papers,* and *Spirit of the Age,* followed on the heels of *The Dial,* forming a veritable underground press.

By the end of the 1830s, some members of the Transcendentalist Club started talking about living together and putting their ideals about a good society into practice. George Ripley, influenced by a utopian socialist movement called Fourierism, decided to set up a commune based on voluntary sharing, goodwill, and cooperation. In 1841, Ripley, along with Hawthorne and a few others, secured loans in order to buy a parcel of land in West Roxbury, just outside Boston. There they would conduct this experiment in transcendental living. The commune dedicated itself to farming, and running a Transcendentalist school. Plenty of time was set aside for the life of the mind, and for the leisurely enjoyment of nature and good company. As with many of the hippie communes of the early 1970s, farming proved to be less agreeable physically than in the imagination. But with Emerson and Fuller dropping by to teach courses, the school was a raging success, attracting bright young students from as far away as the Philippines. And socially, the group living was found to be altogether pleasant and stimulating.

Soon after the establishment of Brook Farm, a number of other American communal experiments rose up. And although they were probably more influenced by the French socialist Fourier than by Emersonian spirituality, according to Rusk, some Transcendentalists were starting to believe that "the numerous experimental communities now being established might really transform American society. . . . Clapp [Elizabeth Clapp, an Emerson acolyte] told him [Emerson] that it must happen soon that these communities would change and control the price of bread as the manufacturing and commercial associations had done the price of cotton and farmers would be driven into associations in self-defense." But this vision of the communards gaining control of the agricultural economy—peculiarly reminiscent of Tom Hayden's 1969 hallucination that hip communities like Berkeley, California, and Ann Arbor, Michigan, would soon form liberated territories from which they would complete "the revolution"—was not to pass into reality.

Among the principal, original Transcendentalists, only Ripley joined Brook Farm. Emerson and Fuller remained at arm's length, staying sometimes for as long as a week or two at a time, but never committing themselves to the life or even the idea. As Rusk commented, "The bare suggestion of anything resembling a communal scheme . . . chilled Emerson the individual . . . [who commented] 'I do not wish to remove from my present prison to a prison a little larger.' " Emerson also needled the communards for their inflated sense of self-importance, calling their scene "a perpetual picnic, a French Revolution in small, an Age of Reason in a patty-pan." For her part, Fuller wasn't completely comfortable with the carefree lifestyle. Blanchard wrote, "Margaret was mildly offended when she led a conversation there and the audience sprawled all over the floor, yawned and stretched, and wandered in and out."

Brook Farm disbanded in 1846, due to a costly fire and personal economic stresses, unrelated to the commune, experienced by Ripley. Unlike many hippie communes, Ripley's experiment was not ripped apart by personality clashes. While it didn't produce the utopia hoped for, it was—on the whole—a successful experiment in alternative living. In the May 1894 issue of *New England Magazine*, Arthur Sumner, who was a child at the commune, recalled that "the life was pure, the company choice. There was a great deal of hard work and a great deal of fun,—music, dancing, reading, skating, moonlight walks . . . flirting."

EMERSON AND THOREAU: PHILOSOPHERS OF CHARACTER, CHARACTERS OF PHILOSOPHY

> More than once . . . someone . . . would like to know when
> Henry was going to start making a respectable living.
> How soon was he going to straighten out? Just what was
> he planning to do? These were questions many a Con-
> cord neighbor also asked and kept on asking until the
> end of Thoreau's life.
>
> CARL BODE

> Ah, how I have thriven on solitude and poverty! I cannot
> overstate this advantage.
>
> HENRY DAVID THOREAU

Emerson was a man of great enthusiasm when it came to his fellow philosophers. First Alcott, then Fuller, and even the madman Jones Very— all captivated Emerson for a time and received his extravagant praise. But none astounded the dean of Transcendentalism as much as Thoreau. Soon after they met sometime in 1836–1837, Emerson declared Thoreau "as free and erect a mind as any I have ever met." He started referring to him as "my young David," and Thoreau was soon his favorite partner on his frequent long walks dedicated to working out philosophical ideas. The young Thoreau virtually idolized Emerson in return, writing that "More of the divine is realized in him than in any." In 1841, Thoreau became the only long-term guest ever to stay at the Emerson estate, living there for two years in return for handiwork.

They had both tremendous similarities and tremendous distinctions in temperament. Both men desired distance from worldly involvement, but this desire was counterindicated by an equally prominent urge to tweak authority where it hurts. Emerson's rebellious streak became the subject of public controversy largely as the result of two lectures given at Harvard, the place where Thoreau had earlier told his fellow students to slack off. The first address, delivered to the Phi Beta Kappa society, was called "The American Scholar." According to Blanchard, "Emerson . . . challenge[d] the most sacred assumptions of scholarship itself, placing the individual's own experience above books. . . . It was . . . an assertion . . . of the worth and dignity of the individual as opposed to the heavy, mechanical structure of tradition. . . . While by no means denying the importance of history, Emerson insisted that it was a living organic process." Naturally, the school-folk were profoundly angered.

A year later, invited by a student body already growing restless with religious authoritarianism, Emerson addressed the Harvard Divinity School. As related by Rusk, he told the students that "Christianity has built up an absolute monarchy [in worshiping the personality of Jesus] . . . this is intolerable." His advice was "to go alone, and dare to love God without a mediator." As far as the Divinity School alumni, administrators, and (later, as word spread) a whole host of other Christian believers were concerned, he might as well have brought Satan to the assembly with him. The major Unitarian periodical, *The Christian Examiner,* angrily denounced the talk as "utterly distasteful," and another reviewer condemned Emerson as "an infidel and an atheist."

While the Transcendentalists were enthusiastic about the talk, townsfolk literally frowned on him for years in the aftermath. Samuel Ripley (a cousin of Brook Farm commune leader George Ripley) commented, "The whole band of clergymen have raised their voice against him . . . and the common people . . . look solemn and sad, and roll up their eyes . . . 'Oh, he is a dangerous man.' " Rusk wrote that "Boston conservatives . . . were taught to 'abhor and abominate R. W. Emerson as a sort of mad dog.' " Emerson, far from the timid man of his youth, was unfazed. He commented, "I am only an experimenter . . . I unsettle all things. No facts are to me sacred; none are profane."

If Emerson looked like a "mad dog" to the old guard, Thoreau must have seemed like a psychotic wolf. Within commonly accepted social norms, Emerson might be said to have had an antisocial streak (which he largely overcame), while Thoreau was flat-out antisocial (and liked it that way).

At twenty-one, Emerson wrote in his diary about his own "absence of common sympathies, or even . . . a levity of understanding . . . a sore uneasiness in the company of most men and women, a frigid fear of offending and jealousy of disrespect, an inability to lead and an unwillingness to follow the current conversation . . . [lacking] that good humoured independence and self-esteem which should mark a gentleman." Here, in his youth, Emerson's discomfort among others is expressed in terms of timidity and self-criticism. By contrast, Thoreau, in the words of biographer Milton Meltzer, "simply did not care for people."

Indeed, throughout his life, if Thoreau found a conversation or interaction unrewarding, he would quickly make it clear that he would rather be in solitude. In *Emerson Among the Eccentrics: A Group Portait,* Carlos Baker writes that even among the Transcendentalists, "Thoreau was laconic, biting, laced with ironic humor. . . . Emerson long remembered that, when asked what dish he preferred for dinner, Thoreau tartly answered, 'The nearest.' "

Unlike Emerson, Thoreau never expressed the slightest self-doubt regarding the way he related (or didn't relate) to his fellow humans. Emerson once complained that there was "something military" about Thoreau's stance toward the world, "not to be subdued, manly and able, but rarely tender, as if he did not feel himself except in opposition. He wanted a fallacy to expose . . . required a little sense of victory." Henry James, Sr., wrote that Thoreau "was literally the most child-like, unconscious and unblushing egotist it has ever been my fortune to encounter in the ranks of manhood." In *Walden,* Thoreau wrote, "The greater part of what my neighbors call good, I believe in my soul to be bad, and if I repent anything, it is very likely to be my good behavior."

When Walt Whitman stunned the world with his book *Leaves of Grass* in 1855, Thoreau was one among the many leading Transcendentalists who journeyed to the poet's New York City home to pay tribute. But the magnanimous Whitman was appalled by Thoreau's "inability to appreciate the average life—even the exceptional life: it seemed to me a want of imagination. . . . It was a bitter difference: it was rather a surprise to me to meet in Thoreau such a very aggravated case of superciliousness."

Still, we have the gifts of both Emerson's and Thoreau's writings— nonconformist insights—clearly products of a severe alienation first deeply felt by both men in their teens. Emerson believed "antisocial" outsider types made a peculiar contribution to society by influencing its members to try for something better. He was likely thinking of Thoreau when he wrote, "The uncivil, unavailable man, who is a problem . . . to society . . . whom it . . . must either worship or hate . . . he helps; he puts America and

Europe in the wrong, and destroys the skepticism which says, 'man is a doll, let us eat and drink, 'tis the best we can do,' by illuminating the world." And only a person with some degree of antipathy toward the common man could have crafted such a revolutionary statement as Emerson's "Society everywhere is in conspiracy against the manhood of every one of its members. . . . Whoso would be a man, must be a nonconformist."

Surprisingly, while Emerson had a far more generous public personality, Thoreau—when he was finally coaxed into the public eye for a lecture series—entertained better, displaying a wildly acerbic wit. One reviewer remarked on his "strain of exquisite humor, with a strong undercurrent of . . . satire against the follies of the time." According to this reviewer, Thoreau's listeners were kept "in almost constant mirth."

Emerson and particularly Thoreau found refuge from the human mediocrity around them in nature, and in dreaming a human society that harmonizes with it. Emerson's love of nature produced ecstasies: "In the woods we return to reason and faith. . . . Standing on the bare ground, —my head bathed by the blithe air and uplifted into infinite space,—all mean egotism vanishes. I become a transparent eyeball; I am nothing; I see all; the currents of the Universal Being circulate through me; I am part or parcel of God." Thoreau meanwhile, who went far more deeply into nature, wanted not just to love it but to interrogate it: "I went to the woods because I wished to live deliberately. . . . I wanted to live deep and suck out all the marrow of life, . . . to cut a broad swath and shave close, to drive life into a corner, and reduce it to its lowest terms, and, if it proved to be mean, why then to get the whole and genuine meanness of it, and publish its meanness to the world; or if it were sublime, to know it by experience."

For Thoreau, nature wasn't just a nice place to escape the world. It was a site from which to critique it and complain. In one of his nature meditations, *A Week on the Concord and Merrimack Rivers,* he elegantly represented the contrast between natural and societal life: "Some men are judges these August days, sitting on benches . . . between the seasons and between meals, leading a civil politic life, arbitrating . . . from highest noon till the red vesper sinks into the west. The fisherman, meanwhile, stands in three feet of water, under the same summer's sun, arbitrating . . . between muckworm and shiner, amid the fragrance of water-lilies, mint, and pontederia. . . . Human life is to him very much like a river."

Thoreau also found his literary peers wanting from their disconnection to nature. He wrote, "The poet has come within doors, and exchanged the forest and crag for the fireside . . . [and] for the house of the Englishmen." One can't help but think of Jim Morrison's 1969 statement "We have been transformed from an ecstatic body dancing madly on a hillside into a pair of eyes staring in the dark." At times, Thoreau nearly reminds us of the Taoist hermit "blockheads" in Chapter 4: "I have given myself up to nature. . . . I have spent a couple of years . . . with the flowers chiefly, having none other so binding engagement as to observe when they opened."

In what is perhaps *Walden*'s most prescient passage, Thoreau shows astonishing insight into mediated culture, alleging that a life lived in abstraction might not be living at all. He wrote, "By a conscious effort of the mind we can stand aloof from actions and their consequences. . . . We are not wholly involved in Nature. . . . I *may* be affected by a theatrical exhibition; on the other hand, I *may not* be affected by an actual event which appears to concern me much more. I . . . am sensible of a certain doubleness by which I can stand as remote from myself as from another. However intense my experience, I am conscious of the presence and criticism of a part of me, which . . . is not a part of me, but a spectator, sharing no experience, but taking note of it. . . . When the play . . . of life is over, the spectator goes his way. It was a kind of fiction, a work of the imagination only."

As great a recluse and nature lover as Thoreau was, he didn't seem inclined—like John Zerzan—to return to the hunter-gatherer stage. He was, in fact, quite honest about his pleasure in returning to the comforts of the Emerson home after his two-year Walden experiment. He wrote, "It was a relief to get back to our smooth, but still varied landscape. . . . For a permanent residence, it seems to me that there could be no comparison between this and the wilderness." As with much Transcendentalist work, it is difficult to say what the take-home lesson is here, except that inconclusiveness is part of its countercultural package.

From the view of solemn Calvinist-influenced New England, the Transcendentalists—nature's wildmen and -women—were far too unrestrained. But they were far from hedonistic. In fact, Emerson, Whitman, and others inclined toward sympathy for the temperance movement—

those who were trying to remove alcohol (and in some cases tobacco, coffee, and tea) from public life, although they opposed coercive state legal sanctions. (It's worth noting that alcohol-fueled violence existed at that time on a scale unimaginable to us now, even if we've spent time in Russia.) To the bohemians of his time, Emerson wrote: "If thou fill thy brain with Boston and New York, with fashion . . . and wilt stimulate thy jaded senses with wine and French coffee, thou shalt find no radiance of wisdom in the lonely . . . pinewoods."

Emerson's and Thoreau's aversion toward sexuality is less explicable. How strange it is that radical espousers of the natural life, for all intents and purposes, ignored sexuality in their writings, with the exception of a few occasions when the scandalizers of religious purists were themselves scandalized by erotic expression. And it strikes us stranger still when we consider their hymns to the horny horned god Pan. After all, Thoreau wrote, "In my Pantheon, Pan still reigns in his pristine glory, with his ruddy face, his flowing beard, and his shaggy body." And Emerson exclaimed, "I love the mighty PAN!" But at the time, the former minister was simply feeling overwhelmed by the natural beauty of his new country home.

There was a strong, probably inherited, element of Calvinist purism in both their natures. Emerson was troubled when he first spent time with Margaret Fuller because she made him laugh "more than I liked." According to Bode, Thoreau "could never enter the feminine domain without blushing." These inherent characteristics aside, the Transcendentalists' rejection (or *transcendence?*) of sensuality, like that of the Gnostic Christians, was not a ploy to please an angry dysphoric deity. It was, in fact, in keeping with the primary Transcendentalist objective to hold the ideal, the spiritual, above the material. Emerson philosophized that "The ingenuity of man has always been dedicated to the solution of one problem,—how to detach the sensual sweet, the sensual strong, the sensual bright, &c. from the moral sweet, the moral deep, the moral fair." (Note that moral and spiritual were practically synonymous in the Transcendentalist world.)

Over and above learning to enjoy Margaret Fuller's company, Emerson eventually located a sense of humor of his own—understated but tart: "Nature will not have us fret and fume. . . . When we come out of the caucus, or the bank, or the Abolition convention, or the Temperance meeting, or the Transcendental club into the fields and woods, she says to us, 'So hot, little sir?' "

Clearly, Emerson had some conflicting temperaments. There was the bountiful spirit that wrote, "There can be no excess to love; none to knowledge; none to beauty." And then there was the prissy side that said of Whitman's fleshy and celebratory *Leaves of Grass* (which he otherwise promoted with his typical ebullience), "There are parts of the book where I hold my nose as I read. One must not be too squeamish, when a chemist brings him to a mass of filth and says, 'see the great laws are at work here also'; but it is a fine art if he can deodorize his illustrations."

While Emerson married and had children, Thoreau remained a bachelor all his life. Although he attained some degree of personal intimacy with his fellow Transcendentalists, there is no indication that this often discourteous man ever experienced any sexual intimacy at all. At the risk of passing judgment, it seems like a sad end for a man who wished to "suck out all the marrow of life."

REVOLUTION: YOU BETTER FREE YOUR MIND INSTEAD?

> Each "cause" as it is called,—say Abolition, Temperance, say Calvinism, or Unitarianism,—becomes speedily a little shop, where the article, let it have been at first ever so subtle or ethereal, is now made up into portable and convenient cakes, and retailed in small quantities to suit purchasers.
>
> RALPH WALDO EMERSON

> The worst, the pure transcendentalists, incapable of effective human relations, terrified of responsibility, given to transforming evasion into moral triumph.
>
> ARTHUR M. SCHLESINGER, JR.

> A preacher is a bully.
>
> RALPH WALDO EMERSON

> How does it become a man to behave toward [his] gov-
> ernment to-day? . . . He cannot without disgrace be as-
> sociated with it.
>
> HENRY DAVID THOREAU, *CIVIL DISOBEDIENCE*

The political dynamics of America as it entered the 1830s were similar to the current ones. Ownership and oligarchical power were solidifying into the hands of the wealthy few. A conservative party, the Whigs, represented this status quo. The Democratic Party presumed to represent a populist challenge to the elite, but was compromised and riddled with corrupt personalities. Hope experienced resurgence when Andrew Jackson, a Democrat, emerged as a moderately more bona fide representative of the populists' concerns. Jackson was well loved among artists and writers, but our gang of nonconformists was not enticed. In a historical essay, sixties Kennedy advisor and liberal Democrat Arthur Schlesinger complained:

> The transcendentalists . . . constituted the one impor-
> tant literary group never much impressed by Jacksonian
> democracy. . . . Both Democrats and transcendentalists
> agreed in asserting the rights of the free mind against
> the pretensions of precedents or institutions. Both
> shared a living faith in the integrity and perfectibility of
> man. . . . Both detested special groups claiming au-
> thority to mediate between the common man and the
> truth. "The soul must and will assert its rightful ascen-
> dancy," exclaimed the *Bay State Democrat*, "over all
> those arbitrary and conventional forms which a false
> state of things has riveted upon society." . . .
>
> But transcendentalism in its Concord form was infi-
> nitely individualistic, providing no means for reconcil-
> ing the diverse institutions of different men and deciding
> which was better and which was worse.

In parallel with Andrew Jackson's electoral reformation, a deeper and more radical form of activism was emerging—the abolitionist movement. By the 1830s, Northerners were becoming more vociferous about their moral objections to slavery in the South. Common folks organized to protect escaped slaves (Thoreau's mother among them) and young idealists were spreading a strong anti-slavery message. Meanwhile their political representatives, even liberal Jacksonians, refused to take up the cause.

In a near-mirror image of the 1960s and 1970s, African-American rights and opposition to an imperial foreign war (in this case, with Mexico) would foment political rebellion in tandem with the entire Transcendentalist epoch. And the Transcendentalists' role in those times maps almost precisely to the part the psychedelic hippie culture played in its ambiguous relationship to the activist movement of its time. Our spiritual and cultural revolutionaries found themselves simultaneously a part of—and in conflict with—the political rebellion.

To the extent that the Transcendentalists had politics, they were rife with contradiction, a situation that does *not* contradict the Transcendentalist worldview. Emerson famously wrote, "A foolish consistency is the hobgoblin of little minds." But while this quote can easily be deployed as an excuse for opportunism, for the Transcendentalists—who had no ambitions for power—it was simply a refusal to put logic at the helm, favoring the heart's—or spirit's—truest desires. For example, if the heart that wants a society that respects individual autonomy and self-reliance also wants a society based on love and community, the usual ideological oppositions may not apply. Every situation has to be looked upon fresh and all these ostensibly contrary human needs must be respected.

Harriet Martineau, a British novelist and political radical, was probably the first voice from the "movement" to excoriate the Transcendentalists for being too dropped out—divorced from the important battles of the time—in a magazine piece published in 1837 in England about her visit to America. A passage from her later autobiography, in which she singled out Margaret Fuller for criticism, is representative of her view: "The difference between us is that while she was living and moving in an ideal world, talking in private and discoursing in public about the most fanciful and shallow conceits which the Transcendentalists of Boston took for philosophy, she looked down upon persons who acted instead of talking finely, and devoted their fortunes, their peace, their repose, and their very lives to the preservation of the republic. While Margaret Fuller and her adult pupils sat 'gorgeously dressed,' talking about Mars and Venus, Plato and Goethe, and fancying themselves the elect of the earth in intellect and refinement, the liberties of the republic were running out as fast as they could." Given this picture of opulent leisure-class indulgence, it's worth pointing out that Fuller—like nearly all of the Transcendentalists—had a small income. She lived a hard life, caring for family members, many of whom had a variety of the sorts of serious illnesses (and early deaths) that were an ordinary part of family life at the time. Occasional escapes to the Emerson household and the Brook Farm commune were the exception, not the rule. And, in fact, even at this early point, several women within Fuller's circle of "Conversations" were the leading anti-slavery activists in New England.

As far as we know, all the Transcendentalists sympathized with the abolitionist cause, though, in early times, few were notably active. As a group they believed that personal transformations would remake the world in a manner more to their liking than any political reform ever could. Rusk explained, "Emerson tried characteristically to trace social and economic conflict to its root in private character, [believing] that the greatest of all reforms would be effected by substituting love for selfishness."

Mirroring the attitudes of many counterculturists in the 1960s—including Kesey, Leary, and Lennon—the Transcendentalists experienced the politicos' insistence that there was a moral obligation to make the revolution *their* way as just another attack on their highly prized autonomy. However righteous the cause, activists were like politicians—always trying to tell you what to do. Emerson expressed contempt for their single-minded fanaticism, wisecracking that he found it necessary to "treat the men and women of one idea, the Abolitionist, the Phrenologist, the Swedenborgian, as insane persons." And even after militantly joining the abolitionist voices, Thoreau would declare, "I came into this world not chiefly to make this a good place to live in, but to live in it, be it good or bad," and "I was not born to be forced. I will breathe in my own fashion."

Meanwhile Margaret Fuller, while in full accordance with the abolitionists, focused her energy on the rights of an even larger group that was denied citizenship—women. In an 1843 issue of *The Dial*, Fuller contributed a piece that asserted the absolute equality of women to men and advocated full political and economic entitlement. In contrast to the abolitionists, this required a highly individualized bravery—Fuller was one of a mere handful of Americans to ever suggest such a thing. Blanchard called it "the most radical feminist document yet produced in America." Fuller was almost universally attacked by members of the literary class for her assertion, not just in America but also in Europe (and by women as well as men). Edgar Allan Poe snidely commented that "humanity can be divided into three classes: men, women and Margaret Fuller." Carolyn G. Heilbrun, in her introduction to Blanchard's biography, wrote, "The belief that because Margaret competed intellectually with men she must have hated them was both widespread and untrue, and it provided, as did the notion that she had 'unsexed' herself by her choice of a literary vocation, a convenient excuse for outburst against intellectual women in general. In her own time, Margaret Fuller became a legendary bogeywoman, symbolizing a threat not only to the male ego but to the family, and thus to the social order." The men of the Transcendentalist movement, on the other hand, remained as comfortable with—and supportive of—Fuller as ever.

Realizing she'd struck an important nerve, Fuller went on to organize a set of even more radical observances about gender conflict and oppression into a book titled *Women in the Nineteenth Century*. This time she really provoked the good and decent folk. She critiqued the sacrosanct institution of marriage for reducing women to property (particularly true within the laws of the time) and even questioned absolute gender distinctions, suggesting a kind of natural state of androgyny. And most scandalous of all, she indicated that prostitutes, who suffered lengthy prison terms in those days, were morally superior to, in Blanchard's words, "the flirtatious . . . society belle, who used sex for economic gain." The prostitute, after all, was at least honest with herself about what she was doing. Fuller argued that the oppression of the prostitute quintessentially characterized the way society treated women in general.

In 1846, Thoreau demonstrated his own quirky brand of radical political boldness when—busted for having ignored his taxes for the previous four years—he refused to pay, citing the institution of slavery, the war with Mexico, and beyond that, an almost blithe disinterest in acknowledging state authority. After he spent a single night in prison, and over his objections, a friend paid his taxes and he was released. Brilliant egoist that he was, Thoreau put this rather extemporaneous act of noncompliance into a greater context three years later, when he wrote an essay motivated in no small part by a desire to justify his position. Initially titled "Resistance to Civil Government," it was published in an obscure Transcendentalist journal called *Aesthetic Papers*. But it would live on, under the title of "Civil Disobedience," as one of the most popular statements of anti-authoritarian refusal in the entire protesters' lexicon. Influential activists ranging from Mahatma Gandhi to Martin Luther King to Daniel Ellsberg would attest to its import, and it would become the bible of nonviolent civil rights activists, draft resisters, antiwar protesters, and even some anti-government militia members in America's late twentieth century.

However useful the essay might have been to liberals like Gandhi and King in throwing off the chains of blatant oppression in favor of basic civil rights, for those who took its full message to heart, Thoreau's "Civil Disobedience" was an anarchistic shout of individual autonomy from government in any form. Indeed, Thoreau told us that he declared his personal independence from the state, presenting the town clerk with the statement: "Know all men by these presents, that I, Henry Thoreau, do not wish to be regarded as a member of any incorporated society which I have not joined."

Whether this subversive tome was a full realization of Transcendentalist politics or simply an outburst that's distinctly Thoreauvian, it was so lucidly boisterous that it "made history" in a way that the rest of the group's writings never did, succeeding in giving the movement a decidedly seditious spin for posterity.

The text contains so many audacious anarchist aphorisms that it's worth pausing this narrative to quote several of them:

> I heartily accept the motto,—"That government is best which governs least;" . . . Carried out, it finally amounts to this, which also I believe,—"That government is best which governs not at all;" and when men are prepared for it, that will be the kind of government which they will have.

> I am not responsible for the successful working of the machinery of society.

> When I meet a government which says to me, "Your
> money or your life," why should I be in haste to give it my
> money?

> Unjust laws exist: shall we be content to obey them, or
> shall we endeavor to amend them, and obey them until
> we have succeeded, or shall we transgress them at once?

> I quietly declare war with the State . . . though I will still
> make what use and get what advantage of her I can.

Thoreau used his tax resistance to do two things: separate himself from responsibility for the actions of the state, and make clear to all the good tax-
paying citizens that they in fact *were* responsible for slavery and the war
against Mexico. His ethical stance was not that of the political organizer
advancing blueprints for a different society; it was personal and existential:
"It is not a man's duty . . . to devote himself to the eradication of . . . even
the most enormous wrong . . . but it is his duty . . . to wash his hands of it,
and, if he gives it no thought longer, not to give it practically his support."
And, in the essay, having complained of the government's war and slavery
policies, he ultimately declared, "It is for no particular item in the tax-bill
that I refuse to pay it. I simply wish to refuse allegiance to the State, to
withdraw and stand aloof from it effectually."

Clearly, Thoreau was not the sort of anarchist whom we see organizing
to overthrow the world's governments and replace them with autonomous
collectives operating by democratic consensus—or anything of that sort.
Thoreau didn't idealize the liberation of humanity; rather, he dreamed of
freedom for the few who consciously choose it: "I please myself with imagining a State . . . which . . . would not think it inconsistent with its own repose if a few were to live aloof from it, not meddling with it, not embraced
by it."

Over time, distinctions between the Transcendentalist philosophic
rebels and the abolitionist/reformist political activists began to blur. Again
like the 1960s, it was a ripe time for change, and these forces started
seeing themselves as moving in the same direction. By the early 1840s,

even Horace Greeley, the establishment liberal reformist publisher of the *New York Daily Tribune,* liked to refer to himself as a Transcendentalist—somewhat to Emerson's chagrin.

The enforcement of the much hated but little used Fugitive Slave Law in Boston in 1854, returning a slave to the South, brought a critical mass to the abolitionist movement. Masses of New Englanders rose up in protest. Most of the Transcendentalists, Emerson included, were now completely on board. According to Carlos Baker, "Emerson lost his respect for the authority of his government. . . . He even made tentative attempts to give literary aid to the extremists."

On October 16, 1859, the biblically inspired anti-slavery radical John Brown and twenty-one of his followers, seeking to initiate an armed insurrection against the South, took over the armory and the town of Harpers Ferry, Virginia, holding the residents prisoner until his capture that same day by Robert E. Lee. Brown was swiftly brought to trial and hanged. Such was the tenor of the times that a considerable minority of anti-slavery activists supported Brown. None were more impassioned than Thoreau, who wrote, "I never hear of any particularly brave and earnest man, but my first thought is of John Brown. . . . I meet him at every turn. He is more alive than ever he was. He has earned immortality. . . . He is no longer working in secret. He works in public, and in the clearest light that shines on this land." The Civil War was not far off and the gentle idealism of the Transcendentalist era would be among the innumerable casualties of that epic slaughter.

TRANSCENDENTALISM MEETS THE GANGS OF NEW YORK

> There will soon be no more priests. . . . A superior breed shall take their place. A new order shall arise . . . and every man shall be his own priest.
>
> WALT WHITMAN

> Walt Whitman, an American, one of the roughs, a kosmos.
>
> WALT WHITMAN

In the 1830s, while the Transcendentalists were cultivating their love of God, nature, and one another, a rough-and-ready working-class bohemianism took root in New York City and other major urban areas. This inchoate rebellion against the ugly realities of the new industrial economy was labeled "loaferism" by New York City's tabloid press, and the participants called themselves b'hoys and g'hals. These were alienated young toughs—punks, in a very real sense—and they disregarded the Protestant work ethic, dedicating themselves instead to low-level crime, romance, looking sharp, and the fine art of hanging out. David Reynolds, author of *Walt Whitman's America*, writes,

> The b'hoy grew from urban popular culture and fed back into it. The source of the figure . . . [was] popular plays based on British author Pierce Egan's urban sketches *Life in London* . . . [based on] streetwise young men who toured the city in a picaresque fashion. . . .
>
> The b'hoy and the g'hirl had their own dress and habits. The b'hoy clipped his hair short in back, kept his long sidelocks greased with soap, and perched a stovepipe hat jauntily on his head. He always had a cigar or chaw of tobacco in his mouth. He wore a red shirt fastened to one side with large white buttons, a black silk tie knotted carelessly under a rolling collar, and trousers that flared slightly over high-heeled calfskin boots. The g'hal wore colorful multilayered clothes, carried a parasol on her shoulders and walked with a swing and a smirk. . . . They loved . . . Shakespeare.

Before becoming the world-famous poet laureate of generous American visions, Walt Whitman was very much a gruff, urban, radical reformist newspaper journalist and editor. Tabloid journalism was the order of the day and Whitman loved it, considering it people's journalism and using it as a platform to denounce the ruling class of his time. Whitman was on the periphery of the b'hoy scene as a journalist who romanticized the b'hoys into a poetic vision of insouciance. In an 1840 essay, he wrote, "Whilst he puffs the smoke of a remarkably bad segar directly underneath your nostrils, he will discourse most learnedly about the classical performances in the Chatham Theater." In another 1840 essay, the b'hoys evoked in Whitman what could pass for an urban version of Thoreau's slackerly ethic: "I have sometimes amused myself with picturing a nation of loafers. . . . Only think of it! an entire loafer kingdom! Adam was a loafer, and so were all the philosophers."

Whitman's youthful experience in rugged urban rebellion was light-years from the genteel spiritual dissidence of New Englanders like Alcott, Emerson, and Fuller, and he was unknown to them throughout their most vital years. But in 1855, within weeks of its publication, Emerson picked up a copy of Whitman's *Leaves of Grass,* one of the many books of poems that were constantly foisted upon him.

His mind was blown. Never could he have imagined that Transcendentalist spiritual exhilaration could be married to such a loving embrace of humanity in all its rude chaos and fleshy appetite. To one friend, he wrote that it was "extraordinary for its oriental largeness . . . an American Buddh[a]." He wrote to Whitman, calling the book "America's most extraordinary piece of wit & wisdom," and advocated Whitman's book to all who would listen.

While Whitman had been much influenced by Emerson's essays, *Leaves of Grass* was the sort of innovation in form that Emerson had suggested but never achieved. Combining poetry and prose, ignoring all existing rules, Whitman's book arguably introduced "free verse" into the world. He also infused his poems with common language and street slang. A prominent reviewer called Whitman "a compound of New England transcendentalist and New York rowdy."

In part, *Leaves of Grass* paid poetic tribute to a fertile but underappreciated poor, outsider culture that was, in Reynolds' words, made up of "The slang-whanging orators who jousted with their audiences. . . . The black-face minstrels who parodied polite culture in free flowing, disjointed songs. The native humorists. . . . The spirit-rappers, free lovers, mesmerists, and trance poets who paraded their odd marvels."

Another Whitman innovation was one that Emerson and a few other Transcendentalists could not abide. *Leaves of Grass* included blatantly erotic passages, including implicit bisexuality. After shocked reactions from fellow New Englanders who could not understand how Emerson could embrace this "filth," he reconsidered and had to admit that he was not comfortable with the ribald aspect of the work. Emerson's esprit de corps with Whitman was also cooled when Whitman quoted Emerson's personal complimentary note on the back cover of a reprint of *Leaves of Grass* without asking permission.

These differences in style and disposition illustrate what made Whitman in some sense the untamed runaway son of Transcendentalism. He took the Transcendentalists' philosophical divergence several giant steps further from Calvinism. Whitman wrote and lived out a joie de vivre that Emerson in some ways only expressed in the abstract. His freedom from puritanical restraint allowed room for a bighearted generosity that let him see God in the outcasts, the prostitutes, and the riffraff. This same natural ease permitted him to enjoy sex and fame. The Transcendentalists had overthrown self-denial in the spiritual and philosophical realm. Whitman echoed their cause, and brought it also into the sensual realm. His "Song of Myself" still stands as one of literature's greatest shouts of unfettered self-affirmation. It provided a model for Allen Ginsberg's "Howl." Tracing this historical line, Whitman may just be the singularly most important literary forefather of "the counterculture" as we know it today.

DISSIPATION

Whitman, like Ginsberg and Burroughs, became an established celebrity, accepted by a broad public that ignored his message but admired his fame and success. A popular cigar was named after him, and that ultimate American greedhead J. P. Morgan became a financial sponsor. The Transcendentalist movement itself dissipated with the terror of the Civil War and the death of its original proponents. But thanks to their efforts, succeeding generations would find it eminently easier to question religious dogma and state authority.

CHAPTER TEN

⊢ BRILLIANT STORMS
OF LAUGHTER

Bohemian Paris, 1900–1940

Tonight deftly amid wild drink and talk, to pierce the
polished mail of his mind. What then? A jester at the
court of his master, indulged and disesteemed, winning
a clement master's praise. Why had they chosen all that
part? Not wholly for the smooth caress. For them too
history was a tale like any other too often heard, their
land a pawnshop.

JAMES JOYCE, *ULYSSES*

She [Josephine Baker] made her entry entirely nude except for a pink flamingo feather between her limbs; she
was being carried upside down and doing the split on
the shoulder of a black giant. . . . She was an unforget-
table female ebony statue. A scream of salutations
spread through the theater.

JANET FLANNER

Our father who is in heaven, please stay there.

JACQUES PRÉVERT

By the start of the twentieth century, Paris had already established itself as the spot where the most radical and innovative artistic offspring of the European romantic trope gathered. During the previous century, Gustave Flaubert had expanded the scope of the novel by introducing multiple points of view. Paul Cessna had done for painting what Flaubert had done for writing, bringing a new dimensionality and multiplicity into the visual realm. The Impressionists—led by Frenchmen like Monet and Renoir—completed an evolution away from strict reproduction in painting, privileging the artist's inner eye. Paul Gauguin had gone native in Tahiti—his brightly colored paintings brought a kind of exuberance that discreet, civilized Westerners found too extravagant. Eternal counterculture hero Arthur Rimbaud had tried to overthrow reality itself with an aggressively visionary, declamatively anarchic, densely imaged free-verse poetry that exploded with a lust for illumination and an anger at dreary daily existence with all the energy of a literary nuke. Charles Baudelaire, among others, had experimented with opium and hashish, allowing the effects to infect their visionary poetics.

Besides establishing the pursuit of novelty as an important element in the arts, nineteenth-century French artists had evolved a bohemian café society characterized by impoverished, hang-out bonhomie, mental stimulation, and distortion through drugs and alcohol, the free pursuit of sexual pleasures (often in the easily accessible brothels of the time), and tendencies toward both personal and political nonconformity. If these characteristics had long been present in many if not most artistic temperaments, nineteenth-century France cemented the image into the popular culture of the West, bestowing on artists a sort of special permission to be naughty and eccentric that has functioned ever since as both a liberty and a trap.

In the first four decades of the twentieth century, this Parisian artistic bohemia exploded into something that bordered on a mass movement. Literally hundreds of artists, writers, and world historic characters whose innovative works (and, in some cases, challenging personas) still resonate today passed through the portals of what literary historian Donald Pizer has labeled "The Paris Moment." For example: Jean Arp, Isadora Duncan, Chaim Soutine, Anaïs Nin, Vladimir Lenin, Juan Gris, Francis Picabia, Jean Cocteau, Joan Miró, Jean-Paul Sartre, Lawrence of Arabia, Claude Monet, W. H. Auden, Robert Desnos, Pablo Picasso, Georges Braque,

Archibald MacLeish, F. Scott and Zelda Fitzgerald, Jacques Villon, e. e. cummings, René Daumal, Rudolph Valentino, André Breton, Amedeo Modigliani, Sergei Eisenstein, Aleister Crowley, T. S. Eliot, Theodore Dreiser, Stéphane Mallarmé, Stephen Spender, Pierre-Auguste Renoir, Sherwood Anderson, Yves Tanguy, Alexander Calder, E. M. Forster, Edgard Varèse, André Gide, George Gershwin, Hugo Ball, John Dos Passos, Erik Satie, Philippe Soupault, Luis Buñuel, Tristan Tzara, Max Jacob, Malcolm Cowley, William Carlos Williams, Salvador Dalí, Sylvia Beach and Adrienne Monnier, Emma Goldman, René Magritte, André Masson, James Joyce, Henri Michaux, Simone de Beauvoir, Samuel Beckett, Edmund Wilson, Mina Loy, Edna St. Vincent Millay, Sinclair Lewis, René Crevel, Ernest Hemingway, King Vidor, Man Ray, Henri Matisse, Henry Miller, Constantin Brancusi, Thomas Wolfe, Leon Trotsky, Max Oppenheimer, George Antheil, Georges Bataille, Giorgio De Chirico, Igor Stravinsky, Thornton Wilder, Sarah Bernhardt, Ezra Pound, Marc Chagall, Marcel Duchamp, Ford Madox Ford, Sergei Diaghilev, Virgil Thomson, Christopher Isherwood, Aaron Copland, Henri Rousseau, Harry and Caresse Crosby, Gertrude Stein and Alice B. Toklas, Josephine Baker, Vaslav Nijinsky, Natalie Barney, Antonin Artaud, Louis Aragon, Paul Eluard, Djuna Barnes, Maurice Ravel, Paul Valéry, Lawrence Durrell, and Max Ernst.

Many of you are likely experiencing a powerful frisson just from reading the above list of people who—whether briefly or extensively, lightly or deeply—touched down in Paris during this fertile period, making contact with some element(s) of the boho scene. As Dan Franck, author of the historical work *Bohemian Paris: Picasso, Modigliani, Matisse, and the Birth of Modern Art,* wrote, "Paris . . . [had] become the capital of the world. On the pavements, there would no longer be a handful of artists . . . but hundreds, thousands of them. It was an artistic flowering of a richness and quality never to be rivaled. . . . Painters, poets, sculptors, and musicians, from all countries, all cultures, classical and modern, met and mingled."

This daemonic convergence was fostered by any number of elements. At the start of the century, a period of peace and harmony among nations allowed for travel and emigration with minimal trouble. Life in Paris was inexpensive and the travel industry (by ship) had grown in size to accommodate middle-class and even relatively poor passengers. International postal services had matured, allowing the wayfarer to communicate back home within a matter of weeks. The newspaper and magazine industry had grown. The distribution of daily papers and monthly magazines, with reporters stationed all around the so-called çivilized world (and to a lesser extent, the colonized world), penetrated every nook and cranny of advanced nations, where they trumpeted romantic fantasies of a free and stylish lifestyle on Paris' Left Bank to receptive minds as far away as Japan, Russia, and the boondocks of the U.S.A. In the 1910s, a vaccination against typhoid decreased the risks involved in travel, and by the 1920s, the automobile was bringing continental Europe closer together. Finally, the population had grown. There were just a whole heck of a lot more people on the globe, so naturally, that percentage of the population prone toward artistic sensitivity, neophilia, and scene-making used the available means to converge on the hot spot of the moment: Paris, France.

CUBISM AND THE AVANT-GARDE BEFORE THE "GREAT WAR"

Almost as if to announce that LSD was expected to make its entrance by mid-century, twentieth-century painting began with a wild splash of bright colors. Influenced by Gauguin, the Fauvists (including a young Henri Matisse) began displaying works that employed riotously vivid colors in 1904 Paris. They were immediately denounced as "savages" by most art aficionados, but the race for novelty—already a developing art trope of nineteenth-century Paris—was now in full force.

The inspiration for the century's big breakthrough had a decidedly "modern primitivist" flavor. In 1907, the expatriate Spanish painter Pablo Picasso was transfixed by an exhibition of African art in Paris. Experimenting with his own interpretation of what he had seen, he came up with the notion of segmenting the human face into large interlocking cubes. The resulting painting, *Les Demoiselles d'Avignon,* was named after a whorehouse. By taking apart the face, the very site of human representation, Picasso had succeeded in revealing the distortion of personality and psyche that was street prostitution. The disjunctive nature of the painting also seemed to say something about the fragmentative nature of speedy urban life, and suggested Freud's assertion that human consciousness itself was segmented into the conscious and the unconscious: the ego, the id, and the superego. The painting also might have been indicating a difficult aspect of the very novelty-seeking behavior Picasso was engaged in. The pursuit of constant change shatters homeostasis, the calm sameness that comes with knowing what to expect in life. In any case, the surface of painting (and thus, suggestively, human consciousness) had been blurred by the Impressionists, and distorted by the Fauvists, but it had never been smashed to bits and reconstructed, a strikingly twentieth-century notion that still dominates contemporary aesthetics.

As so frequently occurs during periods of invention and innovation, while Picasso was working out his new visual language, both Henri Matisse and Georges Braque were working along parallel lines.

After their early Cubist works fractured the visual space of the canvas, Picasso and Braque decided to expand their revolutionary assault. Dan Franck writes,

> The works of analytic cubism (principally the paintings of Picasso and Braque between 1910 and 1912) aim to represent time as well as space. By combining several angles of vision in one painting, the artist is in effect rendering several moments in time—the time necessary to move the perceiving eye of the viewer from angle to angle—as a single movement in space. The cubist painter has overturned the conventional barrier between the depiction of time and the depiction of space— the convention which held that some arts are spatial, others temporal—and has also suggested the artificiality of the conventional notion of the absolutes of clock time by rendering two moments of time as simultaneously existent in the consciousness of the perceiver of an object.

Cubism was, of course, named by a hostile critic. Indeed, the initial response to Cubism was broadly negative. Most of the presumably open-minded fans of Impressionism and Fauvism had the same complaint—the paintings were "ugly." The painters, who at that point survived on the edge of poverty, had difficulty, briefly, selling their work. Commercial viability was helped along when Picasso completed a Cubist portrait of American expatriate, writer, and scene hostess Gertrude Stein. The notoriously self-involved Stein displayed the painting prominently in her famous rue de Fleurus home, which was a community nexus point for artists, writers, art dealers, and art buyers. Stein and the artists conspired in a series of deft theatrical maneuvers for the benefit of some unwitting art collectors that eventually convinced some of them that the paintings were the trend du jour. The collectors, who walked away with original Picassos for a few weeks' lunch money, would get the last laugh. The paintings would prove to be more economically valuable than anyone in the early part of the century could begin to imagine.

The works of Picasso, Braque, and Matisse inspired a host of other artists, and in 1912, the gallery La Boetie in Paris hosted a Cubist exhibition that included paintings by Jacques Villon, Francis Picabia, and a youthful Marcel Duchamp. Picasso and Braque did not participate in the showing, condescending that the Cubist followers were mere imitators. Later, the painters' art dealer, Daniel-Henry Kahnweiler, would *forbid* them to show in Parisian art galleries. He wanted to create a sense of exclusivity that would increase the already high asking price for their paintings, which, meanwhile, were on display in galleries in Germany and England. Thus, due to mercenary interests, the works of Picasso and a number of other avant-garde artists were isolated from the countercultural community throughout the glory days of Paris' mass bohemian hubbub.

The open and generous sharing of information is, of course, a primary countercultural trope, one that political revolutionaries, consciousness/spiritual explorers, and philosophers generally find convivial. Artists and writers, on the other hand, make their living from "information" and find themselves in the ironic situation of erecting boundaries (in effect, turnstiles) around boundary-defying works. Pablo Picasso personified an interesting type, one that appeared frequently among artists in the twentieth century. He was, on the one hand, influenced by both anarchism and communism. But he reserved a greater passion for his own career, his fame, and his money. This caused some separation between the pioneer of twentieth-century avant-garde aesthetics and his earlier associates. But it's doubtful that this caused him much pain. At the level of fame he achieved, new friends and sycophants (not to mention lovers) were easily found.

If Picasso's Cubist paintings were publicly inaccessible outside of Stein's famous soirees, the man himself was no recluse. The lives of the artists of bohemian Paris before the "Great War" (World War I) were a blur of bars, cafés, and house parties that not even the ever-present elements of competitive jealousy could suppress. Picasso's posse included Max Jacob, a generous and highly emotional poet and painter who was usually out of his mind on a combination of drink, opium, and ether, and the great experimental poet Guillaume Apollinaire.

They caroused and drank together, frequenting all the Left Bank bars, many of which were dens of political anarchism. (To get a sense of Paris in the 1910s, one must note that *Le Merle blanc,* a wickedly satirical weekly newspaper with anarchist leanings, sold 800,000 copies every week.) They were honored guests at Stein's weekly open house parties, where they interacted with the rest of the Paris art community, including Picasso's friendly rival Matisse. And they experimented with opium and hashish together, although the ambitious Picasso quickly lost interest in extended periods of ego confusion.

In the mid-1910s, a bar called Rotonde became the hangout for the French boho painter set. It was also popular with Russian revolutionaries visiting or exiled in Paris. Both Lenin and Trotsky were in Paris during this time, and witnesses claimed that they dropped into the Rotonde a few times. Imagining the scenario, Franck also effectively portrays the spirit of the times: "Picturing Lenin, Trotsky . . . and a collection of . . . Bolsheviks in the middle of the smoky dining room of the Rotonde, surrounded by the vapours of ether and cocaine, rather stretches the imagination. But it is enjoyable to think that the Russians might have encountered Modigliani howling his antimilitarist slogans, Soutine grumbling, naked beneath his coat, and Derain . . . manufacturing little cardboard planes skillfully aimed to fall straight into these gentlemen's coffee cups."

Besides Stein, the passionate Apollinaire was the glue that held the community together. A transplanted Italian, he had adapted to his new home, France, with a patriotism that his French friends were busy rejecting. Nevertheless, he was universally loved as a very catholic supporter of all the avant-garde trends of early-twentieth-century Paris, advocating and explaining over the years on behalf of the Cubists, and later, the Theater of the Absurd, the Dadaists, and pretty much any group or individual who showed talent and a sincere willingness to take risks and challenge conformity.

Picasso, Modigliani, the unworldly Chaim Soutine, Matisse, Apollinaire, Braque, Duchamp—many of the prewar avant-gardists would go on to achieve varying degrees of fame and financial security, but a world war, combined with this very success, would interrupt the cohesiveness of the boho scene. Soon after the war, Apollinaire died. In *The Autobiography of Alice B. Toklas,* Stein wrote, "The death of Guillaume Apollinaire at this time made a very serious difference to all his friends apart from their sorrow at his death. It was the moment just after the war when many things had changed and people naturally fell apart. Guillaume would have been a bond of union, he always had a quality of keeping people together, and now that he was gone everybody ceased to be friends."

Extreme Measures: Dada and the Postwar Avant-Garde

Dada was born of a revolt that was shared by all adolescents.

Tristan Tzara

Beauty must be convulsive or not at all.

André Breton

The sudden collapse of European political equilibrium into the horrors of World War I caught the French boho scene unawares. Some joined the war effort, while others protested in the spirit of anarchism, or pacifism, or simple humaneness. The war was a slaughter unlike any witnessed by humanity up to that point. More than eight million people were killed. With no clear aggressor, the conflagration was sort of like a barroom brawl writ large. The democracies of Europe and the United States tried to sell it as a war to save civilization. The sentiment that spread through the boho community in Paris was precisely opposite. Many writers and artists viewed the war as proof that civilization had failed, and that the sweet reason posited by the Enlightenment had only served to muzzle expressions of the subconscious (conveniently discovered by Freud half a decade earlier), which had finally erupted with a volcanic fury. Disciplined uniformed psychos marching in long straight rows under orders to kill and be killed had unleashed more unholy chaos than the disorderly artists of Paris could have ever imagined or, certainly, wished for. If logic, discipline, and bourgeois refinement produced this bloody insanity, then the only way out was irrationality, disobedience, and provocation.

Enter Dada.

Dadaism, a deliberate nonsense term, was the opening shout of an *anti*-art movement that aimed to make all-out war on cultural formality and constraint. In his first Dadaist Manifesto, the poet Tristan Tzara wrote, "Dada is our intensity; it erects bayonets without consequence . . . Dada is art without slippers or parallel . . . we know in our wisdom that our heads will become soft cushions . . . it's still shit but we now want to shit in many colours, to decorate the zoological garden of art with all the flags of the consulates do do bong hibo aho hiho aho."

The Dadaists got their start in, of all places, Zurich, Switzerland, at an avant-garde art club called Cabaret Voltaire toward the end of the war. Artists would gather to read poetry and speak nonsense, to bang out rhythms, shout, howl, and indulge in random, formless song and dance. This cacophony, they felt, was the only artistic statement that remained possible amidst the war. Tzara wrote, "The new artist protests. He doesn't paint anymore." One day Cabaret Voltaire organizer Hugo Ball announced that he was starting a small magazine called *Dada*. Tristan Tzara was struck by the word and began constructing nonsense poetics in its name. Dadaism was born.

While the Dadaists were ready to flush art history in its entirety down the toilette, they did acknowledge one great inspiration from the recent past: Alfred Jarry. Jarry may still qualify as the most eccentric artist the world has ever known. He first gained notice in Paris in 1896 when a play he wrote opened with an actor crying "Merdre!" (a Jarryesque mutation of the word *merde*, meaning "shit"). The shocked late-nineteenth-century audience rose to its feet as one in horror. Clearly, they were ill prepared for the twentieth century.

Jarry was a prankster and practical joker who was always firing off his beloved gun in public (albeit not at persons); his greatest (and most famous) prank was his staging of that play, *Ubu Roi*. The play centered around a thoroughly revolting, gluttonous, obscenity-spewing, and spontaneously murderous character who, at the same time, displays all the pomposity and self-righteousness of a man of political or economic power. While the opening performance in 1896 caused a riot, the play was well received by many elements of the European intelligentsia. Reviewers compared Jarry to Shakespeare and Rabelais. The respected literary journal *Vers et Prose* called the play "one of the masterpieces of French genius." But *Ubu Roi* was not written by Jarry. It was a joke, written collectively a few years previous, by a small group of sixteen-year-old students, Jarry among them. (He was, in fact, only a minor contributor.) They were making fun of their physics professor (who, as fate would have it, eventually became a reactionary political figure). The students' parody of their pompous and authoritarian teacher was praised by leading intellectuals, who credited Jarry for what they took to be a coruscating caricature of figures like Robespierre and Napoleon. Jarry's confusing of authorship was an intentional prank, not merely an act of exploitation. Jarry himself allowed for ambiguity when questioned about it, and his fellow ex-students enjoyed the joke well enough to play along.

The Ubu Roi character was pure id, and Jarry became obsessed with the freeing potentials of his antisocial behaviors. Franck: "He strode about on the stage of his life as a copy of this character. . . . He scandalized the habitués of fashionable drawing rooms with his provocation, his insolence, and . . . with conduct which brandished the banner of libertarianism and anarchism rejecting the plush chairs of official academies." André Breton, soon to become the dominant force in Surrealism: Son of Dada, said, "Starting with Jarry, much more than Wilde, the distinction long deemed necessary between art and life was blurred until it was finally abolished."

As with many authentic pranks, the prankster's ego took perhaps the hardest hit. Jarry's lifelong acting out of the Ubu Roi persona had both the character of liberation and of resignation. He would often complain that this casual joke of a cabal of high school wags was by far his most popular work. Even his brilliant invention of an imaginary "science" he named pataphysics, a methodology for examining reality using paradoxes and anomalies as points of departure, never quite received the acclaim *Ubu Roi* did (although "pataphysical" was later name-dropped in Paul McCartney's Beatles song "Maxwell's Silver Hammer").

Soon after the "Great War," Tristan Tzara migrated to Paris, where he joined forces with a band of poetic insurgents including Louis Aragon, Philippe Soupault, and the forcefully charismatic André Breton. Tzara had written that "dada was born of a need for independence, a distrust of the community," and Franck asserts that the Dadaists' project meant "No more groups. No more theories. Down with the cubists and the futurists: they were nothing but 'laboratories of formalist ideas.' " Of course, the Dadaists *were* a group.

No problem. Tzara had nothing but contempt for anyone seeking explication. Dada poet Francis Picabia wrote, "Dada itself feels nothing, it is nothing, nothing, nothing./It is like your hopes: nothing./like your heavens: nothing./like your gods: nothing./like your politicians, nothing./like your heroes: nothing./like your artists: nothing."

Aspects of Dadaism suggest a sort of angry European version of radical Taoism. The Taoists gently teased the grasping, categorizing, limiting, logical mind with jokes, riddles, and meditative exercises. The Dadaists impatiently threw cultural Molotov cocktails over the psychic barricades at the anal-retentive Europeans. The Dadaists' weapons in this war against civilized thought were nihilistic poetry, pranks, absurd theatrical events, name-calling, and most of all, assaultive invasions of Parisian artistic events that were deemed just a bit too stuffy and self-important. Picasso, for one, was denounced as "an old soldier who had died upon the field of honor"—in other words, once radical but now sterile. (He would later become friends with the Surrealists.)

A typical Dada event is described by Franck:

> On 26 May 1920, the Dada Festival was held in the Salle Gaveau. . . . All the dadaists would have their hair shaved in public. The show would not only be on the stage, thanks to MM. Aragon, Breton, Éluard, Fraenkel, Soupault and Tzara, but also in the audience, which would, it was hoped, be large and quarrelsome.
>
> Tzara opened the show by exhibiting "Le sex de Dada," an enormous wooden phallus balanced on some balloons. Then the "famous illusionist" Philippe Soupault appeared, made up to look like a black man, wearing a dressing gown and armed with a cutlass. He

> freed five balloons on which were written the identities
> of those who were flying high, balloons which had to
> be burst, a pope . . . a man of war . . . a statesman . . . a
> woman of letters . . . and [effete poet] Cocteau, the first
> to die, pierced by the blade of the surrealist poet. . . . In
> the audience there was pandemonium.

Unless one is seeking a sort-of Taoist illumination—or succeeds in overthrowing all that is tight-assed in Western civilization—anti-art, by its nature, can only carry you so far. After a few provocations, what was there really to do? (Many decades later, Marcel Duchamp would solve this conundrum by abandoning art to dedicate his life to chess.) In 1922, grasping these limitations, the ambitious Breton pronounced Dada dead, and announced the advent of Surrealism. (A personality clash with Tzara supplied added motivation.) Surrealism (the term had been casually invented by Apollinaire a few years earlier to describe a theatrical presentation) was basically Dadaism-plus. Breton's redirection was to proclaim a purpose—give art a reason to go on. According to Surrealism, the artist's job was to give expression to the unexpurgated, uncensored unconscious.

Breton's pronunciamento would cast a long shadow. Hundreds (maybe thousands) of reputable artists and writers—ranging from Man Ray to Salvador Dalí to the poet García Lorca to the popular English comedy troupe Monty Python's Flying Circus—would get to hawk their wares under the sign of Surrealism through the remainder of the twentieth century. Surrealism would eventually become just another genre in the twentieth century's media spectacle, irreverent but hardly revolutionary.

But in the Parisian 1920s, the Surrealists were still carrying forward all the elements of the Dada insurrection. And now they were organized, thanks to André Breton's nasty authoritarian tendencies. (Salvador Dalí would later write that Breton was "as rigid as St. Andrew's cross.") Breton's imagination had been fired up by Lenin's successful Bolshevik revolution. Wishing to get in on the fun in his own antic way, he started sponsoring trials and eventually "purges" against other participants in the Surrealist movement. Initially, the trials, over which Breton would rule, had an appropriately playful "Alice through the looking-glass" quality. They were nonsensical and ludicrous, comprehensible only as a sort of parody of Communist Party discipline. But underneath the delirium, Breton meant it, and eventually the Pope of Surrealism's excommunicational activities would become hurtful.

Still, we must credit this alpha leader from Deliria for having the skills necessary to rally the Surrealists to continue the program of Dada disturbance throughout the 1920s. Most of his Surrealist compatriots, such as Man Ray and Max Ernst, would likely have been content to hang out, as they frequently did, sniffing cocaine and making word and image collages. But when Breton called his minions to battle, they showed up—out of respect, no doubt—but also out of a desire to avoid a Bretonian hissy fit, if not Surreal excommunication. Perhaps this relationship is illustrative of a prime countercultural irony—however anarchic and hang-loose the philosophy may be, there has to be at least one poor anxious bastard prodding things along, or the cultural movement dissipates into historical irrelevance (which might also be okay from a certain countercultural perspective, but then what would I be writing about?).

One of the most famous Surrealist provocations seems to have been spontaneous and situational. In July 1925, the Surrealists were invited to attend a formal banquet sponsored by *Les Nouvelles littéraires* for all its contributors. While many Surrealists wrote for it, this was a mainstream literary journal that featured many of France's most distinguished "men of letters." The Surrealists were well behaved as the dinner party proceeded, until the conservative Madame Rachilde was overheard saying, "A Frenchwoman should never marry a German." Appalled at this xenophobia, Breton rose to his feet and told the woman, "What you have said is extremely insulting to our friend Max Ernst." As Franck tells it,

> An apple flew through the air, then another. Breton . . . threw a napkin in Rachilde's face, crying, "Soldier's whore!"
> The battle was on. On every side, food flew. The platter of fish in cream sauce was a catapult, and everything served as ammunition: the fresh vegetables, the silverware, the wine, the glasses, the plates. . . .

Philippe Soupault took a deep breath, grabbed on to
the chandelier, hung there and swung from it, kicking
out at everyone who passed. Rushing in from a neighboring room, Louis de Gonzague Frick threw himself in
turn on the surrealists. André Breton pushed open a
window, shattering it. A crowd had gathered on the
pavement. Max Ernst cupped his hands and shouted,
"Down with Germany!"

Michael Lieris answered, "Down with France!"

"Long live China!" someone shouted.

"Long live the Africans!" cried someone else.

According to Franck, this "was a great scandal. The next day, the whole
of the press lashed out at the surrealists, accusing them of being 'the
terrors of the Boulevard Montparnasse.' The Society of Men of Letters
and the Writers' Association of Former Combatants, in conjunction with
L'Action français, requested the names of these men never be mentioned
again, so as to cut them off from public view for good." Nothing of the
sort would occur. Surrealist outrages sold newspapers.

As disturbing as Breton's power tripping might seem, he was still too
much of an anarchist at heart to ever realize his dreams of unifying Surrealism with the international Communist Party. When a party comrade
asked him when the Surrealists were going to be ready for the *real* revolution, Breton shot back that the Communist Party didn't have a monopoly
on revolution and that his subjective transformation was just as essential as
their political revolution.

No discussion of Surrealism would be complete without mention of
Antonin Artaud. Artaud fell into the Surrealist circle during its early years.
A French poet, dramatist, actor, and student of magic and the occult, Artaud would become perhaps the twentieth century's most unabashed apol-
ogist for opium, and he would write lyrically about his peyote experience
(he asserted that his hours spent high on peyote were the only time he ever
felt at home in this world). Breton excommunicated him from Surrealism
in the mid-1920s for his "mystical tendencies." But Artaud's most creative
period was ahead of him. Influenced by Oriental theater, he developed
"the Theater of Cruelty," the first art theory that explicitly attempted to

break the proscenium between actor and audience. Artaud wrote that his theater would also "break through language in order to touch life." He envisioned in theater the release of such magical potency that the participants' bodies themselves would be transformed and their immortal nature unveiled.

According to actor Jean-Louis Barrault, "Artaud oozed magical desires. He was the metaphysician of the theatre." Insisting on the literally magical transformative power of art, he deeply explored the metaphysics underlying his work. And like Jarry's, his disregard for social convention was total. In the 1930s, Artaud's work began to show an obsession with his own (sensed) persecution, and he spent ten years (1937–1946) in a French mental institution (not a bad choice, actually, considering that he got to sit out World War II). A program of fifty-one electroshock treatments could not change Artaud's view that society sucked. After his release in 1946, he wrote his most furious, yet cogent and transcendent, essays, including "Van Gogh: The Suicide of Society," and performed a radio broadcast titled *To Have Done with the Judgment of God*. He died of cancer in 1948.

JOYCE, POUND, AND BEACH CONSPIRE TO LET THE RIVER OF THE MIND FLOW FREE

> In Sylvia Beach's bookshop, *Ulysses* lay stacked like dynamite in a revolutionary cellar.
>
> CYRIL CONNOLLY

Joyce has attempted—it seems to me, with astonishing success—to show how the screen of consciousness with its ever-shifting kaleidoscopic impressions carries, as it were on a plastic palimpsest, not only what is in the focus of each man's observation of the actual things about him, but also in a penumbral zone residua of past impressions, some recent and some drawn up by association from the domain of the subconscious. He shows how each of these impressions affects the life and behavior of the character which he is describing.

What he seeks to get is not unlike the result of a

> double or, if that is possible, a multiple exposure on a
> cinema film which would give a clear foreground with
> a background visible but somewhat blurred and out of
> focus in varying degrees.
>
> JOHN M. WOOLSEY, UNITED STATES DISTRICT JUDGE,
> DECEMBER 6, 1933

> History, Stephen said, is a nightmare from which I am
> trying to awake.
>
> JAMES JOYCE, ULYSSES

In 1919, shortly after World War I, Sylvia Beach, a young, attractive, independent-minded American woman who had come to Paris to study experimental poetry, opened up a bookstore on the Left Bank called Shakespeare and Company, inspired and supported by her female lover, Adrienne Monnier, whose own Parisian bookstore, La Maison des Amis des Livres, regularly hosted poetry readings, musical recitations, and other literary gatherings. Beach's bookstore and lending library became the most important literary center in Paris for the next two decades, serving nearly every great literary name of the time, including Ezra Pound, Ernest Hemingway, T. S. Eliot, Thornton Wilder—and most of all, the Irish genius James Joyce.

It was a time of transition for Paris' artistic bohemia. Apollinaire was dead. Picasso had adopted the middle-class life of a successful married man and was detected only occasionally in the Left Bank bars and cafés. The Dadaists had imported their frenzy from Switzerland, but most of the French avant-garde, which had been under the spell of Cubism, was still trying to find its legs in the war's aftermath. Paris bohemia needed new blood. In 1920, it arrived. Ezra Pound, an American who had been a vigorous organizer of a dynamic literary scene in England, had convinced James Joyce to join him in Paris. Word got out, and a year later, Ernest Hemingway, Malcolm Cowley, Sherwood Anderson, and Thornton Wilder joined the expatriate flow.

A generous poet who lived to serve the literary avant-garde and its writers, Pound lost little time bringing this new community together, sponsoring readings, events, and informal gatherings, frequently with

Beach's collaboration. In *Sylvia Beach and the Lost Generation,* Noel Riley Fitch writes, "Pound helped to draw many younger writers to Paris. Although . . . poor himself, he lent them money or solicited it from someone who had it. . . . Hugh Kenner named his literary history of the period . . . *The Pound Era.* . . . The man . . . influenced a generation of writers. He discovered talent, including to some extent . . . Eliot and Joyce, and acted as their unpaid agent. He fathered new magazines; read and criticized poetry (he blue-penciled out a third of *The Waste Land*); cajoled editors into publishing Joyce, Eliot . . . and many others; and dispatched letters against and collected signatures of protest against tariffs on books, censorship of literature. . . . Among those he coaxed into coming to Paris was the American poet William Carlos Williams."

At one point, Pound contrived a plan to, in his words, "release as many captives as possible" by attempting to collect donations so that great writers could ditch their day jobs and focus full-time on their work. Ironically, when he succeeded in raising support for his first grant candidate, T. S. Eliot, the great English writer refused it, as a matter of pride.

Pound was consistently involved in creating "little magazines," the phrase used at that time to describe cheaply produced alternative periodicals featuring writers and artists who cared more about the quality of the work than commercial viability. According to Fitch, "He planned the format of a magazine, conceived it in a flurry of passionate reform, then turned it over to others to publish while he moved on to other causes." These uncensored "little magazines," in many ways the offspring of America's Transcendentalist journals of the mid-1800s, were militantly countercultural. The English author (Winifred) Bryher wrote, "If a manuscript was sold to an established publisher, its author was regarded as a black sheep." Virtually every important writer of the twentieth century had early works published in "little magazines" and each, in turn, would "sell out" and become a black sheep in the eyes of the underground.

Beach and Pound worked joyfully hard to create a potent Paris literary scene. But it would be the slightly withdrawn Irishman James Joyce whose eminence would loom over the entire epoch. Joyce was a frequent but awkward presence at literary gatherings, prone to sitting quietly by himself, or conversing only in monosyllables. He was already respected within knowing literary circles for his 1916 novel *A Portrait of the Artist as a Young Man.* Joyce's innovative gift for language play began to either intimidate or confound (or both) all the other writers on the scene from the moment fragments of his new work, *Ulysses,* began to appear in little magazines.

And it wasn't just the writers who were touched by this work. Those who published it generally wound up facing obscenity charges. In fact, when the publishers of New York City's prestigious *Literary Review* found themselves in court for having printed an excerpt, the judge condemned the work as not just obscene but "unintelligible." The district attorney in the case, meanwhile, was most troubled by the "too frank expression concerning woman's dress when the woman was in the clothes described."

With no source of income, a wife and a child, the obsessed bard labored over *Ulysses* for several years, supported at first by a patron, Harriet Weaver, a wealthy literary editor who had published parts of *Portrait* in one of her journals. Thankfully, Weaver was prosperous enough to handle Joyce's needs, which were many. He suffered from a wide variety of medical ailments, including a painful case of glaucoma, which left him nearly blind in one eye. And he and his wife, Nora, had expensive tastes. They insisted on staying at the finest hotels, eating at the best restaurants, and drinking expensive liquor (and plenty of it). When the money ran out, sad and destitute letters would go out to Ms. Weaver, and she would up her investment in what a knowing few were convinced would be the literary masterpiece of the age.

While Joyce worked to complete *Ulysses,* Weaver devised a plan to publish it, but found that no one was willing to print it. Fitch: "Storms of fear and censorship discouraged each attempt [to have *Ulysses* published]. In July the Pelican Press had refused Harriet Weaver's inquiry; in August Miss Weaver gave up her last hope of an English edition because printers, who were subject to prosecution for obscenity and certainly did not have the commitment to art that a publisher might, refused to take any chances on the printing of *Ulysses.*" After a great many fits and starts, Sylvia Beach decided to take on the publishing task herself, and managed to locate a French printing company where no one read English. Now the publisher of *Ulysses,* Beach *too* was on the merry-go-round of Joyce's needs, and began supplying the writer with "advances" on eventual sales of the book.

Aside from his medical and financial needs, Joyce also had trouble finding typists for the manuscript. Nine genteel Paris ladies in a row were so offended by the sexual content that they quit, and one even threatened to throw herself out the window. Finally a group of friends, including Sylvia, had to chip in their time to get the novel into type.

It quickly became clear that *Ulysses* would not be a complete financial loss for the generous women. The few copies of the fragments of Ulysses that had leaked out into the greater world had already created a stir among the intelligentsia, and as soon as Beach announced that the book publication was upcoming, orders started arriving at Shakespeare and Company from all over the globe. Among those who prepaid for the book were Edith Sitwell, H. G. Wells, William Butler Yeats, Winston Churchill, Virginia Woolf, and Aldous Huxley. On February 2, 1922, Joyce's fortieth birthday, *Ulysses* was published.

Never had there been a literary work of such depth and strangeness. Joyce had taken his influences—particularly Walt Whitman's free-verse usage of common language and street slang and Lewis Carroll's light-hearted inventiveness with new words and multiple meanings—and he had fit them to scenarios that involved the coarsest facets of human existence. It was unrelievedly dense, packed with double and triple entendres, and it was all just the story of a day. Or in Joyce's words, "an epic of two races (Israelite-Irish) and at the same time the cycle of the human body as well as a little story of a day." In fact, once Joyce briefly introduces his alter ego, the poet Stephen Dedalus, the story really kicks in with the interior monologue of Molly Bloom taking a shit—and it closes about six hundred pages later with Molly Bloom fantasizing about having a fuck.

The world had seen a few nihilistic Dadaist/Surrealist poems and manifestoes, and even Rimbaud's deranged *A Season in Hell,* but it had never been presented with an entire epic novel by a master of language filled with visions like "Bag of corpsegas sopping in foul brine. A quiver of minnows, fat of a spongy titbit, flash through the slits of his buttoned trouserfly. God becomes man becomes fish becomes barnacle goose becomes featherbed mountain. Dead breaths I living breathe, tread dead dust, devour a urinous offal from all dead. Hauled stark over the gunwhale he breathes upward the stench of his green grave, his leprous nosehole snoring to the sun."

Most of the critics were not happy. But never mind. Once *Ulysses* was published, Joyce showed himself to be a tireless self-promoter. He was in Shakespeare and Company every day, getting Sylvia and her assistants to send out ever more review copies, to call on friendly writers to plant reviews and endorsements all across the Western media. And he was one of the first innovative twentieth-century artists to fully realize what today is a cliché—that scandal is good for your career. Bad reviews—the more shocked and distraught the better—pleased him almost as much as the raves. One reviewer called him "Rabelais after a nervous breakdown," and another called him "Zola gone to seed." Still another called him one of "the devil's disciples." Even Virginia Woolf sniffed that Joyce was "a queasy undergraduate scratching his pimples." He, Sylvia, and Weaver took particular delight in a front-page headline in London's top tabloid paper that read "SCANDAL OF JAMES JOYCE'S ULYSSES!" The article called Joyce "a perverted lunatic." Beach posted it on the wall behind her office desk.

As amusing as these fits of priggish outrage may have been, censorship posed a commercial problem for Beach and Joyce. Particularly in America, after the initial attempted shipment was seized by the New York Port Authority, *Ulysses* became something of an underground book and its publisher became a guerrilla marketer. Beach would send the book out wrapped in other covers (frequently Shakespeare) and would suggest that her customers do the same when traveling with their copies. She even contracted with an American underworld figure in Chicago to smuggle books into the U.S., a risky scheme that proved to be rather successful.

Joyce meanwhile went right back to writing an even more unconventional and confounding novel that he would eventually title *Finnegans Wake*. He told his friends that he was going to "put language to sleep." The novel would be the most radical subversion of the English language committed to print by any major author in history, with the possible exception of William S. Burroughs. As Fitch writes, he "invent[ed] . . . multilingual speech."

As segments of *Finnegan*—under the designation *Untitled*—began appearing in the little magazines, even many of Joyce's avant-garde supporters distanced themselves. His patron, Mrs. Weaver, continued her financial support, but fretted because she couldn't understand or enjoy the work.

His old colleague Pound, who had already moved on to his own form of *political* insanity in Italy, denounced it as "diarrhea of consciousness."

With its recombinant words and impenetrable multiplicities of meanings that very nearly try to stitch together connections between everything in the universe with each sentence, *Finnegans Wake* reads—let's be honest—like an episode from the most brilliant schizophrenic the world has ever seen. And yet it works, not as a "good read," but as a brilliant, extended "sound poem" to be heard aloud, and as a virtually "Talmudic" text to be studied and deconstructed over time. Joyce himself slyly remarked, "I've put in so many enigmas and puzzles that it will keep the professors busy for centuries arguing over what I meant, and that's the only way of insuring one's immortality."

Despite his detractors, by the late 1920s, Joyce could take literature wherever he wanted. On the strength of *Ulysses* alone, he was widely considered *the* great man of letters, and he had his own posse of followers and sycophants. One of them, a young man named Samuel Beckett, would also grow into a writer of nearly unparalleled originality.

By the early 1930s, as he was completing *Finnegans Wake,* Joyce's hard drinking, his troubles with his schizophrenic daughter, Lucia, and no doubt the stress of being famous without being rich had taken their toll. His personality, always demanding, became contentious, and he began to lose his friends and supporters. Also, by this time, the high spirits of the Paris scene itself had long given way to what—in the 1970s—were called "bad vibes." Much as in the Haight-Ashbury at that time (and seemingly forevermore), crowds of less-than-talented and ill-mannered boho camp followers littered the streets. The heavy opium-fueled decadence associated with a party scene around American expatriate avant-garde writers and publishers Harry and Caresse Crosby (the Keith Richards/Anita Pallenberg of their time) had made its influence felt a couple of years earlier. Gertrude Stein effectively conveyed the sense of the moment with her poetic phrase "Before the Flowers of Friendship Faded Friendship Faded."

Finally, even the Joyce/Beach alliance frayed when it became clear to Joyce that mainstream publishers in England and America who were clamoring to print *Ulysses* were not willing to offer financial compensation to both its author *and* its original publisher. The Irish bard pressured Beach to relinquish her publisher's rights so he could effect a deal. His anxiety to get a powerful corporation behind *Ulysses* was understandable. Not only was the book still banned in America, it was also being pirated by a sleazy New York City publisher. Only a major book company would have the wherewithal to fight the legal battles needed to bring *Ulysses* up from underground where it could get mass distribution to meet an existing demand. Beach was deeply wounded by what she perceived as Joyce's lack of loyalty. Joyce, for his part, assumed that Beach had made a handsome profit from the eleven editions she had already published. She never told him that she'd paid him more than the sum of the book's profits over the years. Beach and Joyce remained superficially cordial, but the harsh realities of the established literary world had permanently damaged their friendship. In the immortal words of the Brains, "Money changes everything."

In 1933, the American publishing giant Random House went before the United States District Court in New York and finally won permission to import and distribute *Ulysses* in America. In his decision, Judge John M. Woolsey wrote, "In respect of the recurrent emergence of the theme of sex in the minds of his characters, it must be remembered that his locale was Celtic and his season Spring."

Innocents Abroad: The Lost Generation

> And so life in Paris began and as all roads lead to Paris, all of us are now there, and I can begin to tell what happened when I was of it.
>
> GERTRUDE STEIN, *THE AUTOBIOGRAPHY OF ALICE B. TOKLAS*

> The age demanded that we sing/and cut away our tongue./ The age demanded that we flow/and hammered in the bung./The age demanded that we dance/and jammed us into iron pants/and in the end the age was handed/ the kind of shit that it demanded.
>
> ERNEST HEMINGWAY

> This is the food of paradise. . . . Euphoria and brilliant storms of laughter; ecstatic reveries and extensions of

one's personality on several simultaneous planes are to
be complacently expected.

RECIPE FOR "HASCHICH FUDGE" FROM
THE ALICE B. TOKLAS COOKBOOK, ENGLISH EDITION

The American expatriate invasion of Paris in the 1920s was presaged by
three powerhouses who established a beachhead by making themselves
central figures in the bohemian community. Two, of course, were Sylvia
Beach and Ezra Pound. But a decade and a half before they sauntered into
the cultural limelight, Gertrude Stein, a California writer of enormous
girth who was frequently described as having the "face of a Roman emperor," arrived in France. She hooked up with a fellow California wayfarer
named Alice B. Toklas and the two began hosting a legendary, nearly perpetual salon for the artistic and literary *luminati* of Paris in their studio
apartment. Pablo Picasso and his successive wives, Matisse, Braque, Apollinaire, and Juan Gris were among the artists who frequently availed themselves of the food, drink, and conversation. Stein displayed her friends'
paintings prominently, and as word of the perpetual party reached the
demimonde, they were frequently enjoined by art buyers and dealers,
wealthy society men and ladies, and even the odd occasional diplomat or
political leader. It was a helpful, as well as pleasurable, party scene for Paris'
boho elite.

Despite the celebratory atmosphere, Stein found time to conduct literary experiments. Seized with a desire to take language apart and make it
new again, she worked on a novel called *The Making of Americans* in which
she used rhythm, repetition, and unusual juxtapositions to create a fragmentary writing style that mirrored what her friends the Cubists were
doing with paint.

Although both Stein and Toklas had made France their home, they
never lost their affection for America. Luckily, after the war, America came
to them. Following Beach and Pound were Ernest Hemingway, Sherwood
Anderson, F. Scott Fitzgerald, John Dos Passos, Djuna Barnes, Malcolm
Cowley, William Carlos Williams, Hart Crane, Katherine Anne Porter,
Thornton Wilder, e. e. cummings, Christopher Isherwood, and Nathanael
West. Some stayed long, while others drifted in and out of the scene.

All were, at the very least, seeking relief from America's alcohol prohibition. Most were looking to experience a sexual liberty that was denied them in the land of the Puritans. And many were also fleeing an anti-intellectual greed ethic, symbolized by the election of the Ronald Reagan of the early 1900s, Calvin Coolidge.

Like the native Cubists before them, the Americans ate, drank, flirted, fucked, and talked philosophy night and day in the cafés and bars. This hedonistic way of life may have been natural to the Europeans, but somehow when acted out by the men and women of the young democracy across the Atlantic, it took on an air of disconsolation. Stein labeled her new American friends "The Lost Generation," and Hemingway would later characterize the American expatriate scene as one of "desperate gaiety."

Easily the most acerbic voice of the disaffection experienced by thoughtful young Americans was Lost Generation social critic Harold Stearns. Stearns wrote of a United States culturally encumbered by a "mania for petty regulation" and featuring "less freedom and right of assemblage, less tolerance, more governmental control over political and economic opinion, less liberty for teachers and college professors, more reaction and militarism than was the case the day we declared war on Germany." In a 1920 essay entitled "What Can a Young Man Do?" Stearns offered freedom-seeking American youth this simple advice: "Get out!"

Expatriate poet Glenway Wescott described the attraction in more positive terms, writing, "I had heard that the French were tolerant and that Parisians, especially, were open-minded, curious, and inquisitive about foreign artists who brought with them different ways of living. A writer in Paris could, I learned, do whatever he wanted, no matter who he was or where he came from, no matter how scandalous his behavior might be."

This American expatriate episode was not an archetypal counter-culturalist-exile-in-search-of-utopia story. True, the Americans sought a certain cultural liberty in Europe, but the journeys taken by Hemingway, Fitzgerald, Stein, Dos Passos, and later Henry Miller were not pointed toward numinous divinity or perfect fellowship. In fact, quite the opposite: they came to sophisticated Paris to lose their cherries—to learn the messy and sometimes bitter facts of life and, in a typically American spirit, to overcome them. Donald Pizer, author of *American Expatriate Writing and the Paris Moment,* writes about

the autobiographically based expatriate novel in which
a potentially creative self is frustrated and defeated,
and the memoir in which there is a rich flowering of the
artist on foreign soil. Why does the expatriate experience lend itself to this thematic dichotomy? And why
does the dichotomy find an outlet in these two distinctive forms? [They] saw all around them in the cafés and
streets of Paris countless examples among their compatriots of inadequacy and weakness, ranging from bohemian dilettantism to a perversion of the opportunity
for freedom into self-destruction and the destruction of
others. They, however . . . viewed themselves as apart, as
different, as capable . . . of drawing upon the creative
potency of the Paris moment rather than succumbing to
its faculty for corrupting further an already vitiated or
flawed spirit and will.

Thus, while most of the expatriate works contain some elements of a
rugged sort of personal optimism, they are peopled by sad, deluded, and
venal human specimens and augur the arrival of the unblinking French
Existentialism of the 1950s. The most famous novels that mirror the
American expatriate experience, *The Sun Also Rises* by Ernest Hemingway
and *Tender Is the Night* by F. Scott Fitzgerald, are works in which the writer
uses the energy of Paris bohemia in a journey of self-discovery in which
he confronts the sometimes ugly complexities of human emotions and
relationships, including his own, emerging a sadder-but-wiser—more
sophisticated—American.

DISSIPATION AND AFTERMATH

Crowded out by pretenders and hangers-on, burned out from drink and
the excesses of Harry and Caresse Crosby's party scene (which ended in
Harry Crosby's suicide), the Lost Generation epoch was fading by the early
1930s. But that wouldn't prevent a couple of newcomers from trying
to raise the standard once more. Henry Miller and Anaïs Nin were a pair
of lusty American writers who formed a fiery partnership—sometimes

friends, sometimes lovers—in Paris in the 1930s. They tasted the "sins" of Paris: open sexuality, drink, drugs, and spontaneity, and unlike some of the earlier Americans, they found it almost unequivocally good. Nin would publish her famous diaries of her Paris adventures, revealing more about liberated female sexuality than had ever been committed to print. And Miller, who coupled a hardy, plainspoken, working-class American voice with the sort of earthy stream-of-consciousness stylings of Whitman and Joyce, would write his famous *Tropic of Cancer*. Described by Pizer as a portrait of "the writer as artist in rebellion . . . within a radically re-created mythic Paris," Miller's autobiographical novel provoked the same response from America's censors that *Ulysses* had about a decade earlier. It wouldn't be allowed into the United States until the mid-1950s.

Despite the best efforts of Miller and Nin, Paris as a vital bohemian center had reached the end of its run. The best painters were now older and comfortably established. Picasso had long been rich. Selling the souvenirs of their revolution against stasis for a pretty penny, Surrealist rebels like Breton, Man Ray, Klee, and Duchamp had returned to the safety of the museums. The best of the writers, Hemingway, Dos Passos, Anderson, also famous and successful, were already selling their memories of the earlier days of Paris bohemia to mainstream American magazines like *Vanity Fair, The Atlantic Monthly,* and *Esquire*. Gertrude Stein, Philippe Soupault, and a few others hit the international lecture circuit—always a sign that an epoch is coming to a close. Meanwhile, Ezra Pound, who had moved to Italy in the mid-1920s, had become obsessively angry about the practice of usury within the international banking system. Italy's right-wing populists, the fascists, led by the former anarchist Benito Mussolini, pretended to share this anti-establishment concern, so Pound became part of their movement, even buying into the anti-Semitic canard about the Jews controlling the banks.

Backbiting and dissension frequently characterize the end of an era. Gertrude Stein, in her popular *Autobiography of Alice B. Toklas,* published in 1933, declared herself the greatest writer of the age, and portrayed all her former friends as petulant children and misguided egotists. This provoked a public letter of denunciation, published on the front page of Paris' daily newspaper *The Post*. It was signed by Tristan Tzara, Georges Braque, and Henri Matisse, among others. Even Hemingway's *A Moveable Feast,* published in 1964, was excoriated by other still-living denizens of the Paris scene for its negative portrayals of his fellow bohemians, although by today's standards, the depictions seem mild.

All after-the-fact gossip and complaining aside, countercultures *should* be impermanent, lest they harden into new conformities. But both the styles and the accomplishments of the Paris avant-garde are still reflected—but hopefully not slavishly followed—in art scenes around the world today. The fragmentation of form first used as a mode of expression by the Cubists is no longer radical. It is ubiquitous in pop music—particularly hip-hop and electronica—films, music videos, and television advertising. The liberated dreamscapes of Surrealism are also unavoidable in precisely the same popular mediums. Dadaist outrages—still used in both politics and art, and sometimes sponsored by vodka companies—are also performed by corporations like Benetton and Abercrombie & Fitch. Of course, now only Bill O'Reilly and his million or so viewers actually get scandalized. In literature, multiple points of view are the norm, and the language experiments of Joyce, Stein, and others are considered common elements to be used or discarded depending on the artist's intention and whether or not she wants Oprah Winfrey to comprehend her book.

And of course, some artists and writers still drink to excess, take drugs, lead sexually libertine lives, wear berets, and live for Camembert cheese. Does this show a lack of originality, or is it merely an expression of natural appetites that, once identified and accessed, should never be suppressed? Your choice.

{ Part III

AFTER HIROSHIMA,
"THE" COUNTERCULTURE }

CHAPTER ELEVEN

⊢ REBELS WITHOUT A CAUSE

The 1950s

AFTER HIROSHIMA, *THE* COUNTERCULTURE

I am become death, the destroyer of worlds.

J. ROBERT OPPENHEIMER, 1947

The supporters of Senator Joseph McCarthy feared the Communist Party. . . . Liberal and left wing enclaves feared McCarthyism. Conservatives feared social dissolution, immorality, rock and roll, even fluoridation.

TODD GITLIN, *THE SIXTIES: YEARS OF HOPE, DAYS OF RAGE*

Rock 'n' roll [is] insistent savagery . . . deliberately competing with the artistic ideals of the jungle.

ENCYCLOPAEDIA BRITANNICA YEARBOOK, 1956

On August 6, 1945, the United States of America dropped an atomic bomb on the Japanese city of Hiroshima. History was split in two. Even before we had the chance to count the dead from Hitler's carefully processed, bureaucratic murder of six million or more Jews, Gypsies, homosexuals, and dissenters, that holocaust was technologically upstaged in the theater of human awareness by the impression that an impersonal and instant *global* holocaust might be just around the bend.

Life under the threat of an instant apocalypse has been written up, brooded over, and sung about so often that, even now, as the bomb gets passed down to unsteady nations, unhinged administrations, and, eventually, unaffiliated gangs, a further disquisition risks banality. And indeed our more sophisticated observers sound like cyberpunk SF writer Bruce Sterling, who glibly predicted in a 2003 interview on Well.com that even a full-fledged nuclear exchange is likely to leave nearly a billion human beings still standing:

> You know, those things don't end the world.
>
> A full-scale nuclear exchange between two heavily armed superpowers might conceivably kill everybody, but that is no longer a big likelihood and even in retrospect I think that prospect was overblown.
>
> What you get is a holocaust of unimaginable proportions. The next morning somebody still wakes up and has to find breakfast. And eventually some historian gets to write something like, "Well, there were nine billion of us, and now there are about 750 million of us. And 'we' are no longer 'them,' because their world has perished and now we must do our best to become us."
>
> Clocks continue to tick and leaves still fall off the calendar. Infants are born who have no emotional attachment to the previous way of life. It's sort of soothing to us to think that "the world ends" when everything we know and love is reduced to ashes, but, you know, it just doesn't.

Jaded twenty-first-century analyses aside, in the immediate aftermath of "the bomb," intellectual discourse and popular mythology focused on mass annihilation. Nihilism was sure to follow. And the atomic news also had a subtext—a message that was perhaps experienced more at the level of the body and the nervous system than the intellect: *speed*. And speed produces exhilaration.

Exhilarated Americans were celebrating the instant end of the world war. And the nuke that made the war go away nearly overnight wasn't just about fantastic advances in physics, it was about flight. Not only did we possess a weapon of unfathomable terror; it was *deliverable* anywhere in a matter of hours!

And again: who had this bomb? America! Land of democracy, liberty (more or less), and racial apartheid. And more to our point, the land of entrepreneurial capitalism and technological optimism: inventors of the telephone, the airplane, and the television. Indeed, even without the nuclear power over (approximate) global life and death, these Americans were an awesome bunch of magicians: they made it possible to project voices and images all around the globe and move around the world at several hundred miles per hour. And they were already selling these superpowers to the rest of the world for a tidy sum. Whether deadly or fun, this conflation of time and distance was all of one perversely exciting piece, interpreted as the expansion of human possibilities—or, in the phrase of sixties media philosopher Marshall McLuhan, the extensions of man.

It is in America, at this peculiar nexus of nihilism and exhilaration, technological optimism and excessive military power, a place where expectations and desires once cultivated over lifetimes were starting to become available in matters of moments, the land of jazz and razzmatazz, that the story of counterculture in the second half of the twentieth century begins.

HOWLING THE 1950S AWAKE

While the blast that announced the new global situation was atomic, a much quieter sound exploded the apparent cultural/psychological/political cohesion of America's dominant white conformist culture of the 1950s. It was 1955, and a crowd of alienated young poets and poetry lovers had packed the Six Gallery in San Francisco. Bags of red wine, provided by the novelist Jack Kerouac, were passed around. A small, neurotic Jewish homosexual walked to the front of the room and, with all the solemn drama he could muster, intoned the words:

I saw the best minds of my generation destroyed by
madness, starving hysterical naked,

dragging themselves through the negro streets at dawn
looking for an angry fix,

angelheaded hipsters burning for the ancient heavenly
connection to the starry dynamo in the machinery
of night,

who poverty and tatters and hollow-eyed and high sat
up smoking in the supernatural darkness of cold-
water flats floating across the tops of cities contem-
plating jazz,

who bared their brains to Heaven under the El and saw
Mohammedan angels staggering on tenement roofs
illuminated,

who passed through universities with radiant cool eyes
hallucinating Arkansas and Blake-light tragedy
among the scholars of war,

who were expelled from the academies for crazy & publishing obscene odes on the windows of the skull,

who cowered in unshaven rooms in underwear, burning
their money in wastebaskets and listening to the
Terror through the wall . . .

The revolution had begun.

DIZZY AND BIRD

They teach you there's a boundary line in music, but
man, there's no boundary line in art.

CHARLIE PARKER, *IN MUSIC*

Ginsberg's epochal reading of "Howl" is often singled out as the moment
when an already extant subculture of hipsters and beats finally blew up big.
Indeed, mass media popularization of this culture of visionary rapture and
apocalyptic alienation from the repressed culture of the times followed di-

rectly on its heels, and the hippies—who pretty much dominated the public imagination in the late 1960s—were its direct descendants. But the counterculture that would come to be dominated by the children of the white middle class was largely rooted in the cultural styles and strategies of African-American children of slaves.

The culture of America had long been subject to a dialectic between the puritanical attitudes of her rural settlers and the cultural liberalism of her more urbane revolutionary founders. A third factor, the sensibilities of several million ex-slaves and their descendants, began to impact on the broader American culture early in the twentieth century.

While explicit Judeo-Christian anti-sexuality had been challenged by elements of the eighteenth-century Enlightenment, rationalism was not about to produce a sensual, sexy culture. The Africans, on the other hand, were not carrying a thousands-of-years-old legacy of bodily shame. African tribal customs that revolved around ecstatic, sensual dancing to percussive rhythms had not been completely suppressed by enslavement and Christian conversion. Besides the well-known "spirituals" and "field hollers," after the 1776 Revolution, African slaves in New Orleans and a few other locations were allowed to gather in public on Sundays for (in contemporary terminology) "drum circles." In *Bohemia: The Protoculture Then and Now,* historian Richard Miller vividly illustrated the scene: "Blacks by the hundreds came to . . . sing and dance to bambouli drums beaten in the tradition of the drums of Africa. Around the circumference stood police and around them hundreds of whites, come to watch the sport and to buy refreshments from hawkers selling to both crowds. At a signal from the police, the drummers began a sturdy rhythm with beef bones on casks, a tremendous heartbeat energy roared on until sundown."

After their release from outright slavery following the Civil War, the former slaves were segregated into their own communities and subjected to a long period of not-so-benign neglect (occasionally interrupted by violent racist attacks). Under this cloak of invisibility, they began to invent new rhythm-oriented musical forms. By the 1860s, the raw elements of the blues were heard in rural settings. In the 1870s, a few Africans in New Orleans got the chance to sit at the rich folks' pianos, leading to the beginnings of boogie-woogie (and therefore jazz and rock and roll) music.

Besides expressing melancholy and pain, the blues, originally sung exclusively by males, was a mating call, an expression of sexual potency and longing. By the end of the nineteenth century, the blues had spread, becoming a popular folk idiom throughout rural black communities, and in the early 1910s, it gained public notice in the wider society. The blues communicated a shocking piece of information to white culture: *sex was somehow related to rhythm!*

While rural African-Americans were refining the blues, by the 1890s boogie-woogie was spawning a wide variety of mutant sounds in New Orleans. Like the blues, this new musical genre featured salacious lyrics. Most were metaphoric ("I need a hot dog for my roll"), but others were as direct as any contemporary rap song ("All the whores like the way I ride"). And while the blues brought great emotional intelligence to slow and simple musical repetitions, jazz (it wasn't actually named until 1913) was speedy and—under the influence of white classical and popular music—incorporated a wide range of musical notes and changes. While blues expressed the pains and hungers of oppressed people, jazz was rooted in "voodoo" rituals geared toward evoking spiritual ecstasies. Jazz was an expression of survivor's joie de vivre. It was also a celebration of the pace of urban life at the turn of the century.

By the 1920s, the media was hyping the "Jazz Age," and jazz—played now by black and white musicians alike—was America's most popular music. It was the first (but certainly not the last) time an African-American musical idiom conquered the country.

Like America itself, jazz culture was restless and innovative, always proliferating new styles and genres. In the 1930s, a highly danceable style called swing reflected the peppy spirit of the automotive age. By 1934, with alcohol prohibition repealed, urban Americans both black and white flocked to nightclubs to swing—get loose and, in some cases, high.

Swing was so hot that the musicians could have profited from it for years to come, but some jazz artists were more interested in innovation than profit. In the late 1930s, Fats Waller foreshadowed world music by about half a decade by incorporating West Indian musicians into his *London Suite*. But it was a showman named Dizzy Gillespie and a wild drug abuser named Charlie Parker (nicknamed "Bird") who risked the loss of their solid swing audience and really let the dogs out.

The new jazz style was called bebop, and it did something previously unheard of in popular music—it allowed the musicians to *improvise*. Until the 1940s, musicians had marched in formation, rendering each composition more or less as it was intended. Gillespie, Parker, and other beboppers cut the musicians loose. Suddenly they were individuals with powers of self-expression. Parker wrote, "Music is your experience, your thoughts, your wisdom." And Parker himself was the best of the breed, giving expression to the spontaneous wanderings of the mind and the infinite variability of the emotions through his horn.

Although bebop did okay commercially, it was not universally loved the way swing was—its unpredictable and intoxicating jams sort of separated the hipsters from the squares.

SLOUCHING TOWARD NOWHERESVILLE: THE HIPSTERS

Hipsters, flipsters, and finger poppin' daddies, knock me your lobes.

LORD BUCKLEY, 1955

The only Hip morality is to do what one feels whenever and wherever possible.

NORMAN MAILER, "THE WHITE NEGRO," 1957

You all know the cliché: the 1950s were a period of *Father Knows Best* conformity. Exhausted by the Depression and the world war—but with an economy on the upswing—white America understandably pushed nuclear anxieties away by buying shiny new consumer products like dishwashers, televisions, and snazzy tail-finned automobiles. Meanwhile, the country's principal dissident current, communism and socialism—already under attack by the House Un-American Activities Committee in the late 1940s—was savaged by McCarthyism in the early 1950s. Famous artists like Charlie Chaplin, Richard Wright, Clifford Odets, Lillian Hellman, Leonard Bernstein, Aaron Copland, Dorothy Parker, Bertolt Brecht, Dashiell Hammett, Orson Welles, Pete Seeger, Arthur Miller, and Paul Robeson were among the thousands of voices effectively silenced until 1954, when McCarthy's paranoid excesses finally brought about his downfall.

The American left barely had a moment to catch its breath before it took another hit. In 1955, Soviet premier Nikita Khrushchev revealed the true history of slaughter and repression under Joseph Stalin. Thousands of well-intentioned humanists, who had either underestimated or denied the Stalin repression as capitalist propaganda, discovered that they'd been played for fools. Quite a few bolted all the way over to the far right. With the exception of a handful of hardy anti-authoritarian pacifists and anarchist intellectuals who had despised Stalin without reservations, the American left as a vital intellectual current virtually disappeared for the entire decade. (This is not to ignore the growth of the civil rights movement during this time. The movement certainly gave leftist holdouts something to do with their bodies while they reworked their ideologies.)

Political dissent was virtually prohibited in the early 1950s, and all nonconformity was suspect throughout the decade. But waywardness springs eternal at the fringes of Western civilization. A young and sullen breed that had started to form a subculture in the 1940s filled the rebel vacuum: the hipster. Inspired by the heady, spontaneous sounds of bebop, particularly Charlie Parker, and developing vaguely in parallel with the evolution of French Existentialism and its vision of human life as a blank slate surrounded by a meaningless abyss, hipsters were furtive characters—the perfect rebels for a paranoid age. Seeing no hope for positive change, the hipster had no desire to confront the repressive political apparatus and was barely even interested in offending "straight" conformists. As Caroline Bird complained in a 1957 *Harper's Bazaar* article, "You can't interview a hipster because his main goal is to keep out of . . . society."

Hipsters could be identified by only a few characteristics. They were interracial, a rare sight in fifties America—black and white bohemians, living on the economic fringes, hung out together, largely at jazz clubs. They were a bit slovenly. They might be, in the words of Caroline Bird, "a petty criminal, a hobo, a carnival roustabout, or a free-lance moving man in Greenwich Village." And they had their own linguistic expressions (best expressed in the playful, funny, flowing "raps" of the eternally hip Lord Buckley). More privately, hipsters liked marijuana and, in some cases, heroin—tools for loosening up the rational mind and digging the bebop.

Hipsterism thrived on the very nuclear anxieties that the straights were trying to forget. The possibility of instant apocalypse formed a perfect excuse for turning away from the responsibilities and delayed rewards of ordinary adult life. Why cautiously build a career, a family, and a reputation when there was no future? The hipster was liberated to live for the moment. In his famous paean to this subculture, "The White Negro," Norman Mailer wrote that hipsters were all about "the search for an orgasm more apocalyptic than the one that preceded it," a statement intended both sexually and as a metaphor for any deeply intense and ecstatic experience of being in the moment.

Although the hipster's intense *now* was grounded in despair, and his general mien was gloomy, he still carried a sense of unconstrained aliveness that was missing in the carefully planned office bureaucracies of the "organization man" and his manicured suburbs. In *Understanding the Beats,* Edward Halsey Foster describes the inhuman trap that the "squares" found themselves in: "Men were expected to be logical, efficient, and cool-headed, organizing their lives according to their employers' needs. There was no place for the excitable, intense, and independent personality exemplified by frontier America. That . . . was identified as . . . adolescent, a stage responsible men were supposed to outgrow." This culture produced a barely suppressed undertow of discontent that was papered over with two-martini lunches and an explosion in psychotherapy. So while the middle class disapproved of the hipsters, they were sort of jealous. Responding to this undercurrent, Hollywood produced movies romanticizing them. Foster: "Hipsters' mannerisms were incorporated into the acting styles of Marlon Brando, Paul Newman, Montgomery Clift, and James Dean. Hipster culture was the subject of such popular films as *Young Man with a Horn* (1950) [and] *The Man with the Golden Arm* (1956) featuring Frank Sinatra." Through these films and film stars, consumers could get vicarious hipster kicks from a safe distance.

THE ALIENS MEET

Art and literature are usually the refuge of the bohemians. Besides the jazz musicians, however, most hipsters couldn't even be bothered. There was, though, a small coterie of friends on the fringes of hipster life who formed an exception.

This alliance of literary hipsters started to take shape in 1943 when two newly acquainted Columbia University students went for a walk together. Jack Kerouac and Allen Ginsberg were engaging in an abstract philosophical discussion when Ginsberg launched a slightly more personal line of discourse. As Barry Miles wrote in *Ginsberg: A Biography*, "Allen told Jack how he would stand in the shadow of the mysterious hedges on Graham Avenue and wonder how big space was and where the universe ended. Jack told Allen how he would stand in the backyard of his parents' house at night when everyone was eating supper and feel that everyone was a ghost, eating ghost food. Like Allen, he often looked at the stars and pondered the size of the universe."

The aliens had met. A few days later they met again at the home of another acquaintance, Bill Burroughs. Ginsberg, Kerouac, and their friend Lucien Carr engaged in an abstract discussion about what constitutes art. "That's . . . the stupidest thing I ever heard," Burroughs interjected. The aliens had found their teacher.

If Ginsberg and Kerouac were sensitive and unusual souls, William Burroughs' presence—at thirty, he already possessed a peculiar ghoulish eminence that made him look ageless—suggested a sort of extraterrestrial gangster godfather. Burroughs wasn't just hip, he was preternaturally worldly-wise, and he taught the young literary pups real-life applications for conventional and unconventional philosophy and the literature of drug experiences. (In 1953, the triumvirate became something of a quartet with the inclusion of Gregory Corso. Corso, unlike the others, who had been raised fairly middle-class, was an orphan, and a genuine, hard-core street hipster from the word go.)

The Low Life

Writers, by nature, are spies; observers gathering material. In the late 1940s and early 1950s, Kerouac, Ginsberg, and Burroughs avoided active participation in the desperate excesses of some of their hipster acquaintances. Rather, they observed and sympathized. They could understand and identify with Bill Cannastra, who would dance on broken glass and on the edge of rooftops, and who one day lost his duel with death while climbing through the window of a New York City subway train. And they offered solace and a place to crash to Herbert Huncke, a severe heroin addict who hustled money as a petty thief out on New York's Times Square. For suicidal and strung-out hipsters, this was life, but to the writers, the hipsters' desperate lives were a statement. To Ginsberg, they represented "the first perception that we were separate from the official vision of history and reality." As Foster explains it, "The official vision, the one to which the GIs returned, seemed a fantasy. The real one was a world of horror. . . . Cannastra's death, and the addicts and petty thieves who passed before the windows of the Times Square cafeteria where [they] would spend . . . time with Huncke."

Jack Kerouac was the first of the writers to publish in book form. *The Town and the City* (1950) was a conventional roman à clef in which the author contrasted his idyllic small-town memories with the desperate and tragic pursuits of his hipster friends. Ginsberg meanwhile started off writing conventional poetry, published in Columbia's student newspaper in the mid-1940s, but based on personal advice from the great American poet William Carlos Williams, he tried free verse. By 1949, his poem *Paterson* included the sort of intemperate thunderclap declamatory lines that would make him famous: "screaming and dancing in praise of Eternity annihilating the sidewalk, annihilating reality, screaming and dancing against the orchestra in the destructible ballroom of the world." The language clearly presaged "Howl."

William Burroughs didn't have any particular desire to be a writer, but as a gay heroin addict he did have a story to tell. So in 1952 he authored his first novel, *Junkie*. This tale of hipster heroin addiction, written in the style of a Raymond Chandler detective story, was published as a paperback under the name William Lee and sold extremely well. The next year he wrote a follow-up, *Queer*, in the same style, but the book couldn't find a publisher. Heroin was one thing, but the absolute last thing heterosexuals in the 1950s wanted to do was read explicit descriptions of gay sex, and the last thing homosexuals wanted was to be seen with a book titled *Queer*.

A careful reading of these stylistically tabloid books shows that Burroughs was already working out his tough-minded liberatory themes. He had studied with the linguist/philosopher Count Alfred Korzybski in the late 1930s, and had been impressed by Korzybski's advocacy of stripping languaged communication of its imprecise emotional and ideological assumptions. Korzybski wanted to eliminate the mind-fogging accumulation of conditioned nonsense from human discourse so that people would be able to think clearly, and for themselves, about political and social life.

Burroughs' version of the Korzybski project involved mercilessly, if impersonally, breaking down his own needs as a junkie queer to their component parts. As Foster writes about Burroughs' work, "Sexuality is seen as a compulsion much like the need for drugs. Both addictions emerge into a world divided between the hunters and the hunted. There is no strong affection between people, only obsessive desires and needs." With these early novels, Burroughs began a lifelong literary exploration of the relationship between conditioning and addiction. Heroin, sex, ideology, love, language: it was all habitual. The important distinction between the good citizen and the junkie was that the junkie was painfully aware of his predicament.

While the young writers were developing their literary chops, life on the hipster edge caught up with them. Burroughs and Kerouac were arrested as material witnesses when their friend Lucien Carr killed a homosexual admirer named David Kammerer in (arguably) an act of self-defense. And Ginsberg got arrested when he allowed some of his junkie friends to stash stolen clothes in his car. He spent about a year in a psychiatric hospital as the result, which turned out to be fortuitous, since he met the mad poetic genius Carl Solomon, an inspiration for "Howl."

Whatever the exigencies of hanging out with the wrong crowd, these young writers were developing an identity that was distinct from the hipster low life. For starters, most hipsters—living only for the moment and for the self—didn't really have friends, just connections. But Ginsberg,

Kerouac, Burroughs, and Corso were all loyal comrades, supporting one another as writers and in the search for maverick self-realization. Indeed, the intimacy and sympathy that they achieved with one another is perhaps the most poignant aspect of their alliance. As John Tyrell wrote in *Naked Angels,* "The crucial motivation for their union was the ability to honestly confess to each other their deepest feelings. Such open revelation of private matters contradicted the spirit of the age, but it led to aesthetic and intellectual discoveries."

Also, by the early 1950s Kerouac and Ginsberg were leavening their hipster alienation with an abiding interest in Eastern philosophies, particularly Buddhism. Buddhist themes like peace, enlightenment, and compassion were not generally spoken of in the nihilistic hipster milieu. Even Burroughs, in his own singular way, was developing a positive project: exploring the potential for liberation from cultural and political brainwashing via the mutation and disruption of language patterns.

Finally, our boys were interested in different drugs than the hipsters were. While most hipsters wanted to lie back with pot and opiates, the writers (with the exception of Burroughs) wanted to write, rant, and rave all night on amphetamines. And Burroughs and Ginsberg were also exploring the magical, shamanic, mind-expanding possibilities of hallucinogens, as evidenced by Burroughs' 1953 letters to Ginsberg from the Amazon jungle, where he'd gone to find and experience yage, a powerful DMT-containing psychedelic (when Ginsberg later tried it, he wrote in a letter to Burroughs, "The whole fucking cosmos busted loose"), and Ginsberg's rapturous Blakean mescaline and peyote hallucinations later in the decade.

POP GO THE BEATS

A revolt of all the forces hostile to civilization itself . . . a movement of brute stupidity . . . that is trying to take over the country from a middle class which is supposed to be the guardian of civilization but which has practically dislocated its shoulder throwing in the towel.

NEOCONSERVATIVE MOVEMENT PROGENITOR
NORMAN PODHORETZ

America, I'm putting my queer shoulder to the wheel.

ALLEN GINSBERG

It's a peculiar truism that—in the late twentieth century—decade-defining cultural trends received mass recognition only toward the end of each decade. In 1957, Ginsberg's poem "Howl" and Kerouac's breakthrough book, *On the Road,* were published and distributed across America, making the beats a popular obsession. In the summer of 1967, the hippies were trumpeted by the mass media. Nineteen seventy-seven was the year of punk rock. In 1997 cyberculture went way mainstream with the dot-com explosion. (And, of course, nothing whatsoever happened in the 1980s.)

John Clellon Holmes introduced the term beat to the world, in a November 1952 article in the *New York Times* titled "This Is the Beat Generation." At the time, the terms hipster and beat were used interchangeably. "More than mere weariness," Holmes wrote, "it [beat] implies the feeling of having been used, of being raw. It involves a sort of nakedness of mind, and, ultimately, of soul: a feeling of being reduced to the bedrock of consciousness. In short, it means being undramatically pushed up against the wall of oneself." Jack Kerouac would later express this feeling in the melancholy Buddhist aphorism: "I accept loss forever." The beat, having nothing left to lose, could at least be honest.

While the hipster-beats were leading their extravagantly messy lives, a related group of countercultural poets had gathered around the anarcho-pacifist San Franciscan Kenneth Rexroth. Called the San Francisco Renaissance, this group included Michael McClure, Lawrence Ferlinghetti, and Philip Whalen. Like the beats, they were influenced by the Romantics and experimental poetry, but they were a bit more sedate and self-serious than Kerouac and company. When Allen Ginsberg showed Rexroth William Burroughs' 1949 antisocial literary burlesque of presidential power, "Roosevelt After the Inauguration," Rexroth said, "That's not funny." Ginsberg replied, "It's not supposed to be *true,* Kenneth." Through the rest of his career, Burroughs performed the piece live to gales of laughter.

Despite their differences, the two crowds were friendly. On October 13, 1955, Ginsberg helped to organize a poetry reading featuring mostly SF Renaissance writers. There he performed his first-ever reading of his epic, wailing, visionary complaint, "Howl" (partly written under the influence of peyote), and it blew everybody away.

With Kerouac crying out "GO!" to all of the best lines, and audience members weeping openly, Ginsberg gained confidence and started wailing like an ancient Jewish prophet: "Moloch! Solitude! Filth! Ugliness! Ashcans and unobtainable dollars! Children screaming under the stairways! Boys sobbing in armies! Old men weeping in the parks!/Moloch! Moloch! Nightmare of Moloch! Moloch the loveless! . . . Moloch the heavy judger of men!/Moloch the incomprehensible prison! Moloch the crossbone soulless jailhouse and Congress of sorrows! Moloch whose buildings are judgment! Moloch the vast stone of war! . . ./Moloch whose mind is pure machinery! Moloch whose blood is running money! Moloch whose fingers are ten armies! . . ./Moloch whose eyes are a thousand blind windows!/ Moloch whose love is endless oil and stone!"

Michael McClure later wrote, "At the deepest level . . . a barrier had been broken, a human voice and body had been hurled against the harsh wall of America and its supporting armies and navies and academies and institutions and ownership systems and power-support bases." Perhaps more telling, the publisher Ferlinghetti sent him a telegram the next day that read, "I greet you at the beginning of a great career. When do I get the manuscript?"

Ginsberg wasn't the only one who'd found an unconstrained original voice. At the beginning of the decade, right after the publication of his conventional novel *The Town and the City,* Jack Kerouac had taken an aesthetic clue from the improvisational bebop jazz that he dearly loved. He began writing long, unexpurgated, spontaneous passages—sitting at the typewriter for days on end, wired to the gills on amphetamine and expanded on marijuana, channeling his thoughts and memories through his fingers and into the typewriter keys.

The resulting work, eventually titled *On the Road,* would become the supreme representation of the beat life. It was about freedom and mobility—Huck Finn "lighting out for the territories." The spirit that had propelled the insouciant Taoist/Zen wanderer now had a new tool, the automobile. With characters again based on his real friends, particularly a loquacious and virile hipster force of nature named Neal Cassady, the book was a dropout rhapsody about hitchhiking around America and Mexico virtually penniless, smoking marijuana, digging jazz, hanging out with hookers, and constantly philosophizing about freedom and the wish for a more bighearted America. It was a story without a conclusion or an objective, which *was* the point. *On the Road* was a *river* of a book, and the rhythms of the language, the flashes of illumination, the empathic glimpses of America's marginalized gave its thankful young readers the literary equivalent of the head trip they experienced from a long Charlie Parker solo. This was exactly what Kerouac was after. In an introductory note to his book-length poem *Mexico City Blues,* from around the same period as *On the Road,* Kerouac wrote about his desire to be "considered a jazz poet blowing a long blues in an afternoon jazz session on Sunday."

Although much of it was written in the early 1950s, publication of Kerouac's beat work would have to wait until 1957, after Ginsberg's "Howl" got the juggernaut rolling when it was published by Lawrence Ferlinghetti's City Lights Books. That same year, City Lights successfully beat back an attempt to censor "Howl," which brought Ginsberg massive publicity. Ginsberg immediately put his energy and fame toward getting his friends' works published. In short order, Kerouac's *On the Road* (1957), *The Dharma Bums* (1958), *The Subterraneans* (1958), *Dr. Sax* (1959), and *Mexico City Blues* (1959) would be in bookstores, as would Gregory Corso's poetry collection *Gasoline;* William Burroughs' classic *Naked Lunch*—too corrosive for fifties American eyes—would premiere in Paris (1959). Ginsberg even helped bring attention to writers from the San Francisco Renaissance like Gary Snyder, Philip Whalen, Robert Creeley, and Robert Duncan. It was the beginning of Ginsberg's role as den mother and publicity agent for the late-twentieth-century counterculture.

The three beat main men, Kerouac, Ginsberg, and Burroughs, all had distinctive voices and styles, but there were big commonalities. They all were radical about revealing minutely intimate thoughts and/or aspects of reality that virtually all writers up to that point had shied away from. They all used something close to stream of consciousness as a method (Burroughs didn't embrace stream of consciousness: he had a strong belief in editing and a peculiar angle on craft; but the routines that made up the bulk of his early books *felt* like stream of consciousness) for overwhelming any contrary impulse toward caution and self-censorship. And they all expressed disdain for authority figures, particularly government bureaucrats, cops, and social control professionals like the psychologists who ran mental institutions.

The different ways the writers phrased their disregard for authority were generally indicative of their writing style. Kerouac was liable to sadly but gently bemoan the loss of the wild and free frontier where earlier Americans could get lost and escape daily confrontation with cops and bureaucrats. Ginsberg would angrily identify big authority and its weapons—presidents and atomic bombs—with daily dehumanizations suffered at the hands of cruel conservatism, before wishing love and happiness upon the oppressors. Burroughs would adopt the dominator's voice and gleefully use it to expose the hideous barbarism behind the dignified facade of bourgeois democratic power holders.

During the late 1950s, the beats became massively famous. They were all over the media. Features appeared in all the major magazines and newspapers. They gave readings backed by hip jazz figures. *Life* magazine called the beats "the only rebellion around." (It's worth noting that the beats actually were *not* the only rebellion around. Aside from the glimmers of pop culture disorderliness discussed later in this chapter, young intellectuals had J. D. Salinger's rebel against "phoniness" Holden Caulfield to relate to, and their parents could despair along with David Riesman's *The Lonely Crowd* and William H. Whyte's *The Organization Man*, popular sociological studies that excoriated mass conformism.) Ginsberg and Kerouac appeared on TV talk shows (a big deal back when there were only three networks), and there was even an attempt to make a TV show based on *On the Road*. (When Kerouac wouldn't agree to a deal, they ripped him off, developing the show *Route 66*, a pale evocation of Kerouac's themes.)

In April 1958, *San Francisco Examiner* columnist Herb Caen ascribed the word "beatniks" to the participants in the burgeoning boho culture in San Francisco's North Beach. Immediately, the beatnik became a figure of fun for all America. In this sort of coverage, style replaced content. The media beatnik had a particular look: the male wore a goatee and didn't tuck in his shirt. The female dressed all in black, topped by a French beret. They carried bongos everywhere. It was generally accepted that they didn't like to bathe.

As insulting as it was, this reduction of the hipster bohemian rebellion to a cute stereotype may have subverted mainstream America more than it diminished the beats. It was, after all, still the decade of the "organization man." Anyone who was not clean-cut—neatly dressed, no excess hair anywhere—and didn't submerge his identity in the homogeneity of the industrialized nine-to-five world was viewed as beyond the pale, a total outcast, a suspicious character. After nearly a decade in this restrained condition, any image—however lame or watered down—of people not following the rules was bound to be pretty darned attractive, particularly to the young.

It was the beginning of the television age, and the beats were the first semiotic counterculture. They exiled themselves from mainstream culture not through physical isolation but through art, perception, and—most significantly to the media culture they were both rebels against and very much a part of—mode of dress.

This element of countercultural signification, continued by the youth movements of the 1960s, reached its apotheosis in the 1990s—when tribal subcultures formed almost entirely around mediated identities in which *style* was of utmost importance. At its worst, we entered a stage of history in which signifying counterculture in a manner utterly bereft of content became a rite of passage for a majority of teens and young adults.

This phenomenon began with the beats—not through any fault of the authentic seekers who inspired the movement, but as the result of modern media culture's ability to mimic the effluvia of countercultural movements and values, and turn them into entertainment. It was, after all, only a few years after Allen Ginsberg's historic reading of "Howl" that network television regurgitated the beat movement as prime-time sitcom fare in the persona of Maynard G. Krebs, a character with no more depth than the next major role taken by the actor who played him, Bob Denver—Gilligan in *Gilligan's Island.* (It's amusing, however, to note that Denver became a notorious pothead.)

THE BEATS FOLLOW THEIR BLISS

In the eighteenth century, America's first revolutionary counterculture challenged undemocratic political authority. The counterculture of the Transcendentalists primarily contested the hold religious dogma had over individual thought and spiritual experience. But the freedoms gained by these movements were only partially realized and were consistently endangered due to the perseverance of authoritarian characteristics in both those who would rule and those who would follow. In the 1950s, the McCarthyite hysteria brought this truth into sharp focus. The next project on the road to emancipation would have to be the destruction of the authoritarian personality itself.

This was a pretty sweet deal for the participants, since their main task was to loosen up and explore the creative and humanistic potentialities of doing whatever the hell they wanted. But that wouldn't have worked if these were shallow, selfish men. As it happens, what they wanted to do was explore and expand on human awareness, express and enact greater sympathy for the downtrodden and the outcasts, overthrow tyrannies both large and small, and overcome misery-producing mental programs while sharing the methods and results freely with the public. They enacted all the major countercultural tropes. In fact, they promiscuously allowed themselves to be influenced by nearly every preceding counterculture discussed in this book. They were anti-authoritarian by nature. And they shared information above and beyond the call of duty—if anything, many discomfited readers still find them, Ginsberg particularly, *too* intimate.

And they changed continually. Ginsberg went through a whole variety of mutations, from beat hero to psychedelic guru to Yippie leader before arriving at a genial mix of Buddhism and pacifist activism. He left his body behind in 1997. Burroughs went from a hard individualistic libertarianism to sympathy for the revolutionary left in the late 1960s to cynical comic godfather to New York's punk rockers in the 1970s, finally shocking everybody by announcing that "love is the answer" just before departing for "the Western Lands" (Burroughs' metaphor for death) in 1997, shortly after Ginsberg. Fame didn't agree with Jack Kerouac. He transformed himself from the beat voice of Zen compassion to an embittered, anti-Semitic, paranoid redneck living with his mother, dying in 1969 at the age of forty-seven of cirrhosis of the liver from alcohol abuse.

Most of the young men and women who flocked to Greenwich Village, San Francisco's North Beach, and a few other hip outposts to participate in the "beatnik" phenomenon soon rejoined "normalcy," and some even became conservatives. But significant numbers, even while returning to the comforts of the middle class, would be a part of liberalizing trends in the early 1960s like the civil rights movement, the anti-nuclear-proliferation movement, and increased openness about sexuality. And a great number of gifted writers adopted the beats' "open breath" (Ginsberg's term) aesthetic as well as aspects of their freewheelin' lifestyle. Diane di Prima, who started hanging out among the beats and hipsters in 1953, finally broke the boys' club character of the movement with the publication of her poetry book *This Kind of Bird Flies Backwards* in 1958. Anne Waldman would follow shortly thereafter. Leroi Jones would be the first African-American to enter the beat circle. He and di Prima married and published a beat newsletter called *The Floating Bear* in the late 1950s. In the mid-1960s, Jones became a black separatist and changed his name to Amiri Baraka. (Now the poet laureate of New Jersey, he is currently in hot water for publishing a poem that links 9/11 to American foreign policy and unfortunately includes a line of absurd anti-Semitic conspiracy theory.) Starting in 1961, African-Americans Ishmael Reed and Al Young would write and edit bebop/beat prose composed mostly by blacks and Asians in their *Yardbird Reader,* named after Charlie Parker. By the mid-1960s, it's likely that most young artists, writers, filmmakers, folksingers, and even "new" journalists were influenced by the beats, although playwright Sam Shepard, poet and musician Ed Sanders, avant-garde filmmaker Bruce Conner, gonzo journalist Hunter S. Thompson, and, of course, Bob Dylan demand special mention for brilliantly elaborating beat style.

SEX AND MAD MAGAZINE AND ROCK 'N' ROLL

> Hail, hail, rock and roll/Deliver me from the days of old.
>
> CHUCK BERRY, 1957

> Good golly, Miss Molly/Sure loves to ball.
>
> LITTLE RICHARD, 1958

If the beats were a revolution infecting fifties American pop culture, the pop culture itself had a more broadly subversive impact upon far greater numbers of (mostly) young minds and bodies. There were, of course, the legendary films of youth alienation like *Rebel Without a Cause* and *The*

Wild One. Deeper changes were wrought by Benjamin Spock's top-selling book, *Dr. Spock's Baby and Child Care.* First published in 1946, it became the young parents' bible. So influential he was called "America's baby doctor," Spock uprooted thousands of years of household totalitarianism by advising against the disciplinary abuse of children. (Spock's advice wasn't original. He just broadly popularized less prohibitive methods.) *Mad* magazine, originally subtitled "Humor in a Jugular Vein" and packaged like a comic book to appeal to preteens, mixed together goofy kids' humor with sophisticated and wickedly subversive satire that poked fun at everything in the adult world ranging from politicians and military chiefs to every kid's parents. Hugh Hefner's *Playboy* magazine brought soft-core pornography into the middle-class household, combining mainstream liberal journalism with an eloquent advocacy of sexual freedom, although it came freighted with images of men as slick, self-impressed, shallow consumers, and women as utterly brainless sex toys, that were hardly liberating.

The biggest explosion in teen rebellion against the restrictive pressures of the 1950s was, of course, rock and roll. The early history of rock and roll—named after the sex act, rooted in African-American blues and boogie-woogie music—is probably more familiar than the U.S. Constitution and Bill of Rights to Americans born after 1940, so I won't regurgitate its contents here. Suffice it to say that while rock and roll wasn't precisely countercultural or explicitly anti-authoritarian in the way that, say, a Voltaire essay was, it did establish a separate rebellious youth identity that erupted into full-fledged counterculture revolt in the latter part of the following decade. And it spread all over the world. Among the biggest rock and roll fanatics, a Liverpool art school student who, in 1957, was publishing his own little alternative art/literary magazine titled *The Daily Howl* listened to every Elvis Presley and Chuck Berry record he could find. John Lennon knew something was happening, although he didn't yet know what it was.

CHAPTER TWELVE

When You Change with Every New Day

The Youth Counterculture, 1960–1967

The evolution of ideas [is] a series of escapes from the tyranny of mental habits and stagnant routines. In biological evolution the escape is brought about by a retreat from the adult to a juvenile stage as the starting point for the new line; in mental evolution by a temporary regression to more primitive and uninhibited modes of ideation, followed by the creative forward leap.

Arthur Koestler

There is a time when the operation of the machine becomes so odious, makes you so sick at heart, that you can't take part; you can't even tacitly take part, and you've got to put your bodies upon the levers, upon all the apparatus, and you've got to make it stop. And you've got to indicate to the people who own it, that unless you're free, the machine will be prevented from working at all.

Mario Savio, 1964

The empty-handed painter from your streets/Is drawing
crazy patterns on your sheets.

BOB DYLAN, 1965

Plymouth is tripping out this year.

PLYMOUTH AUTOMOBILE AD, 1967

In the 1960s all of our countercultural tropes came screaming out
into the open at once. It seemed as if some kind of psychic prison had suddenly come unlocked and all the young people were trying to make their
escape. Expanded liberties for individuals in thought, speech, and behavior rubbed against—and tried to merge with—a growing sense of collective responsibility to end war, poverty, and injustice. The Enlightenment's
libertarian ideals rubbed up against the Romantics' poetic drive for deep
human contact, experience, and the liberation of the soul, giving birth to
cultural and political movements based on a desire to bring into being a society that is both humane and ecstatic . . . right away!

At the cutting edge of this countercultural explosion, the Enlightenment's demands for liberties in public discourse mutated into demands for
a liberty within the individual's body (and, by extension, the mind). Not
only should free-consenting individuals have the right to take whatever or
whomever they want (in)to their bodies, said bodies need not be encumbered by unnecessary clothes. Anti-materialist currents set off by movements like the Transcendentalists and the beats mutated into an attempt to
live in the eternal now, as if bureaucratic regulations, the rules of ownership, and the presumed necessity to sell one's time for wages were simply
tiresome roadblocks to be ignored, danced around, or finally to be overthrown. As Richard Miller wrote, it was all about "liberty, meaning the
absence of physical, mental, emotional, cultural, and even biological restraint. . . . This idea . . . is *Autonomy.*"

These ideals and impulses naturally evoked a clamor of riotous activity
and a severe reactive repression. Legends were made, revolutions seemed
feasible, communities and communes rose and fell, individuals had intense

experiences that some will never forget and others will never remember. New philosophies were modeled with almost as much frequency as miniskirts. People's belief systems and minds were expanded, sometimes well past the breaking point. Prison terms were meted out. Protesters were shot. Countercultural political extremists suicided their movement (and ultimately, in some cases, themselves).

Nonconformism and the personal search for identity became a mass movement, in many ways summoning forth new forms of conformity, new group identities. Drugs and rebellion became the thing that all young people do. Massive contradictions were duly noted and still, perfectly intelligent and reasonably people felt that a great liberation—even a *total* liberation—for the one and for the many was at hand.

And then, sometime in the early 1970s, the utopian expectations of the 1960s counterculture just sort of burnt out. An instant ecstatic communal praxis, fueled by psychedelic drugs and spread by the evolving global media, was not to be. But the essential energies and ideas of the 1960s didn't die. They just slowed down.

And in the Beginning There Was an Altered Statesman

In 1960, the signature of change appeared at the top of the social hierarchy when the Democrat John F. Kennedy replaced stolid Republican General Dwight D. Eisenhower as the president of the United States. Kennedy was not particularly liberal. In fact, he started off his administration by increasing military spending to unprecedented levels and expanding nuclear bomb testing. Still, Kennedy was much like our recent philanderer-in-chief—his charisma, his dynamic youthful vibe, his fashionable and pretty wife, his willingness (and ability) to engage in casual, witty banter with the educated media elite, and his friendships with vaguely bohemian artists like Gore Vidal and Peter Lawford combined to create a sense that he was a wee bit hip.

Later revelations would prove that Kennedy was something of a sex-and-drugs president. While his libidinal appetite has been well documented, his drug indulgences are slightly more arcane. Methamphetamine and B$_{12}$ injections from Max Jacobson, known to fashionable New Yorkers as Dr. Feelgood, marijuana in the White House with Mary Pinchot Meyer (as disclosed in the 1979 book *Catherine the Great* by Deborah Davis), and quite probably at least one LSD trip with the same woman (as implied by Timothy Leary, who knew Meyer) indicate that Mr. Kennedy was a bit of an altered statesman.

Drugs aside, JFK was at least somewhat in tune with an emerging generation of idealistic youths. He was sympathetic with the civil rights movement (although slow to act) and, just before his assassination, he reversed his confrontational attitude toward the Soviet Union, calling for disarmament and negotiation. In an oft-quoted speech in June 1963, he waxed visionary: "If we cannot end now all our differences, at least we can help make the world safe for diversity. For, in the final analysis, our most basic common link is that we all inhabit this small planet. We all breathe the same air. We all cherish our children's future. And we are all mortal." In today's cynical climate, this may read like cheap piety, but at that time, Kennedy's words represented a breakthrough.

While Kennedy's progressive image energized the early years of the decade, infusing the times (despite the harrowing Cuban Missile Crisis of 1961) with a sense of possibility, two other events at the start of the decade represent the raw beginnings of a countercultural formation that seemed close to turning Western civilization on its head by the decade's end.

In 1962, Harvard University, under pressure from the CIA, fired Richard Alpert (later Baba Ram Dass) and Timothy Leary, unwittingly setting off a spate of publicity for psychedelic drugs, and giving both the drugs and the former professors a rebellious cachet that sparked the interests of (mostly) college students across America. That same year, a group of college students, including a twenty-two-year-old named Tom Hayden, gathered together and wrote the Port Huron Statement. This eloquent manifesto defined a new, post-communist but radical left politics based on expansive notions of "participatory democracy," existentialist concepts of individual identity forged through activism, and youthful alienation. These two minor blips on America's sociopolitical radar screen would prove to be the launching points for major movements that would later converge into the unholy holy mess that was the late 1960s.

They'd Love to Turn You On

In 1960, at thirty-nine, Timothy Leary was a moderately progressive Harvard psychology professor with a lifelong habit of getting into minor scraps with authority. On a colleague's advice, while vacationing with family and friends in Mexico, he took some psilocybin mushrooms. The results left him, to put it mildly, much impressed. He later wrote of the experience: "It was . . . without question the deepest religious experience in my life. I discovered that beauty, revelation, sensuality, the cellular history of the past, God, the Devil—all lie inside my body, outside my mind."

Leary returned to Harvard that fall determined to conduct experiments examining the psychotherapeutic potentials of this substance. He set up a Harvard psilocybin research project and located a legal supply of synthetic psilocybin pills. Various well-informed and well-read colleagues brought him up to speed regarding already extant psychedelic research and the writings of intellectual self-experimenters like William James and Aldous Huxley. A thriving subculture of scientists, therapists, and CIA spies had been experimenting with various psychedelic compounds throughout the 1950s with wildly conflicting goals. Some scientists thought that the drugs created a temporary psychosis, affording them an opportunity to learn about these pathological states. Another group of psychiatric professionals had discovered that the drugs could evoke a positive, life-affirming, even spiritual experience with therapeutic results. And although no one was quite certain at that time what the CIA was up to, files later released under the Freedom of Information Act revealed that they thought the drugs (particularly LSD) could be used for various "defense" purposes, including the interrogation of prisoners and the incapacitation of enemy troops and civilian populations. (They eventually decided the drugs were too unpredictable to be useful.) So Timothy Leary joined the small but growing list of psychological experimenters who emphasized the healing capacities of these substances.

Allen Ginsberg had already tripped out on mescaline, peyote, and LSD when he got wind of the Harvard research project and made arrangements to be a guinea pig in one of Dr. Leary's little experiments. With his longtime lover Peter Orlovsky, he paid the professor a visit. According to biographer Barry Miles, about an hour into the trip,

Suddenly, out of the window, Allen saw a flash of light, which reminded him of the Star of Bethlehem, and as the music of Wagner's *Götterdämmerung* thundered in the room, "like the horns of judgment calling from the ends of the cosmos—calling on all human consciousness to declare itself into the consciousness," it seemed to Allen as if all the worlds of human consciousness were waiting for a Messiah. "Someone to take on the responsibility of being the creative God and seize power over the universe and become the next consciousness. . . . I decided I might as well be the one to do so—pronounce my nakedness as the first act of revolution against the destroyers of the human image. The naked body being the hidden sign."

Allen thought of Milton's Lucifer and wondered why Milton sided with the rebel in Heaven. He got up from the bed, put on his eyeglasses, and walked downstairs naked, closely followed by Peter. They headed for the study, where Frank Barron, Leary's co-worker, who shared the house, was sitting at his desk. They stopped in front of him. As Leary came into the room, having ushered his young daughter up to the safety of the third floor, Allen raised his finger in the air and waved it. "I'm the Messiah," he said. [If the twentieth century taught us one thing, it's that charismatic visionaries with leadership potential shouldn't listen to Wagner!] "I've come down to preach love to the world. We're going to walk through the streets and teach people to stop hating."

To prove he was the Messiah, Ginsberg asked Leary to remove his glasses, so he could heal his vision. Leary did this, and then pointed out that Ginsberg was still wearing *his* glasses. When Ginsberg wanted to call Kerouac to tell him that "It's time to seize power over the universe and become the next consciousness," he had to go off squinting in search of his address book, at which point he realized some limits to his new godlike powers.

This somewhat ironic deflation of Ginsberg's messianic psilocybin insights didn't curb his enthusiasm for turning people on to the wisdom he had found in the substance. And Ginsberg's fervor awakened in Dr. Leary a capacity for evangelical enthusiasm virtually unmatched in the Western world. This odd couple—Ginsberg bearded, gay, Jewish, a bit slovenly, a hipster poet of often confrontational spontaneous rants; and Leary nattily dressed, smooth as any politician, Irish-American, decidedly hetero, Robert Redford–handsome, and prone to linear, numerically based models of human behavior—made a pact to turn on the world.

Their initial plan rejected media hype in favor of a slow, organic, word-of-mouth process. They would guide important writers, artists, and musicians through psilocybin trips. Presumably, the targeted communicators would catch the enthusiasm and begin to spread the word.

The results were decidedly mixed. Most of the intellectuals and artists who tried the drug found it to be a worthy experience, but they were—each in their own idiosyncratic way—ambivalent about its effects and its promises. Among the dozen or so chosen, Arthur Koestler called it "false, ersatz. Instant mysticism." Ginsberg's beat brother, the great drug veteran Burroughs, had a massive bummer in Tangiers and wrote, "Listen: Their Garden of Delights is a terminal sewer. . . . Their Immortality Cosmic Consciousness and Love is second-run grade-B shit." Perhaps the most prescient and poignant response came from the poet Robert Lowell, who, under the effects of the psilocybin, envisioned a dark wave of violent repression against helplessly vulnerable, mind-opened trippers. Ginsberg tried to reassure him, saying, "Don't worry. Love conquers all." Lowell's response: *"Don't be so sure."* And then there was the mad jazz genius Charles Mingus, who just smiled and asked if they had anything stronger. (He would later become a frequent visitor to Leary's mid-sixties Millbrook, New York, scene, where they did, in fact, have something stronger: LSD.) Some liked the drug a little. Some hated it a lot. Some liked it a lot. None joined the crusade.

Leary continued with his academic research project. While he was no beatnik, his natural style was informal and independent. Sessions were conducted without a medical doctor present in a comfortable home setting by candlelight instead of in the laboratory. And when a student's proposal for an experiment involving prisoners was rejected by the Harvard bureaucracy, Leary used his persuasive skills to make his own arrangements with the prison officials.

In addition to Leary's experiments, Harvard was a center for CIA research into hallucinogens, particularly LSD. And the CIA soon decided that "this town isn't big enough for both of us." In his 1988 book, *Acid Dreams: The CIA, LSD, and the Sixties Rebellion,* Martin Lee reported that "a confidential memorandum issued by the CIA's Office of Security, which had utilized LSD for interrogation purposes in the early 1950s, suggested that certain CIA-connected personnel might be involved with Leary's group. . . . [The memo read:] 'Information concerning the use of this type of drug for experimental or personal reasons should be reported immediately. . . . In addition, any information of Agency personnel involved with Drs. ALPERT or LEARY, or with any other group engaged in this type of activity should be reported.' " Lee also wrote that a distinguished Harvard Medical School doctor, Henry Beecher, who had directed drug experiments on behalf of the CIA, publicly "ridiculed Leary's methodology, stating that it 'reminded him of De Quincey's *Confessions of an Opium Eater.*' " Other denunciations from CIA-associated experimenters appeared in the *Harvard Alumni Review.*

The Harvard administration sat up and took notice. In a public meeting, the psilocybin project was put under heavy bureaucratic scrutiny (for all intents and purposes, shutting it down) and Leary and Alpert were ordered to relinquish their psilocybin stash. On returning the drugs, Leary commented that "These drugs cause panic and temporary insanity in many officials who have never taken them." This sharp and irreverent rejoinder would characterize Leary's relationship with all forms of authority from that point until the end of his life thirty-five years later.

One factor in Leary's dismissive attitude toward social deference was LSD. The much more potent and abstract psychedelic had replaced gentle, natural psilocybin as the drug of choice among the project insiders. Leary began to view all normal social interactions as "a fake prop movie set." The LSD initiate, he would soon advise, should "detach yourself from the external social drama, which is as dehydrated and ersatz as TV."

It was only a matter of months before Harvard found excuses to fire Alpert and Leary, at which point the law of unintended consequences worked its magic. With publicity galore, the disgraced professors were set loose in the mediated world to speak their minds freely, which they did with intelligence and a reckless abandon that intrigued rebellious seekers, especially among the young. Now that they had an enemy, the establishment, the crusade could begin in earnest.

SOUL LEFTISTS

We are people of this generation, bred in at least modest comfort, housed now in universities, looking uncomfortably to the world we inherit.

When we were kids the United States [represented] ... freedom and equality for each individual, government of, by, and for the people—these American values we found good, principles by which we could live as men. . . .

As we grew, however, our comfort was penetrated by events too troubling to dismiss. First, the permeating and victimizing fact of human degradation, symbolized by the Southern struggle against racial bigotry, compelled most of us from silence to activism. Second, the enclosing fact of the Cold War, symbolized by the presence of the Bomb, brought awareness that we ourselves, and our friends, and millions of abstract "others" might die at any time. . . .

We regard men as infinitely precious and possessed of unfulfilled capacities for reason, freedom, and love. In affirming these principles we are aware of countering perhaps the dominant conceptions of man in the twentieth century: that he is a thing to be manipulated, and that he is inherently incapable of directing his own affairs. We oppose the depersonalization that reduces human beings to the status of things.

Men have unrealized potential for self-cultivation, self-direction, self-understanding, and creativity. . . . The goal of man and society should be human independence: a concern not with image or popularity but with finding a meaning in life that is personally authentic, a quality of mind not compulsively driven by a sense of powerlessness, nor one which unthinkingly adopts status values, nor one which represses all threats to its habits, but one which has full, spontaneous access to present and past experiences, one which easily unites the fragmented parts of personal history, one which openly faces problems which are troubling and unresolved; one with an intuitive awareness of possibilities, an active sense of curiosity, an ability and willingness to learn.

. . . Loneliness, estrangement, isolation describe the vast distance between man and man today. These dominant tendencies cannot be overcome by better personnel management, nor by improved gadgets, but only when a love of man overcomes the idolatrous worship of things by man.

. . . We would replace power rooted in possession, privilege, or circumstance by power and uniqueness rooted in love, reflectiveness, reason, and creativity.

PORT HURON STATEMENT,
STUDENTS FOR A DEMOCRATIC SOCIETY (SDS), 1962

In the wake of Khrushchev's Stalin revelations, many former Marxists and socialists had attached themselves to anti-communist liberalism. With the election of Kennedy, they were in proximity to real power. And although more conservative elements dominated the upper reaches of the administration, many liberals held minor positions. The going was slow, but anti-poverty programs, increased federal support for African-American civil rights, and eventually even nuclear disarmament agreements—all policies near and dear to their liberal hearts—were at least on the table.

These post-fifties liberals, having survived McCarthyism, were cautious men and women. To the extent that they still harbored any left-wing or even any expansive civil libertarian sentiments, they were inclined to keep those sentiments to themselves. If they dissented, as some did in response to Kennedy's earlier expansion of nuclear testing, they did so timidly, as polite supplicants begging for consideration. Cold War paranoia about Russia, China, and other communist takeovers, particularly the recent youthful, vibrant, and reckless Castro revolution in Cuba, still suffused the political environment. Like today, being sufficiently patriotic meant being sufficiently militaristic, and the liberals didn't just play the game. For the most part, they believed in it.

In 1960, a left-liberal college organization, the Student League for Industrial Democracy, a group sponsored by the unionist League for Industrial Democracy, changed its name to Students for a Democratic Society—SDS. The name change was decidedly a statement of independence. A new generation was taking charge of the organization. They had no guilt or disillusionment over Stalin—that was their parents' history. As mid-sixties SDS president Todd Gitlin wrote, "The Soviet system . . . they couldn't even take it seriously, even as an enemy; it was an aged and obsolete 'dinosaur,' not a monster in its prime." As children, they'd been aware of McCarthyism, but they *were,* after all, children. Their psyches were more deeply imprinted by *Mad* magazine, rock and roll, the presence of the atomic and hydrogen bombs, James Dean in *Rebel Without a Cause,* and Salinger's alienated seeker after authenticity, Holden Caulfield (*The Catcher in the Rye,* published in 1951, was must reading for all intelligent high school students in the late 1950s). And somewhere in the mythic distance were the rumored beatniks, getting high and having sex while their parents toiled nine-to-five.

College intellectuals of the period were also neck-deep into a trend for existential philosophy, particularly Albert Camus. The message of the Existentialists, in a reductionist nutshell, was that the individual is responsible for her own life; no divinity, no government, no society is going to do it for you. And you'd better grab hold of this life with all the intensity you can muster, because there's nothing afterward. Middle-class liberalism, with its impotent compromises and its abstract, bureaucratic policy solutions to social problems, was not for them. The point of life was to make your stand, here and now. To put your body on the line. And to connect intimately with your fellow human beings. Paul Goodman, an eloquent anarcho-pacifist who had authored a popular 1960 book, *Growing Up Absurd,* had written about "the most important resistance of all resistances— resistance to mass collective loneliness." An early SDS slogan was "One

Man, One Soul." Lenin was rolling over in his grave, and even Trotsky was tossing and turning!

The medium through which the mostly white SDSers expressed their existential commitment and forged their activist identities was the civil rights movement. (The irony of young whites finding their identities in the struggle for black equality would not be lost on the Black Power militants of the mid-1960s.) They aligned themselves with the Congress of Racial Equality (CORE), the Student Nonviolent Coordinating Committee (SNCC), and other groups and individuals. The New Left's version of the *On the Road* experience would involve taking buses and cars to the American South to help challenge racial segregation. It was—no doubt about it—an authentic experience. Along with the black activists and local black citizens, they were spat at, threatened with guns, beaten by police, jailed, and two among them were killed. But after over a thousand civil rights demonstrations, and twenty thousand arrests, they *won* (not completely of course, but substantially). Attorney General Robert Kennedy, after months of hesitation in the face of outrageous violence, finally sent federal troops into Mississippi to force the integration of a school there, and in 1963 JFK introduced a comprehensive civil rights bill into Congress that focused primarily on the desegregation of schools, restaurants, and hotels. It became law a year later, under the leadership of Lyndon Johnson. Racial oppression would remain a fact of American life, but at least outright apartheid had been clearly made illegal.

Back on campus, the college radicals were becoming identified with general rebelliousness and sexual freedom. Mild beatnik affectations were adopted. Their self-confident insouciance was apparent. Their hair was a little shaggier than the rest. In a few spots, like Berkeley, California, the illicit kicks of marijuana became a part of the left-wing scene.

The sexual standards of the time were still very conservative. Premarital sex was taboo, and cohabitation was a serious outrage. The universities were empowered with parental authority. Students chafed under the limitations of separate dormitories and curfews. The New Leftists were conspicuous in their disregard for old sexual standards and school rules. This rebel-with-a-cause attitude made them the sexiest thing on campus. Members and sympathizers increased. And swagger as they might, their intellectual earnestness was also manifest. Gitlin: "There were questions, endless questions, running debates that took their point from the divine premise that everything was possible and therefore it was important to think, because ideas have consequences. Unraveling, rethinking, refusing to take for granted, thinking without limits."

It didn't hurt the New Left that the mainstream ideology of the time was also substantially to the left of today's dominant discourse. The ideology of free-market absolutism that is so popular today (although crony capitalism is actually in practice) was in complete disrepute, surviving only on the fringes of political culture. Leftist theorist Daniel Foss could write, "In public rhetoric, 'capitalism' has been treated as mildly obscene. . . . No serious thinker has any further use for the self-regulating market theory as a descriptive model."

In this welcoming environment, the young, libertine, civil libertarian left picked up steam, and their leadership of a nuclear disarmament protest movement connected to a growing sense of generational alienation. Many college students blamed their parents' generation for bequeathing them an apparently terminal planet.

This political culture's evolution was not seriously interrupted when, on November 22, 1963, the semi-liberal "prince" John Kennedy was shot dead on the streets of Dallas. Despite his alleged assassin, Lee Harvey Oswald's, apparent left-wing and Cuban connection (no, we're *not* going to go there), the public response was more mournful than retributive. And the shock of seeing Kennedy and then Oswald assassinated on TV (over and over again) left people with a lot to process. What to make of the endless replays of dramatically real murders of such political import viewed at the safe distance of a screen from our living rooms? If anything, the pervasive sense of disquiet only made these new existential leftists more attractive to their fellow youths.

BUILDING THE PERFECT HIPPIE, 1964–1967

> On a personal level, Freaking Out is a process whereby an individual casts off outmoded and restricting standards of thinking, dress, and social etiquette in order to express CREATIVELY his relationship to his immediate

environment and the social structure as a whole.... On a collective level, when any number of "Freaks" gather and express themselves creatively through music or dance...it is generally referred to as a FREAK OUT. The participants, already emancipated from our national social slavery, dressed in their most inspired apparel, realize as a group whatever potential they possess for *free expression*. We would like to encourage everyone who HEARS this music to join us . . . become a member of *The United Mutations* . . . FREAK OUT!

FRANK ZAPPA, 1966

We hold these truths to be self-evident, that all is equal, that the creation endows us with certain inalienable rights, that among these are: The freedom of the body, the pursuit of joy and the expansion of consciousness.

STATEMENT FROM THE "LOVE PAGEANT RALLY"
TO PROTEST THE NEW PROHIBITION AGAINST LSD, 1966

Beatniks and politics nothing is new/A yardstick for lunatics, one point of view.

JOHN CARTER AND TIMOTHY GILBERT,
STRAWBERRY ALARM CLOCK, 1967

While the militaristic logic of the Cold War maintained a strong hold on the psyches of most Americans during the early 1960s, the sullen anti-authoritarian countercultural tendencies left over from the beatnik 1950s started to evolve into a more playful, absurdist style. Released in 1964, Stanley Kubrick's *Dr. Strangelove or: How I Learned to Stop Worrying and Love the Bomb* turned nuclear brinkmanship and right-wing patriotism into farce. The film, scripted in large part by the beat-influenced, drug-gobbling comic genius Terry Southern, still stands as one of the most outrageous acts of disrespect toward America's military and political establishments. In painting, the desperate lunge at liberation represented by the Abstract Expressionists and their hard-drinking and -fighting lifestyle gave way to the fey, stylish, ironic/iconic play of pop artists like Roy Lichtenstein and Jasper Johns. In England, as early as 1961, Op Artist Bridget Riley was striking a colorful hallucinatory note, and the Fluxus group (which originated in New York City) caught the British art-going public's imagination with Dadaist-style happenings that replaced that earlier movement's postwar anger with pure whimsy. And Bob Dylan, while he was mostly acclaimed as a bright young star for striking protest songs like "Masters of War" and "The Lonesome Death of Hattie Carroll," behaved like a snotty (and funny) teenage Surrealist in his press interviews, putting down reporters and other adults for being too self-serious and literal-minded.

Another little-noticed bit of subtly anti-authoritarian youth programming came from mid-sixties TV sitcoms, which tended to portray the father or the authority figure as a buffoon. There was Darrin, the clueless middle-class husband of the good witch Samantha, who was antagonized by his wife's elegant nonconformist (not to mention immortal) mother, Endora. And there was Captain Tony Nelson, the army major who didn't have enough sense to take advantage of what his magical "Jeannie," Barbara Eden, had to offer. Both of these emasculated mediocrities lived in constant fear of being fired or punished by their equally idiotic, albeit irritable, bosses. The commanders of *F Troop* and *McHale's Navy* couldn't walk and chew gum at the same time. Their underlings could easily trick them, which they did either for laughs or to solve a problem that would have only been made worse if they followed the orders of the befuddled fool at the top of the work hierarchy. (The perverse *Hogan's Heroes,* in which the clueless "boss" was a Nazi prison camp commandant, took the genre into the realm of unintentional surrealism.)

In any case, the mini–cultural revolution that started in the 1950s was continuing apace, gaining self-confidence, even getting cheeky. But where was the rock and roll? The raw sexuality and rebellious spirit expressed in the early music of Elvis Presley, Eddie Cochran, Jerry Lee Lewis, Little Richard, Fats Domino, and Chuck Berry had come from their authentic love of rhythm and blues. But by the end of the 1950s, their stylings had been copied and watered down by companies who used payola to impose their prefabricated teen idols on the top of the pop music charts.

In England, meanwhile, young men, most of them from the working class and many born during the terror and shame of the Nazi Blitz bomb-

ings, were living in the husk of a fallen empire built on rigid class distinctions. Finding solace in old American rock and roll records from the
1950s, they bought or stole musical instruments and started to play. Combining this influence with earlier American blues, rockabilly, and, in some
cases, British dance hall music, they developed a sound that was all their
own.

For several years, England's rock scene was a local secret. The lads had
time to develop not just their music but their fashion sense. With longish
hair creeping over their collars, high-heeled boots, peg-legged pants, dark
turtlenecks, and other high-collared shirts, their look was a mix of British
dandy and American beat. And for some damned reason, the best musicians were all skinny, pale things. The British rockers, many of them art
school students, looked like the kids that the jocks beat up in high school,
but the local girls were wild for them.

In early 1964, the energetic and frothy pop rock of the Beatles, already
inducing mania among young fans in England, exploded in the United
States. It was Beatlemania, and while the little girls screamed and creamed,
the entire adult population of America momentarily stopped worrying
about the commies and started worrying about *hair*. With the American
media acting almost as frantic as the screaming girls, the Beatles came on
like four lads having a private joke. They were quick and funny in their
press interviews and, like rock star James Bonds, they seemed to maintain
cool heads in the midst of the possibly dangerous hysteria.

Like a good cop/bad cop routine, after the Beatles established a beachhead, the British Invasion sent in the Rolling Stones to let American
teenagers know that fucking usually follows foreplay. While all these
young men (Beatles and Stones) were mildly influenced by hipster memes
and art school educations (at least some of them), and they all shared in
the largely inchoate sense of youth discontent that permeated their culture,
they were not out to "subvert the dominant paradigm" or anything of that
sort. The rock and rollers just wanted to have some fun playing the music
they loved, make a bit of money, and score with birds (girls in Britspeak),
although one look at the surly, feral-looking Rolling Stones told you that
there were other undercurrents lurking that maybe even *they* weren't fully
conscious of.

Over the next three years, rock lyrics and music evolved at a head-spinning pace. In early 1965, while the Beatles were still singing simple clichéd rhymes about puppy love, and the Stones were mimicking the simplest blues tropes, the left's folksinger hero, Bob Dylan, recorded a side of electric rock tunes for an album titled *Bringing It All Back Home*. Suddenly, a rock and roll album was capable of carrying lyrics like: "Disillusioned words like bullets bark/As human gods aim for their mark/Made everything from toy guns that spark/To flesh-colored Christs that glow in the dark/It's easy to see without looking too far/That not much/Is really sacred." But it wasn't until later that year that the Top Forty radio made it explicit that young rock and rollers didn't like adult society. It started, again, with Dylan. Even preteens couldn't help but get the message from his first major hit, "Like a Rolling Stone," that there was a tough and ugly world out beyond the suburbs and we ought to A) be pissed off about it and B) go and check it out. Lyrics like "You never understood . . . /you shouldn't let other people get your kicks for you," struck at the heart of the middle class's fearful attempt to live life at a safe distance and consume experience through media.

In May 1965, Allen Ginsberg visited his friends Bob Dylan and Joan Baez while they toured England, where he was introduced to the Beatles and started a lifelong friendship with Paul McCartney. Although at that time there was only the bare glimmer of lyrical and intellectual content on the "Swingin' London" rock scene, Ginsberg sensed something potent and hip emerging. He proclaimed, "Liverpool is at the present time the center of the consciousness of the human universe."

By late 1965, with Dylan's liberation of Top Forty airspace, the floodgates were opened. One-hit wonder Barry McGuire growled "Eve of Destruction," a didactic statement of youthful distress and apocalyptic paranoia that centered around the bomb but also referenced the civil rights struggle: "Marches alone can't bring integration/When human respect is disintegrating." And the Animals declared, ". . . daddy . . . been working and slaving his life away . . . /We gotta get out of this place." In 1966, the Who escalated the generation gap, asking the older generation, "Why don't you all f-f-f-fade away," and declaimed, "I hope I die before I get old." And the Rolling Stones went toe-to-toe with Dylan for the premature lyrical jadedness crown with "Have You Seen Your Mother, Baby, Standing in the Shadows?," singing about the choice between "the brave old world or a slide into the depths of decline." (It was clear they had chosen the latter. They also posed menacingly in drag as flight stewardesses on the record sleeve.) And they dropped the first hint of LSD in their song "19th Nervous Breakdown": "On our first trip I tried so hard to rearrange your mind." But then Dylan set everybody on their ears with his peripatetic *Blonde on Blonde,* in which—years ahead of everyone else—he identified the beatific psychedelic "Visions of Johanna" as ultimately "cruel" because of the ugly social realities that surround them. And finally the Beatles one-upped everybody with the musically sophisticated psychedelia of their album *Revolver,* which included several spooky LSD-saturated songs from George Harrison and John Lennon, one with lyrics cadged from a Timothy Leary book.

WHAT A SHORT FUN TRIP IT WAS

If the rock stars were getting a bit far out, they were positively stiff compared to American novelist Ken Kesey and his Merry Pranksters. Kesey was turned on to LSD during government experiments at Stanford University in the early 1960s. He had written a powerful hit book, an attack of madness against authority called *One Flew Over the Cuckoo's Nest,* while working at a mental institution, flying high on various hallucinogens the whole time. Then, in 1964, he packed a bunch of friends and LSD into a psychedelic-painted bus and, dressed in cartoonish superhero outfits, they roared off across America to goof on people and see how the country (outside of their home in the always hip San Francisco Bay Area) looked while under the influence. In one instance, they showed up in Phoenix, Arizona, the hometown of conservative Republican presidential candidate Barry Goldwater, in fully costumed glory, flying American flags and carrying a huge placard reading, "A Vote for Goldwater Is a Vote for Fun." With speakers set up outside the bus, this gang of freaks could broadcast music and talk at the people they passed by. They were so loud, friendly, and *confusing* that they were rarely hassled. After all, they obviously weren't those pesky civil rights protesters, and they weren't those tiresome, gloomy, black-clad beatniks. Who *were* these strange happy people wearing capes and masks?

When Kesey and his tribe returned to the Bay Area in 1965 it was clear that something new was brewing. Bohemians had migrated from the beat-nik North Beach over to the Haight-Ashbury, where large ramshackle houses could be rented cheaply. And the entire sensibility of the hip scene had changed. The bomb that had made nihilists out of the fifties hipsters was by now an accustomed fact of life, the lunatic uncle Thanatos who lived in the attic of everyone's psyche. Meanwhile, life went on. The new hipsters were speaking a language of love, community, and ecstasy. This high, upbeat mindmeld was catalyzed, first of all, by the bright transcendent sparkle of newly dawning psychedelic consciousness, thanks to the great batches of clean, strong LSD distributed by the eccentric genius chemist Augustus Owsley Stanley. And while any hipster worth his salt still appreciated the opiated dreamscapes of jazzmen like Charlie Parker and Miles Davis, the new sound on the block made you get up and dance and smile—rock and roll.

By the end of 1965, a young alien named Chet Helms had hitchhiked into town with his friend Janis Joplin, and opened a rock emporium called the Family Dog. The community came out in droves, introducing a new dance style—free-form. The frenzied, sexually charged rock celebrations brought out a different gloss on the psychedelic experience. It was no longer necessary to sit piously in full-lotus meditation before statues of Eastern gods awaiting the clear light of the pure void. A decidedly Dionysian character was added to the acid gestalt. Martin Lee observed, "By 1965, Haight-Ashbury was a vibrant neobohemian enclave. . . . A small psychedelic city-state was taking shape, and those who inhabited [it] . . . adhered to a set of laws and rhythms completely different from the nine-to-five routine that governed straight society. More than anything the Haight was a unique state of mind, an arena of exploration and celebration. The new hipsters cast aside the syndrome of alienation and despair that saddled many of their beatnik forebears. The accent shifted from solitude to communion, from the individual to the interpersonal."

By early 1966, Kesey's Pranksters were sponsoring public LSD happenings, dubbed "Acid Tests." These were massive come-one come-all events. (Invitations to the first test were passed out to people leaving a Rolling Stones concert.) Big bowls of Kool-Aid were filled with great quantities of LSD, and the Pranksters rigged the Acid Test sites with various amplifiers that would add disorienting chatter and sound effects to the already loud music played by the acid-ripped band, the Warlocks (soon to be called the Grateful Dead). Flashing lights and projections of pulsating colors and peculiar images completed the cacophony.

Like Leary, Kesey wanted to turn on the world. But whereas Leary wanted to provide genteel environments conducive to quiet introspection— exploration of deeper realms of consciousness—Kesey preferred shock tactics similar to those that had been employed by the Zen and Sufi masters. Kesey: "The purpose of psychedelics is to learn the conditioned responses of people and then to prank them. That's the only way to get people to ask questions, and until they ask questions they're going to remain conditioned robots."

Meanwhile, the Timothy Leary show continued broadcasting to ever-greater gobs of media attention out of a donated mansion in the upstate New York town of Millbrook. While it was nowhere near as loose as the Prankster/Haight-Ashbury bacchanalia, Leary's scene was slowly drifting away from the cautious scientific/religious mode and into a party atmosphere. On weekends, trendy New Yorkers—among them models, actors, and denizens of Andy Warhol's decadent Pop Art Factory—drove upstate to leave both the city and the planet behind for a while. Leary's psychedelic evangelizing also continued to grow ever more pop-conscious and provocative. In perhaps the most telling example of his brilliantly targeted pitching, during a 1966 feature-length *Playboy* interview he said, "In a carefully prepared, loving LSD session, a woman will inevitably have several hundred orgasms."

In late 1965, the Leary cabal returned the favor for the British Invasion, sending over an emissary, the eccentric Englishman Michael Hollingshead, along with five thousand hits of LSD. Hollingshead proceeded to turn on all the hippest bohos and artists; among the more famous were Keith Richards, Eric Clapton, Donovan, Paul McCartney, and the influential, radical psychotherapist R. D. Laing. The crossing of psychedelic illumination with Carnaby Street style created a cultural ferment that was less radical but more razzle-dazzle, peacock sartorial than the scene in San Francisco. It was a whole different vibe: fey, androgynous, a bit pretentious, and—being British—respectful of their royalty; in this case Princes Lennon, McCartney, Harrison, Jagger, Richards, Jones, and Townshend. They even had their own acid test equivalent, giant psychedelic rave-ups

attended by most of the hip royalty, with a band called Pink Floyd providing the spacey jams.

By 1966, this wild carnival of untamed youth was starting to worry the
authorities, particularly in the U.S. For starters, according to the FBI,
there were nearly 100,000 juvenile runaways, most of them escaping the
dreariness of their parents' expectations in search of the neo-bohemian experience. In the Haight-Ashbury, there were these lunatics throwing wild
all-night parties with crazy flashing lights, nudity, sex, Hell's Angels, and
dilated people babbling cosmic gibberish. And one couldn't help but notice that many of those filthy New Left troublemakers from Berkeley were
showing up as well. By normative social standards, something unseemly
was going on, but since LSD, the catalyst that was unleashing the celebratory chaos, was still legal, there was little they could do.

In defense of the fortress of ordinary reality, the press and the politicians got busy. The media, which had been trying to sound the alarm since
Leary's dismissal from Harvard, became positively apoplectic, according to
Martin Lee, producing headlines like "GIRL 5, EATS LSD AND GOES
WILD" and "THRILL DRUG WARPS MINDS." One government re-
searcher announced that LSD caused chromosome damage, endangering
the well-being of users' children. (He later confessed that this was a complete fabrication.) The federal government sponsored no fewer than three
hearings designed to attack LSD. Psychedelic advocates, including Timothy Leary and Allen Ginsberg, testified, offering sane and reasonable compromise ideas about regulating, rather than prohibiting, the drug. But it
was a zero-bullshit New York City–bred prankster from Leary's Millbrook
camp named Art Kleps who set the tone that would dominate the hallucinatory drug wars for years to follow, telling the U.S. Senate, "We are not
drug addicts, we are not criminals, we are free men, and we will react to
persecution the way free men have always reacted. . . . I'd rather see the
prison system become inoperable. . . . We would have to regard these
places as concentration camps where people are being imprisoned because
of their religion. . . . I would resort to violence."

Across the nation, states started passing laws prohibiting LSD. On October 6, 1966, when a law passed by the California legislature went into effect, several thousand San Francisco–area acidheads gathered in Golden

Gate Park to protest, and celebrate the new consciousness. Despite the ministrations of "the man," the mood was still high and self-confident.

By their panic, as expressed through their prohibitionary legislation, the conservative forces teased out what was perhaps the central counter-cultural progression for this epoch. Rationalist countercultures like the Enlightenment had sought to expand freedom of thought and speech. Transcendental or spiritual countercultures like Zen Buddhism, Taoism, and Sufism, and post-rationalist countercultures like Romanticism and Surrealism, sought to liberate the entire human being from self-abnegating constrictions. But now, as reactive forces moved to suppress this attempt at transcendent and/or post-rational liberation of consciousness through plants and chemicals, the logical response was to demand an expansion in the definition of enlightened liberal democratic rights. Leary called it the fifth freedom, the right of a human being to control her own states of con-sciousness. In a free society, the state ought not prevent people from achieving any mind state, so long as these people don't intrude on others. Once stated, it seems obvious, except to the vast majority of people to whom it *doesn't* seem obvious. And while this very basic idea of cognitive liberty was, and still is, supported by several million counterculturalists globally, it was (and is) beyond the pale of legal, democratic, "enlightened" discourse. No one in mainstream politics (that we know of) has ever dared to imply that they were even familiar with this notion.

Responding to political pressures was not a hippie specialty. Following in the footsteps of Ginsberg and Leary, the freak youth culture was influ-enced by transcendental Eastern religions like Hinduism and the counter-cultural varieties of Taoism and Zen Buddhism discussed earlier in this book. Even taking into account the Merry Prankster wildness, the basic underlying idea was more interior and contemplative: change yourself and eventually that will change the world; than activist: change the world and in the process change yourself. However, a slightly discordant note was being struck in the Haight community by a group of street-level acid an-archists who called themselves the Diggers. They weren't interested in Learyesque (or even Keseyesque) media hype. They were not enamored of the notion that psychedelic consciousness, in and of itself, was going to bring about a groovy, ecstatic, liberated society. They also didn't think well of the New Lefties and their protests. As Gitlin tells it: "They didn't *demand* because, as they saw it, demanding was dependency, it taught that authorities are legitimate enough to be targets of demands. Don't demand food, they said; get the food and give it away." According to the Diggers, acid was just a small part of a much deeper package. People should be active, innovating their own lives and culture. The streets should be a place for challenging, creative interactions. While evolving their own independent alternative economic forms, freaks should help one another live off the detritus of an abundant economy by begging or stealing free food and clothes. They issued a manifesto challenging hippies to "reclaim . . . territory (sundown, traffic, public joy) through spirit," and to "become life actors . . . a caste of free beings." And, true to their words, they opened a free store and started serving a free meal in Golden Gate Park every afternoon at 4:00 p.m. The Diggers were tireless, mostly begging support for the dropout counterculture from merchants, civilians—whomever they could accost for their alternative Salvation Army programs.

While the Diggers believed radical change came about by acting locally, on the streets, here and now, in an unmediated fashion, the creators of Haight-Ashbury's underground newspaper, *The Oracle,* were among those who wanted to turn on the world. To celebrate and publicize the already expanding hippie culture, they decided to hold a "Be-In" in Golden Gate Park.

The Human Be-In, promoted as a "Gathering of the Tribes" and a "Peace Dance to Be Celebrated with the Leaders of Our Generation," attracted nearly fifteen thousand freaks to Golden Gate Park. The press release for the event declared its lofty ambitions: "For ten years, a new nation has grown inside the robot flesh of the old. . . . Berkeley political activists and the love generation of the Haight-Ashbury will join together . . . to . . . celebrate and prophesy the epoch of liberation, love, peace, compassion, and unity of mankind." The "generational leaders" who mounted the stage to try to make comprehensible vocal noises at the hallucinating crowd included Allen Ginsberg, the poet Gary Snyder, Timothy Leary, and the Berkeley radical Jerry Rubin. Rubin lost the stoned masses with his talk about the Vietnam War, but gamely tried to win them back by saying, "Our smiles are our political banners and our nakedness is our picket sign." Leary tried out his new "Turn On Tune In Drop Out" bumper sticker slogan, which resonated only slightly better. Really, the whole notion of leaders or spokespeople was anathema to the boundary-defying, acid-drenched spirit of this still small and very independent countercultural community. The talks were tolerated, but the people were really there to be with one another, and if anybody was going to be worshiped, it would be Jerry Garcia, the hometown hero who, with his band the Grateful Dead, spoke a language of the deep soul and the wandering psyche through his guitar.

The national media ate up the Be-In, and hippies in general, broadcasting images of stoned, ecstatic, grinning young people into living rooms across middle America, where susceptible teenagers and young adults were likely to take up the thought that *this* looked like more fun than four years of college, forty years in an office wearing a suit and tie, followed by a retirement in Palm Beach. And they did.

Everybody started talking about the hippies. The word hippie, which, by 1967, had been adopted by many members of the Haight community (as well as counterculturalists in New York's East Village and a few dozen other smaller hot spots), was originally an expression of contempt. Starting in the 1940s, black hipsters would call white hipsters hippies. (Malcolm X referred to them in his autobiography.) Then in the 1950s, the cooler white hipsters started calling weekend hipster poseurs hippies. The more modern version began appearing in the 1960s. Leary's generally upscale gang of seekers were complaining about the vagabond "hippies" who were following them around and trying to glom onto their scene as early as 1963. Now, for this brief blissful moment, for the year 1967, hippies would become the hippest thing around.

While most pundits saw a gaggle of bratty, drug-addled, overgrown children who didn't want to work or bathe, others were impressed by their sense of peace and community, and suspected that they might represent a new stage of humanity. Liberated from most material concerns by the ubiquitous, overflowing wealth of the time (and, as we would later learn, by their youth), some analysts thought the hippies represented a human future in which technological advances would eliminate human want and the necessity to do boring work. "Let the machines do it" was a common hippie rejoinder to the work ethic, and counterculture writer Richard Brautigan wrote a poem about "a cybernetic ecology/where we are free of our labors/and joined back to nature,/returned to our mammal/brothers and sisters,/and all watched over/by machines of loving grace." A *Time* magazine reporter wrote, "In their independence of material possessions and their emphasis on peacefulness and honesty, hippies lead considerably more virtuous lives than the great majority of their fellow citizens."

MAGICAL MISERY TRIP

The influx to the Haight that occurred during the famous summer of 1967 was a perfect example of media memetics (the idea that cultural forms and behaviors spread in a viral fashion). A reporter from the *San Francisco Chronicle* overheard a worried Digger casually predicting that, thanks to all the publicity and hype from the Be-In, over 100,000 young people would descend on the community during the coming summer. The *Chron* turned this single person's opinion into a front-page warning that the city would be under siege. The rumor was repeated by the mass media across the land (and even across the sea), ensuring that large numbers of young people would do their best to make it come true.

The "Summer of Love" made a mess out of the sweet scene that was shared by the relatively intimate community of self-selected, artistic, and smart acid eaters. Lost youths in the tens of thousands (although somewhat short of the 100,000 feared), hearing the voice on the Top Forty radio telling them to "come to San Francisco/Be sure to wear some flowers in your hair," swarmed into the Haight-Ashbury district. For each young immigrant who understood some of the creative intentions behind the *Oracle*'s brand of hippie social transformation, there were several who wanted nothing more than free and easy kicks. They came looking for, in Lee's words, "The Capital of Forever, where . . . all would be provided and everyone could do their own thing without being hassled." Among them were the huddled masses of screwed-up teenagers and young adults yearning to be free; the troubled kids, the juvenile delinquents, the spacy schizophrenics and psychotics hoping for acceptance and a solution to the tortures in their minds. And right behind them came the criminal predators (like Charles Manson) looking for easy victims among the starry-eyed flower children. What the lost kids found in the "Capital of Forever" was insufficient food, insufficient housing, an overwhelmed core group of hippie street philosophes who could offer only so much comfort and advice, and plenty of drugs. The criminal class brought with them harder drugs like methamphetamine and heroin, which were used to dull the pain and confusion of this paradise lost. Starry-eyed beautiful people were soon overwhelmed by empty-eyed, confused, lost youths.

But what was lost to the Haight was, arguably, gained to the nation and the world. Hippie notions spread like crabgrass. "Peace" and "Love" were scrawled on high-schooler notebooks in the millions from Pinedale, Wyoming, to Binghamton, New York. Teens and young adults gobbled up books on consciousness by Leary, Alan Watts, Aldous Huxley, and a variety of swamis and gurus. Draft resistance increased in the name of hippie-styled pacifism.

The mainstream culture continued its love/hate relationship with hippiedom, and as they debated this counterculture's efficacy in public, hippie ideals and psychedelic drug experimentation spread to unprecedented levels. Hundreds of psychedelic rock bands, some terrible (the Ultimate Spinach, Vanilla Fudge) and some brilliant (Procol Harum, the Jimi Hendrix Experience) sold millions of albums, and goofy trip songs like "Journey to the Center of the Mind" and "Hot Smoke and Sassafras" dominated Top Forty radio. A hippie-sympathetic musical, *Hair*, in which cast members burned draft cards, praised all forms of sexual intercourse, and disrobed, was the Broadway event of the season. Advertisers invited America to trip out with with the Plymouth or else "join the Dodge rebellion." Department stores sold incense, Nehru shirts, beads, and sandals. A revolution in consciousness and an over-the-counter culture seemed to be flowering in tandem.

ENLIGHTENMENT NOT GUARANTEED

The presumption, going at least back to Ginsberg's messianic 1961 visions that psychedelic drugs–induced revelations were conducive to world peace, love, and anti-authoritarian philosophy, was belied by the experiments carried out by the CIA (called the MK-ULTRA program) during the 1950s and 1960s. Besides testing LSD's proficiency as an incapacitant and a truth serum, the spies got it into their heads that it would be a good idea to dose themselves. The idea was that the Russians and the

Chinese could be thinking the same thing as the U.S., and an LSD attack might be imminent. Agents and soldiers needed to be prepared. Hundreds of CIA agents were dosed in the early 1950s. Many of them wrestled deeply with their psyches, rolling around, laughing, crying, and even praising God. According to Lee: "One MK-ULTRA veteran wept in front of his colleagues at the end of his first trip. 'I didn't want to leave it,' he explained. 'I felt I would be going back to a place where I wouldn't be able to hold on to this kind of beauty.'" Despite several responses of this sort, none of the spooks are known to have changed their minds about their sometimes violent mission on behalf of state authority. They did, however, get a bit carried away with the acid, sometimes dosing themselves above and beyond the call of duty. According to Lee, by 1954, there was a growing "sense that the MK-ULTRA was becoming unhinged by the hallucinogen. . . . The straw that broke the camel's back came when a Security informant got wind of a plan by a few . . . jokers to put LSD in the punch served at the annual CIA Christmas office party." The plan was scotched and the after-hours tripping was brought to an end. (Agents who had taken LSD were dubbed "enlightened operatives" by the CIA.)

And what should peace idealists make of Al Hubbard, a former OSS agent with powerful right-wing establishment connections who believed deeply in the spiritual qualities of LSD? During the 1950s and into the 1960s Hubbard was known among cognoscenti as the "Johnny Appleseed of LSD." Among the many who received his druggy beneficence was the famous British author Aldous Huxley, whose 1954 book, *The Doors of Perception,* is perhaps the most influential psychedelic trip report in history. Despite his hundreds of trips and his brilliant grasp of the shamanic powers of hallucinogens, Hubbard remained an all-American, right-wing, patriotic buddy to J. Edgar Hoover to his last days. The only people he despised more than Leary and the hippies were the New Left "commies" who were presuming LSD as one of *their* weapons against capitalism and imperialism.

And then there were Reagan pals Henry and Clare Boothe Luce, publishers of *Time* and *Life* magazines, rock-ribbed ruling-class Republicans, and trip enthusiasts. In 1957, before psychedelics became completely associated with the counterculture, they published R. Gordon Wasson's glow-ing accounts of his psilocybin experiences, but the Luces disapproved of the democratization of the vision drugs. At a party in the 1970s, Clare Boothe Luce told Abbie Hoffman (I guess that famous people, however incompatible, all sometimes wind up at the same parties), "We wouldn't want everyone doing too much of a good thing."

LEFT BEHINDS: IRREVERENCE AND DROPPING OUT AMONGST THE POLITICOS, 1964–1967

> I never found the words to describe what is still my most vivid feeling from the FSM [Free Speech Movement], beyond even the intense surprises of fraternity, community, and power over my citizen life—the sense that the surface of reality had somehow fallen away altogether. . . .
>
> Objects, encounters, events, all became mysterious, pregnant with unnameable implications, capable of astounding metamorphosis. I looked at a wall: yes, it was a wall, but I would not have been surprised if it revealed in the next instant a sheet of white ants cascading to the floor. The night throbbed with power, strange flows of energy; during the days and weeks we imagined an unprecedented movement into being. I felt us carried along by those flows, as if each tactical decision or chance dramatic incident were preordained, the precise inevitable consequence of a play of forces vast beyond our comprehension.
>
> MICHAEL ROSSMAN, 1974

In the mid-1960s, the growth of the New Left proceeded apace, and its themes continued to match the concerns of hip youth culture in general. Gitlin: "perfecting and proliferating . . . identities: culture as politics, the idea of 'liberation'; the movement as a culture, a way of life apart."

In 1964, the student movement developed a unique and powerful identity above and beyond the civil rights movement, forged in conflict in Berkeley, California. Political students, mostly from the peace and civil rights movements, but including even conservative groups, had been setting up tables in a public area (Sproul Plaza) of the university, where they passed out literature and made speeches to increasingly large gatherings. Although this politicking was against school rules, it was tolerated. But in the fall of 1964, under pressure from right-wingers on the Board of Regents, the university cracked down. On October 1, 1964, in an act of civil disobedience, Jack Weinberg put up a civil rights recruitment table. Police came to arrest him, and when they put him into the back of their squad car, they were surrounded by a mob of students who held them captive for thirty-two hours. The Free Speech Movement won its battle with the university and the meme spread: a new generation was on the scene that wasn't going to take any shit.

As the New Left picked up steam, its sense of provocative fun mirrored the shift from beatnik to hippie among the cultural revolutionaries. In Berkeley, radicals went from Free Speech to Filthy Speech, demanding the right to carry picket signs that simply said "FUCK!" on them. When HUAC (House Un-American Activities Committee), an organization that was a remnant of McCarthyism, held hearings investigating the subversive leanings of the antiwar movement during the summer of 1966, Berkeley's most mediagenic radical, Jerry Rubin, appeared stoned and grinning ear to ear, wearing an American Revolutionary War outfit. The message was clear: youth didn't take the establishment seriously. They were thumbing their noses at the powers-that-be.

By April 1965, SDS was on the media's political map as a serious player for sponsoring the first substantial demonstration against the war in Vietnam in Washington, D.C. By October of that year, the New Left was able to organize protests and teach-ins in dozens of towns and college campuses across America. A tenuous relationship between the different youth rebellions—the protest movement and the psychedelic culture—came to a head that October at an antiwar action in Oakland, California. The plan was to have public talks, and then those demonstrators who wished to would put their bodies on the line, marching on the Oakland Army Depot and trying to shut it down for the day. Feeling increasingly attuned to the hippie style, the protest organizers invited Ken Kesey to speak. When Kesey took the stage, he dissed the previous speakers, who had all been angrily screeching their dissent. According to Kesey, if you ignored the content of what they were saying and just paid attention to their body language and the sounds of their voices, they were rather reminiscent of Hitler. Kesey told the gathering that "you're not gonna stop this war . . . by marching. . . . That's what *they* do." Rather, he suggested that they "look at the war, and turn your backs and say . . . Fuck it." The speech dissipated the confrontational energy and everybody went home.

While the young white leftists gained new followers with their resistance to the war and their advocacy of campus freedoms, the young African-Americans who had been the shock troops of the civil rights movement were undergoing their own identity consciousness revolution. Even as Lyndon Johnson pushed JFK's civil rights legislation through Congress, and outright segregation became illegal, blacks realized that they would be confronting an entire tapestry of racist social and economic power, bigotry, and fear—probably for the rest of their lives. In the midst of America's great orgy of material well-being and its youth-cultural saturnalia, their communities were still poor, viciously policed by all-white forces, and marked by the scars of slavery and discrimination. Tired of playing the supplicant, the young black radicals started studying African and American history and amplifying their otherness and feelings of difference from the dominant white culture. They adopted a tradition of black nationalism that, within America, went back to the early twentieth century when W. E. B. Du Bois and Marcus Garvey advocated black pride and some degree of separation from the white society. In the mid-1960s, the black-dominated SNCC kicked white civil rights supporters out of their organization. Proud, angry, charismatic leaders like Stokely Carmichael and H. Rap Brown emerged into the mass-mediated public eye. Much like Leary, they were outrageously quotable—H. Rap Brown's statement "Violence is as American as cherry pie" is proved more true (if that's possible) every decade.

This black political militancy was born within a context of seething discontent within the poor black communities that erupted into violence with astonishing frequency during the mid-1960s. Usually provoked by incidents of police brutality, urban riots had become, in the words of historian William L. O'Neill, "a regular feature of summertime in America." The first truly massive riots of the 1960s occurred in the Watts section of Los Angeles in 1965. Thirty-four people were killed, and large sections of the community, particularly businesses, were looted and burned to the ground. Other cities soon followed suit, including Newark, New Jersey (twenty-five killed), and Detroit (thirty-four killed). They were explosions of pure despair, with all of the damage directed at the blacks' own communities. Mainstream politicians tried to answer with liberal social programs, while radicals both black and white viewed the riots as rebellions that warned of revolution.

Meanwhile, in Oakland, California, in 1966, two young black Merritt College students who were influenced by the political ideas of the Black Power movement decided to get active. Huey Newton, a smart, tough, and rebellious son of civil rights activists, and Bobby Seale, a rather easygoing jokester who liked to cook up elaborate "soul food" feasts for friends and neighbors, shared one thing in common: they both believed Newton was a political genius.

Like all black communities across America at that time, the Oakland ghetto was policed by an all-white force. Racism and brutality were the rule rather than the exception. The cops harassed, beat, and framed black (mostly) men with impunity. While both the black riots and the relentless poverty that provided the context for those conflagrations received bountiful government and media attention, the police savagery that usually catalyzed those riots went underinvestigated and unresolved. Newton's major insight, tied to the trendy notion of black nationhood, was that the white police force in Oakland was exactly like an occupying army in a foreign land—indeed, like the U.S. troops in Vietnam. Having carefully studied America's revolutionary documents—the Constitution and the Bill of Rights—Newton concluded that African-Americans could get guns and police the police. Newton and Seale formed the Black Panther Party for Self-Defense, attracted a few more members, and, armed with rifles, began shadowing the Oakland police to make sure they were doing their jobs properly. Not surprisingly, the cops didn't appreciate the attention. By late 1967, Newton got into a firefight with an Oakland policeman that left him severely wounded and the officer dead. He faced murder charges. It would be the first of many violent incidents between the Panthers and the police during the late 1960s and early 1970s.

While the Panthers scared the shit out of both white and black middle America, the white New Leftists, and even parts of the hippie counterculture, took to them. Mainly, it was simple requitedness. They'd been told to bugger off by black nationalists like Carmichael and Brown. But the Black Panthers were willing to work with the antiwar movement, the New Leftists, and even issued a statement that said, "The hippies are not our enemy." According to Lee: "Some of the Panthers . . . liked to get stoned and listen to Bob Dylan's *Highway 61 Revisited* on headphones. They were particularly impressed by 'The Ballad of a Thin Man,' which taunted 'Mr. Jones,' the archetypical honkie who knows something's happening but doesn't know what it is." Like many a hippie pedagogue, Newton liked to interpret Dylan lyrics for his Panther followers.

As America swung into the year of the hippie, 1967, only about 10 percent of the polled public opposed the Vietnam War. SDS and the New Left were in the doldrums, feeling impotent to do anything about the increasingly distressing carnage. Half a million American troops were now in Vietnam, and about five hundred of them were dying every month. No one knew for sure how many Vietnamese were being dispatched, but it was increasingly clear that American and South Vietnamese Army soldiers were attacking civilian populations, burning villages, dropping more bomb tonnage on this small country than had been used by the U.S. during the entire Second World War, and using chemical warfare agents like napalm, manufactured by the friendly folks at Dow Chemical. Many activists, clergy, and respected American (and international) intellectuals had come to believe that genocide was not too strong a word to describe the U.S. policy.

Of course, for the Vietnamese, for the American troops, for black rioters and Panthers, these issues were matters of life and death. For the New Leftists, it was more a crisis of conscience and identity. Their awareness of the relative distance between their small protestations and these social realities only made the situation more depressing. It amounted to, in essence, a realization that they weren't just alienated from the establishment, they were ultimately personally disconnected from the very issues they cared deeply about.

Meanwhile, hippie lifestyle anarchism was on the rise, and New Leftists were dropping out of the political struggle in droves and going where the zeitgeist was hot and the grass was always stronger. At the June SDS 1967 national convention, a gang of Diggers showed up drunk, stoned, and spontaneous, to rub the leftists' noses in their own uptight impotence.

Abbie Hoffman, a former civil rights activist who had moved to Greenwich Village to become a hippie, attended the SDS conference and was impressed by the Diggers' bravado. In his 1968 book *Revolution for the Hell of It*, he described the scene:

> In came the Diggers . . . all hell breaks out . . . [Digger leader Emmett] Grogan's yelling "One of us is in the can, is there a fuckin' lawyer here? What the hell you faggots looking at, get off your asses, we need help." [Note that the use of the term faggot here connotes not sexuality but wimpish ineffectuality, which in itself is, of course, way problematic.] . . . [Digger] Peter Berg . . . starts to talk. He looks like a young angry Sitting Bull. . . . He's on a trip. Holy Shit, Excitement, Drama, Revolution. The message: Property is the enemy—burn it, destroy it, give it all away. . . . Don't let them make a machine out of you, get out of the system. . . . Don't organize students, teachers, negroes, organize your head. Find out where you are, what you want to do, and go out and do it. Johnson is a commie; the Kremlin is more fucked up than Alabama. Get out. Don't organize the schools, burn them. Leave them . . . they will rot. . . . The kids are getting stoned. . . .
>
> Grogan re-enters, reconvenes the meeting single-handed. He climbs up on the table. Starts slow, sucks everyone in by answering a few questions. . . . All of a sudden he erupts, and kicks the fuckin' table over. He [is] slapping SDSers right and left. "Faggots! Fags! Take off your ties, they are chains around your neck. You haven't got the balls to go mad!"

In contradiction to Grogan's macho provocateur outrage, the New Leftists *were* "going mad" and moving toward their own version of the dropout philosophy. The ideological influence came from a dour but very contemporary German neo-Marxist philosopher named Herbert Marcuse, who had evolved an analysis that left little hope for social change. According to Marcuse, the left's romantic working class was too bought out by material wealth and brainwashed by mass media to ever challenge the system. Capitalism had developed its skills of co-optation and could absorb all forms of rebellion and even apparent revolution back into its system. In *The Making of a Counter Culture,* Theodore Roszak explained the Marcuse view: "It is impossible for thought to escape contamination with the assumptions that underlie the structure and behavior of existing institutions. Language and philosophy become devices whereby man is made to avoid becoming conscious of the existence of the possibility of his own liberation. . . . Sex, 'tolerance' as a generalized principle, freedom of press and speech, as well as other civil liberties—all these have . . . manipulative aspects; 'repressive desublimation' prevents true instinctual liberation, while 'under the rule of a repressive whole, liberty can be made into a powerful instrument of domination.' " The only possible response, carrying with it only the vaguest of hopes, was a "great refusal" to be part of the system. In essence, Marcuse was telling the New Left what Leary was telling the hip youth: drop out.

The main distinction that made Marcuse a hit with a youth culture that was generally uninterested in tortured European Marxist discourses was that he wasn't just against capitalism, he was against technocracy. According to Marcuse, "Intensified progress seems to be bound up with intensified unfreedom. Concentration camps, mass exterminations, world wars, and atom bombs are no relapse into barbarism, but the unrepressed implementation of the achievements of modern science, technology, and domination. And the most effective subjugation and destruction of man by man takes place at the height of civilization." This spoke to the sense, common to both the hippie and New Left cultures, that they were expected to become cogs in an inhuman machine, a machine that was trying (and failing) to automate its Vietnam War. A machine that couldn't reverse its course in that war even after the human beings who were allegedly running it realized it was "unwinnable." It was a machine that offered ineffective "programs" to alleviate the oppression of the poor, instead of humanity, dignity, autonomy, and democratic participation. It was a machine that had lashed their parents to the time clock, forcing them to work at boring jobs that sapped them of spontaneity and life.

Sixties youth attitudes toward technocracy were in apparent contradiction. The kids, at least most of them, wanted the "machines of loving grace." They wanted the electric guitar and amplifier, the pop radio, the light show, the fast-moving vehicles, and the divine products of advanced chemistry. They wanted to live off the excesses of mass production, but they were suspicious of technological civilization. A reasonable response to this contradiction might idealize "appropriate technologies" and nonauthoritarian democratic institutions that don't mimic the functions of their machines, but this tension between technology as a liberator from material necessity and boring labor and technology as a big mean machine in the service of grim power mostly remained unresolved. To Marcuse the picture looked mostly bleak, but even he managed to twist his objections to technocracy into a vague demand for a post-scarcity liberation from boredom and want.

HIPPIES TO THE RESCUE

If 1967 was a year in which the earnest New Leftists lost cultural momentum to the wild hippie counterculturalists, there was one event during that fall where the hippies brought cheer and hope to the antiwar movement. The increasingly psychedelicized Jerry Rubin had moved to the East Coast to coordinate an antiwar demonstration at the Pentagon that was to take place in October. He developed a rapport with Abbie Hoffman, and joined Hoffman when he pranked the Stock Exchange by leading a group of freaks in throwing dollar bills from the balcony onto the Stock Exchange floor, where the traders dropped everything to dive for the free ones and fives. (Guard to the crowd of hippies as they approached the Stock Exchange: "You can't come in here. You're hippies and you're going to have a demonstration." Abbie Hoffman to guard: "We're not hippies, we're Jews, and you don't want to *exclude* us from the Stock Exchange." Fearing accusations of anti-Semitism, the guard let them in.)

Together, Rubin and Hoffman concocted a plan to bring hippies, and their subversive sense of fun, into the Pentagon protest. An acid mystic had advised Rubin that the Pentagon, as a five-sided building pointing east, was a magical symbol of evil. So Hoffman announced that a group of freaks would "levitate the Pentagon" and "exorcise the evil spirits." The building would rise three inches in the air, the demons would flee, and the war would be over. Approximately 75,000 hippies and peaceniks showed up for the October event. As Lee described it, "The motley army of witches, warlocks, sorcerers and long-haired bards who had come to celebrate the mystic revolution lent a carnival atmosphere to the demonstration." Thousands of armed troops defending the building surrounded a contingent of freaks who chanted "Out Demons Out!" and sang "Ring around the Pentagon, a pocketful of pot/Four and twenty generals all begin to rot/All the evil spirits start to tumble out/Now the war is over, we all begin to shout." Beautiful hippie girls flirted with the soldiers and inserted flowers into the muzzles of their guns. At least three soldiers threw down their guns and helmets to join the fun.

In a weird way, the Pentagon exorcism worked. A politically ambitious situations analyst with the RAND Corporation named Daniel Ellsberg, who was working inside the Pentagon on war strategy, was already starting to have doubts about the morality of his work. He sympathetically watched the demo from inside the building, thinking that they needed more effective tactics.

Daniel Foss wrote that "In hippie politics the objective . . . was not to 'put your bodies on the levers' of the machine and so stop its functioning; rather it was to . . . 'Freak out the Machine,' to incite the enemy to self-injury through cultural destruction and the scrambling of meanings." Hoffman's and Rubin's antics at the Stock Exchange and the Pentagon were the first of many events in which this pair would bring this prankster, jujitsu approach into the political arena.

LET A MILLION FLOWER POWERS BLOOM

I am nothing and I should be everything.

KARL MARX

With all of its thorny problems, the youth rebels of the earlier years of the counterculture truly represented "flower power." Not that it was universally *soft* in the way that phrase implies, but there was a great flowering of creativity; young people were in a cauldron of constant change, experimenting with free thought and behaviors, and testing their abilities to inject countercultural memes into the world. They were met with both an astounding tolerance and a brutal harsh resistance (not to mention commercial exploitation), which, if nothing else, proved that mainstream Western culture was far more variegated than anyone would have suspected during the unicultural 1950s. They expanded the boundaries by which individuals sought liberty, both internally and externally, on an increasingly mass basis. And by the very growth of these idealistic and optimistic countercultures, they charged ahead into far more dangerous territory.

CHAPTER THIRTEEN

⊢ WILD IN THE STREETS

The Youth Counterculture, 1968–1972

The cybernetic age entails a change in our frame of reference, man. The traditional spatio-temporal concepts are inadequate. . . . The digital computer is easing us into the electronic/automotive age just as the steam engine pivoted us into the industrial revolution. In those days it was gin. It flowed like water. Kids were suckled on it, societies campaigned against it. Now it's acid. LSD is for us what gin was for the Victorians. It lubricates our acceptance of the new age.

> HELL'S ANGEL PETE THE COYOTE, QUOTED IN
> *PLAY POWER* BY RICHARD NEVILLE, 1969

Be realistic. Demand the impossible!

> SLOGAN OF FRANCE'S MAY 1968 REVOLUTIONARIES

July 21, 1968: It's a sunny day on the Boston Common. Couples lie on the grass, the swan boats flutter in the pond, kids playing Frisbee and catch. One big happy scene. America the Beautiful. You can snap a neat Kodachrome in your mind and send it all over the world. A young girl with long hair, beads, and sandals winks at you and hands you a leaflet. "Last night on the Boston Commons the cops smashed our Be-in. They brought out the dogs. They clubbed and tear-gassed us and arrested 65. Tonight we assemble again. Don't let the pigs take our park. . . . The streets belong to the people." The girl moves on, handing out the leaflets in a very selective manner that looks ever so casual. A leaflet to a black couple. One hesitatingly for the Frisbee players. A leaflet and a hug for two longhair guys, one playing a flute. About a fourth of the people in the area got leaflets. Comrades being gathered for the Second American Revolution. No leaflets for the Tories. The girl had ripped the Kodachrome in two. The eyes blinked open and saw not one but two pictures: THEM–US. . . . The girl and the two longhair guys are transformed, they are Crispus Attucks, they are kneeling praying in a Birmingham church when a bomb comes flying through the window. A heavy voice from behind me smirks up out of the leaflet and drawls, "Hey, boy, you people better not start anything tonight, we don't like your kind in Boston." Yassuh, it was coon huntin' season all over again. The United States of Mississippi had found themselves another nigger.

ABBIE HOFFMAN

They got the guns but we got the numbers/Gonna win yeah we're taking over.

JIM MORRISON, THE DOORS, 1968

The exuberant youthful attacks on the cultural assumptions and political institutions of the Western world that surged through the early and mid-1960s did not fail to provoke the wrath of the establishment and the majority of the common citizenry. A detailed review of the repressive apparatus that was summoned against hippies, New Leftists, and especially Black Panthers would overwhelm this chapter. Suffice it to say that increasingly, cops were harassing, busting, and beating the rebels in droves. Daniel Foss recalled "selective and capricious enforcement of petty statutes; verbal intimidations; use of informers . . . intimidating surveillance . . . arbitrary searches and seizures; disbursing of informal street gatherings; clubbings; raiding of apartments and meeting places." Outside of the more sophisticated urban and college towns where the countercultures dominated youth culture, rednecks and jocks could be counted on to pummel and, in a few cases, kill any kids courageous enough to wear peace buttons or long hair. Thus, the counterculture of the late 1960s was pushed (and, to be honest, pushed itself) into a reactive mode.

In some ways, this wild period of countercultural and human history was the ultimate countercultural epoch. Vast numbers of young people *screamed* for liberation. Boundaries, borders, rulers, rules, static ideas were anathema. Rock star Janis Joplin subverted the very division of time into discrete units, cackling on a live album, "It's all the same fuckin' day, man!" and Graham Nash told Top Forty radio listeners that nation-states and their borders were illusions, singing at the immigration man, "I can't toe your line today/I can't see it anyway." Abbie Hoffman, while he faced down prison and possible death in the streets because—quite frankly—he was trying to provoke some sort of overthrow of the system, could still say that the only movement he believed in was "dancing."

But at the same time, the (as of 1969) pretty much completely merged hippie and New Left scenes—the hip left—lost track of some of its creative, expansive impetus as it narrowed itself down into an assaultive weapon against both real and perceived enemies. On the plus side, the hip left tried to bridge the gap between those who privileged the head: "change yourself"; and those who privileged their social ideals: "change the world." Why shouldn't both aspects of humanness be cranked up to 11? Why not a whole revolutionary human? Leary piped in with one of his typical aphorisms: "Revolution without revelation is tyranny. Revelation without revolution is slavery."

Ideals aside, things got pretty ugly, and some markedly authoritarian tropes sometimes mingled with their most extreme opposite.

COUNTERREVOLUTION

By 1968, Timothy Leary had experienced a series of petty marijuana busts and, thanks to draconian laws, he was facing what basically amounted to a life sentence. One of the busts had been stage-managed by G. Gordon Liddy, at that time the prosecutor from Dutchess County (the location of Millbrook). President Nixon would be so impressed that Liddy would get a job in his White House. Leary kept smiling. Ken Kesey and members of the Grateful Dead faced marijuana charges. And in England, Mick Jagger, Brian Jones, Marianne Faithfull, Keith Richards, John Lennon, Yoko Ono, and George Harrison were all busted for trivial quantities of pot or hashish. On his way to jail, Jagger laughed and frolicked around in his handcuffs.

While much of the repression was undoubtedly the natural response of macho law enforcers to provocations from weirdos and blacks, there was also a massive secret U.S. federal program getting under way to spy on, frame, and in at least one incident, assassinate radicals and/or hippies. Revealed later as the result of investigations related to Watergate, the program was called COINTELPRO, and eventually, as the Nixon administration assumed power, approximately a quarter of a million New Leftists, hippie leaders, and even liberal Democrats as well as rock stars and other popular entertainers would be subjected to a program of close FBI surveillance and infiltration. Additionally, Nixon would keep a private "enemies list" composed mainly of liberals and nearly all of his mainstream media critics. The list would be turned over to the IRS, who, undoubtedly, knew what to do.

By early 1968, longhairs (and by now, the leftists looked pretty much indistinguishable from the freaks) in some areas were being subjected to near daily harassment from law enforcement. But since the counterculture was young, was still gaining momentum, and was frequently defended by respected intellectuals and enthusiastically mirrored by elements of the entertainment culture, the mood in the hip communities was cocky rather than intimidated. They knew that they were the future. Still, the severity of the reaction was creating a different dynamic. Among leftists, and even among some hippies, the new word was revolution . . . by any means necessary, and it grew from a whisper to a shout.

GOT TO REVOLUTION

Hey I'm dancing down the street/Got a revolution got to
revolution
MARTY BALIN AND PAUL KANTNER, JEFFERSON AIRPLANE, 1969

The first manifestation of this new attitude caught everyone by surprise.
Young people in France had not taken to the psychedelic countercultural
style to the extent that they did in America and England, but a substantial
subculture of French students was leaning toward a peculiar set of left-
wing anarchist memes not dissimilar to the Diggers' vision of unmediated
spontaneous relations. Still, they didn't anticipate what happened in Paris
during May 1968. It started with an attempt by the Paris police to shut
down a meeting of students planning anti–Vietnam War protests under
the excuse that right-wing extremists might attack the gathering. Much
like the incident that set off the Free Speech Movement in Berkeley, the
police intervention attracted a throng of students who surrounded their
police vans. A pitched street battle followed during which the students
fought every bit as tough and hard as the cops. In contrast to America, the
French students' willingness to stand up for their rights (which were, after
all, simply to meet and plan a legal protest demonstration) resonated with
the general public. Professors, university workers, and working-class militants joined an increasing number of students in street demonstrations
against the repression that went on day after day, consistently increasing in
size and scope. Finally, the Paris police decided to clear off the streets. The
battle that followed left several hundred injured and France erupted.

Across the entire nation, some *ten million* workers went out on strike.
Many occupied and took control of their factories. They threw out the
management and started holding the sorts of grassroots, democratic,
decision-making meetings envisioned—but rarely practiced—by revolutionary communists, and the students at the Sorbonne University in Paris
did the same. Middle-class and even wealthy French citizens came down
from the suburbs bringing the strikers and demonstrators food and drink.
This was, after all, about basic democratic rights.

Radical anarchist memes spread almost as rapidly as the strike. Students and workers now didn't just want their rights, or a new set of benefits and privileges. They started to talk about a new kind of society. They wanted Charles de Gaulle's national government to surrender! Workers at auto factories chanted "People's Government!" Protest signs started appearing all over France reading "All Power to the Imagination" and "Be Realistic. Demand the Impossible." According to historian Iain Gunn,

> For the mass of workers and students the strike was not just about pay and conditions—it was about power.
>
> Work had stopped, factories were occupied, the TV was off, debate raged. People changed more in a few hours or a few days than they had in a lifetime. People who would have seen themselves as conservatives yesterday, now talked of revolution.
>
> On May 24th, de Gaulle addressed the nation on TV. Even by his own admission it was a flop. He was the old man in charge of the old world. . . . At the height of the protest, the crowd ransacked and set fire to the Bourse, the Paris Stock Exchange building.
>
> After that revolution was truly in the air. . . . Strike committees were more and more taking over the functions of civil administration, joining together to form the embryo of an alternative system of government. Dual power existed.

Eventually, the "French Revolution" of 1968 was dissipated by a combination of forces. About a million hard-core right-wingers, including many neo-Nazis, took to the streets in counterrevolution. And the French Communist Party stepped in to arrange a compromise that granted workers the usual concessions: higher wages, longer holidays, greater benefits.

Needless to say, the French establishment would never again try to stop students from holding meetings or legitimate protests.

That same month, all eyes in America were on the college campuses as student revolt turned militant. At Columbia University, SDS led a group of students and freaks in the occupation of the administration building (and eventually several others). The action was nominally about university plans to build a gymnasium in a park that was used by poor blacks, and university connections to the Vietnam War machine. But all that was really just an excuse. A group of young white radicals had simply chosen this as the moment to trumpet their revolutionary intentions. The radicals' tactics alienated the majority of Columbia students until the New York City police converted them by employing excess brutality in removing the occupiers. The entire university went out on strike for the rest of the school year. Final exams were canceled. And radical "vandalism" paid off. Rifling through the school bureaucracy's papers, the radicals uncovered evidence that the university was indeed involved in classified war research. The evidence was published in a New York underground newspaper, *Rat.*

With this and other radical actions, SDS's fortunes surged. According to William L. O'Neill, by the end of 1968 there were about four hundred chapters and nearly 100,000 members. The SDSer who had led the Columbia revolt, Mark Rudd, got his fifteen minutes of fame. He toured college campuses, screeching obscenity-filled invectives against the war, racism, and authority (particularly as represented by college administrators) to auditoriums packed with cheering students.

And then it was on to Chicago for the Democratic National Convention.

ABBIE'S APOCALYPSE

> The revolution is wherever my boots touch the ground.
>
> ABBIE HOFFMAN

Abbie Hoffman and Jerry Rubin, along with Abbie's wife, Anita, and *Realist* publisher Paul Krassner (he had earlier been a writer for *Mad*) started off the new year (1968) by dropping acid together and cementing their partnership in political pranks by forming a new organization, YIPPIE! It was, first of all, just the way it looks: an exclamation of irrepressible joy at being alive during such a promising and promiscuous time. It was also a moniker under which Hoffman, Rubin, and friends could draw media attention to their clever subversive pranks. And finally, it was the Youth International Party, an attempt to meld the New Left and hippie countercultures into a singular force. Having thrown money on Wall Street, exorcised the Pentagon, dumped soot in the lobby of Con Edison head-quarters, and mailed Valentine cards with marijuana joints (paid for by Jimi Hendrix) to names chosen randomly from the NYC phone book, the Yippies had created a mythic résumé of disruption even before they took a name.

Hoffman believed in media revolution. If activists created events that looked wild, sexy, and funny, the mass media wouldn't be able to resist bringing attention to them. "Media is free," he wrote. "Don't buy ads. Make news." It didn't matter that the Yippies' pranks would be relegated to the final segment that the national TV news used to save for a bizarre or amusing item that would leave their viewers, in Hoffman's words, "happy as cows." In fact, that was perfect. As Hoffman pointed out, TV commercials were always more dynamic than the shows. Yippie coverage would be "commercials for the revolution," occupying just enough time to not become boring like the rest of the news. Young people would get the idea, and they would invent their own ways to prank the establishment to death. In *Revolution for the Hell of It,* Hoffman wrote, "John Roche . . . once said that if Hitler had been captured in 1937, brought to Trafalgar Square, and had his pants pulled down, he could never have risen to power." Pull down the system's pants! This was the essence of the Yippie political strategy. Unfortunately, Roche's observation is not necessarily correct.

The Yippie big event for 1968 was a "Festival of Life" at the Democratic National Convention in Chicago. It was to be an alternative to the festival of death being held by the Democratic Party, which was still managing the Vietnam War, and pushing their own peace advocates to the periphery of their nominating process despite the fact that the liberal peace candidates were winning primaries. (Antiwar candidates Robert Kennedy, Eugene McCarthy, and George McGovern got 80 percent of the Democratic primary vote.)

The Yippies were hardly an organization. They had one small run-down office in New York City with a single telephone, but Hoffman was a media darling, always quotable, always good copy. He organized the Chicago protests through both the mainstream media and the underground press. He spread rumors that perfectly separated the hip from the square. "We're going to put LSD in the water supply." "We're going to get Yippie prostitutes to kidnap delegates and drive them to Michigan." "We have a liquid spray called LACE. It's related to LSD and it makes people take off their clothes and fuck." (Two Yippie couples demonstrated its potency at a press conference.) "We will fuck on the beaches!" They announced that they were nominating a pig for president, and once it got elected, they were going to eat it. If you were under thirty, you recognized these claims as psychedelic put-ons. Even most of the mainstream media got it. But if you were a Chicago authority, your worst anxieties about the intentions of hippie radicals were being blatantly enunciated. Chicago's police chief even stationed men around the city's waterworks. Hoffman called him up to explain that it was technically impossible to saturate the water supply with LSD. "Come on. You *must* have at least one chemist who advises you."

After Mayor Richard Daley's men refused to give the Yippies permission to sleep in Lincoln Park in downtown Chicago near the convention center, most of the musicians who had agreed to appear (including popular folksinger Judy Collins) canceled. *Rolling Stone,* still a voice of the counterculture at that time, told people not to go to Chicago. Original endorsers Timothy Leary and Allen Ginsberg recommended against participation (although Ginsberg went anyway, as did William Burroughs).

The reticence of these former Festival of Life supporters was mirrored by the hip community. Things had been spooky since April 4, when the hero of the civil rights movement and modern American pacifism Dr. Martin Luther King had been assassinated. The ghettos exploded as never before. There were riots in 125 cities, forty-six people were killed, over twenty thousand were arrested, and more than fifty thousand federal troops and National Guardsmen were deployed.

One man who helped to calm this ultimately self-destructive frenzy was Robert Kennedy, a recently announced candidate for the Democratic presidential nomination. Generally considered by most left-liberals as even more of a fraud than his older brother, Kennedy showed understanding, genuine emotion, and real courage in response to the terrible assassination of the civil rights hero. He appeared before mobs of African-Americans offering a ray of hope for a better deal in the near future. And then, two months later, Kennedy himself was shot dead at a celebration for his victory in the California Democratic primary.

The counterculture shared an ominous mood with the rest of the nation. Most weren't willing to follow Hoffman and Rubin into the apocalypse. Only about eight thousand protesters showed up for the "festival." The event was, as Hoffman said, a perfect mess. The Chicago police started attacking demonstrators even before the curfew in Chicago's Lincoln Park went into effect. It was, in the words of a commissioned government report issued afterward, a police riot. This *New York Times* slice of life captures the flavor of the entire four-day affair: "Even elderly bystanders were caught by the police onslaught. At one point the police turned on several dozen persons standing quietly behind police barriers in front of the Conrad Hilton Hotel watching the demonstrators across the street. For no reason that could be immediately determined, the blue-helmeted policemen charged the barriers, crushing the spectators against the windows of the Haymarket Inn, a restaurant in the hotel. Finally the windows gave way, sending screaming middle-aged women and children backward through the broken shards of glass. The police then ran into the restaurant and beat some of the victims who had fallen through the windows and arrested them."

Television coverage of the Democratic convention flipped back and forth between the convention hall and the violent chaos on the streets. The convention was itself full of rancor, as the peace Democrats protested their treatment by the Democratic establishment and expressed their outrage at the police riot outside. When Abraham Ribicoff suggested that if peace advocate George McGovern were being nominated for president instead of Lyndon Johnson's vice president, Hubert Humphrey, "we wouldn't be having Gestapo tactics on the streets of Chicago," Mayor Richard Daley responded in perfect Gestapo fashion by calling Ribicoff a "Jew son of a bitch." CBS news reporter Dan Rather was physically attacked by some of Daley's thugs inside the convention hall. But aside from these sickly scenes, it was for the most part a typically boring political convention. Hoffman's media theory was in practice. For every dreary half hour or so inside the hall, the TV cameras showed a couple of minutes of the battle in the streets, with cops beating wild-looking long-haired people bloody and demonstrators chanting, "The whole world's watching!" It was a different kind of "commercial for the revolution." It wasn't funny. It didn't inspire pranks. It inspired rage.

And when it was over, more than 50 percent of the American people said that they approved of the police actions. In the world of real politics, where revolution by the young was not going to happen today or the next day, the battle of Chicago accomplished only one thing for certain: it ensured the election of the law-and-order Republican, Richard Nixon.

MOUTHING OFF

We are forces of chaos and anarchy . . . and we are very proud of ourselves.

PAUL KANTNER, JEFFERSON AIRPLANE, 1969

As Nixon took office at the beginning of 1969, the conditions for culture war and political conflict escalated, as did the war in Vietnam. The new president announced the "war on drugs" (the gift that just keeps giving), pushing through a "No Knock" law that allowed armed police to break into the homes of drug suspects without warning. (We take this for granted now, but it was previously customary for law enforcement officers to knock and announce that they had a search warrant.) Student and freak demonstrations became increasingly militant. Armed black students at Cornell took over the administration building. Most of their demands were met, and they emerged proudly waving their guns in the air. Hippies and students who took over an abandoned university parking lot in Berkeley to turn it into a "People's Park" were met with the most severe police violence experienced by white radicals up until that point. And they fought back. The National Guard occupied the college town. It looked like a war zone. For days, cops, guardsmen, and freaks lobbed canisters of tear gas back and forth, and eventually the Guard opened fire with buckshot. Around fifty protesters were seriously injured and one young man, James Rector, was killed by a police bullet.

Meanwhile the wild-in-the-streets spirit of rebel youth running riot was not limited to the U.S. (or France). In 1968–1969, there were major disruptions by long-haired, pot-smoking, rock and roll youth radicals in virtually every Western European nation, as well as Mexico, Japan, and communist Czechoslovakia. Even Mao Tse-tung's terrible Cultural Revolution in China, in which he used restless youths to terrorize old bureaucrats and anyone still enamored of old (and therefore presumed axiomatically reactionary) Chinese cultural ways, seemed peculiarly related to the global youth insurgency.

If the American hip left affiliation was becoming more militant on the streets, their actions were flat-out wimpy compared to their rhetoric. Across America (and, to a lesser extent, Europe), underground newspapers that used to be dedicated to rock, drugs, sex, peace, love, and mystical philosophy were telling people how to make Molotov cocktails and publishing pictures of freaks with guns. (The slogan was "Armed Love.") The time was right for revolution, as Mick Jagger sang, and while the Rolling Stones' song was meant to be ambiguous, the freak left was—at the very least—deluding themselves into believing actual armed revolution was nigh.

For the white radicals, it was all really an extension of the same search for meaning that had guided their countercultures in the earlier part of the decade. Only now the attempt to locate their identities became bound up in a willingness to fight against the mainstream political forces, which had grown more hostile under Richard Nixon. Third World revolutionaries—Fidel Castro, Ho Chi Minh, Chairman Mao, and most of all the handsome, long-haired martyr Che Guevara—were romanticized as images of revolutionary success worthy of emulation. The fact that most of these men ran highly authoritarian regimes was buried beneath the alternative narrative, also true, that the Marxist icons had all been rebels in their youths, that they were poetic and visionary in their public expressions, and that their coercive measures seemed motivated more by a terrible rush to achieve the perfect communist utopia (we can help humanity once we get the people out of the way) than by the kind of bureaucratic opportunism that had made the Soviet model so unromantic.

Great quantities of psychedelic drugs sure weren't making very many people lose their egos. If anything, the chemical amplifiers just made the freak leftists envision themselves as the coolest primitive warriors defending the natural, spontaneous rhythms of nature and authentic life against the most evil robotic oppressors that the planet had ever seen, man. (I probably shouldn't sneer at the "authentic humans versus brainwashed robotic conformists" trope, since it continues to delight in massively popular films like the *Matrix* trilogy, which are chock-full of countercultural observations.) In their manifesto, the Ann Arbor, Michigan–based freak-radicals, the White Panther Party, bragged: "Fuck God in the ass. . . . Our program of rock and roll, dope and fucking in the streets is a program of total freedom for everyone. . . . We breathe revolution. We are LSD-driven total maniacs in the universe." An underground paper ran this self-impressed doggerel: "we were a community of crazie hogfarm-mother-fucker-street people acidhappy freaks stampeding down st. marks place, wearing our favorite costumes that jangled and fluttered color when we hugged each other, while we danced to drum rhythms on the cobblestones, we vaulted the cold turnstiles with fat joints in our mouths and visions in our heads and dancing drum beats in our heels . . . we came with the things that are part of our lives; our music, our dances, our bodies, our people, our dope, our acid, our food, our love." (It would be another two and a half decades before Generation X taught the baby boom generation the value of self-deprecating humor.)

Amidst all this intensity, there were still lighter currents. Underground comix by the likes of R. Crumb and Gilbert Shelton made corrosive fun of everybody, including the ultra-revolutionaries. The trippy Beatles movie *Yellow Submarine,* in which the multicolored world of the happy, music-loving people of Pepperland was attacked and rendered black and white by the joyless "Blue Meanies," only to be saved by John Lennon and company to the tune of "All You Need Is Love," had a decidedly larger fan base than the White Panthers' "LSD-driven total maniacs of the universe." Indeed, within the youth culture that the Yippies and White Panthers purported to represent, one was more likely to find supporters of Eugene McCarthy's moderate antiwar campaign for the Democratic Party nomination—a position treated with contempt by the radicals.

If, within the white freak revolution, real political struggle was secondary to ego identity, for the Black Panthers, out of necessity, the priorities were reversed. Not that Huey Newton, Eldridge Cleaver, and Bobby Seale didn't get off on their rock-star-sized reputations; they did. But they were dealing with harder repression and harsher realities than the white kids could ever dream of provoking. Huey Newton was out on bail facing murder charges for his shootout with the white police officer in Oakland. Eldridge Cleaver had also gotten into an armed exchange with the Oakland police, and Bobby Seale was bound and gagged by Judge Julius Hoffman at the trial of the Chicago Eight, in which seven white radicals, including Tom Hayden, Abbie Hoffman, and Jerry Rubin, plus Seale were put on trial for conspiring to create havoc at the 1968 Democratic National Convention in Chicago.

As revealed by the Church Committee hearings in 1975 and later Freedom of Information Act releases, J. Edgar Hoover's top sixties obsession was with preventing the rise of black political leadership, and he became focused on closing down the Black Panthers, who had become folk heroes to ghetto blacks. The great brunt of the FBI's COINTELPRO program was directed at the Panthers. All chapters were heavily infiltrated by agents who tried (with some success) to get them to engage in acts of illegal violence. Fake letters were sent from one Panther to another to (successfully) provoke internal fighting. Dozens of party members were framed, and at least two, Fred Hampton and Mark Clark, were murdered in cold blood by the Chicago police while they slept.

Fred Hampton, leader of the Chicago Black Panther Party chapter, was particularly loved by his community, which made him into a "King"-sized threat in the eyes of the FBI. Along with their militant stance against "the pigs," the Panthers' main attraction was constructive: a group of programs, partly inspired by the Diggers, designed to serve the needs of their neighborhoods. They served a free daily breakfast for school kids, started medical clinics, and set up pest control services. An eloquent, warm personality, Hampton particularly focused his chapter's energies on these more positive manifestations of the Black Panther ideas.

The leaders of the dominant Oakland chapter, on the other hand, were enamored of the same sort of ultra-revolutionary rhetorical exaggerations engaged in by the freak left. Indeed, the Oakland Panthers were very much a part of a Bay Area counterculture triangle that included the radical freaks of San Francisco and the freaky radicals of Berkeley. Eldridge Cleaver, a prodigious pot smoker who had been an editor at the hip white left's most commercial magazine, *Ramparts,* before joining the Panthers, was a frequent presence on the hippie-Yippie scene. According to Martin Lee, "Cleaver, [Panther] Minister of Information . . . offered to make an alliance with . . . the Yippies. 'Eldridge wanted a coalition between the Panthers and psychedelic street activists,' Rubin explained. So they got together, smoked a lot of grass, and composed a 'joint' manifesto called the Panther-Yippie Pipe Dream. 'Into the streets!' Cleaver proclaimed. 'Let us join together with all those souls in Babylon who are straining for the birth of a new day. A revolutionary generation is on the scene. . . . Disenchanted, alienated white youth, the hippies, the yippies and all the unnamed dropouts from the white man's burden, are our allies in this cause.' "

In organizational terms, it didn't mean much. In fact, Huey Newton considered Cleaver a bit of a loose cannon, and was probably less than thrilled at the Panther representative getting righteously baked and signing treaties in the name of his organization, but the Yippies were chuffed. In fact, most members of the freak left soon decided that the Black Panther Party was the "vanguard of the revolution." Huey Newton agreed. He appointed himself the "Supreme Commander of the People" and generated an iconography around himself that mimicked Mao.

This whole peculiar relationship between the revolutionary fantasies of the white radicals and the harsh fantasy-meets-reality of the Black Panthers was parodied in the mid-1970s on a National Lampoon album called *Lemmings,* in which the Marin County–based leftist folksinger Joan Baez is parodied singing "Pull the triggers, niggers/We're with you all the way/ Just across the bay." Meanwhile, in the 1990s, some historians characterized the Black Panthers as having been essentially a criminal gang. Others have defended them as beleaguered-but-brilliant progressives who made some serious mistakes under incomprehensible pressure and went through some major character distortions once it became clear that they weren't going to be the vanguard leadership of a new revolutionary United States. The truth, I suspect, is in between these two views. Alternatively, both visions may be completely accurate, making the Panthers prime exemplars of people's ability to contain vastly contradictory attributes.

Adding to the violent turn, by the end of the decade most of the U.S. soldiers in Vietnam had adopted countercultural attitudes. They opposed the war and didn't much care for ordinary authoritarian military procedures. They smoked pot, and many took LSD to try to make sense out of chaos in the Vietnam jungle. Quite a few, in the midst of the misery of the war, also succumbed to the very strong Vietnamese heroin that was easy to secure from the criminal types who surrounded the regime they were there to defend. They listened to psychedelic rock music and wore protest buttons on their uniforms. And with increasing frequency, they were "fragging" their officers (killing them).

WE DON'T NEED A WEATHERMAN. IN FACT, WE DON'T NEED MEN!

By the spring of 1969, the majority of Americans opposed the war, but they disliked the freak-left that was starting to dominate leadership of the antiwar movement even more. Meanwhile, the youth, college students particularly—though they still viewed the hard-core freak-left counterculture and its acid apocalypse rhetoric with a certain trepidation—*were* inching further leftward. The conviction of the Chicago Seven (Bobby Seale had been removed from the trial by the judge) for conspiracy, an absurd legal construct ruled over by the wacky, clearly biased (later confirmed by FOIA documents) judge, Julius Hoffman, touched off massive riots on dozens of college campuses. (Ironically, the guy who actually caused the most trouble in Chicago, Abbie Hoffman, received the lightest sentence. The judge was charmed, unable to resist laughing at his comic testimony and courtroom antics.) So while the average long-haired kid was more likely to have a poster of Peter Fonda—giving the world the finger in *Easy Rider*—than a poster of Che on his wall, the possibilities for some sort of an effective mass youth political revolt were high. But the very moment they might have mounted sufficient force to bring about social change, the political radicals who had the organizational skills to lead the movement had gone over the edge, hallucinating that they were on the verge of an armed revolution against the most powerful and heavily armed government in human history.

This self-destructive direction of the New Left leadership came to a head when SDS met for its national convention in June 1969. Three factions waved Mao's "little red book" at each other and fought for control of the organization. The rhetoric was getting ever more bizarre. Two of the three factions concluded that the American people, even the protest movement kids, were "the enemy" because they weren't ready to rise up in revolution against racism and imperialism in Vietnam. One group, which controlled the national organization and had the mighty endorsement of the Black Panthers on their side, decided to ditch SDS, instead calling themselves Revolutionary Youth Movement (RYM). They declared their new slogan: "Bring the War Home!" Another faction tried to one-up them by mutating the Chairman Mao aphorism "Serve the People" into a more hostile slogan directed against their fellow whites: "Serve the People *Shit!*" They cleverly named themselves Revolutionary Youth Movement II (RYM II) and drifted off into relative obscurity. (The basic organization still exists today, under the moniker Revolutionary Communist Party. They have a rather large bookstore in a commercially viable section of Berkeley.) The third group, the disciplined cadre of a very straight Maoist cabal called the Progressive Labor Party, actually won the vote to lead SDS, but drifted off into *complete* obscurity. SDS was dead.

Revolutionary Youth Movement, the First, also gave themselves a nickname, taken from lyrics in a snarling youth-alienation Bob Dylan rocker from 1965 called "Subterranean Homesick Blues." They called themselves the Weathermen. In October 1969, the Weathermen (having dropped the RYM) started "bringing the war home" by going to Chicago for "Days of Rage." It wasn't a demonstration per se; it had no theme or set of demands, although it was understood that they were taking vengeance for the summer 1968 police riot. Chicago conspiracy trial convict Tom Hayden showed up to give them a quick little cheerleader speech before beating a hasty retreat. Approximately four hundred Weathermen (Weather*people,* actually, but the women hadn't had their "consciousness raised" yet) wearing helmets and other protective gear and armed with baseball bats and other implements of violence rampaged through the commercial section of Chicago's wealthiest district smashing windows and cars and fighting with the police. Over fifty police officers and nearly half the Weathermen participants were hospitalized. Even the Black Panthers were appalled at the pointless idiocy of the action, labeling it "Custerism." Shortly thereafter, the Weathermen went underground and graduated to bombs, although in their first attempt at bomb making three "urban guerrillas" only succeeded in blowing themselves up. Taking this as a lesson learned, they turned toward "nonviolent" bombings. In these "symbolic actions," they would bomb buildings, mostly housing U.S. military institutions and war contractors, but they would first phone in a warning so that no human beings would get killed or hurt. Indeed, no one after that point was killed or even injured by the Weather Underground. (Yes, the name was finally changed.) One symbolic bomb actually went off in the Capitol Building. A lot of people actually cheered that one. Such was the temper of the times.

The way the Weather Underground used drugs and sex to solidify their group identity was, in some ways, even weirder than their political strategies. Within the countercultural ideal of the age, drugs and sex were catalysts and contexts within which individuals could expand and therefore liberate themselves from narrow psychological precepts. They were ways to affirm the rights of individuals, couples, and small groups to have and share pleasures and visionary states that were presumed to be vouchsafed only to the privileged, the brilliant, and/or the damned, and therefore ways to separate from—or rebel against—the dreariness of quasi-responsible bourgeois life. Under more ordinary, less exultant circumstances, the *use* of drugs and sex could be reduced to mere peer pressure. And at the low end of this hierarchy of mind-blown eroticism, peer pressure could spill over into something that borders on psychic—or indeed even physical—rape. Additionally, these deeply intense and unpredictable experiences could turn in on the intentions of users, producing an abnegation of the self in which the once hopeful voyager found herself utterly emptied and unmoored.

The Weatherpeople used drugs and sex in nearly all these ways. For the Weather Underground, drug and sex experiences were like training exercises for psychedelic, armed guerrilla war. Acid trips were *ordered* by the leadership. They initiated frequent organized sessions in which Weatherpeople would probe their own and each other's weaknesses and their depth of commitment to the Revolution. Stripped of all categories and boundaries on high dose experiences, rather than abandoning politics for a float in the cosmic realm, the Weathermen would experience the "primitive" warrior within—that aspect of the human spirit, or perhaps that part of the genetic program, that is geared toward warfare in its nonalienated, pretechnological sense. All-night war whoops were their version of the hippies' "om."

Monogamous relationships were verboten. Orgies were *mandatory.* One could, we suppose, argue that these tactics were not so different from the ones used by Sufi masters to tease their followers out of their psychic slumbers into full awakeness. But the Weatherpeople's self-shock training was more a peculiar psychedelic reframing of the Stalinist notion of "reeducation" and was aimed toward a strategy for social change.

Divisions within the political counterculture were greatly amplified when women activists realized that the men were creeps. Throughout the

1960s, most women in the New Left culture were treated as second-class citizens, left out of decision-making discussions (beautiful Weatherwoman powerhouse Bernardine Dohrn was an exception), relegated to making coffee and mimeographing leaflets, while men took the glamorous macho public stances. But the women had gone into the streets at public protests and gotten their heads cracked just like the men. Within the hippie culture, it was even worse. In hippie vernacular, men commonly referred to their female partners as their "old ladies," and called the practice of multiple partnership "sharing the women"—as if the women in question were commodities instead of active participants. Domestic division of labor between the sexes tended to follow traditional lines, and the recognized leaders of the movement were exclusively male.

In 1969, the women revolted. Tactics that the freak radicals had used against "the man" were employed by radical women against the men. Movement offices and underground newspapers like *Rat* were occupied and their male publishers and editors were declared "pigs." Particularly within the hard-core "revolutionary" movement, things were seriously hostile. For the most part, the men, being earnest leftists, immediately saw that the women were right and moved to correct the imbalance. But nothing seemed to stanch the flow of rage. As with the black activists of the mid-1960s, the avant-garde of the women's movement called for a complete separation from the New Left men.

Robin Morgan's statement "Goodbye to All That" ("Goodbye, goodbye forever, counterfeit Left . . . male-dominated cracked-glassed-mirror reflection of the Amerikan nightmare"), published in virtually every underground newspaper across the land in 1970, sounded the radical feminists' battle cry. Many movement women abruptly ended their relationships and even marriages with men, and tried to live in a women-only world. Some feminist theorists declared that all male sexuality was, in essence, imperialist rape—the penis, a penetrative implement, invaded women's bodies and colonized them through pregnancy.

It was a well-deserved kick in the ass, but if it was going to be difficult for a gang of stoners to fight a revolution against the planet's greatest empire before, it wasn't going to be any easier with half of the movement at war with the other half. Also, one of the things that had attracted so many people to the movement during the 1960s was that it was one of the few places in American culture where people weren't uptight about sexuality. Throughout the ribald, libertine 1970s, as feminist hostility toward male sexuality held firm, the left became one of the few places in American society where people *were* uptight about sexuality.

On June 27, 1969, the sex wars moved into new territory when police raided a gay bar in Greenwich Village. Homosexual activities were still illegal, so gays were subjected to constant harassment and even imprisonment merely for being sexually active. On that day, the gays said "enough" and a riot erupted. People from all over New York's Christopher Street gay community converged in front of the Stonewall Inn to fight the police and a tactical riot squad. The revolt initiated a new era, as gay liberation organizations formed and asserted their rights to "come out of the closet" and into the open as human beings as deserving of rights as everybody else. Once again, the almost entirely heterosexual leaders of the New Left were slammed by a rising oppressed group. Abbie Hoffman, Jerry Rubin, White Panther leader John Sinclair, Stokely Carmichael, and the Weatherpeople were all singled out for homophobic statements or macho attitudes. Once again, they confessed that they had been wrong, but it was no secret that the leadership of "the revolution" felt wounded and tired—bruised and battered—from within.

Meanwhile, over in England, the heralds of the new world, the bards of the generation, were also fighting amongst themselves. The Beatles too were breaking up. Even the different paths they took as they split off mirrored divergences within the counterculture as the 1960s gave way to the 1970s. John went to America to join the Yippies. George went off shopping for spiritual gurus. Paul went back to nature. And Ringo partied like there was no tomorrow.

PEACE GETS A CHANCE

As the avant-garde of the youth culture was getting all set to suicide itself in a revolutionary fantasy, the kids en masse showed the world that they were still alright when they packed into a field just outside Woodstock, New York, for "three days of peace and music." Rock culture, the musicians, and most of their fans were living out a whole different narrative from the hard-core dropouts and the militants. Since the early days of the

Family Dog, psychedelic rock had evolved internationally into a consciously countercultural global language, speaking to a growing if ill-defined sense of generational unity around expanded liberties, free sexuality, psychedelic drugs, and general rebelliousness. Rock was also a vast, successful commercial enterprise, and rock musicians were contracted with large media corporations who advertised and distributed their messages, frequently with great wit and skill thanks to the "corporate house hippies" the companies hired to keep them clued in. Large rock concerts, now a daily fact of life even in relatively small cities all over the world, mimicked the Dionysian feelings of the early "acid test" Trips Festivals and Family Dog happenings with light shows, free-form dancing, and lots of psychedelic drugs distributed by—and among—the audience members themselves. But these shows were also different. Fans had to pass through the turnstiles and pay some serious money, and when the show was over, they were ushered back out into the night by the frequently harsh employees of the show promoters. One moment, one felt like a blissful spirit breaking all the surly bonds of earthly adversity, and the next, one was being herded cowlike toward the realities outside.

Popular rock musicians, while they were nowhere near as business savvy and (therefore) wealthy as they are today, lived comfortably while pursuing many of the same obsessions—drugs, sex, alternative philosophies—as the freaks on the street. The rock stars were in a position to have their cake and revolt against it too. Keith Richards told *Rolling Stone* that if there was actually a revolution, he and Mick would be right there on the barricades, but there *wasn't* going to be a revolution—a convenient excuse as well as an astute observation. Meanwhile, most of the rock musicians were still speaking the language of peace and love.

More than underground newspapers, more than political speeches at demonstrations, more than cosmic gurus, the sound that was near-constantly in the ears of the great mass of America's counterculturally inclined youths came from their stereos. For the most part, the popular bands provided an island of sanity and ambiguity where the battle lines were not so clearly drawn. David Crosby, Stephen Stills, Graham Nash, Joni Mitchell, and others formed a laid-back hippie scene in Los Angeles where peace and romantic love were still the watchwords. The British bands, particularly the Beatles and the Rolling Stones, supplied a sense of irony that was almost entirely missing on the hyper-earnest American baby boomer scene, as manifested in songs like "Sexy Sadie," "Blue Jay Way," and "Salt of the Earth." Frank Zappa, probably the most didactically explicit anti-authoritarian rock star of the time, pointed his ferocious satire equally at politicians, militarists, hippies, their confused parents, and leftists, and refused to become part of the drug scene. The Grateful Dead ignored the revolution in favor of narratives about adventurous life and cosmic insights. Most of the fans, also, had not completely turned their backs on the better gifts that everyday life held. After all, when there is only rage against the machine and the extremes of hallucinatory consciousness, what becomes of relational romance, learning, children, science, good food, fiction, sports, invention: all the good stuff that comes with ordinary humanness?

The not so desperately hip masses were a sort of "silent majority" (Nixon's term for his supporters) *within* the counterculture, difficult to historicize because they didn't make as much noise as the radical spokespeople. But there they were in Bethel, New York, having a great big peaceful party. The rock revelers and the citizens of upstate New York treated one another with mutual kindness. Even the U.S. Army pitched in with food and supplies so that people frolicking naked in the mud high on acid could eat and drink and have medicine. For one brief moment good vibes had the day. *Time, Newsweek,* the *New York Times,* and other mainstream media outlets across the nation ignored the massive transgressing of drug laws to praise the half a million young people who had remained peaceful and happy despite the rain and the insufficient food.

Time magazine chirped that Woodstock "may well rank as one of the significant political and sociological events of the age. . . . The revolution it preaches, implicitly or explicitly, is essentially moral; it is the proclamation of a new set of values. . . . With a surprising ease and a cool sense of authority, the children of plenty have voiced an intention to live by a different ethical standard than their parents accepted. The pleasure principle has been elevated over the Puritan ethic of work. To do one's own thing is a greater duty than to be a useful citizen. Personal freedom in the midst of squalor is more liberating than social conformity with the trappings of wealth. Now that youth takes abundance for granted, it can afford to reject materialism."

The high coming out of Woodstock during the summer of 1969 even cooled the freak-left down a bit. Abbie Hoffman, who, freaking out on acid, climbed the stage during the Who's performance to deliver a political harangue, only to be bonked on the head with a guitar by Pete Townshend (each would later say the other one was in the right; Townshend said he should have been more politically aware, and Abbie admitted he was behaving like a jerk), pulled through his bummer filled with love for the potential of the "Woodstock Nation." With similar visions of a potential alternative society in mind, many denizens of the freak-left began emphasizing the building of alternative institutions within hip communities over confrontation, and some even went off to form farming communes in the country.

A BANG AND A WHIMPER

One person who wasn't picking up on the groovy new vibe sat in the Oval Office. On April 30, 1970, Richard Nixon expanded the war by sending twenty thousand U.S. troops into Cambodia.

Instantly college campuses and hip communities all across the country went nuts. Over the next few days, the size and militancy of protests were a quantum leap beyond anything the antiwar movement had seen. Army recruiting centers and other war-related sites were under siege. High school and even junior high school students staged militant demonstrations, often in small American towns where they'd never seen anything more controversial than the irreverent, antiwar Smothers Brothers on TV. Even middle-class liberals from the older generation turned out for protests with their fists waving in the air. Several ROTC buildings were burned to the ground or blown up by antiwar militants, including one on the college campus at Kent State University, in Ohio, where the National Guard was called in to respond. On May 4, 1970, students and guardsmen squared off. It was a by now familiar ritual as the opposing forces tossed tear gas canisters back and forth at each other. Then suddenly, the guardsmen knelt, aimed their rifles, and fired. Four protesters were shot dead.

And so the size and militancy of the demonstrations and riots doubled again. Thousands of college campuses closed down for the remainder of the school year. Dozens of high schools went out on strike in protest, and in some cases, the teachers joined in. Around twenty more ROTC buildings burned to the ground. And within a few days of the shooting, the rock band Crosby, Stills, Nash and Young had a battle-cry song called "Ohio" blaring out of every Top Forty car radio in the country ("Got to get down to it/Soldiers are cutting us down"). For a brief moment, young people—students particularly—by the millions were sounding just like the freak-left, and talk about "the revolution" was everywhere.

And then it was time for summer vacation.

"The revolution" never quite returned. Perhaps over the long months of summer, people had a chance to slow down and really think about what had happened to those kids at Kent State, and the initial rage turned to fear. After all, the great masses of hip young people, while they hated the war and the overreactions of state authority, did not have the kind of dedication to total social change that the hard core of the counterculture did. And perhaps, when they momentarily turned their full attention toward "the revolution," they discovered a leadership that was lost in the iconographic worship of Chairman Mao, Chairman Huey, Uncle Ho, and, in some cases, even the Manson Family. So, as Ken Kesey had said in another context, they "turned their backs and said 'fuck it.' " Whatever the reason, as 1970 segued into 1971, students *stopped* attending protests in droves.

Another dissipative factor was the fact that by the early 1970s, many—if not most—of the leading advocates of "the revolution" were in jail, on trial, or in exile. The language of the freak-left counterculture was spoken in terms of cities and numbers, the Chicago Seven, the New York Twenty-one, the Gainesville Eight, and bold imaginative slogans and declarations had long since been displaced by a list of people to free: "Free Huey," "Free Angela [Davis]," "Free John Sinclair," "Free Timothy Leary," ad infinitum. In a rare, bitter 1974 political essay titled "The Outlaw Industry," Leary wrote, "When all is said and done the culminating goal of most radical activism in this country is The Trial." In Leary's analysis, the real (if perhaps unconscious) goal of underground activities was fame, and the fortune that followed. The symbolic outlaw got the fame of martyrdom. The lawyers, biographers, and public advocates got reflected glory plus profit from this "outlaw industry." Leary: "Like the movie and record business, the Outlaw Industry needs a continual supply of new faces and groups."

With revolution no longer in the air, long stretches of pointless misery lay in store for the prisoners and exiles who had gone too deep into the fantasy.

Perversely, just as the spirit of revolution was starting to disintegrate, rock and roll's two most powerful figures apparently decided to try to give it a boost. The eternally contrarian Bob Dylan had ignored the hippies and the New Left throughout the peak years from 1967 through 1970. Then in late 1971 he released a single that was a tribute to George Jackson, a Black Panther prisoner who had been shot in an alleged prison break attempt. Dylan sang, "He wouldn't take shit from no one/He wouldn't bow down or kneel." It was a Top Forty radio hit, and while Dylan couldn't restart "the revolution," he *was* able to get the word shit played over the radio.

While the song permeated the airwaves, Dylan trudged off to meet with Huey Newton and donate some of his profits from the tune. But Dylan and Newton argued over Israel versus Palestine, so there would be no "Panther-Dylan pact."

Meanwhile, that same year, John Lennon and Yoko Ono had started working and playing with Abbie Hoffman and Jerry Rubin in New York City. In the pages of *Rolling Stone* and elsewhere, Lennon endorsed "the revolution" that he had once rejected in a Beatles song, and performed benefit concerts for the Black Panthers and for John Sinclair, who had been given a ten-year sentence for giving two joints of marijuana to an undercover agent. Three days after the latter performance, Sinclair, who had been in prison for two and a half years, was set free.

An ex-Beatle was a power to contend with but, for whatever reason, in 1971 an irreversible shift in youth consciousness had occurred. Even Lennon couldn't rouse his millions of fans to get back into the protest movement. It was clearly time for a different strategy. The presidential election was coming up in 1972. If the counterculture couldn't overthrow the government and make the world safe for rock, dope, and fucking in the streets, maybe it could take over the Democratic Party and change the system from within. The New Left's long journey was finally leading it right back to where it started.

The liberal antiwar candidate George McGovern swept the primaries. Much to his chagrin, Abbie Hoffman, Jerry Rubin, and Ed Sanders endorsed him for president. They wrote a popular book called *Vote!* to try to help bring in the youth vote (it was released too late to have any effect). After all the wild rhetoric, after all the riots and all the acid trips shedding every trace of bourgeois respectability, vast numbers of former "LSD-driven total maniacs of the universe" agreed "the revolution" was over: liberal Democrats were the last best hope.

In sharp contrast to the Chicago convention, the 1972 Democratic convention had many Yippies inside. Abbie Hoffman was enthusiastically escorted inside the convention hall wearing a fake *Mad* magazine press badge. Inside, he met up with old friends from past street battles who were now delegates and was mobbed by enthusiastic young Democrats who asked for his autograph. Delegates turned him on to the ultra-powerful three-minute hallucinogen DMT in the convention bathroom. Allen Ginsberg was also inside, where he spoke before TV cameras on behalf of the first ever gay delegation to a major national convention. This sure wasn't Mayor Daley's Democratic Party.

If the welcoming of the freaks into the mainstream Democratic Party generated excitement and optimism within the counterculture, it generated even more optimism within the Republican Party. Middle America was watching, after all, and they weren't going to vote to let the hippies take over the country. Nixon's campaigners effectively mocked the Democrats as advocates of "Abortion, Acid, and Amnesty [for draft dodgers]." The election was the biggest landslide in U.S. history. Americans rejected countercultural governance by a margin of 60 percent to 37 percent. (Young voters between the ages of eighteen and twenty-six voted for McGovern, but only by a slim majority.)

THE END

> And in the end/the love you take/is equal to the love you make.
>
> PAUL MCCARTNEY, THE BEATLES, 1969

Reflecting on this chapter, the late sixties/early seventies revolution may read like a series of mostly hellish events and psychotic mind-states. But, for all the excesses of repression and revolution, the decade was also characterized by lots of blindingly positive countercultural energy. As Hunter

Thompson wrote, "There was a fantastic universal sense that whatever we were doing was *right,* that we were winning. . . . Our energy would simply *prevail.* We had all the momentum, we were riding the crest of a high and beautiful wave." People pushed their liberties to the limit, let their desires for real change overtake their reason, let the excitement and love that they felt for their collectivity sear their souls. It really felt as though one push in the right direction could break down all the prison walls humanity has ever constructed: in the material world, in the relational world, and within the minds and hearts of each individual. And finally, it was, as George Harrison sang, "all too much." Reacting in part to repression from outside, it turned in on itself with an anti-authoritarian frenzy that sometimes turned authoritarian in the intensity of its insistence.

Probably the major fallacy that guided the entire sixties epoch from idealism to lunacy was utopianism—Ginsberg's hallucination that he could "seize power over the universe and become the next consciousness." As a totalizing philosophy, utopianism is authoritarian in essence. (Jim Morrison sang about the hippie "soft parade": "Everything *must* be this way.") Writ small, utopian experiments like the Transcendentalists' Brook Farm commune can motivate love, generosity, and creativity. And occasional bursts of utopian energy may be necessary to propel countercultural epochs that seek social changes. But when the utopian mind-set ultimately tries to conquer vast populations it comes up against its limits. Utopians demand perfection, and those damned irascible human beings who refuse to fit themselves into the model tend to become enemies. Che Guevara's sixties altruistic "New Man" was a beautiful idea, but he used state power to try and coerce the Cuban people into living up to the ideal's demands. The Western left-counterculture never got quite that far, but people who were in the midst of it used to joke knowingly about "LSD reeducation camps."

Nasty detours aside, the ideal of the hip left really *was* anti-authoritarian, even anarchistic. With the exception of a few groups like the Black Panthers, who had Leninist fantasies about running a centralized vanguard-led revolutionary state, the hip left didn't propose an alternative system. They offered opposition to systems. The core guiding vision was that "the revolution" itself would inspire personal and collective *evolutions* on a mass scale. The behaviors that would allow society to function without a governing system would spontaneously emerge—a voluntary cooperation among networked autonomous individuals and groups would see to it that basic human needs were taken care of. Its theater, its psychedelic pathways to personal growth, its grassroots democratic participation in communes and collectives, its free rock and roll orgies and festive celebrations would be so fulfilling that people would not desire for much else beyond their basic material needs. The consumption and ownership of excess goods, of media images, of commercial leisure activities, would simply wither away. And within a few years, the machines would make us all equally rich anyway. This imaginal narrative is still compelling to many of today's anarchists (although many have abandoned the "equally rich" part in favor of a rejection of technology). It has the advantage that it has never been tried on a mass scale for any extended length of time, and it is not likely to be. So it can never be disproved and will forever remain romantic.

Ironically, it's doubtful whether anything like the excitable counterculture of the 1960s would have happened if the U.S. and global economy were not in terrific health. Those who burned money as a representative of inhumane interests and as a signifier of unnatural relationships knew that either the abundant economy would always produce *more* money or that the money system would be replaced by something more idealistic. As bizarre as it seems now, it was easy at that time to believe both these things at once. As to whether a post-scarcity society based on play and eros was (or is) possible, what was once an article of faith for some of us is now an area for research and inquiry. Certainly, the economic privileges that gave Western sixties youth the leisure to dream such wild dreams have struck up against environmental constraints, the impoverished realities of a more closely integrated global economy, and the tightening economic policies of corporate consolidation and capitalism-with-no-brakes.

Both the styles and contents of the radical period in modern counterculture remain with us today. Indeed, most of the succeeding countercultural episodes measure themselves against the extremity of this epoch. Hopefully, in the future, if a mass countercultural movement again seems close to mounting some sort of extraordinary transmutation of a major nation-state or an entire planet, it will avoid some of the mistakes that these brilliant but confused experimenters made in the rush of history.

CHAPTER FOURTEEN

⊢ THAT WHICH DOES NOT KILL ME MAKES ME HIPPER

The Hedonist/Nihilist Countercultures of the 1970s

Half a million people who didn't have enough sense to come in out of the rain.

ANDY WARHOL, ABOUT THE WOODSTOCK FESTIVAL

Life is disappointing.

ELDRIDGE CLEAVER, 1973

The American 1970s have a bad rap within counterculture. The decade is commonly viewed as the aftermath of the 1960s, a time when dreams of peace and love, or anarcho-communal revolution, were relinquished. People stepped back from the edge, shallowed out, gave up, and tuned in to the mellow sounds of James Taylor and Carole King. And it's true. From *Time* magazine's 1967 cover declaring "Youth" as the "Man of the Year" to the late-sixties fantasies of total political and cultural liberation, expectations toward the baby boom generation as a transformational force had expanded to the bursting point. By 1972, that bubble burst and it became clear that the *hippest* generation was mostly made up of ordinary, selfish, unimaginative human beings ready to make accommodations with the particulars of capitalism and the customary requirements of adulthood—ready to drop back in and compromise with the system. Particularly among those who had been on the front guard of the counterculture revolution, these changes were viewed through a thick haze of disappointment.

It's too bad because, in many ways, the 1970s were a time of countercultural victory. Revolution wasn't in the air, but in the aftermath of the 1973 Watergate crisis, anti-authoritarianism was ubiquitous. Political and (especially) cultural conservatism were in retreat. Films by the likes of Martin Scorsese, Francis Coppola, Robert Altman, Paul Mazursky, and Paul Schrader dominated the theaters, heralding the violent existential revolt of the angry and alienated Everyman against the forces of constriction and conformity; along with hip youths, members of the older generation turned out in droves. Young people watched in stunned amazement as their parents went around with shirts open to the chest, joined swingers' retreats and clubs, and tried cocaine and marijuana. All generations sampled various methods for self-exploration and development that were available on the new spiritual/human potential marketplace. Books like *Zen and the Art of Motorcycle Maintenance* and TV shows like *Kung Fu* pushed a light version of psychedelic hippie philosophy to the top of the pop charts, and California even elected a governor who spoke in spacey cosmic aphorisms. Liberals took over a good chunk of federal and state governments. And if you didn't want to mellow out, slow down, or conform even a little, you could drown your revolutionary blues in a succession of wildly hedonistic, nihilistic rock and roll subcountercultures.

For counterculturalists, the 1970s represented a peculiar mix of total defeat and partial victory. For a substantial aggregate of Americans from all generations, it represented a brief flirtation with vaguely countercultural values, however poorly understood or manifested. With little purposeful focus, this equivocally mass countercultural epoch would easily give way to the cohesive, conservative Reagan "Revolution" at the start of the 1980s. But meanwhile, there was fun to be had.

OH YOU PRETTY THINGS

> Among the young, eroticism and suicide became mass
> phenomena, embraced with the same headlong extrem-
> ism that had been given to revolution. The brief celebrity
> of Artsybashev's *Sanin* (published in 1907) was due to
> the fact that it combined both themes in one. Two sui-
> cides and two seductions . . . a toying with incest; the
> glorification of . . . physical joys; the ridiculing of those
> who waste their time on politics or knowledge; the ad-
> monition to . . . follow instinct and impulse, abandon
> principles, plans, regrets, and to use reason only as devil's
> advocate and instrument for liberating oneself from all
> codes and conventions and principles.
>
> BERTRAM D. WOLFE (DESCRIBING RUSSIAN YOUTH
> AFTER THEIR ABORTED 1905 REVOLUTION)

That dis*illusion*ment can be liberating is no surprise. Disillusioned "sixties" people were no longer expected to make the revolution overnight, and they were no longer constrained by the stringently anti-materialist demands of the hyper-spiritual hippie dropout ethic. Out of the tepees and into the nightclubs! *What a fucking relief.* Some youths decided to put their clothes *back on* to engage in a period of wild sexuality and partying abandon. A new rock culture, called glitter or glam, was the first countercultural rebellion against hippie conformity and the expectations of political correctness.

Glam rock was partly rooted in the pre-hippie rock and roll style of England's dandyish mid-sixties Mod subculture, and glam musicians like David Bowie and Marc Bolan (T. Rex) eschewed the long musical jams popular among hippie musicians in favor of the effervescent, well-constructed three-to-four-minute pop song reminiscent of that period. The uprising of gay culture was another influence. If the left was on the lam, the gays were on the rise, and out-of-the-closet-and-flaunting-it gay men brought a sense of boldness, novelty, sensuality, and playfulness back into a counterculture that had grown grim and peevish during its ultra-revolutionary period. Last but certainly not least, the glam rock culture was rooted in the consanguinity between Andy Warhol's art Factory and the Velvet Underground—the brilliantly experimental (and massively unpopular) rock band Warhol had sponsored in 1966–1967. While the hippies and the New Left were constructing and reconstructing their identities, Warhol's New York City Factory was populated by drag queens, hard-drug fiends, and other freaks who were too original and fucked up to conform even to counterculture versions of the good and the beautiful. In the punk rock history *Please Kill Me,* Warhol "superstar" (Warhol labeled all those who performed in his spontaneous underground movies superstars) Mary Woronov contrasted the Velvet Underground/Warholians with the San Francisco hippies who came to check them out when the band performed in that city: "We weren't like them at all. They hated us. . . . They were like, 'Oh wow man, a happening!' We were like reading Jean Genet. We were S&M and they were free love. We really liked gay people, and the West Coast was totally homophobic. So they thought we were evil and we thought they were stupid."

A revealing distinction between the Warholian and the hippie aesthetic can be drawn by comparing their use of the word plastic. For hippies, plastic was a curse word. Plastics were mass-manufactured objects, easily manipulated and lacking authenticity. Plastic *people* had these same qualities. For Warhol, who labeled his light show for the Velvet Underground "The Exploding Plastic Inevitable," plastic represented a quality of flexibility, mutability, changeability. In the province of authenticity, flexibility can be suspect. The flexible person lacks *commitment*—a primary authenticist value. This contrast, understood intuitively by many a seventies neodecadent, exposed a certain rigidity within the sixties aesthetic. (Must a counterculturalist assume a brittle, defensive posture so as not to be manipulable by mainline ideals and addictions? A complex exegesis would be required to do complete justice to this peculiar conundrum.)

In the aftermath of the frantic search for political, spiritual, and existential authenticity, many hipsters needed a little slack. Some looked to Warhol's aesthetic of ironic distance to help them climb down off the high horse. In *The Philosophy of Andy Warhol from A to B and Back Again,* published in 1975 (even the title contains a lovely *anti*-expansive, minimalist joke), he admitted to loving money, fame, surface beauty, television, gossip, sexual perversity, and *artifice*.

Why was this good? Because it was *irreverent*! The counterculture had built up its own set of judgments and constraints—its approved behaviors. Warhol's crowd, and later the glam rock movement, refused the authority of those judgments. Besides, constant authenticity/sincerity is stultifying. We are (most of us) always thankful when an evening full of earnest talk is alleviated by a shocking joke that stands everybody's expectations on their heads. Ironic distance liberates psychological space, which (ironically) can lead to further authentic growth.

Besides forging a new neo-decadent aesthetic, glam culture produced some great pop music at a time when rock was growing stale. Many of the most interesting albums from this creatively lifeless period emerged out of the genre. *Stranded* by Roxy Music, *New York Dolls* (self-titled), *Here Come the Warm Jets* by Brian Eno, *Killer* by Alice Cooper, and everything recorded by David Bowie spring immediately to mind. Peculiarly, the musical genre was considered chintzy and shallow by most hippies, who still worshiped the Grateful Dead and Eric Clapton. This is largely because the glam aesthetic wasn't about instrumental expertise, and because the scene didn't take itself too seriously. The wild and intentionally tacky androgynous costuming, bizarre stage theatrics, and real or fake bisexuality either blazed so bright (for those who liked them) or were so alienating (to those who didn't) that many were blinded to the high quality of at least some of the work.

If rock and roll in the late 1960s was about tripster consciousness and collective rebellion primarily, and (with the possible exception of the Rolling Stones and the Doors) about sex only secondarily, the glam movement put the sex on the front burner. As Gary Herman wrote in his 1982 book, *Rock and Roll Babylon,* "Sexuality became the great playground of rock in the seventies. In fact, everything pointed in that direction: the permissiveness of the preceding decade, the sexual symbolism of performance itself, the need to exploit unconventional morality. Liberation became personal liberation, freedom from oppression became freedom from sexual repression, the democratic urge towards equality and freedom of association became an individualistic quest for guiltless promiscuity."

The central image and the most creative artistic representative of the glam rock scene was David Bowie (although it would be shameful not to mention the acid-drenched San Francisco underground phenomenon called the Cockettes), who presented himself as an insatiable bisexual mutant who might just be an extraterrestrial. It was, largely, a theatrical piece, a character he was playing both on and off stage that seemed to speak to the zeitgeist, or at least to a peculiar sliver of it.

Bowie was also the first rock star of the 1970s to sell himself as an anti-hippie. "I want to strangle them with their hippie beads," Bowie told *Rolling Stone*. It was a good way to stand out, and no doubt he was expressing a real frustration with that certain self-righteous rigidity already discussed. But his stance, and his glittery clothes, seemed to blind commentators to an interesting fact. His song lyrics were more explicitly, directly reflective of someone who wrestled with countercultural ideas, and with the issues of the hip left, than any other major rock performer, with the exceptions of Paul Kantner (of the Jefferson Airplane) and John Lennon.

His 1971 song "Memory of a Free Festival" got as misty-eyed about the beautiful people as Joni Mitchell's "Woodstock" and was more explicitly acid-saturated: "Someone passed some bliss among the crowd/And we walked back to the road, unchained." (All Bowie lyrics can be found online. It is worth reading this one in its entirety.) In "Cygnet Committee," Bowie identifies with the forces that "planted seeds of rebirth" in the place of money and rattles off a list of sixties counterculture slogans from the hippie/Beatles' "all you need is love" to the White Panthers' "kick out the jams." The song starts by wistfully embracing the dissipating hopes of the hip left but winds its way toward a vision of psychedelic fascism as his voice cries that "we can force you to be free" and portrays freaks running wild down "desolation rows plowing down men, women" and hearing only "the shrieks of the old rich." "Oh You Pretty Things" (1971) limned Nietzsche and more explicitly Leary in portraying youth as a new species fit to leave *Homo sapiens* and Planet Earth behind. "Panic in Detroit" (1973) portrayed an isolated former American revolutionist who "looked a lot like Che Guevara" and is "the only survivor of the National People's Gang" committing a nonspecific terrorist act while undergoing a nervous breakdown. The persona Bowie adopted in "Scream Like a Baby" (1980) reminisced that he "wouldn't buy no merchandise, wouldn't go to war . . . mixed with other colors" and describes a hard-core freak-radical hero named Sam who got taken away by the police for treatment with psychiatric drugs. At the end of the song, Sam suicides himself.

In public appearances and interviews, Bowie—who chose his name because it represents a knife that slices from both ends—has cagily avoided identifying himself with the hippie counterculture (even ambiguously), leaving only a trail of lyrical comments and hints. In a 2001 VH1 special, however, he reminisced fondly about meeting Abbie Hoffman when he (Hoffman) was underground, hiding from the FBI. Hoffman, Bowie enthused, "really understood my entire corpus."

Glam culture had its faults. In fact, it almost had nothing *but* foibles and vices—that was part of its charm. While much of the music contained as much social commentary as other seventies rock genres, there was little or no sense of community or collective responsibility. Hard drugs like heroin, cocaine, methamphetamine, and especially alcohol were voluminously abused. Nihilistic and suicidal attitudes were often embraced. The denizens of the scene had no loftier ambitions than to "rock and roll all night and party every day," and the musicians wanted to become rich and famous enough to do that very lifestyle up right. (They failed. Even Bowie was a B-list rock star—in terms of popularity if not influence—until the mid-1980s.)

Within the Third World communist cultures that the hip left flirted with at the end of the 1960s, decadence was the ultimate transgression, and the authoritarian state claimed the right to alter the decadent individual's behaviors for the good of all. The late-sixties left-hippie counterculture mimicked this purism in its own peculiar way with its insistence on health food, plain peasant clothes, the rejection of (plastic) makeup, and in many other slight ways. In response, within glam culture, "decadent" was the ultimate compliment.

Glam was a trivial counterculture that marked the beginnings of a division of a relatively unified rock-identified youth movement into conflicting tribes. We had gone from trying to turn on the world, to trying to take over the world, to fighting over which genre of rock and roll was hip.

On the other hand, it brought performance and costuming back into rock and roll, which inspired an African-American acid freak named George Clinton to create the psychedelic glam-funk band Parliament/Funkadelic, which in turn spawned the creative, surrealistic edge of today's hip-hop underground.

Dope Desperadoes and Cosmic Cowboys

I'm not gonna let them catch me/Not gonna let them catch the midnight rider.

GREGG ALLMAN, ALLMAN BROTHERS BAND, 1973

With the new decade, life in the streets had grown untenable. The country was going into an economic recession; community groups like the Diggers, who had once kept the hippies fed, had long since slipped away into various personal destinies. Common citizens had grown tired of being panhandled. Addicts searching for money for heroin made the hippie streets unsafe. With the revolution dead, individuals were withdrawing into private enclaves and the generous communities of support for wandering dharma bums were drying up. For those holdouts who wanted to evade the nine-to-five and keep the dropout party going, there was a clear solution. All those hippies and radicals who had rushed to drop back *in* still liked to get high, and now they were receiving weekly paychecks.

Drug dealing, small-time and big-time, became the chosen lifestyle among those hard-core freaks who still couldn't—or didn't wish to—fit in to society. For most, it was just a few dime bags of marijuana sold here and there to keep body and soul together. But bolder, more adventurous hippies built up big businesses, mostly around the importation and sale of marijuana and the newly popular cocaine, flown in "beneath the radar" in private planes from Mexico, Colombia, Peru, and other Latin/South American supplier nations.

In sharp contrast to the glam rock milieu, hippie drug dealers at all economic levels tended to invest themselves into a macho, Wild West, cowboy-outlaw self-image that gloried in gambling and gunfighting metaphors supplied to them by bands like the Eagles, the Allman Brothers

Band, the Charlie Daniels Band, and (let's be honest here) Bob Dylan and the Grateful Dead. The hard-drinking, pot-smoking, coke-sniffing, womanizing dope desperado cut a romantic figure, and the illegality of popular mind-altering substances allowed these dealers to maintain a sense of revolutionary bravado long after the political moment had passed. Expressions of the dope rider culture expanded beyond rock. In 1974, a particularly eccentric Yippie named Tom Forcade, who had run a wire service for underground newspapers, invested his income from marijuana sales into a magazine called *High Times,* which glamorized the dealer culture. A little later in the decade, Cheech and Chong made popular comedy albums and movies also aimed at the culture.

While most of those involved probably got away with living free and high (if paranoid) for various periods of time, the outlaw culture produced its share of inmates. One victim of the dope rider romance was Abbie Hoffman. Hoffman—feeling lost in the absence of *his* revolution—decided to, at once, participate in and write about the new outlaw scene. His first big cocaine deal was a bust, and Hoffman spent years on the lam followed by nearly a year in the prison system, which exasperated the depressive side of his manic-depressive tendencies, ultimately leading to suicide in 1989. (It's worth noting that, at the height of his fame, Hoffman gave away essentially all of his substantial earnings as a writer and lecturer to radical groups. At the same time that he was being busted for coke, he was refusing product endorsement offers. So it seems clear that Hoffman's dope dealing mistake was more in the spirit of adventure than greed.)

The Fall of the House of Nixon

The hip left had succeeded in doing at least one thing right: they drove President Richard Nixon and his minions absolutely nuts. Indeed, probably the only people outside the hip left who took the threatened "revolution" seriously were in the Nixon administration and the various law enforcement agencies. As the Vietnam/Cambodian/Laotian war became increasingly unpopular, the administration slid ever deeper into a paranoid abuse of the FBI, DEA, IRS, and Nixon's own personal henchmen to go after the radicals. As they entered the 1972 election year, the administration had some reasons to be nervous. Not only was the majority unhappy with the conduct of the war, the economy was in serious recession. Worst of all, from Nixon's gut-level view, the antiwar movement had driven Daniel Ellsberg to follow his own conscience and release the Pentagon Papers. All the lies and the dearest secret war plannings of his administration related to Vietnam were all over the news. Nixon—a severely paranoid and secretive man—felt *exposed*.

When John Lennon announced that he would play for Yippie protests at the 1972 Republican National Convention in Miami, the president fretted about a horde of Beatles fans creating a major disruption. He used the Immigration and Naturalization Service to try to boot Lennon out of the country on the basis of an English hashish conviction. And he encouraged Gordon Liddy to concoct wild and illegal schemes, including a plan to kidnap antiwar leaders before the convention and hold them until it was over. He had his henchmen illegally bust into Daniel Ellsberg's psychiatrist's office, hoping to discredit the "treasonous" antiwar hero with proof that he was an LSD user. Nixon and his henchmen were on a tear.

Nixon succeeded in scaring Lennon away from the Republican National Convention and it went on without serious disruptions in the streets of Miami. After the way-left Democratic convention (also in Miami), his campaign became obsessed with exposing the "subversives" in the McGovern for President campaign. Nixon's secret team of "burglars" went off to rifle through Democratic headquarters in the Watergate hotel and office complex in Washington, looking for connections between McGovern operatives and Cuba or other damaging far-left implications. They were busted.

Coverage of the Watergate burglary was minimal as the presidential campaign continued. But once Nixon secured the election, an administration insider started supplying information and leads to the *Washington Post* reporters Bob Woodward and Carl Bernstein.

The rest of the story is in your history books, and this is not the place to review the details. Between the Pentagon Papers, the Watergate hearings, and the Church Committee hearings that followed up on materials exposed during "Watergate," a flood of information about conspiratorial double dealings, lies, violations of rights, even murders, made it clear to the American people that their government, and the man they'd just elected in a landslide, held them in contempt. The Nixon administration fell—a slow, graceless collapse that first took out his absurd, corrupt vice president, Spiro Agnew (his teenage daughter sent love letters to Abbie Hoffman), and various other administration members before Nixon himself finally exited the stage in a flurry of Shakespearean pathos on August 10, 1974. Faith in authority, particularly faith in conservative, Republican authority, was shattered.

The Republican Gerald Ford, who had replaced Agnew as vice president, was now president. Ford, not the sharpest tack in the package, more or less coasted through the next few years. He watched the last Americans leave Vietnam as the victorious communists took Saigon. He watched his son Jack smoke pot in the White House under Secret Service protection. When Jack got George Harrison, who was in Washington, D.C., on a tour, to visit him, the new president greeted them for a photo op on the White House lawn, smiled and shook hands with the former Beatle and his African-American musician friend Billy Preston. The scene led the evening news programs and was on the front pages of most newspapers across the country. Harrison wore sneakers and a button representing the Hanuman Foundation (Richard "Ram Dass" Alpert's spiritual organization) for the occasion. From inside Folsom Prison, Timothy Leary declared, "The war between the generations is over."

WELCOME TO THE MACHINE

> I see the world in very fluid, contradictory, emerging terms, and with that kind of circuitry I just don't feel the need to say what is going to happen or will not.
>
> CALIFORNIA GOVERNOR JERRY BROWN, 1977

> Successful heads have taken over the government.
>
> TIMOTHY LEARY, 1979

In 1974, cosmic philosophy sneaked into the highest office in the nation's most populous state. Jerry Brown, the son of an earlier California governor, Pat Brown, ran a low-key campaign as a conventional Democrat and, like most Democrats that year, won easily thanks to Nixon's fall from grace. Once safely ensconced in office, Governor Brown let his freak flag fly. For starters, he refused to move into the grand, opulent Governor's Mansion that the Reagans had built for themselves, instead renting a cheap apartment in downtown Sacramento. Furnishings were minimal and the bed was on the floor. He also refused the customary chauffeured limo, driving himself around instead in an old blue Plymouth. A *People* magazine cover story trumpeted "California's Hippie Governor."

Brown rarely issued political policy statements that could be comprehended by those who lacked philosophical grounding in the slippery nature of reality. A Jesuit in his youth, he had since leavened the highly disciplined radical, anti-materialist Christian practice with Zen meditation and an interest in Taoist and Zen philosophy. The previous California governor, Ronald Reagan, was as confused as he was perturbed, and the left-liberals weren't altogether happy either. Brown was in no rush to enact leftist programs like the closer regulation of big business, reformation of the criminal justice system, and aid to the poor. He eventually did some of those things, but he embraced the Taoist notion that inactivity is sometimes preferable to activity. He wanted to slow things down, examine legislation not just politically but philosophically. True to the words of Lao-tzu, he wanted to "govern less." He expressed this sensibility with one of his more infamous aphorisms: "Less is more," which provoked shaking heads and wild giggles from mainstream political pundits, and even won him the ridicule of America's hippest daily comic strip, *Doonesbury.* (Brown also aimed "Less is more" at the economics of consumerism.) The Brown administration was a peculiar mix of radical, liberal, and conservative actions, and while his unpredictability made him few friends among the various political factions, the people of California remained happy with his leadership for quite some time.

Brown's go-slow approach to political reform made him vulnerable to charges that his liberalism was mostly show. Critics called him a "governor of symbols." One of the most potent (if possibly empty) images that the Brown administration sent out across the country was the integration of the left-counterculture into the nation's mainstream. Former Acid Test organizer Stewart Brand became one of his favored advisors. He appointed beat hero Gary Snyder chairman of the California Arts Council, and then former Digger Peter Coyote to succeed Snyder. Tom Hayden served as Brown's "research director," focusing primarily on appropriate technologies (an area the Brown administration really did act upon). For a brief period, the two men became such inseparable pals that California journalistic wags started referring to the Brown administration as "the Tom and Jerry show." Even the acid king Ken Kesey accepted an invitation to give a talk to members of the administration. Brown finally provoked a reaction when he nominated "Hanoi" Jane Fonda to the Arts Council. She was loudly rejected by the State Senate, to much public opprobrium and controversy. And law enforcement interests nationwide denounced him after he granted American Indian Movement leader Dennis Banks asylum from extradition to South Dakota to serve time for riot and assault charges.

Brown's countercultural cadre were mostly relegated to politically unimportant roles within the administration, while serious legislation was frequently handled by Brown's chief of staff, Gray Davis, who was sometimes called "the grown-up" by the California media. Nevertheless, the Brown message, in essence, "welcome to the machine," resonated out into the hipster world, receiving a mixed response of curious optimism and cynicism. Brown was the most unique of an entire political tide that was labeled "The Democratic Class of '74." Longish-haired liberal young Democrats, veterans of the more moderate tendencies within the antiwar and civil rights movements, poured into government positions—among them were U.S. senators Gary Hart and Paul Tsongas. In Arkansas, a bright, aggressive young liberal named Bill Clinton was elected governor.

The return of the prodigal sons and daughters into a friendly dialectic with the machine was completed with the election of Jimmy Carter in 1976. Carter was a moderate Democrat and his cabinet was dominated by establishment power brokers and seasoned bureaucrats. His economic policies—as with any American president in the latter twentieth century— were primarily dictated by wealthy corporate interests, and his foreign policy was mostly run by an unapologetic imperial strategist with an unpronounceable name: Zbigniew Brzezinski. But his young advisory staff, labeled the Georgia Mafia, were a bit on the hip side, and on the heels of the Nixon administration, Carter's gang looked like an influx of saints into the Oval Office.

Carter was the first president to incorporate rock and roll into his gestalt. He quoted Bob Dylan almost as frequently as Huey Newton did. His campaign was supported and financed by at least one Southern record company executive and the Allman Brothers performed benefits for Carter during the Democratic primary. (Jerry Brown, the primary runner-up, had the Eagles in his corner.) It seems trite now, but rock and roll still had a definitively countercultural cachet, and the fact that both Carter and Brown picked up bands from the cocaine cowboy branch of outlaw culture didn't fail to amuse knowing observers or titillate "drug conspiracy" fanatics. Carter also sought and won an endorsement from Hunter S. Thompson, famous for his brilliant drug-fueled rants against ersatz American culture and Richard Nixon. Finally, he advocated the decriminalization of marijuana, which pretty much sealed the deal.

The day after his inauguration, with one stroke of his pen, Carter granted a pardon to all the young men who had left the country to avoid the Vietnam War. It was, no doubt about it, a healing moment between counterculture and the system. Criticizing harsh drug policies, Carter said, "Punishment for drug use shouldn't be more harmful to an individual than the drug itself," and his administration planned a retreat from some of the more draconian aspects of enforcement. However, the administration's plans to liberalize drug policy were sabotaged by drug use within its own ranks.

Peter Bourne, Carter's drug policy advisor (this was before the time of the "czars"), was busted for writing a Quaalude prescription for a friend, signed with a false name. Within days, investigative journalist Jack Anderson wrote that Bourne had been seen publicly snorting cocaine at a benefit party for NORML (National Organization for the Reform of Marijuana Laws). If that wasn't trouble enough, rumors that the president's chief of staff, Hamilton Jordan, was seen snorting coke at Studio 54, the notorious disco den of carnality and cocaine hedonism, were trumpeted by the media. Covering their asses against a conservative reaction, the administration put drug liberalization designs into reverse, and the feds returned halfheartedly to the drug war. But that wasn't the end of the Carter administration's drug troubles. In the late 1970s, news sources blasted revelations that there was massive drug use—primarily marijuana and cocaine—going on among the young staffers within the Carter administration. Fortunately for them, conservatism, and the anti-drug fanaticism that accompanies it, was still anemic. On the whole, Americans were still getting over Watergate and the loss of the Vietnam War. Too shocked by the fall of the house of Nixon, pretty much everybody—even conservatives—had already smiled tolerantly on Jerry Ford's pothead son. So the White House partying was nowhere near the kind of scandal that it would be today. (Also, people still hadn't quite come to grips with what a nasty drug cocaine is.) However, the general impression that Democrats endorse hippie hedonism still haunts American's mainstream political discourse, and is often exploited by culture warriors like Newt Gingrich (who, of course, was a college pothead himself).

. The transformative promise of middle-of-the-hip baby boomers rising into positions within the system was pretty much permanently muted with the return to power of the right's conquistador, Ronald Reagan, in 1980. By the time Bill Clinton and Al Gore—two definitive members of the middle-of-the-hip seventies crowd—got into office in 1992, the limitations of both the system and the boomers who had joined it were apparent.

THEIR KARMA FAILED TO RUN OVER THEIR DOGMA: THE NEW AGE

> The Perfect Master teaches perfection, and will bring perfection on Earth—not after the Millennium, but right now, in three years. A revolutionary perfection, realizing all our ideas of peace and justice, brought about not by struggle and conflict but by the perfect working of a perfect organization.
>
> FORMER CHICAGO SEVEN CONSPIRACY RADICAL
> RENNIE DAVIS, 1974

As the counterculture of the 1960s split off into varying countersubcultures, the one that most approximated the mid-sixties psychedelic vibe was labeled "the New Age." At the start, the New Age movement was an attempt by some trippy hippies to *not* get grounded. Rather than fall back to earthly cynicism, or join the political reformists returning to the bureaucratic structures of society, New Agers sought a permanent high through "natural" means. To a great extent, this meant finding spiritual trainers, and joining communes and cults dedicated to "higher consciousness." Indian gurus roamed the Western Lands picking up devotees, who believed that the masters, sometimes with the touch of a finger upon the third eye, could send the seeker to paradise, bliss, contentment . . . what have you. All the seeker had to do was submit, utterly, to the authority and whims of the guru. It was, in some ways, an authentic spiritual paradox—the same one we have already explored when looking at Sufism and Zen. The only way one could truly be liberated was by relinquishing control, letting go. This could be accomplished only by relinquishing your ego (not to mention, in some cases, your house, car, and bank account) to the guru or leader. No doubt, some gurus and teachers gave genuine experiences of cosmic mindfulness and meditative peace for a reasonable price, or even for free, and without raping the souls of the followers. But many others took advantage. After all, "You manage *all* my physical needs and I'll sit around giggling and providing a model for happiness" is a pretty sweet gig if you can get it.

Aspects of the New Age movement were a desperate attempt to preserve the totalizing, utopian hopes of the late 1960s. It had become clear that one could not reasonably expect a full-on consciousness and/or political revolution and the resultant golden age in the near future. But one could *unreasonably* expect it. Pure and strong enough magical desire married to the word of the Maharaj Ji, or the touch of the Bhagwan, might bring down heaven on earth, all in a single great moment of harmonic convergence. Or maybe the space brothers would come to take the turned-on elect to a better place. And if not, one could at least reach personal nirvana by purifying the body, maybe even living on nothing but air.

The peculiarities and disasters of the New Age have been amply exposed, and particularly since the authoritarian wing of that movement has little to do with counterculture, I'm going to give it short shrift. On the other hand, the "human potential" meme espoused by the psychological/ therapeutic edge of the movement mapped to countercultural concerns about human self-development and excellence. Even hypesters like Werner Erhard—a mix of Gurdjieff, Hitler, and a traveling salesman—provided a necessary service at that time. His four-day therapeutic boot camp convinced many a burned-out sixties veteran that they were responsible for creating their own reality. If nothing else, this reduced the toxic flow of *whining* they were emitting into the environment. And finally, the New Age maintained and spread interest in genuine countercultural trends in Zen Buddhism, Taoism, Sufism, paganism, and psychedelic spirituality.

It's easy to laugh at the New Ager's flaky gullibility (and fun!) but, in large part, the bliss-ninny guru-worship phase has passed, and many of those who have stayed within this general spiritual path through the years have grown into committed participants in antiwar and anti-authoritarian activities.

TOUGH LOVE

> D U M B/Everyone's accusing me.
>
> THE RAMONES, 1977

> We weren't stupid enough to be businessmen and we weren't pretty enough to be David Bowie, we're just following our genetic imperative.
>
> DEVO, *SEARCH AND DESTROY*, 1977

> All of social life is organized/From the top down/Through impenetrable hierarchies/To make you into a receptacle/For the culture/That will seduce you into functioning/As a robot for the economy.
>
> GREIL MARCUS, *LIPSTICK TRACES*, 1989

While Californians were swapping crystals and getting Rolfed, in New York City, the pretty things were becoming ugly things—glam rock was mutating into punk rock. The transitional hinge was a gang of tough urban street urchin musicians who dressed in drag. The New York Dolls looked and sounded like the Rolling Stones through a carnival funhouse mirror, with only half the talent but twice the enthusiasm. They didn't play their instruments all that well, but the sound they made was *effective*.

Mainstream rock had grown flabby with self-importance and musical competence. Songs, even by goofy bands like Aerosmith and Uriah Heep, had to dribble on for five to seven minutes, so that we could hear the instrumentalists show off their technique. It was a tired ritual, and it wasn't art.

For all its post-1967 psychedelic pretensions, rock culture never developed a very sophisticated, daring, or avant-garde understanding of art. (Remember how Beatles fans hated Yoko Ono?) Mainstream (classic) rock musicians and fans didn't seem to understand that nobody ever went nuts over the quality of Pablo Picasso's brushstrokes. There were, surely, plenty of painters who could handle their brushes as well as Picasso (or Matisse et al.). What made Picasso's work meaningful was the vision of the artist, the impact his canvas had on the viewer, and the statement it made within the culture in its time (or what it tells us about that time now, and how it relates to our own). In the 1910s, Marcel Duchamp clarified this point by taking found objects and recontextualizing them as art. Andy Warhol's Campbell Soup cans defined Pop Art by capturing something essential about pop culture—mass production and branding. Any painter who knew "two chords" could have played that song, but Warhol had the perceptiveness and humor to play it.

The Ramones' first album, full of two-minute, two-chord statements that joked simply but darkly about the very nonliberated, constrained, dead-end lives of a bunch of lower-middle-class white guys from Queens, New York, was the Warhol statement of the mid-1970s. The Ramones became the laughingstock of the conventional rock world, but their influence on rock music today outweighs that of all the "heavy" bands of the 1970s, even Led Zeppelin and Pink Floyd.

The Ramones were not a bunch of avant-garde artists concocting an appropriate minimalist statement for the post-hippie era somewhere in a loft in Manhattan. They were ordinary guys with a humorous glint in their eye who served as a reminder that there are always people out there sprinkled among the hoi polloi who just "get it" naturally. But a New York rock scene evolved around the Ramones that was made up of conscious avant-gardists who were inspired by the New York Dolls and the Ramones to get instruments and create something weird within the context of pop music. The scene was called punk rock.

The point wasn't even that you could make your statement without having to be a practiced musician. In fact, many of the major bands in New York—Talking Heads and Television, for example—were competent, even good, players. The point was that there was suddenly permission to make quirky, unusual statements; to approach things from odd angles that had nothing to do with pseudo-cowboy outlaws, or groupies, or the demise of the hippie dream. You could even sing "Don't worry about the government," as Talking Heads did.

The NYC punk scene had all the elements of bohemia that we're already familiar with. Centered on the live performance club CBGB on the Bowery, the artists set aside any concerns with appealing to mass audiences and record companies and made the music that pleased them. There was (for the most part) a comradely, supportive spirit amongst the players, there were lots of novel ideas, plenty of interactions with artists working in other media (including Warhol), and the usual variety of mind-altering substances (albeit generally used less than in the mainstream rock world). But in other ways, the scene adopted anti-countercultural (not just anti-hippie) poses. As decadence was the buzzword for the glam scene, "reductionism" was a desired quality among the NYC punks. Some songs by bands like Blondie, Talking Heads, and the Ramones glorified discipline and narrowness of vision. The Ramones used patriotic and even fascistic iconography. Much of this was in a spirit of parody. (One Ramones icon was the American eagle, holding a bomb in one claw and a baseball bat in the other, with the text "In God We Trust" replaced with "Look Out Below.") Other conservative stances were more ambiguously serious.

It was all a continuation of glam's rebellion against the hippie culture. But in this case, instead of rebelling against the purists, some of the NYC punks rebelled against the dissipated aspects of the sixties counterculture. In the mid-1970s, you could still get called a fascist by some hanglooseniks simply for dressing neatly, being efficient, or even keeping a job. Many of the NYC punks sought to sharpen up the marijuana-soaked edges a bit. (The Rimbaudian poet of Dionysian liberty Patti Smith was a highly visible exception. Smith and her band worked brilliantly within the erotic/psychedelic tradition of Jim Morrison and the Rolling Stones. In this case, it was her willingness to push beyond the clichés of that genre and reach a new level of intensity that made her a beloved presence on the scene.)

When the NYC punk influence hit England it turned into something else. Working-class British kids were living through a serious economic depression. They were broke, jobless, and restless. They wanted to identify with rock music, but their wealthy stars—Mick Jagger, Rod Stewart, Pink Floyd, the ex-Beatles—seemed blissfully unaware of their misery. They took the fast, hard, loud energy of the Ramones and turned it into a music of rabid revolt. If the NYC punk scene's complaint was that the hip left revolution was a conformist bore and good riddance, the British punks' complaint was that the hip left had chickened out and failed to actually *make* their revolution.

The story of British punk starts with the contradictions of Malcolm McLaren. McLaren was a genius trickster, an anarchist who wanted to blow the capitalist system sky high, the capitalist owner of a fashionable S&M clothes store always looking for get-rich-quick schemes, an avant-garde conceptual artist, a pretentious hater of all that was pretentious, a rock manager, and (obviously) a consummate ironist. He was carrying two unlikely influences when he helped formulate the English punk zeitgeist.

The obvious influence was the New York City glam/punk scene (McLaren had briefly managed the New York Dolls during a visit to the U.S.). Earlier, in 1968, he had been an English supporter of the Situationist International. A small group of Dada-influenced left-anarchist intellectual extremists, the Situationists were centered in Paris, and had an astoundingly potent influence on the 1968 French revolt. Their slogans, like "It Is Forbidden to Forbid" and "Neither God Nor Masters," appeared all over the country during that interval.

Their chief ideologist, Guy Debord, wrote dense prose critiquing capitalism, Marxism, and—most of all—mediation, and the resulting alienation of the average person from his own subjective experience. Debord's main contribution to counterculture philosophy was to identify the primary control system of capitalist democracy as "the society of the spectacle." (He authored a book of the same name.) Greil Marcus, in his brilliant ranting and rambling (but well-researched) book on punk and Situationism, *Lipstick Traces,* made Debord's vision comprehensible:

> A never-ending accumulation of spectacles—advertisements, entertainments, traffic, skyscrapers, political campaigns, department stores, sporting events, newscasts, art tours, foreign wars, space launchings—made a

modern world, a world in which all communication flowed in one direction, from the powerful to the power-less.... The spectacle naturally produced not actors but spectators: modern men and women, the citizens of the most advanced society on earth, who were thrilled to watch whatever it was they were given to watch....

Having satisfied the needs of the body, capitalism as spectacle turned to the desires of the soul. It turned upon individual men and women, seized their subjective emotions and experiences, changed those once evanescent phenomena into objective, replicable commodities, placed them on the market, set their prices, and sold them back to those who had, once, brought emotions and experiences out of themselves—to people who, as prisoners of the spectacle, could now find such things only on the market....

All desires had to be reduced to those that could be put on the market.

In other words, when capital had been primarily focused on providing basic necessities, and when the world was not completely mediated and interpenetrated, human beings had private lives—their leisure time was not yet colonized. When capital needed new markets, it turned its energies from selling necessities to selling fulfillment in the form of media products, spectacles, and organized commercial leisure activities.

The Situationists hated fame—particularly famous radicals. They repudiated even the most nonauthoritarian applications of leadership, and critiqued the international gallery art scene and the entire notion of the production of art. They denounced hallucinogens as an ultimate "spectacular" product, and were not the least interested in rock and roll. Their alternative was subjectivity and spontaneity. The movement's name derived from the idea of creating "situations" in which the dynamics between people were not subject to normal received influences and broke through social conditioning to force experiences and exchanges of a radically personal and immediate nature.

The Situationists believed that the advent of a truly classless society would liberate the creative unconscious of the people so that art would become indistinguishable from daily life. A classic embodiment of the experiential, experimental Situationist approach was the *Derive,* the practice of wandering aimlessly in groups through the cityscape as a means of exploring *psychogeography,* a term coined by Situationists to denote the influence of the human-constructed urban environment on consciousness.

The positive aspect of the Situationist agenda was pretty much a blank slate, which is not to say that it was nonexistent. Even more than the Diggers and other anarchist tendencies, Situationists believed a new society would emerge naturally out of revolution and the refusal of individuals to acknowledge any limits on their subjective selves. The title of a manifesto by Situationist Raoul Vaneigem, *The Revolution of Everyday Life,* defined the attitude.

It's not easy to imagine a merger between Situationism and a band spewing out a series of Top Ten rock hits, even limited to the small island of Great Britain, but if anyone could elide the obvious contradictions it was Malcolm McLaren. In 1975, back in London after a short stay in New York, he was trying to form a band that could translate the CBGB's punk rock energy into something that made sense for England. He had the good fortune to meet Johnny Rotten, né John Lydon, a perpetually enraged young man who moved onstage like he was being electrocuted and sounded like he was possessed by the same spirit as Linda Blair in *The Exorcist.* The Sex Pistols were formed.

That this Irish-English working-class guttersnipe happened to also be carrying within himself an educated political consciousness and concise lyrical skills would soon become apparent, but when the Sex Pistols released their first single, "Anarchy in the U.K.," in late 1976 it was the *sound* that hit people first. Blast is too weak a word. The record knocked over psychic walls that even the Ramones couldn't get near. It cleared away sleep cobwebs that had been accumulating since the birth of rationalism. This song, and a series of singles that followed, all became major hits in England despite the fact that the radio refused to play them. The impact of these songs was oddly like hearing the first Beatles singles in 1964. There was a freshness, an enthusiasm, a *joy* in the sound that had not been asserted since that time; and it was just so right that—in the disillusioned

1970s—the greatest expression of joy committed to vinyl should also be the greatest expression of rage.

During their brief career, the Sex Pistols engaged in a series of public outrages, including disrupting the Queen's Jubilee, swearing on national television (which was turned into an amazingly *huge* national crisis by England's tabloid press), and a host of other antisocial acts. A multitude of English punk bands emerged on the immediate heels of the Sex Pistols, and thousands of young kids, wearing torn clothes decorated with bizarre and threatening slogans, spiky Mohawk haircuts, tattoos, and safety pins, poured into the street. While this style is something we're used to seeing now in corporate offices (at least in Silicon Valley) and McDonald's commercials, it once represented a genuine hatred of all civilized constraints (not to mention the eternal desire of youth to have a little fun and shock the old people). The Situationist influence could be noted by those in the know in iconography and slogans that popped up on record sleeves, posters, and in punk zines, and in a few of the lyrics. (The opening line of the Sex Pistols' "Holidays in the Sun," "A cheap holiday in other people's misery," came from a Situationist epigram.) Punk, in its totality, did not seek to be a Situationist movement, if such a thing is possible. Whether it was Situationism in action must be—of course—*subjective*.

The first wave of the English punk rock scene dissipated quickly. The Sex Pistols split up after a bizarre tour of the American South, and the other major band, the Clash, became international rock stars—while still maintaining loads of political integrity by all but the most purist estimations.

Punk became a global identity that meant a lot of different things to a lot of very different people. It could be a fashion, or a musical style bereft of content. Even young political conservatives joined the ranks of punk fans and musicians (today there are Christian-right punk bands). On the other hand, what punk wrought was a Do It Yourself (DIY) attitude. Instead of sitting around worshiping the rock stars or gurus who supplied the people with dreams of one free ride or another, punk *fans* were encouraged to pick up their own guitar, or a mimeograph machine, or some old clothes—or whatever was around and cheap—and express themselves. As the 1970s leaked into the 1980s, a hard core of tough, earnest, punk anarchist-oriented groups developed coherent, skillful, resilient alternative institutions that the hip left only dreamed of. Alternative music labels, performance clubs, zines, cassette-trading clubs, independent videos and films emerged out of the punk aesthetic. Political punk collectives and squats helped counterculturally inclined youths survive the Reagan/Thatcher era and supplied the troops for various anti-system protests during that time. And anarcho-punk communes could soon be found nearly everywhere: in Mexico, in Eastern Europe just as the Stalinist walls were coming down, in the Balkans throughout all the troubles there.

This resilient global punk counterculture survives to this day. The greatest irony of punk may be that this most impatient of all eruptions has evolved such staying power.

STANDING IN THE SHADOWS

The 1970s played itself out in the long shadow cast by the "Woodstock Nation" notion, and countercultural forms tended to obsess on either rejecting or trying to reinfuse that legacy. Frequently they were trying to do both at once. But it could be that the decade's actions—ranging from the Brown administration's advances in alternative energy to the DIY survivalist toughness of serious punk culture—may have more pragmatic applicability to our world today than all the acid tests and rhetorical revolutions of the 1960s.

CHAPTER FIFTEEN

⊢ GLOBAL. DIGITAL. *DOOMED?*

Counterculture Leans into the Future

There is no other place I'd rather be/ . . . watching the
world wake up from history.

MIKE EDWARDS, JESUS JONES, 1990

A wire is stuck into the pleasure center of your brain
while someone is vivisecting you; you just chuckle and
reel them out a length of your intestines.

JOHN SHIRLEY, 1989

In 1994, St. Martin's Press published a book about the American art
punk band Sonic Youth titled *Confusion Is Next*. I remember seeing it
while browsing bookstore shelves, and the name struck me as an interesting zeitgeist statement, although perhaps not the *perfect* statement of the
moment. Still, it lodged in my memory bank.

As a writer and editor who was deeply identified with the futuristic
technoculture of the late 1980s and the 1990s, I am sometimes called
upon to forecast future trends. After the 9/11 attacks on America, which
came also on the heels of the tech market bust and the contestable election

of an anti-intellectual oil baron fratboy to lead the world's only super-
power, I found myself at a loss for words—that is, at a loss for clear vision.
"Confusion is next" became my stock response to requests for prognosti-
cation (always acknowledging the source).

Perhaps the only thing that makes "the times" (always?) seem so much
more grandly complicated than previous periods is the fact that we're in
them. On the other hand, the presence on our small globe of ever-larger
quantities of human primates capable of time-binding memory storage,
language, tool making, planning, and *dissatisfaction* seems likely one of
several factors that have been continuously evolving us toward ever more
elaborate situations.

Sheer quantities of complicated humans ensure that cultural trends,
subcultures, and counter(sub)cultures will multiply into an ungraspable
myriad of forms, styles, and memetic aggregations. Additionally, the availability to all of trillions of "informational signals" (in the broadest sense,
which can include fiction, pornography, lies—anything that can be put
into symbolic form) through various communications media on a daily
basis ensures that no individual, or even collectivity, can attain "total information awareness." In a 1989 issue of *Mondo 2000,* Robert Anton Wilson explained the situation in terms of knowledge: "According to *The
Mathematical Experience* by Davis and Hersh, the last human to know all
mathematics was Alexander Ostrowski, who died in 1915. . . . In the late
1940s, John von Neumann estimated that the best-informed mathemati-
cians knew only about ten percent of the then-published theorems. . . .
Davis and Hersh concluded that at the time they wrote (c. 1980) no
mathematician could learn more than one percent of the math that had
been published."

Finally, those of us who have operated within the context of the Western historical world, even within countercultures, have been permitted to
simplify our worldview by excluding the vast majority of humans from
consideration. For better *and* for worse, areas and peoples are now emerging into the awareness of the broad news and historical recording and
broadcasting mechanisms called media. A whole range of perspectives demand to be heard, while the perspective of those of us in the "privileged"
or "advanced" worlds is challenged.

It is, clearly, too much for any individual to wrap his mind around, never mind present inside a chapter within a book. Nevertheless, I will try to show cultural trends, both within the traditional Western world (particularly the U.S.) and beyond it, that lean toward the future.

DAYS OF FUTURE PAST: BRAZIL'S TROPICÁLIA AND OTHER FAR-OUT "OTHERS"

> Tropicalismo wanted to project itself as the triumph over . . . the horrifying humiliation represented by capitulation to the narrow interests of dominant groups, whether at home or internationally. It was also an attempt to face up to the apparent coincidence, in this tropical country, of a countercultural wave emerging at the same time as the vogue in authoritarian regimes.
>
> CAETANO VELOSO, 2002

The primary twentieth-century countercultural narrative has the 1960s at its axis. The usual touchstones are a series of identities and events that focused largely in the United States, with a few references to Europe, which I have discussed in Chapters 12 and 13. A Mexican student revolt in 1968 that manifested similarities in both style and content to the hip left revolt in the West, but which was suppressed with far greater brutality, is sometimes fit into the picture.

Two twenty-first-century books—*Tropical Truth* by Caetano Veloso and *Brutality Garden* by Christopher Dunn—have brought global notice to an unfairly ignored historic, radical, music-centered counterculture from late-sixties Brazil called Tropicália or Tropicalismo. Living in the shadows of a U.S.-supported military dictatorship that had taken control of that country in 1964, Brazilian artists and musicians still had relative cultural liberty for a brief period. An avant-garde of artists worked in concrete poetry and other forms, and manifested influences ranging from Dadaism to an organic Brazilian cultural movement called Cannibalism. Announced in a 1928 manifesto by Brazilian art theorist Oswald de Andrade, Cannibalism sought to resolve the tensions of cultural colonialism by suggesting, in the words of Dunn, "a 'poetry for export' neither deferent to, nor ignorant of metropolitan literary currents. . . . [Oswald] advanced a model for critically 'devouring cultural inflows from abroad.' " In other words, Oswald's "cannibalism" suggested that the colonized could take advantage of hybridizations with the colonizer just as vice versa.

Meanwhile, within popular culture, two musical forms competed for attention: bossa nova, the popular Brazilian folk style; and rock and roll, imported from the U.S. (and later England). Rock lost some of its rebel implications in translation, but eventually Western youth styles of the 1960s began to infiltrate Brazilian culture, bringing with them the long hair, mod clothes, and the overall generational impiety.

In the late 1960s, Tropicália emerged out of a synergy of all these influences: the art avant-garde, rock and roll (the genre particularly limned the psychedelic studio experimentation of the Beatles), and bossa nova. It wasn't just a new music; a new culture gathered around it: film, visual arts, poetry, even a guerrilla theater group participated in a cultural expression that, among other things, managed to get surrealist tableaus and pranks onto prime-time Brazilian television. The musical stars of this movement were Veloso, Gilberto Gil, and a band called Os Mutantes (the Mutants—their 1968 song "Prohibiting Is Prohibited" was taken from a Situationist slogan). Political alienation under the military dictatorship (not to mention ubiquitous poverty) was pervasive and the common people of Brazil identified with the political left. For Veloso, Tropicália was an expression of artists who "wanted the freedom to move beyond the automatic ties with the Left and at the same time to account for the visceral rebellion against the abysmal disparities that tear a people asunder."

The participants in Tropicália identified with both the British and American rock and roll countercultures and their own deep Brazilian cultural roots. But in contrast to American and English rock stars, they also tended to take their intellectual, literary influences—as varied as Borges, Beckett, Sartre, and Apollinaire—very seriously, and to allow highly experimental musical pioneers like John Cage and Stockhausen—who were likely to be name-dropped by the likes of McCartney or Jagger—to actually impinge directly on their sounds.

Picking up on the spirit of 1968, youths led Brazilians into open revolt against the military dictatorship. There were worker strikes, university takeovers, pitched street battles, and the beginnings of an armed resistance.

In December of 1968, the government issued a decree that outlawed all political opposition and imposed total censorship on all media. The youth protest movement was crushed. The Tropicália performers, whose comments in live performances tended to be even more irreverent and anti-authoritarian than their song lyrics, were quickly dealt with. Veloso and Gil were arrested and spent about two months in prison before they were allowed to leave Brazil, going into exile in England. Other members of the Tropicalismo movement were tortured, and many were confined in psychiatric hospitals for long years. The consequences for playful, psychedelic musical experimentation in late-sixties Brazil contrasted with the risks for rock stars in the U.S. and England, who, if they faced prison or exile, did so not because of their lyrical and musical statements but because of violations of culturally normative laws: the possession of illegal substances, sex with minors, or the display of private parts (and, in fact, all the major rock stars got off easy). As Damon Krukowski wrote in *Bookforum,* "Dylan may claim to have suffered at times from his fame, but he never had to hear prison guards mock him with one of his own songs, which is what happened in Brazil to founding Tropicalista Gilberto Gil."

Why does this 1960s "Third World" counterculture point toward the future? First of all, because it points toward an ignored past, and one element of the future surely involves a discovery of—and a confrontation with—disregarded histories. How many other illuminating hybrids—anti-authoritarian episodes influenced (or perhaps not) by Western anarchist, Dadaist, or other countercultural ideas—either current or of the immediate past—remain invisible or outside our focus? Second, these are places we'll want to look to for countercultural activities in the future. In other words, while counterculture has been mostly associated with Western phenomena, the near future will see the growth—or the acknowledgment—of countercultures in the East and the "Third World."

It is not my intention here to romanticize those who have been held outside of Western historical notice, although there can be no doubt that there have been native countercultural epochs in most areas of the world at various times. The hard reality is that, in most non-Western nations, anti-authoritarian memes must still confront a mass fundamentalism (this is, of course, also true of parts of the U.S.) and political totalitarianism—whether religious, Marxist, right-wing, or otherwise—that has not been mitigated by a tradition that incorporates the classical liberal principles of the Enlightenment. Authoritarian attitudes are far more deeply entrenched in other parts of the world than in our troubled First World corporate democracies. Still, events of the last two decades offer abundant evidence that a global incursion of countercultures is already well under way.

In the 1980s, the revolutions within the Soviet bloc were propelled by blue-jeans-wearing, rock-loving, freethinking youth. Today, in the never-ending search of global youth for the current hipster hot spots, Prague and St. Petersburg vie with Amsterdam for the prize. Raves (mass techno-hippie dance parties) even occurred with some frequency in Sarajevo during the worst days of the terror that took place there, and video news broadcasts around the globe repeatedly showed tenement walls covered with countercultural graffiti like the anarchist sign of the A in a circle or the letters L-S-D.

In China, the youths who marched on Tiananmen Square in 1989 referenced American countercultural motifs from the Jeffersonian period as well as from the 1960s. A sudden infusion of Western pop culture, with its gleeful irreverence and open eroticism, had helped to create an environment in which greater freedom was demanded. While overt political dissent was suppressed in China, personal freedoms—and the small countercultural communities that usually come with them—are blossoming in urban regions. A particularly strong literary avant-garde has sprung up in this land where—just two decades ago—art was closely watched by the government and confined to the peculiar style of Maoist social realism that today is mimicked for its pleasing kitsch value by artists all over the planet, including in China. In *China's New Cultural Scene,* Claire Huot describes Weng Shu as a writer whose "signature is manifest all over China in all cultural forms: literature, television, music, film, art, theater." His popular experimentalism is reminiscent of Walt Whitman and Gertrude Stein. Huot described it as "invented lingo, a combination of subverted political formulae with streetwise slang." And then there's the more radical Can Xue, who "calls herself a barbarian. . . . Her work is a resistance against culture and language.

"Culture is an ordering of the world by man [*sic*]; it is what civilization entails: cities, institutions—such as marriage, work units, literature, medical knowledge—and . . . language. Can Xue's works make fun of all of these either by refusing to acknowledge them or by exposing their civilized pretensions." Reports that Mao rolled over in his glass-encased public mausoleum remain unconfirmed. (On the day I completed the manuscript for this book, an article appeared in the *San Francisco Chronicle* about a current Chinese government crackdown against arts groups and other informal organizations. This serves as a handy reminder of the incompatibilities between counterculture and authoritarian government.)

And in the conservative Catholic nation of Mexico, countercultures thrive. According to Guillermo Peña—an iconoclastic Mexican performance artist who splits his time between Mexico City and San Francisco— Mexico City boasts all the countercultural and subcultural tribes that San Francisco does, from libertine sexual experimenters to neo-hippie environmental purists. When I interviewed him for *Axcess* magazine, he told me that alternative media is more popular in many areas of Mexico than media on subjects of mainstream interest. And, in 1994, Mexican/Mayan guerrillas calling themselves Zapatistas united in open warfare against the corporate New World Order under a leader who calls himself "Subcomandante Marcos."

Marcos' irreverent prankster persona, public appearances, and writing clearly evince countercultural influences, and Zapatista-sponsored gatherings bring together anarchistic and free-thinking tribes from all over the globe to discuss such currently trendy topics as the use of the Internet to decentralize economics and politics, and the notion of Autonomous Zones.

In light of the degree to which global media allow ideas to penetrate the tightest fortresses, it can be predicted that even in the most culturally locked-down regions—for instance, Syria and North Korea—there are now at least a few closet counterculturalists lurking, awaiting an opportunity to share their insights into unmitigated mass conformity with humor and style.

GEEKS AND FREAKS

Bill [Gates] and the gang looked so scruffy and young
and very unlike a Fortune 500 company. Long hair,

> beards, sloppy casual dress—these people looked like
> they were just coming down off a ten-year acid trip.
>
> DAVID BUNNELL, MONDO 2000, 1989

Less than a decade ago, the digital revolution blew through here like the proverbial white(boy) tornado. To mix cousin metaphors, there was a blizzard of hype, but there was also a mass distribution of computing power.

Technoculture is largely rooted in the post-Hiroshima countercultures. In the 1970s, while some hippies ran to the woods to escape civilization, a coterie of visionary science-fiction-influenced innovators, inventors, and engineers fastened on to the potentials inherent in information and communication devices—particularly telephones and computers. One group of clever youths, aligned with the Yippies and their ideologically convenient belief in getting free stuff from big corporations, called themselves phone phreaks. They were obsessed with making free long-distance phone calls. One among them, a brilliant, hairy street freak named John Draper, discovered that the whistles that were given away in boxes of Cap'n Crunch cereal, when used in a phone booth, tricked the phone company into giving free calls. Draper became known as Captain Crunch, and the phone phreaks/Yippies began publishing their various phreaker techniques—among them corporate phone credit numbers—in a Xeroxed newsletter called *TAP.*

Meanwhile, in Berkeley, California, a former *Berkeley Barb* (underground newspaper) "military editor," Lee Felsenstein, started the Homebrew Computer Club. The underground press was failing, and although it was several years before the first PC, the rough beginnings of the Internet (called ARPANET) showed that computers would become a resource for people sharing information, alternative or otherwise. Hip creative geeks and tinkerers started gathering together around Homebrew Computer Club events. Among other projects, hobbyists were trying to hack out a personal digital computer.

In 1977, two lads who had participated in both the Homebrew Computer Club and phone phreaking, Stephen Wozniak and Steve Jobs, finally gave birth to the first viable personal computer, the Apple II. Aside from their hopes for a successful business, Jobs and especially Wozniak were among a growing number of idealists who believed that personal computers were a great equalizer, giving individuals a medium through which they could compete in expressive power with the powerful forces that owned the other channels of communication.

HACKING IT 1.0:
FREE TOTAL ACCESS TO COMPUTERS

This hacker culture (the word hacker used to indicate computer programmers and hobbyists, not just outlaws) evolved a number of attitudes or ethics that were influenced by both the anti-authoritarian spirit of the counterculture and what they saw as implicit in the nature of computing and communication. In his book *Hackers: Heroes of the Computer Revolution,* Steven Levy came up with several basic hacker tenets. The most important ones were: "1) Access to computers should be free and total. 2) All information should be free. 3) Mistrust authority—promote decentralization."

The idea of free, total access to computers harked back to the days before home computing, when computers were locked up in computer labs at universities and scientific and military institutions. So first, the principle was simply that all lab members and, in fact, any visiting friends with a knack and a taste for computing should be able to get their hands on the machine. But the principle went much deeper. Hackers in those days functioned as a sort of spontaneous, anarchistic collective organism working together to build up this novel thing called computing. Total access to computers meant "open source." Individuals could get on the machine and root around, looking at anything they wanted, including all the coding. They could make improvements on the operating system if they wished. And as Richard Stallman, one of the original MIT hackers, told *Mondo 2000* magazine in 1989, "This system was not a static entity. What seems most extraordinary about it today, of course, is that there could be that much trust. It worked!" Free and total access to computing meant that software was also designed to be shared freely, without too much concern even about attribution. After all, other hobbyists were going to bring other programs to the party, and everyone was constantly improving on and adding to the open source software, so why fuss?

For Jobs and Wozniak, the principle of access to computers had another meaning: simply getting computers into the hands of masses of home users. Once the desktop PC became a commercial fact of life, *free* and *total* were abandoned. Some now claim that this was necessary to create the business ecology that motivated the mass availability of useful computers and software, while others insist that the passions of computer hobbyists and users would have led them to fill the software void, and that the best software would have had a better chance of finding its way into the machines of the users.

The Grinch who stole the free software Christmas was a diminutive long-haired marketing genius who, like the other geeks of his generation, listened to acid rock and even dipped his toe into the kaleidoscopic river of psychedelic consciousness a few times. But Bill Gates was no anarcho-communal techno-hippie. His hyper-competitive parents had instilled in him a big hankering for success, and for Gates that meant money. Gates' other passion was software development. Unlike personal computers, software posed a singular marketing dilemma. Once somebody had a copy, she could theoretically let every living human being on the planet make his or her own copy from the original, and still have her copy. Particularly for those who had the bandwidth to transfer software on the Internet, there was simply no physical property, no exchange of goods, involved. Within the hacker community, it was accepted that someone who wrote a particularly fine program might ask users to voluntarily send a small fee as a way of supporting the work, and some programmers made a few thousand bucks that way, but very few people took it seriously as a business. The exception was Bill Gates, who put his faith in intellectual property laws that would make it illegal to copy software. Ultimately, of course, Gates was proved right. He clearly not only won that horse race, he bought the stadium and the county it was located in.

Free software and open source have remained battle sites within computer culture ever since. In the late 1990s, open source software gained some ground with the popularization of Linux, an open source system that has spawned a number of businesses and been embraced by many major corporations. Most home users, however, find it difficult to use, and it remains to be seen whether this or another open source system will someday replace Microsoft as the standard.

HACKING IT 2.0: INFORMATION SHOULD BE FREE

Both open source and free software clearly also fall under the second of Levy's hacker principles: all information should be free. But this ethic also speaks to the tendency of information to escape boundaries. Stewart Brand indicated this—and in the process credited information with a primary human, countercultural characteristic—in his famous dictum "Information wants to be free. Information also wants to be expensive." (Brand intentionally invoked a multiplicity of significations. I am focusing on only one of them.)

In other words, the computer, particularly when tied to the telephone (the Internet), was a tool for sharing information freely, instantly, at any distance, and with little possibility of interference. Computers allowed for a new form of communication called many-to-many. Before the Net, individuals could communicate privately with each other at a distance via telephones and letter writing. Broadcasters and publishers could carry communication from one source to many individuals in a self-limiting fashion. With the Internet, individuals could send instant e-mail to each other, engage in real-time text-based group conversations or games, and leave information at a site on the Net where it would be instantly available to everybody else on the planet who had Net access. And they could access any information posted by anyone from anywhere else on the planet simply by logging on.

The implications were manifold. Text-based communities allowed people separated by great physical distances to contact other people who shared similar interests, however arcane those interests were. The only lesbian biker vegetarian Republican Nine Inch Nails fan in Hoisington, Kansas, could now find several dozen others who shared similar interests, becoming less lonely and better informed about when Nine Inch Nails was performing in the nearest city and where to find a gay bar, vegetarian restaurant, and Republican activists while in town. Individuals and small groups could publish and distribute (and eventually broadcast) their materials without having to get the approval and support of a publisher or an editor. And the Net made censorship difficult, if not impossible. Of course, most living humans still couldn't afford telephones, never mind computers. And authorities could always ban the Internet outright. Or they could pass laws to intimidate people with the consequences of free speech if caught. Or they could learn—as they have—how to block some of their citizens from viewing particular Web sites and bulletin boards. But the basic hacker principle remains in play. Net blocking is an imprecise and inefficient process. Anyone with reasonably sufficient computer skills can still access any information on the Internet from anywhere in the world.

The hacker activity that earned them their naughty reputation also falls under the "information should be free" banner. Early hackers believed that in an information culture, secrecy was a power freak trait used only by those trying to gain power or unwarranted profit. Hacking became identified with gaining information that was supposed to be off-limits. Based on this image, Hollywood produced films during the 1980s and 1990s that glamorized the hacker as a sort of countercultural revolutionary intelligence agent who could get at any information and reveal to the world that the evil corporate/political/military piggies had done something so abominable it would bring down the system; or they would reveal the cure for cancer—which was being withheld by similar nefarious forces for reasons of profit. It was a groovy fantasy, but there's very little evidence of this sort of thing. The reality often involved something like an illegal entry into a (what else?) telephone system database, leading to the sharing of really dull, banal operational information that was interesting or useful only as a trophy that showed off the hacker's ability to beat security and get inside where he has not been invited.

This early hacker belief in liberating information has become a mutable doctrine at best. It went through a variety of complex iterations, particularly during the mid-1990s, when a peculiar, fanatical, libertarian-anarchist hacker subculture called "cypherpunks," dedicated to the development and disbursement of unbreakable encryption technology, appeared on the scene. Since encryption technology aimed to guarantee people and organizations *privacy* and *anonymity,* its advocates seemed to be promoting the opposite of the hacker strategies for penetrating secrets. A lengthy discursive process among many hacker types attempted to iron out these seemingly absolutely contradictory positions. The main point of agree-

GLOBAL. DIGITAL. *DOOMED?* {347}

ment was that everyone was entitled to use whatever technology existed any way they wanted. If the government had data security, then the individual was also entitled to it. Beyond that, some leaned toward the defense of the privacy of the "little guy" and the liberation of information from the powerful and the bureaucratic. Others believed that people who were smart enough to technologically ensure their privacy deserved that protection while everybody else could get fucked, which corresponds pretty well with actual reality. Some cypherpunk ideologues, meanwhile, held the belief that unbreakable data encryption would destroy all governments, an argument too arcane and, frankly, too ludicrous to exfoliate here. More generally, the contradiction between the desire for absolute open communication—an important countercultural quality—and the right to privacy—a needed defense against authoritarian intrusion (not to mention theft)—isn't resolved by technology or by a set of hardened principles. Which of these characteristics counterculturalists should emphasize is situational and can usually be determined using ethical common sense.

The free information meme, meanwhile, found another host when it begat file-sharing technology for the Internet, enraging the recording industry and making the film industry nervous in the process. One of the main purposes of the *early* Internet was to allow scientists to all be able to view the same research paper without having to make and ship dozens of copies. By the late 1990s, kids could all listen to the same copy of a song without having to buy any of the millions of copies that were manufactured and shipped, and the recording industry was doing everything within its power to stop them.

The choosing up of sides among the longtime counterculture-identified rock performers over this issue served as a fine example for how many iterations removed we were from the presumptive hip generational unity that was felt in the 1960s. While most counterculturalists support file sharing as a matter of principle, free "art" is not always easy on artists who must continue to live in a money-based society. (One of the most depressing phenomena of the last decade has been finding countercultural rock stars from earlier decades, now mega-multimillionaires, among the most determined to squeeze every last penny out of intellectual property laws.)

HACKING IT 3.0: MISTRUST AUTHORITY

Computer geeks have little respect for titles, seniority, political power, law enforcement authorities, work hierarchies, social hierarchies, or the decision-making wisdom of owners. This does not mean they will automatically *dis*respect those positioned in power and authority, it just means that they will usually treat such people like anybody else. If what someone is doing or saying is useful or interesting, they will be treated with some regard; if not, they will be dismissed or ignored if possible. As mathematician/science-fiction writer Rudy Rucker said, "If you regard information the most, then you don't care about convention. It's not 'Who do you know?'; it's 'How fast are you? How dense [i.e., information rich]?' "

Many hackers hold rabidly pro-free-enterprise libertarian political views. Intellectual property laws, like the ones that try to prevent the sharing of software or online files, form a complicated nexus for pro-capitalist anti-authoritarians. These laws invite the state right into people's living rooms and bedrooms, where it presumes the right to intervene in sometimes spontaneous voluntary sharing relationships. Substantially enforcing property rights on immaterial stuff that can be instantly shared without any loss to the original owner requires either a vast police state of informers or a reliance on people's inner cop.

Stallman said, "Software is different from material objects where, you grow a certain amount of wheat, it makes a certain number of slices of bread . . . it only makes so many sandwiches. That is not true with programs. You can copy a program and you cannot, in the same sense, copy a loaf of bread. So anyone who tries to stop you from copying a program is doing real harm to society—setting up scarcity where there isn't any. They're also poisoning the spirit of . . . the free interchange of ideas. . . . Making people feel guilty about something as natural and loving as sharing . . . with your neighbor is a sad thing."

HACKING IT 4.0: PROMOTE DECENTRALIZATION

Hacker culture presumed that the Internet would decentralize power in the world. And to a degree, it has. A couple of geeks in a garage can run a business that used to require a staff of twenty. Musicians can reject the big bad record company and disperse their own music. A reliable self-motivated worker can avoid the centralized office and do his job from home, even if that home is thousands of miles away, passing in the results of his labors at the end of the workday. Hipsters can leave the city and still participate virtually in sophisticated subcultures (but you still have to watch out for those real-world rednecks!). The antiwar movement opposing the U.S. invasion of Iraq was able to organize the biggest global protests in history without large organizations and mass meetings.

More interestingly, the availability of trillions of bits of conflicting, valid, and invalid information and disinformation decenters collective attention. It is difficult to locate a consensus reality in a world where everybody is watching, listening to, and thinking about different things. Of course, one of the things digital romantics underestimated was the power that the intentions and actions of real-world players can still wield to defy the abstract, assumed effects of technological change. Thus, the decentralized al Qaeda network partly *re*centralized the attention of the world's most virtual nation through a simple act of violence. Patriotism, war, homeland security efforts, and coincidentally nascent global epidemics call people back into a shared reality, however bifurcated their political views on how to deal with these situations. Interestingly, conflict comes from our new, centralized togetherness. People are paying closer attention to one another's views on these shared concerns, and familiarity clearly breeds contempt between opposing forces.

Decentralization is sometimes prettier said than done. I will probably lose the love of a few of my hard-core anarchist and libertarian readers by claiming that a rush to decentralize political nation-states is likely to look more like the Balkans, or Mississippi in the 1950s, than an anarchist utopia (although if Northern California decides to secede, sign me up!).

All kinds of peculiar alliances emerged out of the belief in technoculture's decentralizing impact. For instance, Newt Gingrich, a man who made attacking the libertine behaviors of the sixties counterculture a centerpiece of his political persona, developed friendly relations with some fairly countercultural representatives of technoculture around mutual devolutionary, deregulatory interests.

Techno-libertarians like Kevin Kelly worked to show the necessity of modeling information economics after biological systems. In biology, the simpler the rules are (i.e., the less predetermined the organism is), the more freedom there is to evolve successful novelty and complexity. Therefore, the "neo-biological" libertarian model concludes: keep government rules away from business. Intellectuals around the left-anarchist Zapatistas, meanwhile, embrace a similar organic model for social organization called "rhizomatics," limned from the postmodernists Gilles Deleuze and Felix Guattari, concluding: keep government *and* big business dominance out of the way of organic community cooperation.

Decentralization is a deeply countercultural trope; what could be more decentralized than an individual, or a small group, living in accordance with their own conception? At the same time, as a practical matter, a world largely divided by vicious, reactionary warlords would be pretty rough on freethinkers and sensitive, creative types. (I acknowledge the anarchist argument that state leaders *are* vicious warlords, but there are stark qualitative differences that you do *not* want to experience directly.)

STARK RAVING MONDO

> As soon as they announce that skull implants are available, I'm gonna line up for mine. I'd like to add a few languages, be able to go without sleep.
> STEVE JACKSON, *MONDO 2000,* 1991

In 1984, a novel by a bohemian science-fiction writer named William Gibson hit the bookstores. Initially inspired by the sight of young people playing video games while wearing portable audio Sony Walkmans, Gibson's *Neuromancer* posited a techno-media-saturated world whose protagonists are street-smart hipster punks who live to jack into computer cyberspace, a consensual hallucinatory digital terrain inside the computer made up of all the data in the infosphere: the matrix.

Neuromancer was just one representative of a new literary style that was labeled "cyberpunk" by an editor of a science-fiction magazine. It was science fiction created by a post-sixties generation of writers whose referents were punk-inflected hipster countercultures. Influenced by the microchip, genetic engineering, and designer drugs, they ditched the big spaceships, big computers, and unaltered Captain Kirk–style heroes in favor of surgically and biologically enhanced characters dealing with the dense power that can be crammed into the tiniest of physical matter, including, in some stories, suitcase nukes and advanced biological terror weapons.

In a 1986 introduction for a representative cyberpunk short story collection called *Mirrorshades,* Bruce Sterling, a leading light in the cyberpunk firmament, described cyberpunk as "an unholy alliance of the technical world and the world of organized dissent—the underground world of pop culture, visionary fluidity, and street-level anarchy, this integration has become our decade's crucial source of cultural energy. The work of the cyberpunks is paralleled throughout Eighties pop culture: in rock video; in the hacker underground; in the jarring street tech of hip-hop and scratch music."

At the end of the 1980s, a thriving computer industry/culture (although tiny by today's standards), located primarily in Silicon Valley and composed mostly of way-too-smart guys who were more naturally conversant with a wide range of mathematical and scientific discourses than with the requirements of the business world, was married in the countercultural imagination to the cyberpunk science-fiction writers. Psychedelic technology buffs, led by Timothy Leary, performed the wedding ceremony and an irreverent new magazine (full disclosure: I was co-publisher and editor-in-chief) named *Mondo 2000* sent out the public announcements. Academic postmodernist culture critics were also in attendance, serving up mixed emotions and language cocktails composed largely of hybridized adjectives.

For a brief celebratory period in the early 1990s, a flood of public imaginings outstripped technical innovation, even as innovation itself was on the rise. Hipsters fantasized fully realized sensory-saturating, hallucinatory, shared, computer-generated realities where people could exchange the visual and auditory contents of their imaginations, a new form of communication so rich and different that it might just mutate us into a different sort of human being. The actual technology, called virtual reality (VR), was (and still is) in a very raw stage of development, so its headier possibilities could only be envisioned. Nevertheless, this peculiar countercultural mélange of tripsters, computer geeks, and cultural theorists came together to confer and party about this idea of alternative, computer-generated realities and the psychological and communicative changes they might bring about.

If you read *Mondo 2000* in the early 1990s, you were also looking forward to brain upgrades, smart robots, a nanotechnology-based leisure lifestyle, and other life-changing technological events too numerous to ponder in this space. None of this was to be taken too seriously (although some people did). Reports on real technological advances, however hyperbolic, still indicated some distance between the present moment and the further-out visions but, I'll confess, the overall myth fostered by *Mondo* and the "cyberdelic" culture around it was that a radical shift in what it means to be a human being was within our grasp by the end of the millennium. The initial editorial, written by "Queen Mu" and myself, declared, "This magazine is about what to do until the *millennium* comes. We're talking about Total Possibilities. Radical assaults on the limits of biology, gravity, and time."

The wild technological changes that actually have occurred since the early 1990s—among them the cloning of mammals, stain-free nanotech clothing, ubiquitous computing, and multimedia over the Internet—seem snail-paced compared to the transformations envisioned by some of us during the early 1990s.

A simpler but more culturally and commercially viable stream in cyberdelic counterculture—the acid house/rave movement—emerged in Great Britain in the late 1980s. The music that gave birth to this counterculture had originated among African-American musicians and disc jockeys from the tough streets of Chicago. Using digital synthesizers, these club entertainers created a robotic nightclub dance music called "house" that was stripped of human voice and emotion. The house genre quickly mutated into "acid house," a sound that pushed the inhumanity into stranger territories. In the words of online techno-hippie pundit Jah Sonic, "Acid house is the purest, barest distillation of house, the outer limit of its logic of inhuman functionalism. With acid, black music has never been so alienated from traditional notions of 'blackness' (fluid, grooving, warm), never been so close to the frigid, mechanical, supremely 'white' perversion of funk perpetrated by early eighties pioneers like D.A.F. and Cabaret Voltaire."

Somehow, the acid house music traveled to a psychedelic-drug-saturated hippie dropout party scene on the island of Ibiza, where the tripsters found the rhythms conducive to the production of benevolent communal trance states via a combination of psychedelic drugs and all-night dancing. This information quickly made its way to England, and by the end of the 1980s, acid house had conquered nightlife in that trend-crazed country.

Acid house parties, called raves, were initially an underground phenomenon, albeit a *large* underground phenomenon. Unlicensed illegal mass parties in urban warehouses and in open fields brought together British hipsters in a spirit of communal autonomy from club owners and law enforcement authorities, while pirate radio stations brought the musical style and cultural attitudes to the English airwaves.

A series of tropes evolved around the rave culture. One folk wisdom had it that the best music for trance dancing played at 120 beats per minute—believed to be the baby's heartbeat in the womb. MDMA (Ecstasy), a gentle stimulant-psychedelic, was the recommended mind-altering drug for getting maximum benefit from the acid house experience. (MDMA had been popular primarily among California New Age psychotherapists for its ability to allow patients to feel that they were in a benevolent place where it was safe for them to release their defenses and review traumatic emotional material dispassionately and from a mildly transcendent perspective.) Rave spokespeople asserted that they were realizing the democratization of music culture promised by the punk slogan "No more rock stars." The singular, romantic, self-important performers had been replaced by the DJ, who mixed together other people's sounds and was not the center of attention—attention was centered on the dance and the "communal vibe" (or perhaps the psychedelic light show and trippy images thrown up by VJs, a clear linkage to the Trips Festivals of yore).

Rave visionaries revived the utopian hopes of the 1960s, believing that the vibe coupled with the communications technology and the open information channels now available to people through the Internet could effect a rapid, global, mass transformation of consciousness. As stylistically silly and playful (big floppy hats, glow-in-the-dark pacifiers) as it was cosmically ambitious, rave culture also provided a mellow alternative to the more macho aspects of the other technomusical counterculture, hip-hop. The scene embraced a healthier mix of races and sexual preferences than the hippie scene of the 1960s and, despite the fact that pretty much all the DJs were male, was generally more respectful of women than other nightlife environments.

A sophisticated, ambiguous reading of acid house, posted on the Web by music writer Simon Reynolds and well-known (yes, Virginia, some did become stars) house musician Paul Oakenfold suggests that the utopianism was mostly nonsense, and that the culture was really about momentary ecstasis (and there's nothing wrong with *that*!),

> where acid rock imagined utopia as a garden of pre-modern innocence, acid house is futuristic, in love with sophistication and technology. Acid house imagines a James Bond/Barbarella leisure paradise of gadgetry and designer drugs. House is a kind of pleasure factory (an orgasmotron, in fact) and as Marx wrote, the factory turns human beings into mere appendages of flesh attached to machinery. If house, acid, new beat, etc., are radical, it's a radicalism that's inseparable from their simple effectiveness, pure pleasure immediacy. Here's a pop culture based around the death of the song, minimalism, repetition, departure from the stability of the key and harmonic structure in favour of sonority and sound-in-itself. . . . No delay, no mediation, but a direct interface between the music's pleasure circuitry and the listener's nervous system.

Rave culture went global in the early 1990s. In the U.S., it became directly associated with the digital counterculture. It also quickly became commercialized, the willingness of hundreds of thousands of new enthusiasts to pay high prices to participate in the all-night psychedelic dance parties proving irresistible not only to old-style nightclub owners but to many of the original raver visionaries themselves.

Rave culture became a mix of smaller outlaw parties and popular commercial raves for the masses that still maintained some semblance of the initial acid house spirit. Beyond that, acid house DJs became de rigueur at fashion events, corporate parties (at least in the Silicon Valley/San Francisco Bay Area), and society events.

Meanwhile, raving countercultural gangs continued to expand on the more liberatory sociopolitics implications of the early acid house scene into the late 1990s. One such group was the loose-knit San Francisco–based S.P.A.Z.—a "Semi-Permanent Autonomous Zone" with a constantly shifting, international roster of participants. Through most of the 1990s, S.P.A.Z. toured the United States every summer in a caravan of vehicles, throwing surreal parties with mutating art installation environments and a blend of live and DJ-oriented experimental music. Each S.P.A.Z. tour returned to the West Coast with a significantly altered cast of characters, some members of the crew having decided to remain behind at various points en route, other musicians and artists having hooked up with the tour along the way to end up returning to San Francisco with the reconfigured entourage at summer's end. Overlapping with S.P.A.Z. in recent years was the similarly structured (or unstructured) U.K.-based post–acid house network Spiral Tribe.

Another loose-knit confederation based in San Francisco was the super-psychedelic arts collective C.C.C. (Consortium of Collective Consciousness), whose converted South of Market San Francisco warehouse, while maintaining a discreetly low-key neighborhood presence, nonetheless periodically hosted legendary word-of-mouth/invitation-only dusk-till-dawn trance-dance parties in an environment that can only be described as extraterrestrial in sensibility. This location also served as an ongoing hostel for itinerant trance-dancing travelers from across the globe, and housed the office of the collective's successful book publishing company specializing in countercultural guide titles for young backpacking global travelers—or "world stompers," as one of the company's books calls them.

As a popular mass youth phenomenon, rave parties have spread to every nook and cranny of America, as well as to much of the world. At its best, this mass popularization can look like Germany's Love Parade, an enormous (approximately half a million attendees on average) annual four-day street celebration in Berlin that realizes the White Panthers' program of rock, dope, and sex in the street (but without that messy total-revolutionary-transformation-of-society bit). Since 1989, the Love Parade has come off with a great deal of good spirit and minimal trouble, bringing tourist dollars into the happily tolerant German Republic. The imaginative, freely freaking attendees, who require no rock stars, make Woodstock look like a Shriners convention.

At its worst, as the rave culture drifted off into the suburbs and backwaters of America, it became linked to drug disasters that brought down the wrath of parents, police, and politicians. A few mostly young, immature, ill-informed kids who have been attracted to raves—most of them looking to get high on Ecstasy—have hurt or killed themselves, sometimes from overdoses or dehydration from Ecstasy itself and other times from other street drugs that were passed off as Ecstasy. The numbers are minuscule compared to the number of kids who have disasters with prescription drugs, alcohol, or even *aspirin,* but that didn't prevent the media from invoking an Ecstasy hysteria eclipsed only by the more justifiable crack cocaine panic of the 1980s. In 2003, the United States Congress attached a new law nicknamed the "Rave Act" to the "Amber Act," an emotionally fraught piece of legislation that created a national system for responding to child abduction, and which very few congresspeople dared vote against. The "Rave Act" part of this legislation, signed into law by President George W. Bush, makes the sponsor of any public event legally responsible for *any* illegal drug exchanges or use that occurs at their event. The initial bill actually singled out raves as the likely enforcement target, but that language was changed as clearly prejudicial. Taken literally, every rock concert and most mass sports events, country music shows, and even some Republican Party rallies are technically in violation of this bizarre piece of legislation. In the words of a missive from the Drug Policy Alliance, which organized the opposition to this law, "Because of its broad language, the proposed law would even potentially subject people to twenty years in federal prison if guests smoked marijuana at their party or barbecue." In essence, acid house is the first musical culture in America to be declared more or less illegal, and the U.S. government has dragged most public gatherings into this legal quagmire with it.

THE BOMB: HIP-HOP BLOWS UP BIG

Years before the acid house movement connected technologically based music to a unique set of neo-hippie values, an African-American ghetto-based counterculture had emerged, initially in the Bronx district of New York City in the mid-1970s. Revolving around a technomusical style that vividly reflected shattered, fragmented, post-industrial life from the perspective of those whose communities were being abandoned as a blighted urban wasteland by postmodern capitalism's migratory opportunism, hip-hop/rap culture was a perfect example of the countercultural urge to view abandoned terrain as an opportunity for creative, subversive play.

As a musical style, rap was a return to the African/African-American tradition discussed in Chapter 11, emphasizing rhythm and voice, instrumentation that could be gathered without great expense. Early performances took place at parties and in the streets, using turntables and digital drum machines to back up simple spoken-word poems geared toward celebration.

Shaping a lifestyle in tandem with the mostly white punk subculture that centered around New York's East Village and the CBGB nightclub on the Bowery, hip-hop culture developed its own DIY outlaw art aesthetic that was particularized by graffiti art (called "tagging"). These elaborate, cartoonish, psychedelic paintings created with (frequently shoplifted) spray cans were affixed to any unoccupied public "canvas," primarily subway trains, commercial buildings, and the walls of large apartment complexes. The text generally consisted of the taggers' imaginative pseudonyms. Tagging was a people's medium for those excluded from more commercial avenues of self-expression, and for anyone with eyes to see, it brought brilliance and art to the dreary gray architecture of everyday urban life. As Nelson George, author of *Hip Hop America,* wrote, "For those looking for manifestations of rebellion, for some last gasp of public defiance before the '60s spirit completely died, graffiti fit the bill." While the style remained an element of urban street life (and does to this day), it was also quickly recognized and absorbed into the worlds of avant-garde (and eventually mainstream) museums, and artists like Jean-Michel Basquiat and (white and gay) Keith Haring were among those graffiti artists who developed international reputations.

The earliest hip-hop recordings emerged in the late 1970s. But it wasn't until the digital sampler was added to the hip-hop recording toolbox in the mid-1980s that the culture became memetically linked to hacker issues about the ownership of information and joined itself to the avant-garde traditions of collage, found, and appropriated materials. The sampler allowed musicians to take small fragments of previously recorded sounds and use them to create or spice up an original piece. A hip-hop recording was likely to mix up a drumbeat sampled from a James Brown record, a guitar riff from a heavy metal band, and fragments from old TV shows or advertisements that subtly reminded listeners that black youths had to process the same white, mainstream inanity as hip white youths and from an even more culturally alienated standpoint.

Most early rap/hip-hop was apolitical. While the rhymes often acknowledged the ugliness and alienation that surrounded the artists, bragging, partying, and sex were the main obsessions. In 1988, with the release of *It Takes a Nation of Millions to Hold Us Back,* Public Enemy brought black nationalist militancy, and defiance against the powerful and the greedy owners and governors of America, to the fore, attracting an astonishing fan base among young whites as well as blacks. Over the years, their most productive writer and rapper—Chuck D—evolved into an eloquent spokesperson for nineties (and twenty-first-century) counterculture, defending civil liberties, speaking out against the Iraq wars, and advocating Napster-style file sharing; and Public Enemy has provided an example of how musicians can gain value from the Internet without attacking their own fans for freely sharing music.

Hip-hop evolved and devolved into dozens of new directions from those earlier times to become the dominant sound in America's mainstream music industry. Conscious political rap followed on the heels of Public Enemy, performed by artists like KRS-One and the hippieish black music collective Arrested Development. Today, Michael Franti, formerly of the Disposable Heroes of Hiphoprisy, is the most famous among many political hip-hoppers who play a vital and tireless role in civil liberties and anti-militaristic battles.

A peace-and-love-oriented psychedelic hip-hop trend nicknamed

"Daisy Age" emerged at the end of the 1980s, primarily represented by the band De La Soul. De La Soul themselves identified with something called the "Native Tongues posse." The group included A Tribe Called Quest and Queen Latifah and, as Jim DeRogatis recollected in a 2003 *Chicago Sun-Times* article, they "avoided sexist boasting and clichéd tales of . . . violence in favor of timeless celebrations of individuality." In the late 1980s and early 1990s, Oakland, California, artists the Digital Underground and Del tha Funkee Homosapien—influenced by George Clinton—recorded and performed irreverent, surrealist, psychedelic hip-hop music. And today, artists like Blackalicious, Kool Keith, and DJ Spooky continue to work the mind-expanded edge while another genre called trip-hop combines hip-hop and acid house themes.

Of course, the rap sound that has most offended, excited, upset, and succeeded in America is gangsta rap, primarily because it has so loudly and vividly reflected the country's main values since the Reagan era: tribal/gang/national warfare as the default position when you don't get your way, greed, vicious competition, masculine supremacy, and mindless hedonism/consumerism sometimes alternating with attacks of conscience expressed in clichéd, Dr. Phil–level pop psychological confessions of guilt and loss. But even gangsta has some countercultural roots and subtexts. The original gangsta band, N.W.A (Niggaz with Attitude), were in many ways the black Sex Pistols, reinterpreting that band's total, nihilistic rejection of all illusions of bourgeois propriety for an even harsher social reality. In 1991 N.W.A's second album, *efil4zaggin* (Niggaz4Life backward), hit number one on the *Billboard* charts even though radio stations refused to play it, reminding some commentators of the Sex Pistols' banned hits in Britain.

Any doubt within rock culture about N.W.A's punk approach was erased when they were interviewed by *Spin* magazine. In a manner reminiscent of previous confrontations with Pistols Johnny Rotten and Sid Vicious, the rappers insulted everybody they could think of, singling out venerated black institutions like the Muslims, Martin Luther King, and the recent cause célèbre Rodney King. It was uproarious, hilarious, and pure surrealism—unrepressed, uncensored expressions of the id.

After N.W.A acrimoniously split up, two of its members, Ice Cube and Dr. Dre, went on to have successful commercial careers. Unfortunately, the gangsta approach became formalized and predictable, more an expression of the *gangster* values of unalloyed capitalism than a hyper-real, cartoonlike exposure of society's unconscious. The master of our current psychotic zeitgeist, Eminem, manages to simultaneously embrace and parody these values, something that is, after all, a grand rock tradition.

Some of the gangstas, as progenitors and advocates of unconstrained free expression (not to mention voracious potheads), may yet develop a more broadly countercultural voice. If they do, they will certainly be in a position to influence a substantial listenership.

The Millennial Frenzy of the Corporate Hipsters

> Join the cyberpunks at Pac Bell.
> PACIFIC BELL BILLBOARD ADVERTISEMENT, SAN FRANCISCO, 1996

"Irrational exuberance" comes in many styles. The spirit touches Baptists singing the praises of the Lord. In the late 1960s, the Yippies and White Panthers felt its effects, with a little help from their friends. In the late 1990s, the stock market caught the buzz from a heady combination of futurological Internet hype and casino-style speculation. They were led along by a mysterious cyber-priesthood of young twenty-something hipsters who—like Werner Erhard and his minions in the 1970s—"got it." Hundreds of millions of dollars were invested in dot-com companies run by young men and women sporting nose rings and casual wear, skating to work while yakking enthusiastically into their cells. And before they saw a penny in revenue, their stock values rose to unprecedented levels, and many became on-paper multimillionaires literally overnight.

Was this the same generation that had just spent several years whining that the baby boomers had sold out? You bet! But don't blame them too much. They were caught up in the exuberance themselves.

For the most part, nobody remembers what these mysterious young hipsters were selling, not even the hundreds of thousands of ordinary middle-class stock purchasers who blew their life savings on whatever-the-hell-that-was. But everybody remembers the cultural styles and ethics; the

TV ads promising a rich, rewarding, hyper-sexy, 24/7, always-on future in a fully linked-up world without borders or boundaries, as represented by smiling Tibetan Buddhist monks holding laptop Macintosh iBooks. And we remember the ad with the obnoxious hip geek with his long red hair tied back in a ponytail Xeroxing and passing a rave flyer to his fat, balding, clueless old boss and smirkingly explaining how to get on the day-trade gravy train. And we remember *Wired* magazine's breathless rock-star-like coverage of a dot-com start-up run by a kid who wasn't even old enough to buy his own drinks; how we thrilled to the dynamic depiction of young people sitting in cubicles staring at monitors all day, and then hitting the odd occasional all-night rave.

Was it a counterculture? Well, it was certainly something of an *office* counterculture: informal dress, irreverent free speech, less hierarchical secrecy and deference to the boss than in traditional companies, an ethic that trusted individuals to do their work without close supervision, flexible (if long) hours, and increased mobility.

And beneath it all was the stirring of a utopian vision weirdly similar to the one that guided the hip sixties left: the end of economic scarcity (predicted as "the long boom"), the liberation of the individual from a dull lifetime of wage slavery within a single institution (every man and woman a "free agent"), a seeming diminution of the power of authoritarian memes as corporate geeks of all ages strived mightily to be hip and all of it watched over by the postmodern president winging it on the fly, dissembling with jazzy smoothness, without ideological commitment or fine moral precision. Only this time, post-scarcity anarchy would be brought to us by the very capitalist system that sixties utopians rejected.

Okay. So it was wack, everybody lost his or her shirt, and now it's time for John Ashcroft to give us all a well-deserved spanking. Still, maybe we've learned something. Next time we start to hallucinate that incredible abundance and new vistas of personal liberty are right around the bend, do a quick head count. First of all, does everybody here have something to *eat*? Is there enough water to go around? And how many psychos are plotting mega-violence, what's their skill set, and what is their arsenal like? Finally, if, as *Time* magazine proclaimed in a 1994 cover story, "Everybody's Hip," who or *what* are all those carbon-copy morons on reality TV?

TECHNOCULTURE'S DISCONTENTS: THE NEW HIP LEFT

The computer hobbyists of the 1970s who initiated the high-tech counterculture that evolved into such a powerful and equivocal force by the mid-1990s really formed a small minority of the hippies and activists who were trying to figure out what to do with their lives once "the revolution" was over. Far greater numbers of sixties veterans remained true to their countercultural roots by building up the environmental movement (generally labeled the ecology movement at that time). For many, the sixties revolt had been in opposition to technocracy. It was primarily enacted in terms of alienation from the political and corporate classes' agenda of domination and control, and its corresponding attempt to reduce individuals to robotic servants of the industrial machine. By the 1970s, this critique had flowered into a positivist agenda that organized itself around a Thoreau-inflected deep love and respect for nature and a need to model a more organic, eco-friendly lifestyle.

Early-seventies ecological theory described nature in terms of whole systems that need to be understood and respected, as opposed to exploitable parts that can be used and discarded any which way (it's worth noting that cybernetics, source of the trendy technoculture prefix "cyber," is the mathematical study of whole systems). At the hippie edge of this trend, new pagan (nature religion) spirituality evolved along feminist lines, expressed as Goddess worship. (This equation of women with nature has been vehemently opposed by other feminists as just another reduction of women to a highly sexualized, unintellectual, primitivistic force.)

New tribes of neo-hippie "eco-warriors" began to spring up to organize politically to defend wild nature against the ravages of greed and industrialism. According to the online subculture encyclopedia Wikipedia, "The first significant radical environmentalist group was Greenpeace, which made use of direct action to confront a variety of transgressors, including whaling ships and nuclear weapons testers." In 1979, a group of eco-anarchists in the Western U.S. formed Earth First!, vowing to protect the "wild places" by any means necessary. They were inspired by the Edward Abbey novel *The Monkey Wrench Gang*, in which an unlikely foursome—

including a Vietnam vet and a radical feminist—roam America sabotaging machines that destroy the wilderness.

By the mid-1980s, Northern California became a focal point for an ongoing confrontation between the eco-warrior counterculture and the lumber industry, which was clear-cutting vast areas of the redwood forests. Radical environmentalist tactics ranged from spiking trees so that the electric saw would break when loggers tried to cut them down, to sitting in the trees and refusing to come down, to more traditional avenues of mass protest and civil disobedience. As they mixed with punk and Deadhead crowds, the cultural assumptions of the eco-warrior crowd spread. "Redwood summers" filled with protest actions became something of a popular lifestyle option among counterculture types from all generations, even attracting celebrities like punk rocker Jello Biafra, Jerry Brown, and Grateful Dead drummer Mickey Hart. Eventually, California senator Dianne Feinstein, in cooperation with the Clinton administration, pushed through a policy compromise between logging industry and environmental concerns that—in typical Clintonian fashion—satisfied no one but managed to dissipate the confrontational energy. Redwood summers continued on, and Julia Butterfly Hill, undoubtedly the most attractive woman ever to live in a tree, even became a mediagenic folk hero, but the size and spirit of that particular confrontation had dwindled. (Rest assured the Bush administration is doing everything within its power to provoke another round.)

The radical environmentalists were (and are) deeply anti-authoritarian. Most are anarchists who believed that life is best organized in small autonomous villages without any need for centralized government. Far more successfully than the hip left of the 1960s, they repudiated centralized organizations and charismatic leaders in favor of consensus decision-making and ad hoc organizing into temporary affinity groups (ironically, made much easier by the Internet). In a letter to the Marxist political journal *Monthly Review,* Louis Proyect accurately described the values of environmental anarchists as "egalitarianism; opposition to all hierarchies; suspicion of authority, especially that of the state; and commitment to living according to one's values."

In the mid-1990s, the environmental/anarchist counterculture joined forces with more traditional leftist groups, representatives of poor people from all across the globe, some unions, some liberals, and even some right-wing nationalists to create a force that has been labeled the "anti-globalization movement."

Most movement historians point to the Zapatista uprising on January 1, 1994, in opposition to the North American Free Trade Agreement on the day it went into effect as the opening salvo of the movement. But within the context of American culture and media, it was in Seattle, Washington, in November 1999 that the new hip left suddenly went from being viewed as a laughably weak, archaic caricature of the once potent hip left of the 1960s to a fearsome force to be reckoned with. Seemingly out of nowhere, massive numbers of protesters flooded the streets to protest and disrupt, through civil disobedience, a meeting of the World Trade Organization, a primary organizational representative of corporate global interests. The demonstrators blocked traffic, preventing delegates from attending the gathering, effectively shutting down the first day of activities and making themselves and their issues a locus for discussions within the media and the corporate globalist establishment from that point on. A few members of a young ultra-radical anarchist affinity group that called itself the Black Bloc smashed a few windows and threw a few objects into the streets, provoking police violence. Given the post-1970s media lack of interest in hip left activities up to that point, the impact of the "Battle of Seattle" on America's body politic felt vaguely like it might have felt if we'd gone directly from the 1950s to the Chicago convention in 1968.

While media pundits portrayed the protesters as new reactionaries, frightened by the glorious changes being wrought by the new technology that was turning the world into a global village, the reality was more complex. The main body of protesters was not really against globalization (i.e., global cooperation), technology, or even capitalism and trade. They objected to the actual specific policies being put into place by the NAFTA treaty, the World Bank, the WTO, and other powerful corporate globalist organizations, and their undemocratic assumption of that decision-making power. A full discussion of these policies is a topic for another book, but within an environmentalist context, the WTO arrangement that allows private companies to use a global court to overrule national or local environmental law that gets in the way of their doing business is perhaps the best representative of dozens of very real offenses.

ANARCHIST SCOLDS

The new hip left has the potential to be the most important anti-authoritarian political force in the contemporary world because it stands directly in opposition to the increasing powers of gigantic corporation. Global corporate monoliths are, in essence, merging with most of the world's governments and positioning themselves to dictate the actual physical and material conditions under which people everywhere will live, what kind of air they will breathe, what kind of buildings will surround them, what kind of work they will do or whether they will be excluded from working at all, what kind of products they will consume, and what kinds of programs will be available through the mass media and even (if they can manage it) the Internet. They are invading everybody's privacy to globalize (i.e., integrate) their consumer base to match the integration of their business interests, and they are using formerly private information to exclude people from health care, jobs, credit, and housing. They are creating a closed system in which the individual's choices and opportunities are ensnared within a web of corporate databases that cannot be contested. Benito Mussolini defined fascism, and his definition was the complete integration of the state with corporations.

Unfortunately, the new hip left also includes what this writer considers remarkably reactionary elements. An extreme example would be those who want to return humanity to the hunter-gatherer state. And while most environmentalist neo-hippies advocate "appropriate" technology, a substantial number are neo-Luddites, virtually opposed to all technology. This rising anti-Promethean counterculture gains strength in the face of extraordinary abuses of technological invention by forces of greed and power. You can find them, along with the right-wing religious fundamentalists, vehemently opposing not just cloning but stem cell research; not just the patenting of new biologicial mutant food forms but biotechnology itself.

Many environmental radicals also have an extremely strong urge to tell everybody how to live: what to drive (preferably a bicycle), what to eat (no meat), what to smoke (legalize pot but persecute tobacco smokers), what to wear (no leather, makeup, nothing expensive), and how to spend their leisure time (don't watch television). Popping into a Starbucks may be a thought crime. Popping into a Burger King may be murder. Driving an SUV may be a war crime!

Okay, moralistic peer pressure beats the hell out of urine testing and the despoliation and murder of small communities for their oil resources (as per Chevron in Nigeria), but besides holding the unattractive position of national scold, the hip left has a bigger problem. They don't offer a realistic alternative vision. A functioning, decentralized, distributed anarchy on a nine-billion-person planet isn't going to happen, kids. Not in my lifetime and not in yours. A more realistic, gradualist approach to a less authoritarian future is called for. But hey, very few want to seem unhip to their rad friends by confronting this dreary truth.

Of course, that's just my opinion.

TAG. YOU'RE IT

It's June 23, 2003, and, along with everyone else, I'm leaning into the future. Mainstream pundits are predicting droughts, epidemics, wars with weapons of mass destruction, and an increase in antisocial violence. Hell, there was even a hail of locusts in some small Midwestern town a few days ago. By the time you're reading this book, we may well have experienced social convulsions that dwarf recent episodes.

But take heart. First of all, future projections are always wonky. In the late 1990s, we were presumed to be on a straight path to a utopian long boom. Now we're sputtering down the road toward total human degradation. And secondly, *here we are!* Across human history, our species has risen to the occasion by bringing forth bold and wildly creative individuals and cultures that somehow sustain and even expand the countercultural spirit of autonomy and mutual bounty. This time, it's your turn.

⊦ BIBLIOGRAPHY

PART I: THE MAKINGS OF COUNTERCULTURES

CHAPTER ONE: ABRAHAM AND PROMETHEUS: *Mythic Counterculture Rebels*

Aeschylus, *Prometheus Bound.*

Ginsberg, Allen, *Kaddish and Other Poems, 1958–1960,* City Lights Books, 1961.

Goethe, *Poems,* 1853.

Hertzberg, Arthur, with Aron Hirt-Manheimer, *Jews: The Essence and Character of a People,* HarperSanFrancisco, 1998.

Kerényi, Carl, translated by Ralph Mannheim, *Prometheus: Archetypal Image of Human Existence,* Princeton University Press, 1991.

Kuhrt, Amelie, *The Ancient Near East,* Routledge, 1995.

Lerner, Michael, *Jewish Renewal: A Path to Learning and Transformation,* HarperPerennial, 1995.

Nietzsche, Friedrich, translated by Douglas Smith, *The Birth of Tragedy,* Oxford University Press, 2000.

Roszak, Theodore, *The Gendered Atom,* Conari Press, 1999.

Rushkoff, Douglas, *Nothing Sacred: The Truth About Judaism,* Crown, 2003.

Shelley, Percy Bysshe, *Complete Poems,* Modern Library, 1994.

Soden, Wolfram von, *The Ancient Orient: An Introduction to the Study of the Ancient Near East,* Wm. B. Eerdmans, 1994.

Werblowsky, R. J. Zwi, *Lucifer and Prometheus,* Routledge & Kegan Paul, 1952.

Wilson, Robert Anton, *Prometheus Rising,* New Falcon Publications, 1993.

CHAPTER TWO: A DIFFERENT TYPE OF HUMAN EXCELLENCE: *Defining Counterculture*

Free (a.k.a. Abbie Hoffman), *Revolution for the Hell of It,* Pocket Books, 1968.

Leary, Timothy, *Flashbacks: A Personal and Cultural History of an Era,* Jeremy Tarcher, 1983.

Marcuse, Herbert, *One-Dimensional Man,* Beacon Press, 1964.

Roszak, Theodore, *The Making of a Counter Culture,* Doubleday, 1969.

PART II: ACROSS THE SPAN OF TIMES AND PLACES

CHAPTER THREE: POLITICALLY INCORRECT: *Socrates and the Socratic Counterculture*

Davidson, James, *Courtesans and Fishcakes,* HarperCollins, 1997.

Guthrie, William Keith Chambers, *Socrates,* Cambridge University Press, 1971.

Leary, Timothy, *Flashbacks: A Personal and Cultural History of an Era,* Jeremy Tarcher, 1983.

Munn, Mark, *The School of History,* University of California Press, 2000.

Plato, *The Portable Plato,* edited by Scott Buchanan, Viking, 1948.

Plato, translated by Benjamin Jowett, *Apology; Crito; Phaedo; Symposium; Republic,* Classics Club, 1942.

Russell, Bertrand, *A History of Western Philosophy,* Simon & Schuster, 1945.

Spielberg, Herbert, ed., *The Socratic Enigma*, Bobbs-Merrill, 1964.

Stone, I. F., *The Trial of Socrates*, Little, Brown, 1988.

Wilson, Pearl Cleveland, *The Living Socrates*, Stemmer House, 1975.

CHAPTER FOUR: LEAP INTO THE BOUNDLESS: *Taoism*

Chuang Tzu, *The Complete Works of Chuang Tzu*, translated by Burton Watson, Columbia University Press, 1968.

Clarke, J. J., *The Tao of the West: Western Transformations of Taoist Thought*, Routledge, 2000.

Fung Yu-lan, translated by Derk Bodde, *A History of Chinese Philosophy Volume 2, The Period of Classical Learning*, Princeton University Press, 1983.

Kaltenmark, Max, *Lao Tzu and Taoism*, Stanford University Press, 1969.

Lao-tzu, translated by Stephen Mitchell, *Tao Te Ching*, Harper & Row, 1988.

Schipper, Kristofer, *The Taoist Body*, University of California Press, 1993.

Watts, Alan, *The Way of Liberation: Essays and Lectures on the Transformation of the Self*, Weatherhill, 1983.

Watts, Alan, with Al Chung-liang Huang, *The Watercourse Way*, Pantheon, 1975.

CHAPTER FIVE: THE HAND THAT STOPPED THE MIND: *The Zen Counterculture*

Fung Yu-lan, translated by Derk Bodde, *A History of Chinese Philosophy, Volume 2, The Period of Classical Learning*, Princeton University Press, 1983.

Hyers, Conrad, *The Laughing Buddha: Zen and the Comic Spirit*, Longwood Academic, 1991.

Kerouac, Jack, *The Dharma Bums*, Penguin, 1976.

Nisker, Wes, *Crazy Wisdom*, Ten Speed Press, 1990.

Smith, Huston, *The Religions of Man*, HarperPerennial, 1992.

Snyder, Gary, *Riprap and Cold Mountain Poems*, Shoemaker & Hoard, 2004.

Suzuki, D. T., *Essays in Zen Buddhism*, Grove Press, 1949.

————, *An Introduction to Zen Buddhism,* Grove Press, 1964.

Watts, Alan, *The Way of Zen,* Vintage, 1957.

————, *Zen and the Beat Way,* Tuttle, 1997.

Wu, John C. H., *The Golden Age of Zen,* Doubleday, 1996.

CHAPTER SIX: LOVE AND EVOLUTION: *The Occult Counterculture of the Sufis*

Bayman, Henry, *Science, Knowledge, and Sufism,* http://home. att.net/~nungan/sufiway/home.htm.

Bennett, J. G., *Gurdjieff: Making a New World,* Bennett Books, 1992.

The Drunken Universe: An Anthology of Persian Sufi Poetry, translation and commentary by Peter Lamborn Wilson and Nasrollah Pourjavady, Omega Publications, 1987.

Ernst, Carl W., *Sufism,* Shambhala, 1997.

Farzan, Massud, *Another Way of Laughter: A Collection of Sufi Humor,* E. P. Dutton, 1973.

Rumi, *The Essential Rumi,* translated by Coleman Barks with John Moyne, HarperSanFrancisco, 1995.

————, *Mystical Poems of Rumi 1: Jalal al-Din Rumi,* translated by A. J. Arberry, University of Chicago Press, 1968.

Schimmel, Annemarie, *Mystical Dimensions of Islam,* University of North Carolina Press, 1975.

Sells, Michael A., ed., *Stations of Desire: Love Elegies from Ibn 'Arabi and New Poems,* Ibis, 2000.

Shah, Idries, *The Sufis,* Doubleday, 1964.

————, *Tales of the Dervishes,* E. P. Dutton, 1967.

Smokey, Richard, and Jay Kinney, *Hidden Wisdom,* Penguin/ Arkana, 1999.

Wilson, Peter Lamborn, *Sacred Drift: Essays on the Margins of Islam,* City Lights Books, 1993.

————, *Scandal: Essays in Islamic Heresy,* Autonomedia, 1988.

CHAPTER SEVEN: REMAKING LOVE: *The Troubadours and the Heretic Spirit of Provence*

Briffault, Robert, *The Troubadours,* edited by Lawrence F. Koons, Indiana University Press, 1965.

Daniel, Arnaut, *Pound's Translations of Arnaut Daniel: A Variorum Edition with Commentary from Unpublished Letters,* Garland, 1991.

Shah, Idries, *The Sufis,* Doubleday, 1964.

CHAPTER EIGHT: CULTURAL AND POLITICAL REVOLUTION: *The Enlightenment of the Seventeenth and Eighteenth Centuries*

Ayer, A. J., *Voltaire,* Random House, 1986.

Barzun, Jacques, *From Dawn to Decadence: 1500 to the Present, 500 Years of Western Cultural Life,* HarperCollins, 2000.

Blanning, T. C. W., *The Culture of Power and the Power of Culture,* Oxford University Press, 2002.

Gottschalk, Louis, with L. C. MacKinney and E. H. Pritchard, *The Foundations of the Modern World, 1300–1775,* Harper & Row, 1969.

Paine, Thomas, *Common Sense, The Rights of Man, and Other Essential Writings of Thomas Paine,* introduction by Sidney Hook, Meridian/Penguin, 1969.

Simon, Julia, *Mass Enlightenment: Critical Studies in Rousseau and Diderot,* State University of New York Press, 1995.

Voltaire, *Philosophical Dictionary,* translation and introduction by Peter Gay, Harcourt, Brace & World, 1962.

Zinn, Howard, *A People's History of the United States, 1492–Present,* HarperCollins, 1980.

CHAPTER NINE: TO EACH HIS OWN GOD: *The American Transcendentalists*

Baker, Carlos, *Emerson Among the Eccentrics: A Group Portrait,* Addison-Wesley, 1996.

Blanchard, Paula, *Margaret Fuller: From Transcendentalism to Revolution,* Delacorte Press/Seymour Lawrence, 1978.

Emerson, Ralph Waldo, *The Essays of Ralph Waldo Emerson,* introduction by Alfred Kazin, Belknap Press of Harvard University Press, 1979.

Hansen, Ellen, ed., *The New England Transcendentalists: Life of the Mind and of the Spirit,* Discovery Enterprise, 1993.

Meltzer, Milton, and Walter Harding, *A Thoreau Profile*, Thomas Y. Crowell, 1962.

Reynolds, David S., *Walt Whitman's America: A Cultural Biography*, Alfred A. Knopf, 1995.

Rusk, Ralph, *The Life of Ralph Waldo Emerson*, Columbia University Press, 1949.

Taylor, Bob Pepperman, *America's Bachelor Uncle: Thoreau and the American Polity*, University Press of Kansas, 1996.

Thoreau, Henry David, *The Portable Thoreau*, edited and introduced by Carl Bode, Viking Penguin, 1947.

Whicher, George F., editor and introduction, *The Transcendentalist Revolt: Problems in American Civilization*, D. C. Heath, 1949.

CHAPTER TEN: BRILLIANT STORMS OF LAUGHTER: *Bohemian Paris, 1904-1940*

Barzun, Jacques, *From Dawn to Decadence: 1500 to the Present, 500 Years of Western Cultural Life*, HarperCollins, 2000.

Fitch, Noel Riley, *Sylvia Beach and the Lost Generation: A History of Literary Paris in the Twenties and Thirties*, W. W. Norton, 1983.

Franck, Dan, *Bohemian Paris: Picasso, Modigliani, Matisse, and the Birth of Modern Art*, Grove Press, 1998.

Hemingway, Ernest, *A Moveable Feast*, Charles Scribner's Sons, 1964.

———, *The Sun Also Rises*, Charles Scribner's Sons, 1954.

Joyce, James, *Ulysses*, Random House, 1934.

Pizer, Donald, *American Expatriate Writing and the Paris Moment: Modernism and Place*, Louisiana State University Press, 1996.

Plant, Sadie, *Writing on Drugs*, Farrar, Straus & Giroux, 1999.

Schalin, Leonard, *Art & Physics: Parallel Visions in Space, Time & Light*, Quill/William Morrow, 1991.

Stein, Gertrude, *The Autobiography of Alice B. Toklas*, Vintage, 1990.

Part III: After Hiroshima, "the" Counterculture

Chapter Eleven: Rebels without a Cause: *The 1950s*

Foster, Edward Halsey, *Understanding the Beats,* University of South Carolina Press, 1992.

Ginsberg, Allen, *Howl and Other Poems,* City Lights Books, 1957.

Gitlin, Todd, *The Sixties: Years of Hope, Days of Rage,* Bantam, 1987.

Kerouac, Jack, *The Dharma Bums,* Penguin, 1976.

————, *On the Road,* Penguin, 1999.

Lotringer, Sylvère, ed., *Burroughs Live 1960–1997,* Semiotext(e), 2001.

Mailer, Norman, *The White Negro,* City Lights Books, 1957.

Miles, Barry, *Ginsberg: A Biography,* Simon & Schuster, 1989.

Miller, Richard, *Bohemia: The Protoculture Then and Now,* Nelson-Hall, 1977.

Shipton, Alyn, *A New History of Jazz,* Continuum, 2001.

Chapter Twelve: When You Change with Every New Day: *The Youth Counterculture, 1960-1967*

Foss, Daniel, *Freak Culture,* E. P. Dutton, 1972.

Free (a.k.a. Abbie Hoffman), *Revolution for the Hell of It,* Pocket Books, 1968.

Gitlin, Todd, *The Sixties: Years of Hope, Days of Rage,* Bantam, 1987.

Leary, Timothy, *Flashbacks: A Personal and Cultural History of an Era,* Jeremy Tarcher, 1983.

Lee, Martin A., and Bruce Schlain, *Acid Dreams: The CIA, LSD and the Sixties Rebellion,* Grove Weidenfeld, 1985.

Miles, Barry, *Ginsberg: A Biography,* Simon & Schuster, 1989.

————, *Paul McCartney: Many Years from Now,* Henry Holt, 1997.

Newton, Huey P., *To Die for the People,* Vintage, 1973.

O'Neill, William L., *The New Left: A History,* Harlan Davidson, 2001.

Roszak, Theodore, *The Making of a Counter Culture*, Doubleday, 1969.

CHAPTER THIRTEEN: WILD IN THE STREETS: *The Youth Counterculture, 1968-1972*

The Beatles, *The Beatles Anthology*, Chronicle, 2000.

Foss, Daniel, *Freak Culture*, E. P. Dutton, 1972.

Free (a.k.a. Abbie Hoffman), *Revolution for the Hell of It*, Pocket Books, 1968.

Gitlin, Todd, *The Sixties: Years of Hope, Days of Rage*, Bantam, 1987.

Leary, Timothy, with Robert Anton Wilson and George Koopman, *Neuropolitics*, Starseed/Peace Press, 1977.

Lee, Martin A., and Bruce Schlain, *Acid Dreams: The CIA, LSD and the Sixties Rebellion*, Grove Weidenfeld, 1985.

Lotringer, Sylvère, ed., *Burroughs Live 1960–1997*, Semiotext(e), 2001.

Miles, Barry, *Ginsberg: A Biography*, Simon & Schuster, 1989.

Neville, Richard, *Play Power: Exploring the International Underground*, Random House, 1970.

Newton, Huey P., *To Die for the People*, Vintage, 1973.

O'Neill, William L., *The New Left: A History*, Harlan Davidson, 2001.

Roszak, Theodore, *The Making of a Counter Culture*, Doubleday, 1969.

Rubin, Jerry, *Do It! Scenarios of the Revolution*, Simon & Schuster, 1970.

Samberg, Paul, ed., *FIRE! Reports from the Underground Press*, E. P. Dutton, 1970.

CHAPTER FOURTEEN: THAT WHICH DOES NOT KILL ME MAKES ME HIPPER: *The Hedonist/Nihilist Countercultures of the 1970s*

Anderson, Patrick, *High in America: The Incredible Story Behind the Marijuana Lobby and One Man's Effort to Keep America Stoned and Out of Jail*, Viking Press, 1981.

Herman, Gary, *Rock and Roll Babylon*, Putnam, 1982.

Leary, Timothy, *The Intelligence Agents*, Peace Press, 1979.

Marcus, Greil, *Lipstick Traces: A Secret History of the Twentieth Century,* Harvard University Press, 1989.

McNeil, Legs, and Gillian McCain, *Please Kill Me: The Uncensored Oral History of Punk,* Grove Press, 1996.

Rossman, Michael, *New Age Blues: On the Politics of Consciousness,* E. P. Dutton, 1979.

Search and Destroy #1–6: The Complete Reprint, V/Search Publications, 1996.

Warhol, Andy, *The Philosophy of Andy Warhol from A to B and Back Again,* Harcourt, 1975.

CHAPTER FIFTEEN: GLOBAL. DIGITAL. *DOOMED?*: Counterculture Leans into the Future

Dunn, Christopher, *Brutality Garden: Tropicália and the Emergence of a Brazilian Counterculture,* University of North Carolina Press, 2001.

George, Nelson, *Hip Hop America,* Viking Penguin, 1998.

Huot, Claire, *China's New Cultural Scene,* Duke University Press, 1990.

JahSonic.com.

Kelly, Kevin, *Out of Control: The Rise of Neo-Biological Civilization,* Perseus Publishing, 1994.

Levy, Steven, *Hackers: Heroes of the Computer Revolution,* Anchor, 1984.

Rucker, Rudy, R. U. Sirius, and Queen Mu, eds., *Mondo 2000: A User's Guide to the New Edge,* HarperPerennial, 1992.

Sterling, Bruce, ed., *Mirrorshades,* Arbor House, 1986.

Veloso, Caetano, *Tropical Truth: A Story of Music and Revolution in Brazil,* Alfred A. Knopf, 2002.

⊦ Index

Congress of Racial Equality (CORE),
257
Conner, Bruce, 244
Connolly, Cyril, 209
Constitution, U.S., 25, 159, 276
and democracy, 157
Conversations on the Gospels (Alcott), 169
Coolidge, Calvin, 218
Cooper, Alice, 315
Copland, Aaron, 197, 232
Corso, Gregory, 234, 237
countercultures:
aim of, xvi
anti-authoritarianism of, 29, 31–32,
161
change embraced by, 29, 32–33
characteristics of, 29–33, 161, 162
and communication, 33, 34–35
co-opting of, 35–36
cords of connection between,
xvii–xx
definition of, 26–28
and diversity, 33, 34
diversity of, 29
drugs and, 39–41
and exile or dropping out, 33,
36–37
fundamentalist movements as, 27
generosity of, 37
history, ahistory and, xvii, 24–26, 28
humor in, 37–38
individuality of, 29, 30, 64, 162
and innovation, 33–34
and libertine lifestyles, 38–39
and modern cultures, 41–42
myth's importance in, 3–4, 21–23
persecution of, 33, 35
Promethean essence of, 11–12
universal features of, 33–37
*see also specific individuals and
movements*

Cowley, Malcolm, 197, 210, 217
Coyote, Peter, 323
crack cocaine, 356
Crazy Wisdom (Nisker), 88
Critias, 59
Critique of Pure Reason, A (Kant), 167
Crosby, Caresse, 197, 215, 219
Crosby, Harry, 197, 215, 219
Crosby, Stills, Nash and Young, 306
Crowley, Aleister, 30, 52, 110, 111,
197
Crumb, R., 295
Crusades, 122, 132
Cuba, 256, 309
Cuban missile crisis (1961), 249
Cubism, xx, 198–202, 210, 217, 221
Cultural Revolution, 25, 56, 293–94
culture, definition of, xxii–xxiii
*Culture of Power and the Power of
Culture, The* (Blanning), 142
cyberculture, 238
cybernetics, 362
cyberpunk movement, 350–51
"Cygnet Committee" (Bowie), 316
cypherpunks, 346–47
Cyrano de Bergerac, 145

Dadaism, xx, 29, 201, 202–6, 210,
221, 330
D.A.F., 352
Daily Howl, 245
daisy age music, 358–359
see also hip-hop
Daley, Richard, 291
Dalí, Salvador, 197, 206
Daniel, Arnaut, 119, 120
description of, 121
influence on Dante of, 134
Dante Alighieri, 9, 134
Davis, Angela, 306
Davis, Deborah, 249

Ken Goffman, a.k.a. R. U. Sirius, is a well-known cultural commentator and co-founder of *Mondo 2000,* the iconoclastic magazine that defined the digital culture of the early 1990s. He is the author or editor of seven books, including *Mondo 2000: A User's Guide to the New Edge* and *The Revolution,* and he co-wrote Timothy Leary's last book, *Design for Dying.* He has been a columnist for *Artforum International* and the *San Francisco Examiner.* He lectures internationally on subjects ranging from the implications of new technology to alternative politics. He lives in Mill Valley, California.

Dan Joy is a writer, editor, and inadvertent performance artist from San Francisco.